THE NEW CAMBRIDGE COMPANION TO
AQUINAS

This new *Companion to Aquinas* features entirely new chapters written by internationally recognized experts in the field. It shows the power of Aquinas's philosophical thought and transmits the worldview which he inherited, developed, altered, and argued for, while at the same time revealing to contemporary philosophers the strong connections there are between Aquinas's interests and views and their own. Its five sections cover the life and works of Aquinas; his metaphysics, including his understanding of the ultimate foundations of reality; his metaethics and ethics, including his virtue ethics; his account of human nature; his theory of the afterlife; his epistemology and his theory of the intellectual virtues; his view of the nature of free will and the relation of grace to free will; and finally some key components of his philosophical theology, including the Incarnation and Atonement, Christology, and the nature of original sin.

ELEONORE STUMP is the Robert J. Henle Professor of Philosophy at Saint Louis University. Her books include *Aquinas* (2003), *Wandering in Darkness: Narrative and the Problem of Suffering* (2010), *Atonement* (2018), and *The Image of God: The Problem of Evil and the Problem of Mourning* (2022). She is coeditor (with David Meconi) of *The Cambridge Companion to Augustine*, 2nd edition (Cambridge, 2014), and (with Adam Green) of *Hidden Divinity and Religious Belief: New Perspectives* (Cambridge, 2016).

THOMAS JOSEPH WHITE, OP, is Rector of the Angelicum, Rome. He is the author of *Wisdom in the Face of Modernity: A Study in Thomistic Natural Theology* (2011), *The Incarnate Lord: A Thomistic Study in Christology* (2015), *The Light of Christ: An Introduction to Catholicism* (2017), and *The Trinity: On the Nature and Mystery of the One God* (2022).

OTHER VOLUMES IN THE SERIES OF CAMBRIDGE
COMPANIONS

Continued at the back of the book

The New Cambridge Companion to
AQUINAS

Edited by
Eleonore Stump
Saint Louis University
Thomas Joseph White
Pontifical University of St. Thomas Aquinas, Angelicum

CAMBRIDGE
UNIVERSITY PRESS

CAMBRIDGE
UNIVERSITY PRESS

University Printing House, Cambridge CB2 8BS, United Kingdom

One Liberty Plaza, 20th Floor, New York, NY 10006, USA

477 Williamstown Road, Port Melbourne, VIC 3207, Australia

314–321, 3rd Floor, Plot 3, Splendor Forum, Jasola District Centre,
New Delhi – 110025, India

103 Penang Road, #05-06/07, Visioncrest Commercial, Singapore 238467

Cambridge University Press is part of the University of Cambridge.

It furthers the University's mission by disseminating knowledge in the pursuit of
education, learning, and research at the highest international levels of excellence.

www.cambridge.org
Information on this title: www.cambridge.org/9781316517222
DOI: 10.1017/9781009043595

First published 2022

A catalogue record for this publication is available from the British Library.

Library of Congress Cataloging-in-Publication Data
Names: Stump, Eleonore, 1947- editor. | White, Thomas Joseph, 1971- editor.
Title: The new Cambridge companion to Aquinas / edited by Eleonore Stump
  (Saint Louis University), Thomas Joseph White (Angelicum, the Pontifical
  University of St. Thomas).
Description: [New York] : Cambridge University Press, [2022] | Series: Cambridge
  companions | Includes bibliographical references and index.
Identifiers: LCCN 2022003230 (print) | LCCN 2022003231 (ebook) |
  ISBN 9781316517222 (hardback) | ISBN 9781009044332 (paperback) |
  ISBN 9781009043595 (epub)
Subjects: LCSH: Thomas, Aquinas, Saint, 1225?-1274. | BISAC: PHILOSOPHY /
  History & Surveys / Medieval
Classification: LCC B765.T54 N46 2022 (print) | LCC B765.T54 (ebook) |
  DDC 230/.2092–dc23/eng/20220301
LC record available at https://lccn.loc.gov/2022003230
LC ebook record available at https://lccn.loc.gov/2022003231

ISBN 978-1-316-51722-2 Hardback
ISBN 978-1-009-04433-2 Paperback

For our teachers

He waters the mountains from his higher realms. The earth will be filled with the fruit of your works. (Psalm 104:13)

From eternity, the Lord and King of the heavens has established this law, that the gifts of his providence make their way to lower things through intermediaries.

And so in this psalm the Lord set forth that law, understood with regard to the transmission of spiritual wisdom, under the metaphors of corporeal things, namely, watering the mountains, and the rest.

In this way, the minds of the learned, who are indicated by "mountains," are watered from the higher realms of God's wisdom, and through their service the light of God's wisdom makes its way to the minds of their audience.

Thomas Aquinas, *Rigans montes de superioribus suis*
(inaugural lecture, 1256)

Contents

Contributors

Jeffrey E. Brower is Professor of Philosophy at Purdue University. He is the author of *Aquinas's Ontology of the Material World: Change, Hylomorphism, and Material Objects* (2014) and a contributor to *The Oxford Handbook on Aquinas* (2012).

Therese Scarpelli Cory is the John and Jean Oesterle Associate Professor of Thomistic Studies at the University of Notre Dame, and a member of the Pontifical Academy of St. Thomas Aquinas. She is the author of *Aquinas on Human Self-Knowledge* (2014) and numerous journal articles.

Simon Francis Gaine, OP, is the first Pinckaers Professor of Theological Anthropology and Ethics in the Thomistic Institute at the Pontifical University of St. Thomas, Rome, and a Fellow of Blackfriars Hall, Oxford. He is the author of *Will There Be Free Will in Heaven? Freedom, Impeccability and Beatitude* (2003) and *Did the Saviour See the Father? Christ, Salvation and the Vision of God* (2015).

Michael Gorman is Professor of Philosophy at The Catholic University of America in Washington, DC. He is the author of *Aquinas on the Metaphysics of the Hypostatic Union* (2017) and numerous journal articles.

Tobias Hoffmann is Professor of Medieval Philosophy at Sorbonne Université. He is editor of *Weakness of Will from Plato to the Present* (2008), *A Companion to Angels in Medieval Philosophy* (2012), and *Aquinas and the Nicomachean Ethics* (with Jörn Müller and Matthias Perkams, 2013), and author of *Free Will and the Rebel Angels in Medieval Philosophy* (2021).

Gaven Kerr is Lecturer in Philosophy at St. Patrick's Pontifical University Maynooth. He is author of *Aquinas's Way to God: The Proof in* De Ente et Essentia (2015), *Aquinas and the Metaphysics of Creation* (2019), and a number of journal articles.

Angela Knobel is Associate Professor of Philosophy at the University of Dallas. She is author of *Aquinas and the Infused Moral Virtues* (2021) and a number of journal articles.

Brian Leftow is William P. Alston Professor of the Philosophy of Religion at Rutgers University and an emeritus Fellow of Oriel College, Oxford. He is the author of *God and Necessity* (2012), *Time and Eternity* (1991), and numerous journal articles.

Dominic Legge, OP, is the Director of the Thomistic Institute and Assistant Professor of Theology at the Pontifical Faculty at the Dominican House of Studies in Washington, DC. He is the author of *The Trinitarian Christology of St. Thomas Aquinas* (2017).

Colleen McCluskey is Professor of Philosophy at Saint Louis University. She is the author of *Thomas Aquinas on Moral Wrongdoing* (Cambridge, 2017) and coauthor of *Aquinas's Ethics: Metaphysical Foundations, Moral Theory, and Theological Context* (2009) and numerous articles.

Timothy Pawl is Professor of Philosophy at the University of St. Thomas, Minnesota. His books include *In Defense of Conciliar Christology: A Philosophical Essay* (2016), *In Defense of Extended Conciliar Christology: A Philosophical Essay* (2019), and *The Incarnation* (2020).

Andrew Pinsent is Research Director of the Ian Ramsey Centre for Science and Religion at the Faculty of Theology and Religion, University of Oxford. He is also a priest of the diocese of Arundel and Brighton, England. His publications include the edited volume *The History of Evil in the Medieval Age: 450–1450 CE* (2018) and numerous journal articles.

James Dominic Rooney, OP, is Assistant Professor of Philosophy at Hong Kong Baptist University, Fellow of the Thomistic Institute (Rome), and a Dominican friar of the Province of St. Albert the Great, Chicago. He is the author of *Material Objects in Confucian and Aristotelian Metaphysics: The Inevitability of Hylomorphism* (2022).

Eleonore Stump is the Robert J. Henle Professor of Philosophy at Saint Louis University and a third-order Dominican. She is Honorary Professor at Wuhan University and at the Logos Institute, St. Andrews, and a Professorial Fellow at Australian Catholic University. She is the author of *Aquinas* (2003), *Wandering in Darkness: Narrative and the Problem of Suffering* (2010), *Atonement* (2018), and *The Image of God: The Problem of Evil and the Problem of Mourning* (2022). She is coeditor of *The Cambridge Companion to Augustine*, 2nd edition (with David Meconi, Cambridge, 2014) and *Hidden Divinity and Religious Belief: New Perspectives* (with Adam Green, Cambridge, 2016).

Thomas Joseph White, OP, is the Rector of the Pontifical University of St. Thomas (Angelicum) in Rome. He is the author of *Wisdom in the Face of Modernity: A Study in Thomistic Natural Theology* (2011), *The Incarnate Lord: A Thomistic Study in Christology* (2015), *Exodus* (2016), *The Light of Christ: An Introduction to Catholicism* (2017), and *The Trinity: On the Nature and Mystery of the One God* (2022).

Thomas Williams is the Isabelle A. and Henry D. Martin Professor of Medieval Philosophy at Georgetown University. He has published widely on medieval philosophy and theology. He is coauthor of *Anselm* (2008), editor of *The Cambridge Companion to Medieval Ethics* (Cambridge, 2018) and *The Cambridge Companion to Duns Scotus* (Cambridge, 2003), and translator of *Augustine: Confessions* (2019), *John Duns Scotus: Selected Writings on Ethics* (2017), *Thomas Aquinas: The Treatise on Happiness and Treatise on Human Acts* (2016), and *Anselm: The Complete Treatises* (2022).

Abbreviations

CG	*Contra errores Graecorum*
CT	*Compendium theologiae*
DEE	*De ente et essentia*
Diu. nom.	*Expositio super librum Dionysii De divinis nominibus*
DPN	*De principiis naturae*
DSS	*De substantiis separatis*
DUI	*De unitate intellectus contra Averroistas*
In BDH	*Expositio super librum Boethii De hebdomadibus*
In BDT	*Expositio super librum Boethii De trinitate*
In CA	*Expositio super librum De causis*
In DA	*Sententia Libri De anima*
In DC	*Sententia super De caelo et mundo*
In DMR	*Sententia super De memoria et reminiscentia*
In DS	*Sententia super De sensu et sensato*
In Eph	*Expositio et Lectura super Epistolam Pauli Apostoli ad Ephesios*
In Gal	*Expositio et Lectura super Epistolam Pauli Apostoli ad Galatas*
In Heb	*Expositio et Lectura super Epistolam Pauli Apostoli ad Hebraeos*
In I Cor	*Expositio et Lectura super Primam Epistolam Pauli Apostoli ad Corinthios*
In II Cor	*Expositio et Lectura super Secundam Epistolam Pauli Apostoli ad Corinthios*
In I Tim	*Expositio et Lectura super Primam Epistolam Pauli Apostoli ad Timotheum*
In Meta	*Sententia super Metaphysicam*

In NE	*Sententia Libri Ethicorum*
In PA	*Sententia super Posteriora analytica*
In Peri herm.	*Sententia super Peri hermenias*
In Phy	*Sententia super Physicam*
In Rom	*Expositio et Lectura super Epistolam Pauli Apostoli ad Romanos*
In Sent.	*Scriptum super libros Sententiarum*
QDA	*Quaestio disputata De anima*
QDC	*Quaestio disputata De caritate*
QDM	*Quaestiones disputatae De malo*
QDP	*Quaestiones disputatae De potentia*
QDSC	*Quaestio disputata De spiritualibus creaturis*
QDUVI	*Quaestio disputata De unione verbi incarnati*
QDV	*Quaestiones disputatae De veritate*
QDVCom	*Quaestio disputata De virtutibus in communi*
Quodl	*Quaestiones de quodlibet I–XII*
SCG	*Summa contra Gentiles*
ST	*Summa theologiae*
Super Ioann.	*Lectura super Ioannem*
Super Matt.	*Lectura super Matthaeum*

A Select List of Aquinas's Works

For a list of Aquinas's works in English translation, see https://aquinas-in-english.neocities.org/

GENERAL TREATISES

Scriptum super libros Sententiarum (*Commentary on the Sentences of Peter Lombard*): c.1252–7

Summa contra Gentiles: c.1259–65

Summa theologiae: c.1265–73

Compendium theologiae: c.1265–73

SPECIAL TREATISES

De ente et essentia (*On Being and Essence*): c.1252–6

De principiis naturae (*On the Principles of Nature*): c.1252–6

De regno ad regem Cypri (*On Kingship, to the King of Cyprus*): c.1267

De substantiis separatis (*On Separate Substances*): c.1271

De mixtione elementorum (*On the Mixture of Elements*): c.1270

DISPUTED QUESTIONS

Quaestiones disputatae De veritate (*Disputed Questions on Truth*): c.1256–9

Quaestiones disputatae De potentia (*Disputed Questions on Power*): c.1265–6

Quaestio disputata De anima (*Disputed Question on the Soul*): c.1265–6

Quaestio disputata De spiritualibus creaturis (*Disputed Question on Spiritual Creatures*): c.1267–8

Quaestiones disputatae De Malo (*Disputed Questions on Evil*): c.1266–70

Quaestiones disputatae De virtutibus (*Disputed Questions on the Virtues*): c.1271–2

Quaestio disputata De unione verbi incarnati (*Disputed Question on the Union of the Incarnate Word*): c.1271–2

Quaestiones de quodlibet I–XII (*Quodlibetal Questions I–XII*): c.1252–6 and c.1268–72

BIBLICAL COMMENTARIES

Expositio super Isaiam ad litteram (*Commentary on Isaiah*): c.1248–54

Postilla super Ieremiam et Threnos (*Commentaries on Jeremiah and Lamentations*): c.1248–52

Expositio super Job ad litteram (*Commentary on Job*): c.1261–5

Glossa continua super Evangelia (Catena aurea) (A Continuous Gloss on the Four Gospels): c.1262–4

Lectura super Matthaeum (*Commentary on Matthew*): c.1269–70

Lectura super Ioannem (*Commentary on John*): c.1270–2

Expositio et lectura super Epistolas Pauli Apostoli (*Commentaries on the Epistles of St. Paul*): possibly 1265–73

Postilla super Psalmos (*Commentary on the Psalms*): c.1273

COMMENTARIES ON ARISTOTLE

Sententia Libri De anima: 1267–8

Sententia super De sensu et sensato: c.1268–9

Sententia super Physicam: c.1268–9

Sententia super Meteora: c.1268–70

Sententia libri Politicorum: c.1269–72

Sententia super De memoria et reminiscentia: c.1270

Sententia super Peri hermenias: c.1270–1

Sententia super Posteriora analytica: c.1270–2

Sententia Libri Ethicorum: 1271–2

Sententia super Metaphysicam: c.1270–2

Sententia super libros De caelo et mundo: c.1272–3

Sententia super libros De generatione et corruptione: c.1272–3

OTHER COMMENTARIES

Expositio super librum Boethii De trinitate (*Commentary on Boethius's* De Trinitate): c.1257–9

Expositio super librum Boethii De hebdomadibus (*Commentary on Boethius's* De hebdomadibus): c.1257–9

Expositio super librum Dionysii De divinis nominibus (*Commentary on Pseudo-Dionysius's* The Divine Names): c.1261–8

Expositio super librum De causis (*Commentary on the* Book of Causes): c.1272

POLEMICAL WRITINGS

Contra impugnantes Dei cultum et religionem (*Against Those Who Impugn the Cult of God and Religion*): 1256

Contra errores Graecorum (*Against the Errors of the Greeks*): c.1263–4

De perfectione spiritualis vitae (*On the Perfection of the Spiritual Life*): 1269–70

De unitate intellectus contra Averroistas (*On the Unicity of the Intellect against the Averroists*): 1270

Contra doctrinam retrahentium a religione (*Against the Teachings of Those Who Prevent Men from Entering the Religious Life*): 1271

De aeternitate mundi (*On the Eternity of the World*): c.1271

Epistola ad ducissam Brabantiae (*Letter to the Duchess of Brabant*): c.1271

LITURGICAL AND RELATED WORKS

Principia: "Hic est liber mandatorum Dei" et "Rigans montes de superioribus suis" (*Inaugural Lectures: "This Is the Book of God's Commandments" and "Watering the Hills from His Places Above"*): c.1256

Collationes in decem praecepta (*Homilies on the Ten Commandments*): c.1261–73

Officium de festo Corporis Christi (*Office for the Feast of Corpus Christi*): c.1264

Collationes in orationem dominicam, in Symbolorum Apostolorum, in salutatem angelicam (*Homilies on the Lord's Prayer, the Apostles' Creed, and the Angelic Greeting*): c.1268–73

Hymn *Adoro te devote:* date unknown

Introduction

Eleonore Stump and Thomas Joseph White, OP

The Cambridge Companion to Aquinas, edited by Eleonore Stump and her friend and former teacher Norman Kretzmann († 1998), appeared almost thirty years ago. In the time since the publication of that volume, an enormous amount of research on Aquinas's thought has appeared. The time is right, then, for a redoing of that *Companion* volume. But because so much time has elapsed since the first *Companion* volume appeared, it was not feasible just to revise it and reissue it as a second edition. Instead, it was necessary to start over completely. With the exception of Eleonore Stump, all the contributors to *The New Cambridge Companion to Aquinas* are new and have written original papers for this volume; and even Stump's paper in the first *Companion* volume has been replaced by an entirely fresh essay.

The challenge for this new *Companion* volume has been to pick topics that are faithful to Aquinas's thought and transmit the worldview he inherited and developed, while at the same time revealing to contemporary philosophers the strong connections there are between Aquinas's interests and views and contemporary philosophical research. Erring too much on one side would yield work that is untrue to the historical Aquinas. Erring too much on the other side would result in work of interest to no one but antiquarians. We have been mindful of this challenge, and we have done our best to find a way to address it in *The New Cambridge Companion to Aquinas*. In striving for this result, we have been aided by having been able to enlist contributors who are recognized experts in the thought of Aquinas

1

and also known for their philosophical acuity. We are grateful to all of them for their generous care in producing the excellent chapters of this volume.

We are also grateful to Eleonore Stump's research assistants William Hannegan and Cecilia Nicklaus, who provided valuable help with the footnotes and much other work involved in getting the manuscript ready for the press. Barbara Manning, Eleonore Stump's secretary and the *sine qua non* of her office, was also a great aid in keeping track of the myriad details of the project.

The first section of this volume consists in one chapter on Aquinas's life and work written by Dominic Legge. It gives a thorough historical overview of Aquinas's career and also sketches the character of the man himself, in a human and sympathetic way.

The second section is on Aquinas's metaphysics and his view of the structure of reality in general and of human nature in particular. Four of the five chapters in this section attempt to capture the most basic parts of Aquinas's worldview, which influence all his other thought. The first of these four chapters, written by Jeffrey Brower, presents and explains the philosophical toolkit that Aquinas inherited and put to far-ranging use, including his account of hylomorphism, among other topics. The second, written by Thomas Joseph White, is on Aquinas's understanding of the ultimate foundation of reality, both in its abstract philosophical form, as concentrated in Aquinas's views on essence and existence, and in its theological form, as outlined in Aquinas's account of the simplicity and Trinity of God. The next chapter, written by Gaven Kerr, uses the Thomistic thought outlined in the previous two chapters to show the way in which Aquinas's metaphysics provides a metaethics, by connecting the nature of goodness to the nature of being. The fourth chapter, written by James Dominic Rooney, explores the way in which Aquinas connects his metaphysics to his understanding of nature and causality in the created world. Finally, the fifth chapter in this section, written by Eleonore Stump, explores the nature of the human person on Aquinas's view, not only the metaphysical nature of human beings but also the nature of the human self.

The third section is on Aquinas's epistemology, and it consists of three chapters. The first, written by Therese Scarpelli Cory, is on the general nature of knowledge, as Aquinas sees it. The second, written by Angela Knobel, is on the intellectual virtues, using the intellectual virtue of understanding as representative of Aquinas's thought on this topic. And the third, written by Michael Gorman, is on the relation of the intellect to the will and the emergent freedom of the interactive system of the intellect and the will.

The fourth section is on ethics, to which the volume devotes three chapters. The first one, written by Tobias Hoffmann, explains the nature of human goodness by considering Aquinas's account of grace and the will. The next chapter, written by Colleen McCluskey, moves from Aquinas's metaethics to explain Aquinas's understanding of the moral virtues, which are central to Aquinas's normative ethics. And the final chapter in this section, written by Andrew Pinsent, explains a central and often neglected part of Aquinas's ethics, which Aquinas presents as the gifts and fruits of the Holy Spirit.

The fifth and final section of the volume is on philosophical theology, and it contains four chapters. The first one, written by Brian Leftow, is a short chapter on the nature of original sin, as Aquinas sees it, because this part of Aquinas's thought is foundational for other major elements of his philosophical theology. The second chapter, written by Timothy Pawl, is on Aquinas's understanding of the nature of the Incarnation of Christ, which is the remedy for the problem of original sin. The third chapter, written by Thomas Williams, is on the problem of evil and atonement. And the final chapter, written by Simon Francis Gaine, is on Aquinas's account of resurrection and other related topics usually grouped under the heading 'last things.'

As a comparison of this volume with the original *The Cambridge Companion to Aquinas* makes evident, we have greatly expanded both the number and detail of the topics covered. For this expansion, we sacrificed other topics, perhaps most notably a chapter on Aquinas's politics. But the trade-off allows this volume to present Aquinas's basic philosophical worldview in much greater depth than the earlier volume did. The result is more fidelity to Aquinas's own thought and also much more of interest to contemporary philosophers. The topics we chose reflect as well as we thought possible both the main structure of Aquinas's worldview and also the major areas of philosophy as they are currently understood in the contemporary discipline. In consequence, both the topics and the excellent work of the contributors have fulfilled the aim with which we undertook *The New Cambridge Companion to Aquinas*. The result is a volume that faithfully transmits the thought of Aquinas but that can also engage not only those antecedently interested just in Aquinas's work but also those who are interested in the same topics that occupied him.

PART I **Life and Works**

I   Thomas Aquinas

A Life Pursuing Wisdom

Dominic Legge, OP

Thomas Aquinas was born to an aristocratic family in Roccasecca, near Naples, probably in 1226.[1] At an early age, he was sent to be schooled by the Benedictine monks at the famous abbey of Monte Cassino.[2] It seems that his family planned that he would one day become its abbot – a fitting position of honor and prestige for the youngest son of Italian nobility.[3]

In 1239, at the age of thirteen or fourteen, Aquinas was sent to the newly established university at Naples,[4] where he had two important encounters: He studied the philosophy of Aristotle and Avicenna,[5] and he met the fledgling Dominican Order. The Dominicans did not have the impressive reputation, social standing, or institutional clout of St. Benedict's order; they were mendicants – that is, they depended on alms – and as the *Ordo Praedicatorum*, were dedicated to preaching and teaching. The Dominicans therefore had a strong commitment to study and the intellectual life, and a notable presence in the universities of Europe.

The young Aquinas was impressed by this new order and its friars (*fratres* or brothers). Without obtaining the permission of his parents, he took the religious habit (white and black monastic clothing) of the Dominicans in 1244. This marked a definitive break with his family's plans for his future as a Benedictine abbot. The Dominicans immediately sent him north, journeying to the large Dominican priory in Bologna.

His family tried to stop him. His mother came to Naples too late. She sent a rapid courier to some of his older brothers, then in the company of the Emperor and his soldiers just north of Rome. They gathered a small force that intercepted Aquinas on the road, seized him, and tried to tear off his Dominican habit – unsuccessfully (though they did rip it), because Aquinas, who was notably tall, large, and strong, physically resisted.[6] The family placed him under house arrest in the family castle for a year, hoping to weaken his resolve to join this upstart new order. His brothers even sent a prostitute to his room to seduce him; Aquinas drove her away. Aquinas continued to wear the Dominican habit, spending his time in prayer and study, and reading through the entire Bible.[7] (He was repeatedly visited by the friar who inspired him to become a Dominican, who would wear two habits, leaving one with Aquinas as a change of clothing.)[8]

The young Aquinas's tenacity offers a telling insight into his character. It is akin to the famous gesture of Francis of Assisi, who removed the rich clothing provided by his father in order to assume a poor life in the poorest clothing, against his father's wishes.[9] Aquinas's scholastic works do not often disclose much of his personal life, but when he treats (years later, as a theologian) the subject of religious vows, his personal conviction is evident.[10] He writes that, when called by God to follow Christ's own example – living in voluntary poverty as a religious in order to preach the gospel – a young person should obey God rather than his parents: "Better to obey the Father of spirits (Heb. 12:9) through whom we live than to obey the generators of our flesh."[11] "In this domain, our relatives according to the flesh are more enemies than friends."[12]

DOMINICAN STUDENT IN PARIS AND COLOGNE (1245–1251/2)

Aquinas's family gave up. Released from house arrest in 1245, he was sent to live and study at the Dominican priory at Paris, associated with that city's famous university. He probably stayed there for three years.

In 1248, the Dominican Order decided to send the renowned Dominican professor Albert the Great to Cologne to found a new *studium generale* (a graduate faculty for Dominican students from across Europe and an early predecessor of the University of Cologne). Aquinas, then about twenty-two years old, accompanied Albert. For the next three or four years, Aquinas studied in Cologne under Albert. (Aquinas was probably ordained a priest in Cologne.)

A famous story about Aquinas, found in the earliest histories of his life, dates from this stay in Cologne. Aquinas was physically large but was humble and spoke little. The other Dominican student brothers began to call him "the mute [or 'dumb'] ox," not realizing his tremendous intellectual gifts. One day, Aquinas unknowingly dropped a slip of paper outside his monastic cell on which he had written notes he had taken during a session led by Albert the Great. Another student found it and took it to Albert, who read it and marveled at Aquinas's insight. Albert assigned Aquinas to be the "respondent" (or student-debater) in a "disputation" (a classroom debate) on a difficult question the next day. Typically, a student would lay out the issue and make provisional arguments for and against the main thesis, and then the "master" (or professor) would give the final answer, the "determination" of the question. But in this case, Aquinas gave such a full account that Albert exclaimed, "Brother Thomas, you do not seem to be doing your job, but mine!" Aquinas replied, "Master, I do not see how I could discuss the question in any other way." Albert then said to the class, "We call him a mute ox, but he will bellow so loudly with learning that it will sound throughout the whole world."[13]

Impressed with his student's acumen, Albert designated Aquinas to serve as his assistant. Albert charged Aquinas with compiling careful notes of Albert's courses on Pseudo-Dionysius's *Celestial Hierarchy* and *Divine Names*, and on Aristotle's *Nicomachean Ethics* – works that would have a major influence on Aquinas's own thought.[14]

BACHELOR OF THEOLOGY AT THE UNIVERSITY OF PARIS (1251/2–1256)

In 1251 or 1252, the Master of the Dominican Order directed Albert to recommend a theology student for the prestigious position of "bachelor" at the University of Paris: Albert chose Aquinas, despite his young age (twenty-five or twenty-six). (A bachelor in the medieval university was akin to today's graduate student who teaches while working on a terminal degree under a "master" or full professor.)

In the thirteenth century, the path from bachelor to master in theology consisted of three stages: The bachelor would teach "cursory" lectures on Scripture, then would prepare (and teach from) a lengthy commentary on the standard "textbook" of theology, Peter Lombard's *Sentences*, and finally would assist his master at formal university disputations. In his first academic year, Aquinas completed the first stage, leading to his first two published works: a *Commentary on Isaiah* and a *Commentary on Jeremiah*.

In his second and third academic years as a bachelor in Paris, Aquinas completed the second stage, commenting on Lombard's *Sentences* in roughly 200 class sessions. At the same time, Aquinas was writing his *Commentary on the Sentences* – his first major work – which he published in his fourth academic year.[15] Book I treats God in himself, as one and triune; Book II treats creation, sin, and evil; Book III treats the Son's Incarnation and the theological virtues; Book IV covers the sacraments and concludes with the resurrection and the last judgment.

Aquinas's commentary went far beyond Lombard's text (a compilation of the various opinions (*sententiae*) of Church Fathers on the key questions of theology), and many of his most famous positions are already visible. Not in every case, however: Aquinas later changed or developed his view on a number of important points, especially in light of philosophical insights, or as he conducted new research into patristic and conciliar sources. This is the case, for example, with his analysis of the union of natures in Christ. Because the text is long, one will sometimes find Aquinas offering his most detailed explanation of some of his signature positions (for example, that the Trinitarian processions of the divine persons in God are the origin, cause, and exemplar of the "procession" of creatures from God by creation).

While completing his official course of studies, Aquinas also composed two short philosophical works at the request of his Dominican brothers – probably, other friars living in the same priory. (This was not unusual for Aquinas, who was generous in responding to such requests: Roughly one-third of Aquinas's works were written at the request of Dominican brothers or other friends and superiors.) *On Being and Essence* (*De ente et essentia*) shows Aquinas offering his own treatment of these first concepts of our intellect, showing a notable familiarity with Avicenna.[16] *On the Principles of Nature* (*De principiis naturae*) aims "at illustrating the principles that we can use to read the structure of natural reality."[17]

The University of Paris of the 1250s was a tumultuous place, marked by a bitter conflict between the "secular" masters (university professors who were diocesan clergy and so did not belong to a religious order) and the "mendicants" (the Dominicans and the Franciscans). The issues were complex, but the "seculars" especially objected to the growing number of new mendicant masters and the number of mendicant chairs they held. While Aquinas was lecturing on the *Sentences* in 1253, the secular masters went so far as to expel the mendicant masters from the university. The mendicants continued to teach their courses (Aquinas, not a master but undoubtedly affected, probably kept teaching too), and the pope reinstated them a few months later. The hostility grew to such a point that the Dominicans were afraid to leave their priory out of fear of the seculars' students. In 1255, when a new Dominican master was set to give his inaugural lecture, the Dominican priory had to be protected by an armed guard of archers sent by King Louis IX to prevent any incident.[18]

AQUINAS'S FIRST PARIS REGENCY (1256–1259)

The following year, in the spring of 1256, Aquinas was granted the degree of master in theology and was appointed to a Dominican chair at the university, where he would serve as regent master in theology through the academic year of 1258-9. Aquinas's installation in his new position was hurried, perhaps to avoid any organized opposition by the seculars. The university's chancellor gave Aquinas only one day's notice that he would deliver his official "inaugural lecture" in a public ceremony the next day.[19] Aquinas had no lecture prepared. A story originating with Aquinas (it was published during his lifetime) recounts that, that night, Aquinas dreamed of an older Dominican (St. Dominic?) who said, "Do not fear; God will help you to bear the burden of being a Master. And as for the lecture, take this text, '*You water the mountains from your dwelling above; the earth is filled with the fruit of your work* (Ps. 103:13).'"[20]

Aquinas's inaugural lecture (*Rigans montes*) was based on this Scripture verse. Aquinas explained that the water descending from above is a metaphor for the communication of spiritual wisdom, which descends from God to the teachers like rain falling on the mountains, and thence flows down to the minds of their listeners. Teaching is a high task, and one must depend on God to carry it out. Aquinas ended with these words:

> Although no one is ready for such a ministry of himself or from himself, he can hope to be made sufficient by God . . .. Let us pray that Christ will grant it to us. Amen.[21]

In addition to lecturing, "disputing" was one of the principal tasks of a master of theology. On every school day, Aquinas probably lectured in the morning and led an "ordinary" disputation with his students in the afternoon: The master would choose a question (normally following a sequence of preplanned themes), students would argue for and against, and then the master would give the final answer, responding to the objections of the other side. The proceedings would often be revised by the master and published. Like other university masters, Aquinas was also expected on occasion to hold more demanding "public" or "extraordinary" disputations that students and masters from other schools could attend. Called *quodlibetal* or *de quodlibet* (literally, "on whatever"), the master did not choose the theme in advance: Questioners in the audience could pose a question on any theme, to which the master was then expected to reply – a challenging and dangerous business in such a charged university atmosphere.

During Aquinas's first Paris regency, he prepared for publication his disputed questions *On Truth (De veritate)*. It is his most important work of this time, covering truth, knowledge (human, angelic, and divine), the mind, teaching, faith, conscience, the good, the will, free choice, passions, and grace. Aquinas also published five *quodlibetal* questions from this period. Such disputations normally took place twice a year (in Advent and Lent), but masters could decline to participate – and they often did. Aquinas did not: He was "one of the most prolific disputants of the thirteenth century."[22]

Aquinas also preached as a part of his formal university duties. This included occasional "university" sermons, addressing assembled members of the theology faculty on Sundays or major feast days. The sermon would be given in the morning during Mass, often with a second address following in the evening before Vespers.[23] Aquinas also preached in other contexts – we have his sermons on the Our Father, the Hail Mary, the Creed, and the Decalogue. They show a different side of Aquinas: the priest preaching to the lay faithful on the basics of the Catholic faith.

NAPLES AND ORVIETO (1259–1265)

The Dominicans rapidly rotated masters through the University of Paris, to build up a cadre of highly qualified teachers to send throughout Europe. Thus, at the conclusion of the 1258–9 academic year, Aquinas ceded his chair to his senior bachelor, William of Alton.

Aquinas's next task was to attend the Dominicans' General Chapter of 1259. Humbert of Romans, the Master of the Order, called together five Dominicans who had recently served as Parisian masters of theology – including Albert the Great and Aquinas – to draft legislation for the Order's intellectual life.[24] They strengthened the position of lector (an in-house professor in each Dominican priory), directing that houses without a lector should transfer their young friars to a house with one. It called for young friars to study philosophy (presumably preparatory to theological training, as was required of the "secular" clerical students at Paris and Oxford).[25] Students were not to have duties hindering their studies. What is more, every friar was to attend the lector's class sessions, including the prior and other professors, when possible, and Mass was not to be scheduled to conflict with the academic exercises in the priory.[26] This legislation was key for the future of the Dominican Order, solidifying its commitment to study (including philosophy) as a primary religious observance in the service of its work of the salvation of souls. Albert and Aquinas – both careful students of Aristotle and proponents of philosophy as necessary for the pursuit of divine wisdom – had a hand in drafting it.

After this, Aquinas returned to Naples (his home priory), perhaps after a stay in Paris. In 1260, Aquinas was appointed a "Preacher General" by his province. This prestigious position exempted Aquinas from many other responsibilities and awarded him a permanent *socius* or traveling companion. Reginald of Piperno (or Priverno) was assigned this role; he would become Aquinas's disciple, friend, and confidant. He would serve as his secretary until Aquinas's death.[27]

In the final year of his first Paris regency, Aquinas started writing the *Summa contra Gentiles* (the original title was probably *On the Truth of the Catholic Faith Against the Errors of Nonbelievers*).[28] Aquinas would work on it until 1264 or 1265. The structuring idea of this long systematic work is the pursuit and communication of wisdom, and the destruction of the opposite errors, first using the power of natural reason (Book I covers what reason can know about God, Book II is on creation, and Book III is on divine providence), and then using the light of faith (Book IV treats the Trinity, Christ's Incarnation, the sacraments, and the last judgment). Aquinas argues that God has revealed the highest wisdom through Christ, to which we have access by faith. But since those who reject the faith do not accept the authority of Scripture and the Church, Aquinas marshals arguments from reason to demonstrate what reason can know about God, to illustrate and render plausible what the Catholic faith believes, and to show that no rational arguments can undermine or disprove it.

In September 1261, Aquinas was assigned to the Dominican priory in Orvieto, a small city north of Rome, to serve as a priory lector. This had nothing like the prestige or importance of the University of Paris. Yet this move was notable for two major reasons: It gave Aquinas time to write; and a month after his assignment, the just-elected Pope Urban IV moved to Orvieto, thus placing Aquinas near the pope, his library, and the papal archives.

During his time in Orvieto, Aquinas lectured on the book of Job, probably while writing on divine providence in Book III of his *Summa contra Gentiles*. The result was his *Commentary on Job*, which focuses especially on providence and the mystery of evil and suffering. Aquinas also may have lectured on some of St. Paul's letters during this period; his revised text would later be published as part of his *Commentary on St. Paul's Letters*.

In Orvieto, Aquinas began writing another synthetic work, the *Compendium of Theology*, at Reginald's request. Aquinas organized it on a theological plan centered on the theological virtues: "St. Paul taught that the entirety of the perfection of the present life consists in faith, hope, and love, as if summing up our salvation in these three short headings."[29] During this same period, Aquinas responded to multiple requests for his advice, producing a short letter on buying and selling on credit (*De emptione et venditione ad tempus*), and a longer work responding to questions from "the cantor of Antioch," who seemingly was in contact with Muslim critics of Christianity (*De rationibus fidei*). At the pope's special request, Aquinas also wrote an expert theological assessment of a compilation of quotations attributed to Greek Fathers of the Church (*Contra errores Graecorum*).

Pope Urban also commissioned Aquinas to compose a commentary on the Gospels, known as the *Catena Aurea* or "Golden Chain," exclusively using quotations from Church Fathers, strung together like a running commentary from the pen of a single author. (Aquinas was initially asked to work on only two Gospels; his Franciscan contemporary, St. Bonaventure, was asked to prepare the other two, but Bonaventure demurred and so all four fell to Aquinas.)[30]

This was an enormous project of patristic research, and it prompted Aquinas to delve even more deeply into the thought of the great theologians of the Church's first millennium. Aquinas tells us in a dedicatory preface that he commissioned translations from Greek into Latin of some patristic works. Aquinas may have found some of his sources in the papal library and archives brought to Orvieto. Probably, he also found the decrees of the great ecumenical councils of the first millennium, largely unknown to medieval theologians. He began to quote them from this point forward – and they prompted some notable developments in his theology.[31]

Aquinas's own words give us a precious insight into how hard he worked at – and how much he valued and profited from – this enormous labor in the search of wisdom:

> The judgment of right reason prefers the good of wisdom, by which we may come to the fount of goodness itself, to every human good. For wisdom never grows distasteful: whoever eats it continues to hunger for it, and whoever drinks it does not cease to thirst for it . . ..
> It grants a never-ending fruit to its ministers, so that those who bring it to light would possess eternal life. And thus it is sweeter than pleasures, more secure than offices or kingdoms, and more useful than all riches.
>
> I have applied myself to just such a delightful task: the ministry of explaining the wisdom of the Gospel, hidden for ages in

mystery and brought forth into the light by incarnate wisdom of God, by compiling the comments of holy Doctors . . . . I have applied myself diligently to this study, with much labor, in order to complete this exposition of the four gospels.[32]

The pope also commissioned Aquinas to compose the liturgy of Corpus Christi, the feast added to the Church's worldwide calendar by Urban IV in honor of Jesus's institution of the Eucharist at the Last Supper. (Although some question Aquinas's authorship of these hymns and liturgical texts, there is a growing consensus that Aquinas wrote them.) Made up of prayers, Scripture readings, hymns, and a short devotional treatise on the Eucharist, this work allows us to see a different side of Aquinas: a man of piety, a man of prayer, and even an impressive poet.

ROME: THE *SUMMA THEOLOGIAE* BEGINS (1265–1268)

Pope Urban IV died in 1264, and the papal curia left Orvieto. In the following year, Aquinas attended another provincial chapter, which decided that Aquinas would go to Rome to found a new Dominican *studium* or school. Aquinas himself may have been behind this move: As one of the authors of the 1259 legislation on the Order's intellectual life, he would now be in charge of designing a comprehensive program of studies for the theological education of Dominican student brothers in his province.[33]

It is hard to overestimate the importance of this assignment, because it gave birth to Aquinas's most famous work, the *Summa theologiae*. In Orvieto, Aquinas had Dominicans of all ages attending his lectures. In Rome, he had students starting their theological study – and that called for a new method and a new textbook. Aquinas's own words explain it best:

> Because the teacher of Catholic truth should not only teach the advanced but should also educate beginners . . . our intention in this work is to hand on what pertains to the Christian religion in a way

suited to the education of beginners. For we have noted that newcomers to this teaching have often been hindered: partly by the multiplication of useless questions ... partly because [it is] ... not taught in an order suited to learning ... and partly because frequent repetition generated weariness and confusion in the minds of the students. Zealous to avoid these and other such hindrances, and with confidence in the divine help, we will try to proceed briefly and plainly (insofar as the subject matter allows) to those things that pertain to sacred doctrine.[34]

Aquinas's audacity is striking: His goal was nothing less than to set forth the entirety of Christian doctrine in an organic synthesis that would permit beginners to grasp its principles, its coherence, and its internal logic.

The *Summa theologiae* is arguably the work that best shows Aquinas's singular gift for synthesis. He manifests a grasp of the intelligibility of the whole of theology, and an ability to integrate insights from diverse sources into that whole. Of course, this is "wisdom" as Aquinas understands it: to see the whole and its cause, and to understand each part in that light. The *Summa theologiae* provides a framework that organizes the whole and yet remains open to integrating new knowledge, wherever found.

Even though it was written as a theological work, it also contains an impressive range of philosophy, from proofs for God's existence, to a philosophy of nature and of human knowledge, and even extending to questions of justice and politics. Aquinas likewise presents a formidable and comprehensive philosophical analysis of human passions, imagination, memory, and virtue, and an analysis of human free agency. Indeed, Aquinas's breadth of knowledge and intellectual interests were staggering, and he was extraordinary in his own day for the degree to which he integrated diverse sources: Scripture and the Church Fathers, both Greek and Latin; the decisions of church councils; Greek philosophy and especially Aristotle; Cicero; Christian Neoplatonism; Jewish philosophy; Arabic philosophy; a wide array of views of his immediate predecessors and contemporaries; and even what we now might call experimental science.

The *Summa* is organized with an overarching theocentric perspective: God is the source and first principle of all things; all things point back to him. Man is a microcosm of this theocentric dynamic of creation: He comes forth from God in creation and returns to God through grace, above all through the saving work of Christ's Incarnation, atoning death, and life-bestowing resurrection. Aquinas divided the *Summa* into three main parts.

I The *"Prima pars"* (First part) treats of God and the procession of creatures from God, culminating in the creation of man.

II The massive *"Secunda pars"* (Second part) covers man as the image of God, who therefore is a principle of his own action according to his intellect and free will. It is subdivided into two sections:

  A The *"Prima-Secundae"* (First [section] of the Second part) treats man's last end, and the structure and principles of his action (including the passions, virtues and vices, law and grace).

  B The *"Secunda-Secundae"* (Second [section] of the Second part) deals with specific virtues and vices, especially the theological virtues of faith, hope, and love, and the cardinal virtues of prudence, justice, fortitude, and temperance.

III The *"Tertia pars"* (Third part, unfinished at Aquinas's death) addresses "Christ, the way of our returning to God," treating the mystery of the Incarnation, all that Jesus did and suffered for our salvation, and then the sacraments instituted by him to communicate his grace to human beings.

Aquinas began the *Summa theologiae* in Rome (he would continue working on it until his death), but it was far from his only occupation. As a master living in a Dominican priory, Aquinas's day started with prayer. He rose very early to pray in silence in the priory church and said Mass with his *socius* as altar server. The early sources on Aquinas's life highlight this daily devotion to the Mass and to the

Eucharist: "He celebrated a Mass each day, unless he was prevented by sickness, and he assisted at another said by his *socius* or someone else, at which he frequently served."[35] He may have given as many as two lectures a day, and he regularly held disputations with his students. Outside the classroom, he worked with his secretary (eventually, it was a team of secretaries) on his writing projects. Aquinas's output was prodigious in this period of his life (1265–73). Jean-Pierre Torrell estimates that, at the peak of his productivity, Aquinas composed roughly thirteen pages (2,400 words) per day.[36]

In fact, at this point in his career, Aquinas seems to have coordinated his teaching with his writing of the *Summa* – for example, while in Rome, he produced his *Disputed Questions on Power*, *Disputed Question on Spiritual Creatures*, and *Disputed Question on the Soul*. He also commented on the *Divine Names* of Pseudo-Dionysius, which deals with human knowledge of God, and he composed his first commentary on Aristotle, *On the Soul*. In the same period, Aquinas was writing the parallel sections of the *Prima pars* of the *Summa theologiae* dealing with God in himself (and our knowledge of God), angels, and the human soul.[37]

During this extremely busy time in his life, when he was at the height of his powers, Aquinas systematically applied himself to commenting on the works of Aristotle. This started in Rome and continued in his subsequent assignments, even though it was not part of his job – he was charged with preparing students in theology. It seems simply to have been Aquinas's idea, required neither by his duties nor by his superiors, and he made it a major priority: All told, he commented in whole or in part on ten of Aristotle's works.

RETURN TO PARIS (1268–1272)

Aquinas returned to Paris in the fall of 1268, where he occupied once again a Dominican chair at the University of Paris. A second term in such a position was unusual, and Aquinas probably arrived well after the academic year had started. Was this an emergency assignment? Rome had been invaded in July 1268; the priory where Aquinas lived was sacked. At the same time, a triple crisis gripped the University of

Paris: (1) There was renewed conflict between the mendicants and the secular masters; (2) some partisans of Aristotle in Paris were radically misinterpreting Aristotle's thought in a way contrary to the faith; and (3) some theologians reacted against Aristotle as a danger to the Christian faith.

On the first issue, Aquinas responded by publishing a defense of the mendicant orders (*De perfectione spiritualis vitae*) early in 1270, and a second work (*Contra doctrinam retrahentium a religione*) in 1271 responding directly to the attacks from the secular masters. He also preached university sermons and held disputed questions on related themes.[38] He addressed the second issue in his short work *On the Unicity of the Intellect*, where he attacked the so-called "radical Aristotelians" or "Latin Averroists" for their claim that there was only one agent or active intellect for all human beings. In this, Aquinas was the robust defender of the integrity and autonomy of the human mind as endowed with the light of reason.[39] On the third issue, Aquinas defended Aristotle, especially on the key question of whether the world is eternal. It cannot be proven by reason that the world had a beginning in time, Aquinas argued; this can only be known by faith – and so Aristotle should not be faulted for thinking otherwise.[40]

Aquinas also had substantial university duties to fulfill. As *Magister in Sacra Pagina* (Master of Sacred Scripture), his primary task was to comment on the Bible. From Aquinas's second Paris regency, we have his richest scriptural commentaries. Probably starting in 1269–70, Aquinas produced his *Commentary on Matthew*. (It is a *reportatio* – a secretary's notes of an oral lecture, usually unrevised by the author.)[41] Aquinas shows himself a true master as a theologian and also as a scholar of the Church Fathers, whose insights are found on nearly every page. Aquinas underlines at the outset that "among the Evangelists, Matthew especially focuses on the humanity of Christ," which is the instrument through which the Son entered "into the world, lived in it, and passed out of it."[42]

Even more rich for the theologian is Aquinas's *Commentary on John*, probably composed in 1270–2. Aquinas revised, at least in part, the lecture notes taken by his secretary, giving us the best view of how Aquinas deployed his mature theological insights in a running commentary on the gospel text. Indeed, one could argue that this is Aquinas's crowning work, on what he thought was a text revealing the apex of wisdom. To use Aquinas's own words: "The Gospel of John contains everything that the other disciplines have in a partial way, and so it is the most perfect." It brings the philosophical search for wisdom to a supernatural perfection. "While the other gospels principally treat the mystery of the humanity of Christ, John in his gospel specially and above all penetrates into the divinity of Christ without ignoring the mystery of his humanity."[43]

FINAL TEACHING ASSIGNMENT AT NAPLES AND DEATH (1272–1274)

In 1272, Aquinas's provincial chapter directed him to found a *stadium generale* of theology at a location of his choice. Aquinas returned to Naples, where he taught a course on the Psalms (generating his *Commentary on the Psalms*) and completed his *Commentary on the Letters of St. Paul.* He also was working on the final part of his *Summa theologiae,* dealing with Christ and the sacraments. The enduring contributions contained in this part of the *Summa* are hard to overestimate. Aquinas put forward his definitive accounts of the reasons for the Incarnation, of the metaphysics of the union of natures in the one person of the Son, and of Christ's knowing and willing. Aquinas especially devoted himself to exploring the mysteries of Christ's life (*ST* III qq.27–59), producing a body of systematic theological reflection on the actions and sufferings of Jesus that was unprecedented in medieval theology. In his theology of the sacraments, and supremely in his theology of the Eucharist, we find some of Aquinas's most distinctive and famous theological insights.

As the *Summa theologiae* was nearing completion, Aquinas seems to have had some kind of profound mystical experience while celebrating Mass on the feast of St. Nicholas (December 6, 1273). After the Mass, he stopped working on the *Summa.* Reginald, his *socius* and secretary, repeatedly pressed Aquinas about why he was not writing. Aquinas replied: "Everything I have written seems to me as straw in comparison with the things I have seen and that have been revealed to me."[44] Though he did continue to respond by letter to requests for his expert theological opinion, Aquinas did not resume work on the *Summa*.

Aquinas's health rapidly began to decline. Summoned by Pope Gregory X to attend the Council of Lyons, Aquinas departed Naples in February 1274. Already weak and making a long journey in winter, Aquinas's health worsened after he hit his head on a low-hanging branch. He made several extended stops but did not recover. Realizing that the end was near, he asked to be taken to the nearby Cistercian abbey of Fossanova so that he could end his days in a religious house. While there, he devoutly received the Eucharist and the last rites of the Church. In the presence of several witnesses, Aquinas made a final profession of faith in the Eucharist and submitted all his teachings to the judgment of Rome. He died on the morning of March 7, 1274.[45]

CONCLUSION

Thomas Aquinas devoted himself to the search for wisdom. For the medieval Dominican friar, this search – which included groundbreaking historical research, philosophical and theological disputations in the heart of the greatest universities of his day, frequent lecturing and teaching, commenting on major works of philosophy and theology, as well as his own ambitious writing projects – was not only an academic project or a scholarly exercise. The search for wisdom was a central and organizing theme for his life as a whole. It is the best framework for understanding the unity of his thought across his many works.

Aquinas often exhorted his students to seek wisdom with all their strength and with every resource of their minds. He thinks this is the mind's very purpose, the true goal of any intellectual life – and, rightly understood, of the Christian life. At the start of the *Summa contra Gentiles*, Aquinas writes:

> The pursuit of wisdom is more perfect, more sublime, more useful, and more joyful, than all other human pursuits. It is more perfect because, to the extent that man devotes himself to the pursuit of wisdom, he already has a certain share of true happiness . . . . It is more sublime, because through wisdom, man especially approaches to a divine likeness . . . . Therefore, since likeness is the cause of love, the pursuit of wisdom especially joins one to God in friendship.[46]

The life of wisdom was not an abstraction for Aquinas. He deliberately and consistently consecrated his work and his very person to its pursuit – or, to put it another way, to the quest to know and thus to love God who is eternal wisdom.[47] This is how Aquinas understood his own Dominican vocation. For example, the quotation from the opening lines of the *Summa contra Gentiles* continues:

> Therefore, with trust in divine mercy, pursuing the task of a wise man (although this surpasses our own powers), our intention is to make clear (in our own small way) the truth which the Catholic faith professes, eliminating the contrary errors, so that I might make my own the words of Hilary [of Poitiers]: "I am mindful that I owe this to God as the greatest task of my life, that my every word and thought would speak of him."[48]

This is an extraordinary statement coming from Aquinas, who rarely speaks in the first person. It is as if Aquinas here unveils to his readers not only the centrality of wisdom for his own personal life, but also the inner desire and the spiritual disposition that motivate his work and – he says – guide every word that he writes or speaks.

What is wisdom, according to Aquinas? In the opening chapters of the *Summa contra Gentiles*, Aquinas explains that the wise man principally seeks after the truth – and, above all, the highest truth.

> The name of 'wise,' absolutely speaking, is solely reserved to one whose reflection is focused on the end of the universe, which is also the origin of the universe. Thus, according to the Philosopher [Aristotle], it belongs to the wise to consider the highest causes.[49]

Aquinas concludes that God is the first and highest cause of the universe and its ultimate end, and that God is the truth.

This gives rise to a twofold path to knowing the truth: by reason (or philosophy) and by faith (and theology, the discipline founded on faith). Aquinas holds that God is the source both of faith and of reason, and that the human being needs both in order to come to his final end. Reason and faith are eminently compatible, because God cannot be the source of a contradiction or of error. Consequently, Aquinas has a serene confidence in reason; rightly employed, it will never be able to demonstrate that a claim made by faith is false.[50] Likewise, Aquinas holds that, although many of the truths of faith (e.g., that God is triune) cannot be proven by philosophy, believing those truths is eminently reasonable.[51] The need for this twofold way of knowing the highest truth comes from the weakness of our minds, which cannot see God by the power of their natural light. Aquinas insists that reason and faith do not produce a set of double truths; rather, they are two ways by which our mind comes to know the One who is infinitely above us: "God himself, who is the truth, one and simple."[52]

After his death, Aquinas was canonized as a saint, proclaimed a "Doctor of the Church," and often held up as a great philosopher and theologian. Yet, if we take Aquinas at his word, perhaps he would want to be remembered as one who persevered in the life he embraced as a young man: to "pursue the task of a wise man ... to make clear the truth that the Catholic faith professes, eliminating the contrary errors, so that ... 'my every word and thought would speak of God.'"[53]

NOTES

1 J.-P. Torrell, *Initiation à saint Thomas d'Aquin: Sa personne et son œuvre*, new edn. (Paris: Les Éditions du Cerf, 2015), pp. 19–20; A. Oliva, *Les débuts de l'enseignement de Thomas d'Aquin et sa conception de la Sacra Doctrina avec l'édition du prologue de son Commentaire des Sentences* (Paris: Librairie Philosophique J. Vrin, 2006), pp. 188–97; S. Tugwell, *Albert and Thomas: Selected Writings* (New York: Paulist

Press, 1988), p. 201, 291–2. My citations of Torrell are to the 2015 revised French edition, but most English speakers will find the translation of the earlier edition to be quite helpful: see J.-P. Torrell, *Saint Thomas Aquinas. Volume 1: The Person and His Work*, translated by R. Royal (Washington, DC: The Catholic University of America Press, 2003).

2 Torrell, *Initiation à saint Thomas d'Aquin*, p. 24.

3 P. Porro, *Thomas Aquinas: A Historical and Philosophical Profile*, translated by J. G. Trabbic and R. W. Nutt (Washington, DC: The Catholic University of America Press, 2016), p. 4.

4 Torrell, *Initiation à saint Thomas d'Aquin*, p. 24.

5 Porro, *Thomas Aquinas*, p. 4; Torrell, *Initiation à saint Thomas d'Aquin*, p. 26. See also William of Tocco's *Ystoria Sancti Thome de Aquino* c. 10; critical edition prepared by C. le Brun-Gouanvic, *Ystoria Sancti Thome de Aquino de Guillaume de Tocco (1323)* (Toronto: Pontifical Institute of Mediaeval Studies, 1996).

6 Tocco, *Ystoria Sancti Thome de Aquino*, c. 9; Petro Calo, *Vita S. Thomae Aquinatis*, c. 7 in D. Prümmer (ed.), *Fontes Vitae S. Thomae Aquinatis* (Toulouse: Privat, 1917); Bernard Gui, *Vita S. Thomae Aquinatis*, c. 6 in K. Foster, *The Life of St. Thomas Aquinas: Biographical Documents* (Baltimore: Helicon Press, 1959).

7 Tocco, *Ystoria Sancti Thome de Aquino*, c. 10.

8 Gui, *Vita S. Thomae Aquinatis*, c. 8.

9 M.-D. Chenu, *Aquinas and His Role in Theology*, translated by P. Philibert (Collegeville: Liturgical Press, 2002), p. 7.

10 See Torrell, *Initiation à saint Thomas d'Aquin*, p. 37.

11 *ST* II-II q.189 a.6. All translations of Aquinas's texts are my own.

12 *Contra doctrinam retrahentium a religione*, p. 9.

13 Tocco, *Ystoria Sancti Thome de Aquino*, c. 13; Gui, *Vita S. Thomae Aquinatis*, ch. 10; see Tugwell, *Albert and Thomas*, pp. 209–10.

14 Torrell, *Initiation à saint Thomas d'Aquin*, p. 48; Porro, *Thomas Aquinas*, p. 5.

15 Oliva, *Les débuts de l'enseignement*, p. 241.

16 Porro, *Thomas Aquinas*, pp. 12–26.

17 Porro, *Thomas Aquinas*, p. 6.

18 J. A. Weisheipl, *Friar Thomas d'Aquino: His Life, Thought, and Work* (New York: Doubleday, 1974), pp. 82–8.

19 Oliva, *Les débuts de l'enseignement*, p. 200.

20 Gui, *Vita S. Thomae Aquinatis*, c. 12.

21 *Rigans montes de superioribus suis.*

22 D. S. Prudlo, *Thomas Aquinas: A Historical, Theological, and Environmental Portrait* (New York: Paulist Press, 2020), p. 146.

23 L. J. Bataillon, "Introduction" in *Sancti Thomae de Aquino Opera omnia: iussu Leonis XIII P.M. edita* ("Leonine edition"), vol. 44/1 (Rome: Commissio Leonina, 2014), p. 127*.

24 Prudlo, *Thomas Aquinas*, pp. 152–6.

25 Porro, *Thomas Aquinas*, pp. 118–20.

26 "Ordonnances du chapitre général (1259)" in Prümmer, *Fontes Vitae S. Thomae Aquinatis*, fasc. 6, c. 15, pp. 559–62.

27 Aquinas wrote one of his works (the *Compendium of Theology*) at Reginald's request, addressing him in the opening lines as "my dearest son, Reginald" and exhorting him to a life of faith, hope, and charity.

28 Porro, *Thomas Aquinas*, p. 121.

29 *CT* I.1.

30 Tolomeo of Lucca, *Historia Ecclesiastica Nova* 22.24 in A. Ferrua (ed.), *S. Thomae Aquinatis Vitae Fontes Precipuae* (Alba: Edizioni Domenicanae, 1968), p. 358.

31 M. Morard, "Thomas d'Aquin Lecteur des Conciles," *Archivum Franciscanum Historicum* 98 (2005): 341–2.

32 *Catena Aurea in Mk*, dedication.

33 L. Boyle, "The Setting of the *Summa Theologiae* of St. Thomas – Revisited" in S. J. Pope (ed.), *The Ethics of Aquinas* (Washington, DC: Georgetown University Press, 2002), pp. 4–5.

34 *ST*, prologue.

35 Tocco, *Ystoria Sancti Thome de Aquino*, c. 29.

36 Torrell, *Initiation à saint Thomas d'Aquin*, p. 308.

37 Torrell, *Initiation à saint Thomas d'Aquin*, pp. 211–37.

38 Torrell, *Initiation à saint Thomas d'Aquin*, p. 237.

39 Prudlo, *Thomas Aquinas*, pp. 199–202.

40 Torrell, *Initiation à saint Thomas d'Aquin*, pp. 238–42.

41 E. Stump, "Biblical Commentary and Philosophy" in N. Kretzmann and E. Stump (eds.), *The Cambridge Companion to Aquinas* (Cambridge: Cambridge University Press, 1993), p. 253.

42 *Super Matt.* c.1, lect. 1, n.11.

43 *Super Ioann.*, prologue, nn.9–10.

44 Prümmer, *Fontes Vitae S. Thomae Aquinatis*, p. 377.

45 Prudlo, *Thomas Aquinas*, pp. 242–5.

46 *SCG* I.2.

47 *ST* III q.3 a.8.

48 *SCG* I.2.

49 *SCG* I.1.

50 *In BDT* q.2, a.3.

51 *SCG* I.6–7.

52 *SCG* I.9.

53 *SCG* I.2.

PART II Metaphysics and the Ultimate Foundation of Reality

2   **First Principles**

Hylomorphism and Causation

Jeffrey E. Brower

Matter and form are two notions lying at the very heart of Aquinas's broadly Aristotelian conception of reality. Aquinas inherits these notions from Aristotle (*hyle* and *morphe* in Greek), and his understanding of each is shaped to a large extent by the various uses to which Aristotle himself puts them. Even so, the precise nature of Aquinas's hylomorphism, as well as its centrality in his thought, are of independent significance. Indeed, it would be impossible to understand Aquinas's fundamental divisions of reality – including the division of *God* and *creature*, *substance* and *accident*, *body* and *spirit* – apart from his own particular conception of matter and form. It would also be impossible, apart from this same conception, to appreciate the elements of an explanatory framework that Aquinas deploys in almost all his writings – including *potentiality* and *actuality*, *principles* and *causes*, and the fourfold division of causes into *material*, *formal*, *efficient*, and *final*. In short, to acquire a familiarity with the details of Aquinas's understanding of matter and form is almost to become accustomed to his distinctive vision of reality.

Early in his academic career, one of Aquinas's Dominican confreres asked him to explain the fundamental principles of Aristotle's natural philosophy. In response, Aquinas produced a short work, *On the Principles of Nature*, which provides an opinionated introduction to Aristotle's understanding of matter and form in the contexts of change and physical explanation. In this chapter, I undertake a similar task for Aquinas, but with a view to explaining the fundamental principles of his philosophy as a whole. Although I will have much to say about Aquinas's understanding of matter and form in the contexts of change and physical explanation, my discussion will also extend to his understanding of matter and form in the contexts of metaphysics and explanation in general. We might think of this chapter, therefore, as aiming to produce a short work, *On First Principles*.

My discussion in what follows is divided into two parts. In the first, I focus on Aquinas's hylomorphism and the fundamental divisions to which it gives rise. Here I give special attention to the role of matter and form as principles. In the second part, I turn to Aquinas's views about causation and the broader explanatory framework of which they are a part. Here I give special attention to the role of matter and form as principles of a specific type – namely, principles of being.

MATTER, FORM, AND PRINCIPLES

Any systematic treatment of Aquinas's hylomorphism must begin with his views about change. For change is the context in which Aquinas introduces the notions of *matter* and *form*, as well as that of a *hylomorphic compound*. Moreover, it is in this same context that he identifies matter and form as two of the three fundamental principles of change, the third being privation.[1]

Matter, Form, and Change

Consider two paradigmatic examples of change that Aquinas often appeals to in developing his views.

Accidental Change
- *Change of shape*: Some bronze goes from being lump-shaped to being statue-shaped, as a result of the activity of some artisan.
- *Change of temperature*: Some water goes from being cold to being hot, as a result of being placed over a fire.[2]

Aquinas describes the type of change involved in both examples as *accidental change*, for both involve a substance (some bronze or water) that changes with respect to certain of its non-essential properties or accidents (shape or temperature). Accidental change is not the only type of change that Aquinas distinguishes; there is also what he calls *substantial change*. Even so, Aquinas standardly appeals to examples of accidental change to illustrate the nature of change in general.

Aquinas thinks of change as requiring both sameness and difference. Consider the water that goes from being cold to being hot. If the water at the beginning of the change were not identical to the water at the end, there would not be any *thing* that changed. By contrast, if the water at the beginning of the change were not different in some way (say, in temperature) from the water at the end, there would not be any thing that *changed*. And, of course, a similar point applies to other changes. As all of this helps to make clear, Aquinas thinks of change in general as requiring the existence of beings that play the functional roles that substances and accidents play in accidental change. For the sake of clarity, we might refer to these roles as the *enduring substratum* and *temporary property roles*, respectively. For insofar as one and the same substance exists over time, and serves as a subject for accidents, it plays the role of an enduring substratum. And insofar as an accident is an entity that both characterizes its possessor and is acquired or lost over time, it plays the role of a temporary property.

It is a short step from this understanding of change to Aquinas's hylomorphism. For, like Aristotle, Aquinas introduces the term 'matter' (*materia*) to stand for whatever plays the role of enduring substratum in change, and he introduces the term 'form' (*forma*) to stand for whatever plays the role of a temporary property. What is more, whenever there are entities playing these two roles, Aquinas thinks that there is also a hylomorphic compound that comes into being or passes away. In this respect, too, he takes himself to be following Aristotle. That change involves not only matter and form but also compounds is plausible in Aquinas's example of change of shape. For when a lump of bronze acquires the shape of a statue, it is natural to say both that a statue comes into being and that a lump-shaped object passes away. But Aquinas thinks that the same can be said of his example of change of temperature. For when some water acquires the form of heat, a compound of water and heat – call it *hot-water* – comes into being and a compound of water and coldness – call it *cold-water* – passes away. And Aquinas thinks that the same can be said for changes of other sorts.[3]

On Aquinas's hylomorphic analysis, therefore, change requires entities playing not only the enduring substratum and temporary property roles, but also what we might call the *temporary complex role* – that is, the role of a complex that comes into being or passes away whenever some substratum acquires or loses a property. And just as he introduces the terms 'matter' and 'form' to stand for what-ever play the former roles, so too he introduces the term 'compound' (*compositum*) to stand for whatever plays the latter role. What is more, when Aquinas speaks of compounds in the context of change (as opposed to creation or annihilation), he speaks of them as being *generated* and *corrupted* – that is, coming into being *from* some pre-existing matter or passing away *into* some matter that survives their destruction. Indeed, on Aquinas's preferred analysis, change just con-sists in the generation and corruption of compounds.

Functional Hylomorphism in Physics versus Metaphysics

As the foregoing suggests, Aquinas takes matter, form, and compound to be functional notions that must be understood, at least initially, in terms of the roles they play in change. Since Aquinas thinks of change as falling within the province of natural philosophy or physics, we can state his functional hylomorphism to a first approximation as follows.

Functional Hylomorphism in Physics

- *Matter* $=_{df}$ A being (whatever it is by nature) that can acquire or lose a form over time, and hence can play the role of an enduring substratum.

- *Form* =$_{df}$ A being (whatever it is by nature) that can be acquired or lost by matter over time, and hence can play the role of a temporary property.
- *Compound* =$_{df}$ A being (whatever it is by nature) that can be generated or corrupted when some matter acquires or loses a form over time, and hence can play the role of a temporary substratum–property complex.

Aquinas thinks that beings of all three functional types are required to explain the occurrence of change. But it is important to emphasize that he also thinks that the beings playing the relevant functional roles must be distinct from one another. Insofar as the matter of any given change can exist without the forms or compounds with respect to which it changes, it is clear that such matter must be distinct from its temporary forms and compounds. But it is also clear that the compounds associated with a given change are distinct from both the matter and form of which they are composed. For, strictly speaking, Aquinas insists, it is only compounds (not matter and form) that can be generated or corrupted.[4]

Although my statement of Aquinas's hylomorphism is accurate as far as it goes, it cannot be taken to represent his complete understanding of matter, form, and compounds. There are two reasons for this. First, this statement leaves open the precise nature of the beings that can play the roles of matter, form, and compound – although Aquinas's examples of accidental change are certainly suggestive in this regard. Second, and perhaps more importantly for present purposes, this statement fails to capture Aquinas's functional hylomorphism in its complete generality. I will return to the first issue shortly ('Complete Hylomorphism'); here, I will briefly expand on the second.

In my statement of Aquinas's hylomorphism above, the notions of matter, form, and compound are all relativized to change, and hence defined in terms of roles played over time. But a little reflection reveals that the notions need not be so relativized. For, clearly, if matter is capable of serving as a substratum for different forms *over time*, it must also be capable of serving as a substratum for a form *at a time*. Likewise, if a form is capable of being acquired and lost *over time*, then it must also be capable of being possessed *at a time*. And that is also the case for compounds. In short, what I have referred to above as Aquinas's *functional hylomorphism in physics* presupposes a more metaphysical understanding of matter, form, and compound, which we might state as follows.

Functional Hylomorphism in Metaphysics
- *Matter* $=_{df}$ A being (whatever it is by nature) that can possess a form at a time, and hence can play the role of a substratum.
- *Form* $=_{df}$ A being (whatever it is by nature) that can be possessed by matter at a time, and hence can play the role of a property.
- *Compound* $=_{df}$ A being (whatever it is by nature) that exists when some matter possesses a form, and hence can play the role of a substratum–property complex.

As these two statements of Aquinas's functional hylomorphism are intended to indicate, Aquinas thinks of matter and form as playing different explanatory roles in different domains. In the context of physics, he thinks of them as principles of change: that is, as things that play an essential role in explaining the generation and corruption of compounds over time. By contrast, in metaphysics, he thinks of matter and form as principles of being – that is, as things that play an essential role in explaining the existence of compounds at a time.

Now, as I noted earlier, matter and form are not the only principles of change for Aquinas. And as we will see in due course, they are not the only principles of being either. But before examining Aquinas's views about principles any further, we must first consider what he says about the different types of being that can play the roles that he assigns to matter, form, and compound.

Complete Hylomorphism

Aquinas's examples of accidental change highlight the nature of three different types of being that can play the roles of matter, form, and compound, respectively – namely, substances, accidents, and complexes of each. For Aquinas takes the matter in his examples to be a material substance (namely, some water or bronze); he takes the forms to be a type of non-essential property or accident (namely, coldness, heat, or some sort of shape); and he takes the compounds to be complexes of substances and accidents (namely, cold-water and hot-water, lumps and statues). Although Aquinas often refers to the complexes associated with accidental change simply as *compounds*, when he is expressing his views most precisely, he refers to them as *accidental unities*.[5]

If Aquinas thought of all changes as accidental, we could perhaps identify his matter, forms, and compounds with substances, accidents, and accidental unities, respectively. But, as noted earlier, Aquinas insists that some changes are substantial (as opposed to accidental), and this in turn complicates his understanding of the types of being that can play the roles of matter, form, and compound.

Initially, Aquinas's talk of substantial change might appear to be confused. For if an accidental change involves a substance acquiring or losing an accidental form or property, what could a substantial change possibly involve? When Aquinas speaks of substantial change, however, he is thinking of changes in which substances play the role of compounds rather than that of matter. To illustrate, consider the following two paradigmatic examples of substantial change, which are slight variations on examples to which Aquinas himself appeals in explaining his views.

Substantial Change

- *Evaporation*: Some water is transformed into air, as a result of being heated over the fire.
- *Human death*: Socrates goes from being alive to being dead, as a result of drinking hemlock.[6]

Nowadays we think of evaporation as a process by which a pre-existing substance (some water) merely changes its state (from liquid to vapor), and hence undergoes an accidental change. By contrast, Aquinas thinks of it as an elemental transformation – that is, a change by which one substance (in this case, air) is generated from the corruption of another (in this case, water). In this respect, he thinks of evaporation as similar to human death – which he also takes to be a substantial change involving the generation of one substance (a corpse) from the corruption of another (a human being).

Insofar as evaporation and human death are changes, Aquinas thinks that there must be something that plays the role of matter and form in each. But insofar as these changes involve generation and corruption of substances (rather than accidental unities), he denies that what plays the role of their matter and form can be substances or accidents. On the contrary, Aquinas insists that what plays the role of matter and form in any substantial change is *prime matter* and *substantial form*.

Aquinas's views about prime matter are notoriously obscure. As its name suggests, Aquinas thinks of prime matter. as matter in the primary and proper sense (as opposed to the merely functional sense of a substratum). For the same reason, he takes its possession to distinguish complex, material substances (or bodies) from simple, immaterial substances (or spirits). Even so, how are we to understand its nature? Commentators have provided no clear answer. Indeed, the difficulty has led some to deny that prime matter exists at all. Although I cannot defend my own preferred answer here, I think prime matter is best understood as a type of non-individual stuff – that is, a distinctive type of being that is infinitely divisible and incapable of existing apart from material substances.[7]

As for substantial forms, they are naturally understood as a distinctive type of property that combines with prime matter to generate material substances or bodies.[8] Indeed, Aquinas thinks of different types of body as compounds of prime matter plus different types of substantial form. Aquinas refers to the substantial forms of inanimate substances – including the elements and mixtures of them – as mere *bodily forms* (*formae corporeitatis*), since they bestow on their possessors the characteristics and causal powers associated with mere bodies. By contrast, he refers to the substantial forms of all organisms – including plants, animals, and human beings – as *souls* (*animae*), since they bestow on their possessors the characteristics and causal powers required to be biologically alive (*animatae*).[9]

Aquinas's complete hylomorphism, then, includes two types of matter (prime matter and substances), two types of form (substantial forms and accidents), and two types of compound (material substances and accidental unities). Bodies are the only type of substance that has prime matter and substantial form. Even so, Aquinas insists that, with the exception of God, who alone has no distinct forms or properties, all substances have accidents, and hence serve as the matter for certain forms or properties. Aquinas recognizes that such insistence has the odd consequence that even immaterial substances or spirits, such as angels, can be regarded as material in a certain sense. But he thinks that the consequence itself is harmless, given that such materiality is merely functional.[10] In order to bring out the significance of all this for Aquinas's understanding of the world, we can represent his complete hylomorphism as indicated in the diagram at Figure 2.1 (using boxes to represent matter, forms, and compounds; solid arrows to represent the relation of form to matter; dotted arrows to represent the relation of both matter and form to compounds; and a dotted box to highlight the distinctive nature of prime matter).

As this diagram indicates, Aquinas thinks of the world as dividing into two realms: an incorporeal realm, which includes all immaterial substances and compounds; and a corporeal realm, which includes all material substances and compounds. What is more, Aquinas thinks of his hylomorphism as having its primary application to the corporeal realm – since it is only substances and compounds in this realm that possess matter in the primary and proper sense (i.e., prime matter). Indeed, in the corporeal realm, Aquinas thinks that we get nested hierarchies of compounds of such matter – since the

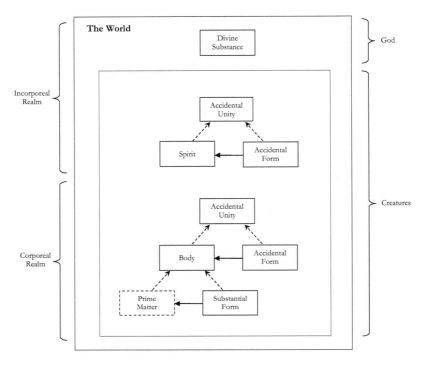

FIGURE 2.1 Aquinas's complete hylomorphism.

substances of this realm not only are composed of prime matter and substantial form, but also serve as the matter for accidental forms. By contrast, in the incorporeal realm, Aquinas thinks of his hylomorphism as having only limited application; for none of the substances in this realm are composed of any prime matter, and although Aquinas thinks of created immaterial substances as playing the role of matter for accidental forms, he denies that God is either composed of any matter or serves as the matter for any distinct forms.[11]

Potentiality, Actuality, and Privation

In examining Aquinas's views about change, I have been focusing so far on just two of its principles – matter and form – and ignoring privation altogether. What is more, I have said nothing at all about potentiality and actuality. And yet Aquinas uses the last two notions to analyze all three of the principles of change.

Consider again Aquinas's example of some water becoming hot. As we have seen, Aquinas is happy to describe this change as involving some matter acquiring a new form, and hence the generation of a new compound. As it turns out, however, he does not think that this is the most perspicuous description of the change. On the contrary, he insists that the change should be described as one involving the actualization of a potentiality – more precisely, the actualization of a potentiality of matter to receive a form that it previously lacked.[12] Let us unpack this new description with a view to what it implies about the principles of change.

Matter and Potentiality

In order for water to acquire the form of heat, it must have the potentiality to receive this form. Evidently, therefore, the matter of a given change is not merely an enduring substratum, but one that has a potentiality to receive the type of form associated with the change itself. Aquinas sometimes uses 'potentiality' (*potentia*) in a broad sense to cover any sort of possibility, but in the context of change he uses it in a narrower sense to refer to what we might call *natural capacity* – that is, the sort of capacity that created substances have for accidents, that certain animals have for sight, and that water has for a certain range of temperatures (say, 0–100°C).[13] As each of these cases is intended to suggest, there is more to natural capacity than mere possibility. It is not merely possible for created substances to possess accidents or for certain animals to possess sight, but contrary to the nature of each to lack such things. Likewise, it is not merely possible for water to possess temperatures within a certain range, but contrary to its nature to lack some temperature within that same range.[14] What is contrary to a thing's nature is often impossible, but not always. Thus, even if water cannot exist without possessing some temperature or other, animals can be blind.

Form and Actuality

Just as the role of matter in change must ultimately be understood in terms of potentiality, so too, Aquinas thinks, the role of form in change must ultimately be understood in terms of actuality. Indeed, in the context of change, Aquinas just defines matter as *being in potentiality* and form as *actuality*:

> Anything that is a being in potentiality [in any respect] can be called *matter*. So too, anything through which something has being [in actuality in any respect], whether substantial or accidental, can be called *form*.[15]

And, of course, if the potentiality associated with matter is just a natural capacity, then the actuality associated with form must involve the actualization of such a capacity.

Privation and the Absence of Form

Although matter and form, understood in terms of potentiality and actuality, are necessary for explaining change, Aquinas denies that they are sufficient to explain it. Earlier I said that Aquinas thinks of change in terms of sameness and difference. But, as it turns out, that's not quite right. To see why, consider some water that remains cold for a period of time. It may be true that the very same water is cold at one time and odorless at another. But this sort of difference is not sufficient to establish change. For change involves not merely difference, but opposition or incompatibility.

It is precisely because change requires not only sameness and difference but also incompatibility that Aquinas includes privation among the principles of change. When some water acquires a new temperature, it doesn't merely actualize a natural capacity to receive some form, but rather it actualizes a natural capacity to receive some form *that it previously lacked*. And it is only when the natural capacity is conceived together with its privation that its actualization can be said to remove it (though even here it would be better to speak of the removal of the privation).[16]

In the final analysis, therefore, Aquinas thinks that, for a change to occur, there must be not only (a) some matter (or enduring substratum with a potentiality to receive a form) and (b) some form (or actuality, which actualizes the relevant potentiality of matter), but also (c) a privation (or absence of the form corresponding to the same potentiality). It is precisely because change requires (a)–(c) that Aquinas includes privation among the principles of change. And it is precisely because privation is not itself a being, but rather a specific type of absence, that he also excludes privation from the principles of being.

MATTER, FORM, AND CAUSES

If change is the context in which Aquinas introduces his views about matter and form, his discussion of causation provides a context for their development and extension. Indeed, in the context of causation, Aquinas locates his views about matter and form within a broader theory of explanation that includes a fourfold division of causes.

Material versus Formal Causes

Aquinas uses 'cause' (*causa*) as a synonym for 'principle of being' (*principium in esse*).[17] On this usage, not all principles are causes, as the case of privation makes clear, but all causes are principles.

Nowadays it is standard to think of 'cause' as applying only to efficient or productive causes – that is, to things such as the fire or artisan in Aquinas's original examples of change.[18] Obviously, Aquinas is using the term in a broader sense. But contrary to what commentators sometimes suggest, we should not identify the notion of cause with that of explanation. For not all explanations have to do with being, as those involving privation make clear. Better, therefore, to identify explanations with principles (rather than causes), and to think of causation as a specific type of explanation.[19]

When Aquinas describes the type of explanation associated with causation, he does so in terms of relations of influence (*influxus*) and dependency (*dependentia*).[20] A cause, he says, *influences* the being of its effect, whereas the being of the effect *depends on* the cause. As this statement suggests, Aquinas thinks of influence and dependency as converse relations: x influences the being of y iff y depends on x for its being. Aquinas's talk of *being* (*esse*) in this context should be taken broadly enough to include not merely the effect's existence, but also its nature or character. Evidently, therefore, what Aquinas has in mind by causation can be understood along the lines of what philosophers nowadays call *metaphysical determination* – that is, a relation that holds between two (or more) things just in case one is ontologically dependent on the other(s). On this understanding, different types of causation correspond to different types of metaphysical determination.[21]

Interestingly, when contemporary philosophers speak of metaphysical determination they almost always have in mind the specific type of causation that Aquinas associates with matter and form. Thus, just as Aquinas thinks of compounds – such as hot-water or a statue – as depending on their matter and form as an effect on its material and formal causes, contemporary philosophers think of complex objects as being metaphysically determined by their proper parts or constituents. Indeed, contemporary philosophers often distinguish something like *influence* and *dependency* here, speaking of the proper parts or constituents as *grounding* the existence of the complex of which they are a part and of the complex itself as depending on the grounds as *that in virtue of which* it exists.[22]

Matter and form can be thought of as different types of grounding cause for Aquinas. Indeed, I think they are best understood as joint grounding causes of a single hylomorphic compound, which in turn depends on its matter and form in different ways. Thus, consider our bronze statue. It is a compound that exists in virtue of some matter and form – or better, in virtue of some particular portion of bronze possessing a particular shape. Even so, the statue depends on its matter alone for its being bronze, whereas it depends on its form alone for its being statue-shaped. More generally, matter and form are joint grounding causes of a single compound, with the matter alone grounding its general character and the form alone grounding its more specific character.

Conceiving of matter and form as grounding causes not only illuminates how Aquinas is thinking of causation in their case, but it also sheds light on certain aspects of his views about hylomorphism and causation more generally. Let me briefly mention three.

First, this conception serves to emphasize that only hylomorphic compounds can have material or formal causes for Aquinas.[23] As we have seen, material and formal causes are the grounds of some effect, and, intuitively, grounding is a relation that holds between distinct beings. For nothing can be explanatorily prior to itself.[24] Evidently, therefore, for something to qualify as a material or formal cause, it must play the role of a substratum or property. As Aquinas sees it, however, some beings, such as God and the angels, are not composed of any matter or form. Thus, it would be a mistake to think of them as having material or formal causes. And even in the case of beings that are composed of matter and form, it would be a mistake to conceive of their matter as a material cause of their form or of their form as a formal cause of their matter. For the matter and form do not ground each other.

Again, conceiving of matter and form as grounding causes helps to explain why both matter and form qualify as principles and causes, but privations qualify only as principles. As Aquinas sees it, all explanations aim to provide answers to "Why?" questions via the identification of principles; but only explanations of a certain type – namely, causal explanations – attempt to do so via the identification of beings or entities.[25] Thus, if we want to know why some water comes to be hot, we must identify three principles: matter (= the water), form (= heat), and privation (= lack of heat). But note that only two of these three principles are plausibly identified as grounding causes. For, intuitively, only existing things can serve as grounds; privations or absences cannot. Indeed, Aquinas seems to think that all privations are explained in terms of matter and form. Thus, if some matter (say, water) has a privation at some time (say, a lack of heat), then this is to be explained in terms of its possession of another form (say, coldness).[26] In light of this, it might be tempting to say that matter and form are grounds (or causes) of privation. But that would be a mistake as well. For just as only beings or entities can serve as grounds (or causes), so too only beings or entities can be grounded (or caused). Indeed, as this serves to emphasize, Aquinas takes causation to be a relation that can hold only between distinct *beings*.

Finally, conceiving of matter and form as grounding causes helps to explain why Aquinas thinks that there is more to causation than material and formal causation. For even if we have a complete grounding explanation of some entity – that is, the material and formal causes in virtue of which it exists and has the character it does – we can still ask why that entity exists (rather than not). Aquinas thinks that this point is easiest to see in the case of compounds that come into existence via change. Thus, in his statue example, which involves some bronze coming to be a statue in virtue of acquiring a new shape, he points out that matter and form cannot be the complete explanation of why it exists:

> Some bronze, which is potentially [but not actually] a statue, does not make itself into a statue, but requires an agent to change the form of the statue from potentiality to actuality.[27]

When some bronze goes from being lump-shaped to being statue-shaped, there must be something that causes the actualization of its potentiality for receiving a form that it previously lacked. But neither the matter nor the form of the change can do that. On the contrary, Aquinas insists that the sort of cause we are looking for here is an efficient cause – that is, one that explains the existence of an effect by producing it, where production is distinct from grounding. Aquinas identifies the efficient cause here with the artisan who produces the statue by skill or art. But in his temperature example, he identifies the efficient cause with the fire that produces hot water by its heat. What is more, Aquinas thinks the need for an efficient cause extends well beyond these sorts of examples, and even beyond compounds that come into existence via change. Indeed, Aquinas thinks that in the case of all beings other than God – whose very nature guarantees his existence – the question arises as to why they exist (rather than not). Thus, even if not all beings require a material or formal cause, Aquinas thinks that all beings other than God require an efficient cause.[28]

As is well known, Aquinas's views about efficient causes are bound up with his views about causes of yet another type, which he calls *final causes* or *ends*. But since causes of both types raise important difficulties, they require separate treatment.

Efficient Causes

As already suggested, when Aquinas speaks of *efficient causation*, what he has in mind is production – that is, a relation that holds between ordinary productive causes (such as artisans and fires) and effects produced by them (such as statues and hot water).[29] Aquinas habitually refers to productive causes of any type as *agents*. Although this way of speaking might seem strange, since nowadays we tend to think of agency as a function of intelligence, Aquinas thinks of it as the exercise of an active causal power to produce an effect. But since such production is a kind of *doing*, he refers to the exercise of such powers as *actions*. Moreover, since he thinks that all substances have active causal powers, whether intelligent or not, he thinks that all substances are capable of acting and hence of serving as agents. The difference between intelligent and non-intelligent agency, therefore, has do with the type of causal powers exercised. Thus, when artisans produce a statue, they exercise a power over which they have some control, and hence engage in voluntary action. By contrast, when a fire heats some water, it exercises a power over which it has no control, and hence engages in merely natural action. Now, as it happens, Aquinas thinks both intelligent and non-intelligent agents act for ends, which in turn serve as their final causes. To understand why he thinks this, as well as what he has in mind by ends, we must first situate his views about active causal powers within his broader views about potentiality and actuality.[30]

When an agent acts, it does so by exercising an active causal power. As we might expect, Aquinas thinks that the exercise of an active causal power must be understood as the actualization of a potentiality. Thus, just as he thinks of change in terms of the actualization of some potentiality of matter to receive a form, so too he thinks of action in terms of the actualization of some agent's potentiality to produce an effect. It is important to emphasize, however, that active causal powers are a very special sort of potentiality for Aquinas.

I noted earlier that potentialities are best understood as natural capacities rather than mere possibilities. Thus, water's potentiality for some temperature is to be understood in terms of its natural capacity *to receive* temperatures within a certain range (say, 0–100°C). This is a purely passive or receptive capacity. By contrast, Aquinas thinks of fire's potentiality to heat as an active (rather than passive) capacity – indeed, one that makes essential reference to efficient causation or production. For fire's potentiality to heat is a natural capacity *to produce* temperatures within a certain range – although the precise range will vary depending on the nature of that in which it produces such temperatures. Thus, in the case of water, fire has the natural capacity to produce temperatures within a range determined by the nature of water itself (say, 0–100°C). But in other objects, it may have a capacity to produce a larger or smaller range of temperatures, although the upper bound will always be fixed by the nature of fire itself (say, 600°C in the case of an ordinary wood fire). As all of this helps to make clear, not all potentialities for Aquinas are merely receptive capacities, and not all of them can be understood apart from efficient causation or production. Indeed, what makes active causal powers a special type of potentiality is that they are essentially *productive* capacities – that is to say, natural capacities for *efficiently causing certain types of effect* in other things.

Final Causes

With the above account of efficient causation in hand, it might seem as if we have all the types of cause needed to provide a full explanation of the existence of different types of things. For, in the case of any object other than God, we will be able to explain why it exists (rather than not) in terms of the agent that produces it, whether that agent creates or merely generates it. And in the case of any hylomorphic compound, such as our hot-water or statue, we will also be able to explain why it exists as a specific type of being in terms of its grounding causes. What further explanation of a thing's existence could we want? To understand Aquinas's answer to this question, and in particular his appeal to final causes, we must first see why he thinks the account of causal powers given so far fails to provide a complete explanation of efficient causation.

Consider again some cold water that has been placed over a fire, and suppose, as Aquinas does, that the water has the passive causal power to be heated and the fire has the active causal power to heat. We know what will happen: The fire will immediately begin exercising its active power to heat and continue exercising this power until the water is either boiling or removed from the fire.[31] That is to say, the fire will initiate a process which, if unimpeded, will continue until a very specific capacity of the water is actualized – namely, the capacity for being heated to 100°C. But given only what we have said about causal powers so far, this is puzzling. Suppose the water starts out at 20°C. In that case, the water will have the passive causal power to be heated to any temperature between 20°C and 100°C, and that is because the fire has the corresponding active causal power to produce any one of these same temperatures in it. But why, if unimpeded, does the fire always produce the highest possible temperature? Indeed, why does it always produce some temperature or other, rather than, say, sometimes merely existing with its capacity to heat remaining dormant or unactualized? In short, why do agents always exercise their active causal powers on suitable patients (rather than not), and why do they always exercise them in the specific ways that they do (rather than in some other way)?

To answer these questions, Aquinas thinks, we must conceive of active causal powers as teleologically directed – that is, as having a final cause or end at which they are directed.[32] Now, in a certain sense, all causal powers – and, indeed, all potentialities – have a kind of directedness. For a potentiality is always a potentiality *for* some type of actuality, regardless of whether it is a mere possibility or capacity, whether it is active or passive, and whether it is causal or merely receptive (see Table 2.1). But in the case of active causal powers there is more to their directedness than this. In their case, there is also a positive inclination – and not merely for the exercise of a power, but for a specific actualization of it. Thus, the active causal power of fire is not merely a capacity to produce heat or even a mere positive inclination to do so. On the contrary, it is a positive inclination to produce heat of a specific temperature. The precise temperature varies with the nature of the fire in question. But, in general, a fire is positively inclined to produce heat in things as close to its own temperature as possible – say, 600°C in the case of an ordinary wood fire.[33] In the case of water, 100°C is as close to 600°C as it can get; hence, 100°C is the specific temperature that fire is inclined to produce in water.

Aquinas thinks that all substances have active casual powers and hence are inclined to act in certain ways. Thus, water not only has the capacity to receive temperatures within a certain range, but also a positive inclination to be room temperature or "cold" – say, 20°C. Thus, if unimpeded, water that is warmer than this temperature will begin to cool and water that is colder than this temperature will begin to warm (see again Table 2.1). And, of course, in virtue of this active causal power, water will also have an effect on its immediate environment – say, cooling its container or weakening the strength of the fire.

It is precisely because agents have teleologically directed causal powers that Aquinas thinks of agents as always acting for ends. Nowadays, it is customary to think of only intelligent agents as acting

Table 2.1 *Types of potentiality*

Potentiality	Water's potentiality for heat (or coldness)	Fire's potentiality for heat
Possibility	Possibly hot (or cold)	Possibly heating
Capacity	Capable of being hot (or cold)	
		Capable of heating (= casual
Power	Capable of having heat (or coldness) produced in it	power for producing heat)
Inclination	Inclined to be cold	Inclined to heat

for ends. But for reasons that are perhaps now apparent, Aquinas thinks of intelligent agency as just a special case of a more general phenomenon. When artisans produce a statue, they do so in virtue of exercising an active power. And if we want to know why they exercised this power (rather than not), the explanation will appeal to a positive inclination they had for exercising that power. In the case of intelligent agents, such inclinations often trace to conscious desires or needs (although just as often such desires or needs are traceable to habits, skills, or other settled dispositions); and unlike natural agents, intelligent agents have control over the exercise of (at least some of) their powers, and hence can resist their actualization directly. Even so, the explanation of action in their case will be the same. Thus, the explanation for why an artisan produces a statue in certain circumstances will be the same in form as the explanation for why fire produces heat in water that is placed over it – namely, that in such circumstances, the agent possesses a positive inclination, which is such that, if unimpeded, it will result in the effect produced.

Because Aquinas thinks that all beings other than God must have an efficient cause, and because he thinks of efficient causation as ultimately being explained in terms of the ends to which causal powers are inclined, he refers to the ends themselves as the "cause of causes" or "final causes."[34] Aquinas's talk of ends as causes, however, can seem puzzling. For in what sense can an end, which does not yet exist, serve as a cause? And what could the causation of a non-existent cause possibly consist in? In light of the foregoing, however, we can see that it is not really the ends produced by action that play an explanatory role in efficient causation or production, but end-directedness or inclination. Indeed, in the case of final causation, it is the end-directed powers themselves that serve as causes, it is their exercise that serves as the effects, and it is their inclinations that serve as the relation of causation.[35]

Aquinas often distinguishes efficient and final causes from material and formal causes by saying that the former are extrinsic, whereas the latter are intrinsic causes.[36] For our purposes, however, it might be better to distinguish them as productive (rather than grounding) causes – since each contributes, though in very different ways, to the production of certain effects. Indeed, if we think of efficient and final causes in this way, we can summarize their relationship both to each other and to the other types of cause, as indicated in Table 2.2.

Table 2.2 *Four causes*

Types of causation		Cause	Effect	Causal relation
Grounding (intrinsic)	**Material**	Matter (substratum)	Compound (substratum–property complex)	Grounding
	Formal	Form (property)		
Productive (extrinsic)	**Efficient**	Agent (substance with active causal powers)	Contingent being (creature)	Producing
	Final	End (active causal power)	Action (exercise of an active causal power)	Inclining

There is much more that could be said about Aquinas's views about matter, form, and causation, but the foregoing will have to suffice as an introduction to the main contours of his views about each.[37]

NOTES

1 Aquinas presents his views about change in two main contexts – namely, *DPN*, especially chs. 1–2 and *In Phy*, especially Bk I. for further references and more detailed development of the issues discussed in this section, see J. Brower, *Aquinas's Ontology of the Material World: Change, Hylomorphism, and Material Objects* (Oxford: Oxford University Press, 2014). Cf. also J. F. Wippel, *The Metaphysical Thought of Thomas Aquinas: From Finite Being to Uncreated Being* (Washington, DC: The Catholic University of America Press, 2000).

2 Aquinas introduces the first example in *DPN* 1 and the second in *In III Phy*, lect. 2.

3 But see Brower, *Aquinas's Ontology of the Material World*, especially §3.2 and §11.2, for complications regarding Aquinas's understanding of change.

4 *DPN* 2.

5 See C. Brown, *Aquinas and the Ship of Theseus: Solving Puzzles about Material Objects* (London: Continuum, 2005), p. 64, note 27 for a list of references to various ways in which Aquinas refers to compounds of substance and accident.

6 Aquinas discusses evaporation and human death in a number of contexts, but see *In IV Phy*, lect. 8, and *ST* I q.50 a.4, respectively, for clear examples of each.

7 See Brower, *Aquinas's Ontology of the Material World*, especially ch. 5, for discussion of these issues and the controversies surrounding them.

8 The case of the human soul is an important exception. Insofar as it is capable of surviving the death of the human being, and hence existing apart from matter, it is naturally thought of as a substance rather than a property. See Chapter 6 for more discussion.

9 See again Brower, *Aquinas's Ontology of the Material World*, especially chs. 3–5 and 9, for discussion of these issues and the controversies surrounding them.

10   *QDSC* 1.

11   See *ST* I q.3, especially aa.7–8, for Aquinas's denial that God has any distinct matter or form, or is part of any compound.

12   See, for example, *DPN* 1–2 and *ST* I q.1 a.9.

13   See *ST* I q.25 a.1 and a.3 for some of the different senses of 'potentiality' and 'possibility,' and their relationship to one another. Cf. J. Brower, "Aquinas's Metaphysics of Modality: Reply to Leftow," *Modern Schoolman* 83 (2005): 201–12 for a discussion of Aquinas's views about possibility.

14   As this example suggests, moreover, some natural capacities are one-many; for water has a natural capacity to receive each of the temperatures within the relevant range.

15   *DPN* 1.36–39. All translations are mine.

16   Aquinas is often at pains to emphasize that privation is not the mere lack of form, but rather the lack of form for which there is a natural capacity. Thus, both rocks and animals lack sight; but only animals can be blind. Cf. *DPN* 2.

17   Cf. *In I Sent.*, d.29 q.1 a.1: "Every cause is related as a principle to the being of what is caused by it." See also *DPN* 3.

18   Actually, nowadays it is standard to think of causes in terms of *events* (rather than *substances*), so perhaps it would be better to speak of the efficient causes in Aquinas's examples as events involving fire or an artisan. Hereafter, I ignore this complication.

19   It must be noted, however, that Aquinas allows that 'principle' can be used in a broad sense to apply to anything that is prior to another in any way, whether explanatorily or not. See *DPN* 3. It might be best, therefore, to identify explanations with a proper subset of principles.

20   For discussions of the importance of both influence and dependency for understanding Aquinas's views about causation in general and efficient causation in particular, see C. Cohoe, "There Must Be a First: Why Thomas Aquinas Rejects Infinite, Essentially Ordered, Causal Series," *British Journal for the History of Philosophy* 21 (2013), pp. 838–56; J. Johnson, "Final Causality, Cognition, and Self-Motion in Aquinas's Natural Philosophy" [manuscript] (2021); M. Rota, "Causation" in B. Davies and E. Stump (eds.), *The Oxford Handbook to Aquinas* (Oxford: Oxford University Press, 2012), pp. 104–14. For evidence that these same notions are also important for understanding later medieval views about causation, see J. Tuttle, "Suárez's Non-Reductive Theory of

Efficient Causation," *Oxford Studies in Medieval Philosophy* 4 (2016), pp. 125–58.

21 Cf. Cohoe, "There Must Be a First," note 13, which makes a similar suggestion.

22 See R. Bliss and K. Trogdon, "Metaphysical Grounding" in E. N. Zalta (ed.), *The Stanford Encyclopedia of Philosophy* (2016) [online], https://plato.stanford.edu/archives/win2016/entries/grounding/ for an introduction to contemporary views about grounding.

23 At least in the strict and proper sense. Aquinas is happy to make use of the analogy of material and formal causation outside of strictly hylomorphic contexts – for example in the context of his action theory or logic.

24 Indeed, it is precisely for this reason that grounding is typically taken to be irreflexive, as well as asymmetric.

25 Cf. *In II Phy*, lect. 5.

26 *DPN* 2.

27 *DPN* 3.5–7.

28 See, for example, *ST* I q.44 a.1.

29 Aquinas thinks that productive causes can, at least in certain circumstances, also sustain the effects that they produce, but here I will ignore complications associated with sustaining-causation.

30 'Power' is rooted in the same Latin term as 'potentiality' (*potentia*), and marks a further sense in which this term can be used. For a book-length treatment of Aquinas's views about causal powers and efficient causation, see G. Frost, *Aquinas on Efficient Causation and Causal Powers* (Cambridge: Cambridge University Press, 2022). For a book-length treatment of Aquinas's views about human agency, which situates them within his broader views about causal powers and efficient causation, see C. L. Löwe, *Thomas Aquinas on the Metaphysics of the Human Act* (Cambridge: Cambridge University Press, 2021).

31 I say that we know this will happen, but what I really mean is that we know this will happen *provided there is no impediment or external interference*. Let us take this proviso as granted throughout.

32 For a contemporary theory of causal powers that shares much in common with Aquinas's, including an appeal to their teleological directedness, see N. Kroll, "Teleological Dispositions," *Oxford Studies in Metaphysics* 10 (2017), pp. 3–37.

33 Indeed, Aquinas thinks that "every agent produces an effect similar to itself." See, for example, *QDA* 12.

34 See, for example, *DPN* 4.

35 See *ST* I-II q.1 a.1 ad 1, where Aquinas says that 'end' (*finis*) can refer either
    to what is produced by action (and hence is not its cause) or to what
    inclines the agent to act (and hence is its cause). It is only in the latter
    sense that active causal powers qualify as ends. It may seem as if my
    discussion ignores the emphasis that Aquinas places on the role of
    cognition in final causation (e.g., in his Fifth Way). But I agree with
    Johnson that this role has more to do with explaining why substances
    achieve the ends to which they are teleologically directed rather than with
    explaining teleological directedness itself. See J. Johnson, "Nature Does
    Nothing in Vain: Reexamining Aquinas's Fifth Way" [manuscript] (2021).

36 See, for example, *DPN* 3.

37 I am grateful to the editors, Michael Bergman, Susan Brower-Toland,
    Caleb Cohoe, Gloria Frost, Chris Hauser, Joel Johnson, Can Löwe, Scott
    MacDonald, and especially Eli Schille-Hudson, for helpful comments
    and discussion.

3   Essence and Existence, God's Simplicity and Trinity

Thomas Joseph White, OP

INTRODUCTION

The aim of this chapter is to introduce Aquinas's account of ultimate explanations in metaphysics. What are the constituent principles of created reality? What do they indicate about God in his unique existence, nature, and divine simplicity? How may one reasonably understand the Christian doctrine of the Trinity in light of the affirmation of divine simplicity? To consider these questions I will proceed in three stages, examining first Aquinas's distinctive claims regarding the distinction of essence and existence in creatures; second his interpretation of the traditional Christian affirmation that the divine nature is simple; and third his concept of Trinitarian persons as subsistent relations, a teaching that helps illustrate the logical compatibility of Aquinas's Trinitarian theology, his doctrine of God, and his metaphysics of creaturely composition.

THE REAL DISTINCTION OF ESSENCE AND EXISTENCE: DEFINITIONS

As a young scholar, Aquinas initially explored his views on essence and existence against the backdrop of Avicennian metaphysics, from which he developed his own definitions.[1] When we speak about the essence of a thing, for Aquinas, we denote the definition of its natural kind, what a thing is.[2] On his view, the essence is not the individual substance itself (a singular human or oak tree), but that in virtue of which a given substance is the kind of thing it is (the human nature or the oak tree nature). To determine the essence of a thing we must identify its genus and species, the latter being determined by a specific difference.[3] Thus, if, for the sake of illustration, we presume the truth of the definition of the human being as a rational animal, the human being is essentially an animal (genus) who is distinctively rational (specific difference), and thus a rational animal (species). Genus and species understood in this way are not properties of essences. They pertain to the essence itself, which is ontologically prior to a thing's properties and manifest through them. If the oak tree is essentially a living thing, specifically different from non-living things in virtue of its vegetative form of life, it will do the kinds of things proper to its essential nature, such as nourish itself, grow, and reproduce. Accidental properties emerge from beings of various kinds in virtue of their essences. Some of these are proper accidents – inalienable characteristics of an essence that pertain to the thing in virtue of what it is – while others are not.[4] It is proper to a human being, for example, to digest food, to have intelligence, and eventually to make decisions of elective freedom. It is not proper to the human being *qua* human to have this or that specific color or musical talent.

Universal concepts of various natural kinds of things in the world are derived by our minds from knowledge of the essences of things. The mind discerns similitudes of the individual realities that have a common nature and abstracts this common nature so as to grasp it in a universal mode.[5] The essence of each thing is singular (this individual human or oak tree), but the essences things have from God accord with God's common ideas of them, so they resemble one another formally in themselves due to God's transcendent knowledge and causation of them, and not only due to our way of perceiving them.[6] We know things imperfectly at first, in an initial way, and make progress.[7] We may simply grasp the difference of a human being and a canine by noting that one is a biped that speaks while the other runs on four legs and barks. The fact that we arrive only gradually at a more perfect reasoned definition of essences in things does not mean that the attribution of them lacks foundation in the realities themselves. On the contrary, it is because there are natural essences in things that we can come to know them and understand their definitions and properties in stable and enduring ways.

It is important to note that Aquinas distinguishes essence from form. Form is a principle that actuates and gives determination to the pure potentiality of matter, and so individual material things are composed of both form and matter. A human being, for example, is a singular substance composed of both immaterial soul and material body. Both principles are essential to the thing. Consequently, when we define what a human being is essentially we must include both the form and the matter in the definition: A human being is essentially a soul–body composite, not merely a soul. Unlike form, then, the essence of a thing includes its matter. Our essential definition abstracts from the *signate* matter as such (the matter of this individual here) and considers its matter universally as something that is essential to its kind.[8]

Prior to Aquinas, Avicenna speculated that existence (*esse*) is a kind of accident or mere property of essence in all created things. On Avicenna's view, essences pre-exist in the mind of God and are given being as an accidental property. This view seeks to explain why things can be or not be, since *esse* is not essential to them. Aquinas takes issue with this account. He agrees that *esse* is not identical with essence, but denies that it is merely accidental. Instead, Aquinas conceives of the relation of *esse* and essence in terms of act and potency.[9] The *esse* is the act of being (*actus essendi*) of a given substance, something that pertains to it in all that it is, not merely accidentally.[10] On Aquinas's view, every created substance is a being composed of *esse* and essence in which the *esse* gives the essence actuality, while the essence limits or contracts the *esse*. Any given individual essence can potentially be or not be, and exists in act only in virtue of its *esse* or concrete act of existence. We have noted above that the definition of essence includes or "contains" both the form and matter of the individual. What, then, does the notion of *esse* add to the notion of an individual essence as a form–matter composite? The *esse* is the act of being whereby the essential form–matter composite truly exists, that which makes it really "to be." In this sense, it is the ultimate principle of actuality found in all things that are real. As Aquinas says, "...what I am calling existing [esse] is the actuality of all actualities, and for that reason the perfection of all perfections ... And so nothing else determines it as actuality determines potentiality. Rather, something else determines it as potentiality determines actuality."[11] Every essence has a limited but real existence by which it is actual in being. Every form–matter composite is in potency to exist or not exist, as a substance. Every purely spiritual being, such as an angel or separated substance, also has the potency to exist or not exist in virtue of its act of being, or esse.

It follows from Aquinas's rather original view that the form–matter distinction is less extensive in application than the esse–essence distinction and is contained within the latter. The former distinction applies to all material beings, while the latter applies to all creatures as such, material or spiritual, insofar as they are caused to be, and have a radical potential to exist or not exist. For Aquinas, the form does actuate the potency of matter as Aristotle thought; but, in another respect, he argues that the form can exist or not exist in act, and therefore it is in potency to be or not to be as a created reality. He thus creatively extends the use of Aristotle's act–potency distinction beyond the range of form–matter composites, so as to apply it to the composition of esse and essence in all created things. In doing so he superimposes his medieval philosophical account of created being upon an Aristotelian doctrine of form and matter, while seeking to preserve the latter.[12] In a seminal text from the SCG II, he speaks of the matter this way:

> [Separated] intellectual substances are not composed of matter and form; rather, in them the form itself is a subsisting substance; so that form here is that which is and being itself [esse] is act and that by which the substance is. And on this account there is in such substances but one composition of act and potency, namely the composition of substance and being [substantia et esse] ... On the other hand, in substances composed of matter and form there is a

twofold composition of act and potentiality: the first of the
substance itself which is composed of matter and form; the second,
of the substance thus composed, and being [esse] ... It is therefore
clear that composition of act and potentiality has greater extension
than that of form and matter. Matter and form divide natural
substance, while potentiality and act divide common being.[13]

The doctrine of esse–essence composition in creatures, conceived as act and potency, is thus extended to include separated
substances (angels) who have essences without matter. Aquinas
claims that each separate substance is its own species. Since angels
are not physical, they are not individuated by matter; instead, each is
individuated by its own essence. However, this individual essence is
given existence, and therefore is a composite being, not of form and
matter but of esse and essence.[14]   In all created things–separated
substances, humans, animals, plants, or physical realities–the essence
of the creature receives and delimits esse.[15] That is to say, no created
reality possesses in itself the plenitude of being. Instead, all individual
creatures have existence and participate in being.[16] Their essences are
not identical with their being, or with being as such. Instead, they
receive their being from the creator.

Thomists have argued accordingly that Aquinas's notions of
esse and essence help one address the problem of the one and the
many. On the one hand, the notion of essence allows us to grasp the
unity and multiplicity of natures, in virtue of which multiple individuals are grouped according to common kinds and attributes. Multiple
chimpanzees rightly are categorized essentially in a group distinct
from multiple humans because of a real natural difference that obtains
between individuals of each kind. The notion of essence excludes each
kind from every other, and includes each individual of a given kind
within a given nature. The notion of esse, on the other hand, signifies
that which distinguishes every being in its singularity from every
other, even within a given kind. Two human beings are, after all,
utterly metaphysically distinct, each having a singular existence. In
this respect the notion of esse helps one grasp the alterity that exists

between all individuals. At the same time, it also signals a very different form of commonality than the notion of essence does. A given human being, a chimpanzee, an oak tree, a star, each exist in a singular and irreducible way. However, by that same measure, each also has something in common at the level of being, even though they have distinct natures. Existence is found in all things, and, in this sense, unites them in being. Aquinas's notion of "participation" in common existence (*esse commune*) follows from this idea.[17] Each singular reality has existence, and in this respect participates in a greater whole, the totality of created being. This does not mean that all things are somehow substantially one in being (a view Aquinas rejects), nor does it mean that all things participate in a Platonic form of being, or idea of being. Essence is the source of formal determination, not existence, but existence actuates each form, as a final perfecting cause. Consequently, everything that is real, that exists, has something in common *as actually existing*, over and above the consideration of its essence. Being is the ontological "common denominator" in all of reality.

THE REAL DISTINCTION: DEMONSTRATIONS

Aquinas thinks that there is a real distinction and composition of essence and existence in each created reality. He gives a number of arguments for this idea.[18] He does not think that the two principles are distinct things, or that they can exist in separation from one another. In fact, he advances the opposite idea: Each concrete substance is composite or ontologically complex, because it has an essence and existence, and is only intelligible in light of these two co-principles. How does Aquinas justify the assertion that there is a real distinction between essence and existence in the realities themselves, and not merely a logical distinction derived from thought alone? Here I will briefly indicate three of the arguments he makes: the genus argument, the argument from act and potency, and the perfection of existence argument.

The genus argument builds on the points noted in the previous section. The basic genera of reality noted by Aristotle pertain to categorial modes of being: substances, natures, quantities, qualities, relations, habits, and so forth. Each of these categories denotes a genus of being having a kind of formal content. For example, quality as a category can refer to a kind of property that resides in a substance, such as musical talent or the color purple, distinct from quantity, which refers to figural shape, dimensional size, or weight. These properties reside in natures, as we have noted, which are the unifying principles that "reunite" and ground the various accidental categories. The genus argument begins from the recognition that existence is not something common to one genus of being alone, or to one natural kind of thing alone.[19] So, for example, both human beings and lions exist, and existence is common to both. Likewise, even within a given kind of reality, the existence of a given human's quantity is distinct from his existent qualities, such as knowledge or color. The quantity of a given reality may change without that reality ceasing to exist in nature, or its qualities can develop or disappear, while other properties continue to exist. What these examples show is that existence is not merely reducible to or simply co-extensive with any genus either of nature or of properties, but enters into everything. However, this means existence is not identical with genus but must be something within every genus of being. If one were to argue the contrary, then existence would be identical with either a given nature (like that of the lion) or with a given property (like quantity). In this case only lions would exist or only quantities would exist, and consequently we could not say that any other (non-lion) natures existed or that any other (non-quantitative) properties existed. These are absurd proposals, and so the appeal to the idea of a "genus" of existence is a self-refuting proposition. However, if existence is not contained within or reducible to any genus, then it follows that existence is not reducible to any nature or essence. If this is the case, there must be a real distinction between essence and existence in the realities themselves, since every essence falls within a given genus.

The argument from act and potency is simpler. Each natural reality we encounter can exist or not exist. All things in our material world come into being and go out of being. If this is the case then each thing considered in its nature as such is ontologically in potency to exist actually or not exist actually. This potency to exist or not exist pertains not only to each thing substantially, as when an oak tree may come into being, but also to its properties, as when it may attain a given maturity or produce seeds. Properties too, then, may come into being or not come into being. Therefore, both the substance and its properties are in potentiality to be or not be in act. Let us presume, for the sake of this argument, that each instance of act–potency distinction entails a real distinction, not a merely logical one. If, then, the existence–essence distinction must be understood as an instance of act–potency composition, and if act–potency composition pertains to something real in things themselves, then the distinction of existence and essence is ontologically real, not merely logical.[20] Were one to reject this argument, it would entail the denial of a real distinction of potency and act at the level of being itself in the things around us. This is contrary to our common-sense observations, however, since we see that things clearly do come to be and cease to be, and likewise develop existent properties that come into being. If we were to deny a real distinction of potency and act in these regards, we would be unable to speak about the ontological capacity of natures to be or not be, whether substantially or in certain respects. So it is reasonable to infer that there must be a distinction of *esse* and essence in things that can be or not be.

The perfection of existence argument begins from the hypothesis that there is at least one thing in which there is a real identity of essence and existence.[21] What would follow if there were such an identity of nature and being in a given reality? Here, Aquinas seems to presume something like the following. If a given reality were to have being (existence) essentially, then it would have in itself all that pertains to existence essentially. There would be nothing that could fall into the formal definition of being, so to speak, that this reality would fail to possess, in its very essence. It would follow from this presupposition, however, that any addition to this reality in the order of existence would be impossible. It could not accrue accidents or properties by which it could be qualified in some way, as existing in a new way, because it would already possess being essentially, meaning in the fullness of perfection. What is already perfect cannot accrue new actualization and perfection. Aquinas then goes on to note, logically, that there could exist only one such being, and not a plurality of such, since any such being would contain the fullness of existence, a perfection that cannot be shared with another formally (since any such "others" would themselves have the same and identical fullness of existence). Consequently, if there are realities that do not possess the fullness of existence, they must not possess existence essentially. Instead, they must be characterized by a real distinction of essence and existence. We should note that Aquinas is alluding in this argument to God who is singularly perfect in being and who alone is essentially existence, and who possesses in himself no distinction of essence and existence. However, he is not arguing here from the consideration of mere notions of perfection in existence and essence to the affirmation of the existence of God (in a way analogous to Anselm in the ontological argument). Rather, he is only arguing that *if there exists* any being that is existence essentially, it must be perfect in being, and there can be only one such being. Nor is Aquinas arguing that this being, if perfect, must absorb or assimilate all other being into itself, but only that if it exists as perfect, it must be in some way the origin and causal source of all that exists in creation, as that which receives being from God. Precisely because all the beings we experience are not identical with all that is in the order of existence, there must obtain ontologically within each of them a real distinction of essence and existence.

Aquinas does also argue from the real distinction of essence and existence in realities that are created to the existence of God, by a distinct form of argumentation.[22] Once the real distinction is acknowledged, at least in all the realities around us that we experience, then we can begin to see that all that we know to exist in nature has an external cause of its existence. It does not exist by nature, or merely in virtue of its essence. But if anything that actually exists has an external cause of its existence, and does not exist by nature, then its existence can only be explained adequately in reference to that which is the cause of its existence. However, to explain individual realities of this kind, we cannot merely appeal to an infinite number of other actually existent realities that are each themselves caused. Each of these is explained in turn only by reference to something external. Consequently, to explain adequately all that participates in being, or that receives existence from another, it is necessary to appeal to something that has existence essentially, in which there is no real distinction of essence and existence, that is the creator and actual cause of all else that exists. For Aquinas, then, one must appeal metaphysically to God the creator to obtain the most expansive explanation of all that exists.

DIVINE SIMPLICITY

The Christian idea of divine simplicity is a commonly misunderstood notion. The idea has its roots in patristic Trinitarian theology, in which thinkers such as Gregory of Nazianzus and Augustine sought to speak of the transcendence and alterity of the divine nature. Because God is the creator of being who gives existence to all that is, he is distinct from creatures and is not ontologically composite in ways that they inevitably are in virtue of their created status. This idea is compatible with the notion of God as a Trinity of persons, as we shall see. Indeed, it is required for any coherent Trinitarian theology, since classical orthodoxy states that the three persons are not only one in nature, but truly one in being, so that they each partake fully of the one unique nature of God.[23] The three persons are not three beings or gods, but each is truly the one God. Therefore, the Trinitarian persons must be non-composite in a way that three created persons are not.

Non-Composition and Apophaticism

The medieval theologians worked out differing theories of divine simplicity. Aquinas develops his own views in a number of major texts, one of which is *ST* I q.3, which I will examine here. In this text he considers a number of forms of ontological composition found in creatures that cannot obtain in the creator, and so he proceeds to negate these distinctions in turn when speaking about God, so as to indicate the apophatic character of our knowledge of the divine nature. God is unlike creatures in ways that oblige us, when speaking of him, to re-qualify our language, since the latter is characteristically drawn from our knowledge of merely created realities. Here, I will consider briefly only four of the non-compositions envisaged by Aquinas, those pertaining to matter and form, individual and nature, essence and existence, and substance and accident. We will see that Aquinas's notion of the "real distinction" studied above plays a central role in his conception of divine simplicity.

Form and Matter

Aquinas follows Aristotle in affirming that there is a real distinction of form and matter found in each physical substance. The form is the natural determination while the matter indicates the material parts and the underlying principle of pure potency that they imply. Our abstract notion of a given essence (human being, kangaroo, gold) is universal but is acquired by abstraction from the consideration of multiple material individuals. The universal notion of a nature corresponds to the form–matter composite, considered in abstraction from its individuating material conditions. We think, for example, of that in virtue of which a human being is essentially human, independently of this or that material circumstance or condition, such as being black or white, young or mature, healthy or ill. Aquinas notes that there cannot be any composition of matter and form in the divine nature for the simple reason that God is not a material body and has no physical substance.[24] If he were material, God would be in potency, in virtue of his materiality, and would be constantly subject to re-determination through his engagement with other realities. Consequently, he would be caused to be (at least in some respects) by other things. But if this were the case, God would not be the creator of being who unilaterally gives existence to all others, but would himself be dependent upon other things in the universe for his existence. God is the creator, however, so he is not in this state, and therefore cannot have a material body. Furthermore, Aquinas thinks that one can demonstrate philosophically that God is pure actuality, without any potentiality to become something more perfect; and if this is the case, then he can have no material composition, since this would entail in him the presence of potentiality and the denial of his pure actuality.[25] We should note that, in arguing in this way, Aquinas is not denying that God can take upon himself a human nature, and have a material body, as in the Incarnation, but only that if he does so, the human nature he has is not identical with his divine nature as such, which is not composed of matter and form.

It follows from this line of argument that God cannot be conceived of in the way we ordinarily conceive of all other things around us: by abstracting a universal concept of their nature from the experience of many concrete individuals. God is not a being in the world, one characterized by "essence" in the sense discussed above – i.e., having a nature consisting of a form–matter composite. We cannot read off from the world, then, a nominal definition of God merely by looking at the physical creatures around us, since he is utterly different in nature than any and all of them. Nor can he be represented in any image or symbol, since God's nature utterly transcends the world of physical sensibility.

Essence and Individual

The second affirmation of non-composition follows closely upon the first.[26] Each reality we experience is characterized by an essence it shares in common with other individuals. In a field of orange trees, for example, we see multiple individual instantiations of a common kind, as we would when surveying a field of horses or a crowd of humans. Therefore, we can never say that a given individual we experience is identical with its natural kind. It is false to say, for example, that

"Socrates is humanity," since this would entail that no one but Socrates is human. Aquinas does famously teach that non-material creatures are different in this respect. As noted above, he thinks that each angel is distinct in essence, and has its own species. However, in a late text he also argues that angels as creatures are composed of essence and existence. In this case, the individual is identical neither with the essence nor with what is distinct from the essence (the *esse*), but results from the composite of the two (essence and *esse*). Therefore, there is also a real distinction in separated substances of essence and individual suppositum.[27]

In God, however, neither of these forms of composition of individuality and nature obtains. First, God is not individuated by matter, as if he were to be literally one material god among others, standing out in a crowd. In this respect he is utterly unlike individuals we experience in the physical world. God is individuated by his divine nature. That is to say, he is the only one who possesses the divine nature. This philosophical idea corresponds to the famous Israelite claim, "The Lord alone is God."[28] Nor is God's essence distinct from his existence, as we shall come to shortly.

It follows from such arguments, for Aquinas, that in God there is no composition of individuality and nature. God is individual or unique in virtue of the nature that he alone possesses. If this is the case, then God is not rightly understood as a species of person alongside other created persons, one in whom there is reason and free will but simply to a more perfect or infinite degree. He cannot be placed in common with others according to a defining set of generalized characteristics. Instead, we have to understand him as the author of all created individuals of all natural kinds, who simultaneously transcends the compositions we identify in them.

Essence and Existence

Aquinas famously argues that, in contrast to creatures, there is no distinction of essence and existence in God. No created thing simply exists by nature. Nor is anything in which the real distinction obtains an efficient cause of its own being. All that can be or not be has a cause of its existence. God, by contrast, exists necessarily, by nature, and has no cause of his being.

> [W]hatever a thing has besides its essence must be caused either by the constituent principles of that essence ... or by some exterior agent – as heat is caused in water by fire. Therefore, if the existence of a thing differs from its essence, this existence must be caused either by some exterior agent or by its essential principles. Now it is impossible for a thing's existence to be caused by its essential constituent principles, for nothing can be the sufficient cause of its own existence, if its existence is caused. Therefore that thing, whose existence differs from its essence, must have its existence caused by another. But this cannot be true of God; because we call God the first efficient cause. Therefore it is impossible that in God His existence should differ from His essence.[29]

Aquinas likewise argues for this form of non-composition based on God's pure actuality and perfection in the order of being. If God's nature is perfect and purely actual, then he differs radically from creatures who are in potency to exist or not exist. Instead, he possesses the plenitude of being by nature. Furthermore, there is nothing in the order of existence that does not derive from his perfect nature. But if he were to have an existence distinct from his nature, he would merely participate in existence like everything else does, and thus would be limited and imperfect in being. God does not receive his being from another, however, so he does not participate in being, and thus is not composed of essence and existence.

If Aquinas is right about this claim, a number of significant consequences can be indicated. We tend to think of existence in abstract terms as that in virtue of which a nature has singular being or is actually existent rather than being merely possible or potential. Therefore, when thinking of created realities, we do not depict existence as something substantive in itself, as if it were a nature on its own (and this is similarly said of goodness, or truth). Meanwhile, we also think of every entity as merely one existent among others, associated with them in a common community of existence (*esse commune*). God, however, cannot be thought of in either of these ways, according to Aquinas. He is neither merely one entity among others, like one substance adjacent to others that participate in common existence, nor is he an impersonal universal idea, like goodness or existence (abstractly considered). Rather, he is one who alone possesses in himself the infinite plenitude of being, infinite existence, and who can personally communicate it to others as a gift. Nor can God be identified with the existence common to all things or with the transcendental features of being found in creatures.[30] Rather, he is the author of all that exists insofar as it exists, of all singular existents and of their natures, and by this very measure God is more intimate to creatures than they are to themselves, not as one who is identical with them but as the transcendent cause of what is most interior to them, their very being, or created *esse*. If God is present in all things in this unique way, as the creator, then his causal activity never functions as an ontological rival to their autonomy of being, but is rather its foundation. God sustains in being all subsistent natural realities with their own proper activities and interactive histories. Even as he is the author of finite existence, he can also be actively present in extraordinary ways in the midst of his creation, without doing violence to the natural order, as when, for example, God becomes human, without in any way diminishing the integrity of the human nature he assumes.

Substance and Accidents

Aquinas also argues that there are no compositions of substance and accident in God.[31] Since the divine nature is immaterial, this form of non-composition applies most evidently to his acts of immaterial knowledge and love. In human beings such activities imply the acquisition of progressive perfections, as when a child learns mathematics or a person develops in character through mature moral deliberation. Were God subject to this kind of development, his nature would undergo an ontological history of progress or regress depending upon his thoughts, decisions, actions, and engagements with creatures. Aquinas interprets scriptural passages that depict God in this way as metaphorical in nature, and argues that if they were ascribed to God in strictly metaphysical terms they would be anthropomorphic.[32] If God is purely actual, he cannot develop potencies in view of eventual perfection. Indeed, if his engagements were the occasions for him to do so, then creation would have as important a role in perfecting God ontologically, entering into a reciprocity of creative causality with God, within a larger pantheistic process. Furthermore, God is existence in all he is, as noted above. If this is the case, he cannot develop new accidental perfections by addition to a substance, as occurs in creatures. Were this to occur, God would develop in the order of existence accidentally by accruing properties, and thus he would not possess the plenitude of existence by nature. Behind Aquinas's thinking here is a claim about the order of ontological dependence. Accidental properties inhere in substances and depend upon them. In this sense, they are causally derivative. God, however, is not self-caused and contains no composition in which he can be said to be perfect in one respect, while causally dependent and gradually developing in another.

It is sometimes thought that this form of argumentation forbids Aquinas from affirming that God truly knows or wills creatures, or that he can love and relate to creatures. This is not true at all, and indeed Aquinas affirms the opposite for what pertains to God's knowledge and love. However, his view does entail that when God knows and loves he does so in a way very different from intellectual creatures. God's knowledge and love are identical with his essence, for Aquinas, and they are perfect in being, so that if God knows and loves creatures, it is only ever because he first knows and loves his own infinitely perfect nature and creates all things in this light, such that all created things participate in finite ways in God's own infinite wisdom and goodness.[33] This "theocentricity" of God's own life is in no way egoistic. On the contrary, precisely because God's knowledge and love of creatures stem from his own infinite perfection, they are not generated from any desire for self-improvement. God creates in ontological gratuity, giving being to creatures as a sheer gift of wisdom and goodness. He does not and cannot perfect or improve himself in the process, by more mature acts of knowledge and love that come to characterize him progressively in regard to creatures. In this sense, we must accept a kind of apophatic register when thinking of God's inner life, since it does not transpire through habit, or by successive acts of relative improvement or failure, as does ours.

KNOWLEDGE OF THE TRINITY

Christian theology traditionally claims that the inner identity of God as a communion of persons is unveiled to the human race by way of divine revelation in the person of Jesus of Nazareth. Traditional creedal definitions of the Trinity affirm that there are three distinct persons in God – the Father, Son, and the Holy Spirit – who are one being and essence, and who are each truly the one God.[34] Based on his understanding of natural knowledge of God, Aquinas argues that philosophical reason can neither demonstrate the reality nor disprove the possibility of the mystery of the Trinity.[35] The reason for this claim is roughly the following. Philosophical reason can demonstrate that there exists a transcendent first cause of all else that is, the creator, who is one in being and simple, in the senses mentioned above. Nevertheless, philosophical reasoning about God does not provide us with immediate intellectual access to the creator in his very being and essence. Even if the Trinity is the hidden cause of all that exists, the Father, Son, and Holy Spirit communicate existence to the world in virtue of their shared nature and power. The effect produced then reflects their inner mystery only insofar as they are one and simple in being, not insofar as they are a communion of three persons. Because God is simple, then, we cannot say philosophically whether God is Trinity or not. Ironic as it may seem to some, the affirmation of divine simplicity functions for Aquinas as a safeguard against the rational pretension to dismiss the mystery of the Trinity as something contrary to reason. Such a dismissal would be, from the philosophical point of view, irrational, precisely due to the natural knowledge we have of God's apophatic simplicity and thus of his transcendence of our immediate comprehension. Personal knowledge of the Trinity as such arises only in virtue of God's free and purposeful self-disclosure in New Testament revelation. This intimate know-ledge of who God is in himself is a gift of grace God shares with the human race, over and above common creation, and is given in view of the beatification of human beings, by means of faith, hope, and char-ity in this life and the beatific vision in the next.[36]

IMMATERIAL PROCESSION OF PERSONS AND RELATIONS OF ORIGIN

Despite its hiddenness, Aquinas does not consider the mystery of the Trinity to be something intellectually insignificant or wholly unintel-ligible. On the contrary, the knowledge provided by Christian revela-tion of who God is casts a light upon the meaning of the whole creation, and human personhood in particular. This is the case for Aquinas especially when one takes into account the Augustinian idea that each human soul has a similitude to the Trinity, according to an analogy of immaterial processions.[37] The person of the Son is the eternally begotten Word (*Verbum*) of the Father, and the Holy Spirit is the eternally spirated Love of the Father and the Son.[38] Understood in this way, the Trinity illumines one's understanding of the human subject as an intellectual and voluntary agent. Human persons are made in the image of the Trinity since they have immaterial facilities of intellect and will, rooted in the immaterial spiritual soul, which is the form of the body. As such they are personal beings who are able to live lives oriented toward truth and love, in activities of both body and soul.

However, if God is non-composite in nature, how can Christianity reasonably ascribe to God an inner life in which there are eternal immaterial processions and a real distinction of persons?

Responses to this question were developed initially in the early Church in the fourth and fifth centuries in response to the Arian crisis, by thinkers such as Basil, Gregory of Nazianzus, Gregory of Nyssa, and Augustine. The first three of these, known collectively as the Cappadocian fathers, sought to defend the doctrine of the Council of Nicaea, which affirmed that the Father and the Son are consubstantial (*homoousios*) and thus one in essence and being. They did so by claiming that the persons are distinguished principally by relations of origin.[39] The Son originates from the Father eternally as his immaterially begotten *Logos* or *Verbum* and in doing so receives from the Father all he is as God, all that pertains to the divine nature in its simplicity. This is true in turn for the Spirit, who proceeds from the Father through the Son. Augustine sought to develop this claim by appeal to the doctrine of divine simplicity in *On the Trinity*, where he noted that, due to the simplicity of the divine nature, there is no real distinction of essence and individual in God.[40] All that has "deity" just is the one God. Therefore, if the Father, Son, and Spirit each truly possess the divine nature, they each truly are the one God. It follows that we can only distinguish them by relations of origin, and do so best by appealing to the aforementioned similitude from acts of knowledge and love.[41] Just as immaterial thought proceeds from a human knower, and voluntary love arises from the knowledge of the good, so an order of relational procession exists in the Trinity. The Father in knowing himself begets the Son eternally as his Word and Wisdom, communicating to him the fullness of his divine life and nature, and so also spirates the Holy Spirit as love from and with the Son.[42]

PERSONS AS SUBSISTENT RELATIONS AND SUBSISTENT MODES OF BEING

Aquinas takes up each of these ideas and gives them an articulation of his own. In the epoch just prior to Aquinas, medieval theology had been colored by Trinitarian debates stemming from the writings of Gilbert of Poitiers (d. 1154) and Joachim of Fiore (d. 1202), both of whose opinions the Catholic theological guild had rejected.[43] Gilbert began from the idea that the essence of the three persons in God must be one and the same, since they are each the one God. He then argued that the relations of origin between the persons must be extrinsic to their essence, since the essence unites them but the relations distinguish them. This led to the conclusion that there is a distinction between each of the persons and their relative properties, since each person is God in essence prior to being related to the others. Relations are therefore accidental or extraneous to the substance of a person, much as they would be in human persons. God the Father is not his paternity (his relation to the Son) but possesses paternity as an extrinsic property, while sharing the divine essence in common with the Son. This way of thinking results in conceiving the three persons by relative similitude to three human beings who are essentially identical in nature (as human), and related to one another according to accidental properties (as father and son, for example). This position was rejected by the Council of Reims in 1148 due to its deficient grasp of the simplicity of the divine nature of the Trinity, in which the relations of the persons are not accidental additions to a substance.

At the other extreme, Joachim wrote in reaction to an opinion of Peter Lombard, who argued that one must not say that the essence of God begets or spirates (a claim that is in fact correct). Joachim mistakenly took this claim to imply logically that the essence in God can be treated as a kind of additional fourth subject, extraneous to the three persons. He countered by arguing that the essence of God itself begets and spirates, attributing processional activities to the nature of God as such, rather than the persons. He likely wished to indicate that the processions of the Trinity just are what God is (the Trinity is the processional life of Father, Son, and Spirit), but he arrived at the affirmation that the essence itself differentiates in composite ways, in virtue of the divine processions. This view was rejected at the Fourth Lateran Council in 1215, also keeping in mind the simplicity and perfection of the divine nature.

Aquinas saw rightly that both of these problematic positions fail to understand sufficiently the implications of the doctrine of divine simplicity. If the nature of God is simple, then there cannot be personal relations in God that are extrinsic to his essence.[44] Nor can God's nature be subject to diverse composite activities of self-differentiation, like begetting and spirating.[45] The three persons are distinct but they are only truly one in essence because they each partake fully of the one divine nature of God.

In the wake of these controversies, and in order to cast greater light on the mystery of the Trinity, Aquinas developed his own account of a common medieval notion of Trinitarian persons as "subsistent relations."[46] This idea has no pure analogue to anything in our ordinary human experience, and is used to denote a mystery proper to divine revelation, rather like the notion of the hypostatic union for the Incarnation or transubstantiation for the Eucharist. Aquinas argues that all ontological relations as we normally experience them are grounded either in quantity or action and passion. For example, one thing can be relatively taller or shorter than another quantitatively, or one thing can act upon another that is acted upon, as when a mother is really related to the child she is begetting and the child is really related to the mother who is giving birth to her. As such, relation denotes a way of being toward another or of being connected to another.

When we speak of real relations in the Trinity, we have to transpose something from our ordinary experience onto God by analogy. In all the realities we experience, relations imply two things: a foundation in a prior accident (quantity or action and passion), and a relationship of one to another that emerges from the foundation. This first aspect of relationality does not obtain in God, because there are no accidental properties in God. It is only in the second of the two senses just mentioned, then, that we can speak of there being relations in the Trinity. The persons in God are relations in all they are, wholly related to one another in mutual reciprocity. If God is simple, how are these distinct relations instantiated? They are instantiated in the distinct processions in God by which one person or two persons communicate the plenitude of the divine life to another. The Father is eternally related to the Son as he who begets the Son as his Word, and the Son is eternally related to the Father as one begotten of the Father. The Father and the Son together are eternally related to the Holy Spirit as their mutually spirated love, and the Spirit is really related to them eternally as the principle from whom he proceeds as love. In these relations of generation and spiration, the persons communicate the plenitude of the divine essence, such that the Father who is subsistent God gives all that he has essentially as God to the Son (without surrendering it himself) and the Father and the Son communicate all that they have essentially as God to the Spirit. On this view, all that is in any of the three persons *qua* persons is wholly relative to the other two, in virtue of the two eternal processions of divine self-communication, and each of the three persons is essentially and truly the one God. Due to divine simplicity, anything seemingly "accidental" in God must in fact be substantial, so if there are real relations in God, each relation must be subsistent. The persons of the Trinity are therefore subsistent relations.

In contradistinction to Gilbert, Aquinas argues that the divine persons are rightly connoted substantively by their relative properties. Otherwise said, the Father is his paternity, because he is relative in all he is as Father to the Son whom he begets eternally. The Son in turn is also relative to the Father as his begotten Word who receives all that he is as God from the Father eternally. The Father and the Son are eternally relative to the Holy Spirit who they spirate eternally as their mutual love, and the Holy Spirit in turn receives eternally all that he is from the Father and the Son, as one who is truly God. Gilles Emery notes that, when Aquinas speaks of Trinitarian persons, he invites us to make use of an intellectual practice of "redoubling."[47] Each Trinitarian person is rightly thought of under a twofold aspect, as one who is ever only relative to the other two in all that he is, and as one who possesses the fullness of the divine being and essence, and thus is truly God. For example, the Father is wholly relative to the Son and Spirit as the active principle of their generation and spiration, respectively, and he is also one who possesses in himself the fullness of the divine essence, which implies all the divine attributes such as simplicity, perfection, goodness, eternity, and so on. Each of the persons can be thought of, then, in this twofold way, as unique in his distinctive relationality and as one who possesses all that we normally attribute to the godhead.

This view of Trinitarian life gives rise to the notion of Trinitarian perichoresis or mutual indwelling. If the Father communicates all that he is as God to the Son and Spirit in generation and spiration respectively, then the Son contains in himself all that is in the Father and the Spirit, and likewise the Spirit contains in himself all that is in the Father and the Son.[48] As a consequence, the persons indwell in one another perfectly, in virtue of their shared divine essence, even while being truly distinct as persons.[49] We should note that this doctrine of perichoresis is implied by the doctrine of divine simplicity. It is principally because the three persons are truly one in being and essence that they must be wholly immanent to one another personally, so that there is nothing pertaining to one person formally as God that is not found in the others. Their communion is therefore infinitely perfect and utterly immanent, even as it is, by our conceptual standards, transcendent and somewhat incomprehensible. This does not mean that the communion of persons in God is wholly inaccessible to us. By grace, the Trinity comes to indwell in the souls of human beings, and when one communes with one person inwardly (such as the Holy Spirit), one also possesses immediate access to the other two (i.e., the Father and the Son who send the Spirit).[50]

Aquinas also speaks about the divine nature subsisting in three distinct personal modes, and this, too, has a logical connection to the idea of divine simplicity.[51] There is only one divine nature, but since the three persons each possess that nature according to their relations of origin, which are subsistent, then the mode in which they are each the one God is distinct to each of them. The Father subsists as God in a paternal way, as one who generates the Word and spirates the Spirit. The Son subsists as God in a filial way as one begotten, who spirates the Spirit with the Father. The Spirit subsists in a spirated mode, as in one who receives all he is from the Father and Son as their mutual love.[52] This idea of personal modes of subsistence is important when thinking about Trinitarian activities such as creation, redemption, and sanctification. Whenever the persons of the Trinity act *ad extra*, they do so as one, in virtue of their shared deity.[53] However, they also do so in distinct personal modes.[54] The Father acts in his principality as the font of Trinitarian life, so that even in creation he is the Father of the Son and Spirit, from whom all things proceed. He creates through his Word, who bears a relation to creatures as the transcendent exemplar of intelligibility in all created things. The Father and the Son create in their Spirit, who is love and therefore a transcendent source of the goodness found in creatures. The persons of the Trinity have proper ways of being God even when they act together as one in virtue of their unity of being and divine life.

What we can observe from these reflections is that the doctrine of divine simplicity, far from being an obstacle to coherent reflection on the mystery of the Trinity, plays a significant role in medieval reflection generally and in Aquinas's Trinitarian theology in particular.

THE TRINITARIAN CHARACTER OF CREATED BEING

As we have noted above, Aquinas does not think that we can derive natural knowledge of the Trinity from the philosophical consideration of created things. He does, however, believe that we can gain new insight into the meaning of creation in light of Trinitarian revelation. If God is truly a mystery of eternal life and interpersonal communion characterized by immaterial processions of truth and love, then aspects of created being can be expected to reflect this mystery, in their own way. Augustine developed this idea in *On the Trinity*, where he characterized the trinitarian imprint in creatures according to the notions of "unity and form and order," each reflecting a respective uncreated person.[55] Aquinas takes up this idea and argues in the following way:

> For the Son proceeds as the word of the intellect; and the Holy Spirit proceeds as love of the will. Therefore in rational creatures, possessing intellect and will, there is found the representation of the Trinity by way of image, inasmuch as there is found in them the

word conceived, and the love proceeding. But in all creatures there is found the trace of the Trinity, inasmuch as in every creature are found some things which are necessarily reduced to the divine Persons as to their cause. For every creature subsists in its own being, and has a form, whereby it is determined to a species, and has relation to something else. Therefore as it is a created substance, it represents the cause and principle; and so in that manner it shows the Person of the Father, who is the "principle from no principle." According as it has a form and species, it represents the Word as the form of the thing made by art is from the conception of the craftsman. According as it has relation of order, it represents the Holy Spirit, inasmuch as He is love, because the order of the effect to something else is from the will of the Creator.[56]

In effect, Aquinas claims that every substance we experience reflects the mystery of the paternity of God in virtue of its substantial autonomy. It reflects the Son by its intelligible species, which has its transcendent ground in the divine Word. The tendency in all things to act in view of various ends in accord with the ordering of nature reflects their capacity to achieve various forms of perfection and goodness. This is indicative of the exemplarity of the Holy Spirit, who in his divine love is the source of created goodness in things.

If we interpret Aquinas only slightly beyond the scope of his explicit formulations, we can revisit the distinction between existence and essence noted in the earlier part of this chapter and think of it in a Trinitarian light. We noted that, for Aquinas, each created being is composed of essence and existence. Consequently, it participates in existence, as each concrete being contracts or delimits *esse*. The perfection of being is actuated in a limited way in each created thing. In light of the Trinitarian re-reading of creatures, we can note that the creator's gift of *esse* reflects the Father's communication of autonomous being to all things, and the participation of this *esse* in distinct essential forms reflects their creation in the Word, according to distinct species of being, themselves reflective in finite ways of the infinite splendor of the Word.[57] The Father communicates the infinite fullness of being to the Word, and in doing so also communicates freely with and from the Word the finite fullness of being to the creation. Likewise, creatures have a finite fullness of being in virtue of which they are good, and can pursue various perfections in accord with their respective natures, embodied activities, and perfecting actions. Their goodness is not subsistent per se, but participated, and their perfecting actions are merely accidental, not substantial; but despite their ontological finitude and imperfection in these respects, they truly reflect something of the uncreated goodness of the Holy Spirit, who is a creative source of personal love in God. Just as the Father and the Son spirate an infinite mutual love for one another who is the Holy Spirit, simply in virtue of who they are eternally, so too they also freely communicate in and with the Holy Spirit a fullness of finite goodness to the creation. The goodness of creatures and their tendencies toward perfection are obliquely reflective of this eternal uncreated spiration of a person who is love.

CONCLUSION

Aquinas's conception of ultimate explanation is nuanced. On his view, one's understanding of the real distinction and composition of existence and essence in creatures can lead to real but indirect philosophical knowledge of God. It also allows one to construct a conceptually ornate and unified account of divine simplicity. This understanding of God can be used in turn to defend the possibility of Trinitarian revelation but not to demonstrate its reality. At the service of this same revelation, the doctrine of divine simplicity can also contribute constructively to a theory of Trinitarian persons as subsistent relations, a notion that allows one to articulate a compelling depiction of the Trinity in terms that are both monotheistic and tripersonal. Aquinas's theological understanding of the Trinity makes specific use of the notion of divine simplicity in this regard and in turn allows one to re-read the composition in creatures in light of the processions of the Word and the Spirit. Creatures are thus understood in their composite metaphysical dependency as finite and temporal expressions of the Trinity. All that exists derives from God's eternal processional life of wisdom and love.

NOTES

1 The *DEE* from his early period remains a fundamental reference, and he develops his mature account later in *Quodl* 8, q.1, a.1, his *In BDH*, *SCG* II, c.52–4, and *QDP*, q.7, *In CA*, and the *DSS*.
2 *DEE*, c.1.
3 *DEE*, c.2.
4 *DEE*, c.6; *In PA* I, lec.10.
5 *ST* I, q.79.
6 *Quodl* 8, q.1, a.1.
7 *Expositio in Symbolum Apostolorum*, preface; *ST* I, q.79, a.9, ad 3.
8 *ST* I, q. 75, a. 4.
9 *In Meta* 4, lec.2, 556–8.
10 *DEE*, c.2 and 5.
11 *QDP*, q. 7, a. 2, ad 9. Translation by R. J. Regan, *The Power of God* (Oxford: Oxford University Press, 2012).
12 See in this regard the helpfully clear text of *SCG* II, c.52–4.
13 *SCG* II, c.54. Translation by J. Anderson, *Summa Contra Gentiles*, vol. II (Garden City, NY: Doubleday, 1956).
14 *DEE*, c.4.
15 *SCG* II, c.52.
16 *In BDH*, c.2.
17 *SCG* I, c.26; *QDP*, q.7, a.2, ad 4 and 6.
18 See J. F. Wippel, *The Metaphysical Thought of Thomas Aquinas: From Finite Being to Uncreated Being* (Washington, DC: Catholic University of America Press, 2000), c.5.
19 See *SCG* I, cc.24–5; *SCG* II, c.52.
20 See *SCG* II, c.54; *QDP*, q.7, aa.1–2.
21 *DEE*, c.4; *SCG* II, c.52.
22 *DEE*, c.4; *SCG* I, c.22.
23 See on this subject, White, 2016a and 2016b.
24 *ST* I, q.3, a.2.
25 Ibid.
26 *ST* I, q.3, a.3.
27 *Quodl* 2.
28 Ps. 18:31.

29 *ST* I, q.3, a.4. Translation by English Dominican Province, *Summa Theologica* (New York: Benzinger Brothers, 1947).

30 *ST* I, q.3, a.5.

31 *ST* I, q.3, a.6.

32 *ST* I, q.1, a.9; *ST* I, q.19, a.7, ad 1.

33 *ST* I, q.14, q.19, q.20. See the discussions of divine simplicity in E. Stump, *Aquinas* (New York: Routledge, 2005), c.3.

34 See, for example, the Nicaean Creed, the Athanasian Creed, or the teaching of the Fourth Lateran Council, simply to indicate prominent examples.

35 *ST* I, q.32, a.1.

36 See *ST* II-II, q.1, a.1; *ST* II-II, q.2, aa.7–8.

37 *ST* I, q.93, aa.4–8.

38 *ST* I, q.27.

39 See. for example, Gregory Nazianzus, *Oration 31 (Fifth Theological Oration)*, n.9; Augustine, *The Trinity*, V, cc.4–6.

40 Augustine, *The Trinity*, V, cc.4–5.

41 Augustine, *The Trinity*, V, cc.6 and 11.

42 Augustine, *The Trinity*, V, cc.14–16; XV, c.6.

43 On what follows on these figures, see G. Emery, *The Trinitarian Theology of St. Thomas Aquinas* (Oxford: Oxford University Press, 2007), 90–1, 141–8.

44 See Aquinas on Gilbert in *QDP*, q.8, a.2.

45 See Aquinas on Joachim in *ST* I, q.39, a.5.

46 See *ST* I, qq.28–9. The notion arises specifically in q.29, a.4.

47 On this, see Emery, *The Trinitarian Theology*, c.5; *ST* I, q.40, a.1.

48 *ST* I, q.42.

49 *ST* I, q.42, aa.5–6.

50 See *Super Johan* XVII, lect.5.

51 *ST* I, q.39, a.8; *ST* I, q.42, a.3; *ST* I, q.45, a.6.

52 *ST* I, q.29, a.4; *ST* I, q.34, a.2, ad 1.

53 *ST* I, q.45, a.6.

54 *ST* I, q.45, a.7; *ST* I, q.39, a.8.

55 Augustine, *The Trinity*, VI, c.10.

56 *ST* I, q.45, a.7. Translation by English Dominican Province, *Summa Theologica*.

57 *ST* I, q.39, a.8; *ST* I, q.34, a.2, ad 3.

4 Goodness and Being, Transcendentals, Participation

Gaven Kerr

The doctrine of the transcendentals is a truly medieval doctrine. Up until the thirteenth century, philosophers and theologians were familiar with the study of being through the ancient philosophers and their schools, particularly Plato and Aristotle. What was important for Plato, Aristotle et al. was to offer an account of being in terms of those constitutive principles without which nothing would be. So, for example, being was taken to be accounted for in terms of participation in the forms (Plato), or through the dichotomies of substance and accident, matter and form, act and potency (Aristotle). What such projects seemed to exclude, or at least did not address explicitly, was the character of being itself. The question of the character of being itself was not explicitly elaborated until the thirteenth century, when the chancellor of the University of Paris, Philip, produced his *Summa de bono* (1225–8), the first eleven questions of which elaborate the doctrine of the transcendentals or what he called the *communissima*. Philip was quickly followed in this project by the Franciscans at the University of Paris, notably Alexander of Hales, whose *Summa theologica* or *Summa fratris Alexandri* (1245) contained a treatise on the transcendentals in Book 1. Finally, Albert the Great, Aquinas's teacher, himself dealt with the transcendentals in several works which appeared prior to Aquinas's emergence as a master of theology.[1] Accordingly, in the first half of the thirteenth century, a distinct treatment of being in itself emerged whereby we could predicate certain properties of being which are found everywhere being is found and yet serve to characterize being in some way. Unlike Plato's forms or Aristotle's compositional structures, these transcendental properties are not merely productive of a being, but attendant upon every instance of being.

There were, of course, anticipations of the consideration of being in terms of the transcendentals prior to the thirteenth century. In *Metaphysics*, Book 2, Aristotle correlated the being of a thing with the truth of a thing.[2] Similarly, in *Metaphysics*, Book 4, he held that being and the one are both said in many ways and so share the same common nature.[3] Furthermore, the Neoplatonists frequently characterized being in terms of unity, truth, and goodness, and even in the case of Plotinus, the fundamental character of being was that of the One.[4] Finally, the Islamic philosopher Avicenna held that being, thing, and unity are primary conceptions of the intellect into which our concepts are resolved.[5] What these examples illustrate is that there was present in the tradition a vague notion of being as itself characterized by unity, truth, and goodness. However, it was not until the thirteenth century that a concerted focus on these so-called transcendental properties of being was developed.

The focus of this chapter is Aquinas's thought on the transcendentals. This involves a consideration of his metaphysics and not only how we can think about being in terms of the constitutive principles of beings – e.g., potency, form, act, etc. – but also how we can think about being itself as one, true, and good. For Aquinas, these transcendental perfections coincide with being but reveal something about the nature of being not originally signified by the term 'being.' It follows, then, that the character of individual beings is determined not only by their metaphysical components, but also by their participation in being itself.

This chapter is broken down as follows. We consider first Aquinas's thought on the transcendentals, focusing on those which appear most commonly throughout his works: unity, truth, and goodness. Having done that, we consider how beings derive their character as one, true, and good through their participation in being. Finally, we consider how Aquinas's metaphysical thinking in this regard informs his thinking on the goodness of beings in general.

THE TRANSCENDENTALS

In traditional Aristotelian fashion, Aquinas takes the subject matter of metaphysics to be being *qua* being; he offers his own term for this subject matter: *ens commune*. What he means by the latter is the being that all things have in common; such a study of being will be applicable to all beings and exclude none. Hence, metaphysics does not carve up one domain of being and study only that; nothing is left out of being in its study in metaphysics.[6]

This generalized study leaves us with a problem; for what can we really say about being other than that it is and that its complementary opposite, non-being, is not? We are in danger of affirming being as an all-encompassing reality from which nothing escapes. Indeed, this was the Parmenidean problem in ancient philosophy such that there is nothing outside of being which can differentiate it, in which case all differentiating characteristics are illusory, and being is the only reality.

It is to the credit of Plato and Aristotle that they recognized that Parmenides and his followers were thinking of being in a univocal fashion – i.e., that it could have only a single definition applicable in all cases, so that all modifications and differentiating features would be illusory. Both Plato and Aristotle recognized that there is a plurivocal notion of being. Being is not a genus only differentiated by what is outside of it (in which case differentiated by nothing); rather, being is an analogous notion said in many ways.

Aquinas himself inherits and develops this analogical way of thinking about being.[7] Following Avicenna, he recognizes that being is what the intellect first conceives and to which it reduces all its concepts. Accordingly, being is the fundamental reality of which we are familiar.[8] But insofar as being is not a genus, there is nothing that can be added to being to specify it. Hence, in order to differentiate our notion of being and thereby fill out our metaphysics as a science of being, we can only add to being certain concepts which express a mode of being not expressed by the term 'being' itself. Aquinas argues that this can be done in two ways.[9]

First, we can express a certain mode of being which considers being in a rather special or determinate manner. And in this case, we speak of different grades of being. Traditionally these have been divided into what exists in itself (substance) and what exists in another (accident). Substance and accident do not add anything to being not already envisaged by being, but they do express certain of its modes. Not only that, in investigating substance and accident, the metaphysician investigates what is proper to all beings, since all beings can be categorized as such, in which case the original subject matter of metaphysics, as being *qua* being, is honored. Furthermore, the study of substance and accident will in turn involve their metaphysical constituents such as essence and existence (*esse*), matter and form, act and potency. This kind of metaphysical investigation is one we all know and love when engaging with Aquinas's metaphysical thought, and it is to the fore in works such as *De ente et essentia*, *De principiis naturae*, and *De substantiis separatis*, not to mention forming the backdrop for much of Aquinas's thought in his systematically theological works such as the *Summa contra Gentiles* and *Summa theologiae*.

Second, we can express a certain mode of being which considers being not in some determinate manner – e.g., as substance or accident – but in a more general manner consequent upon every being. Aquinas argues that this mode of being can be taken in two ways. First, it may follow upon every being considered absolutely; second, it may follow upon every being considered in relation to another.

Considered absolutely, this common mode of being can be expressed either affirmatively or negatively. The only thing we can affirm absolutely of every being is its essence, and to designate this we use the term 'thing' (*res*). On the other hand, negatively speaking we can say that every being is undivided, and we express this lack of division as 'one' or 'unity' (*unum*).

Considered relatively, there is a general mode of being consequent upon every being based on the distinction of one thing from another, and to express this we use the term 'something' (*aliquid*). Furthermore, there is a mode of being, not based on the distinction of one thing from another, but based on the relation of one thing to another. In order to have such a relation, we need some individual being that is in a sense all things and to which being is related; this is the rational soul, since through intellect and will the rational soul can become all things.[10] The modes of being consequent upon the relation of being to the rational soul pertain to how being relates to the intellect and will. If we take being as related to the intellect, we have the true (*veritas*) since truth is the agreement of intellect and thing. If we take being as it is related to the will, then we have the good (*bonum*), since the good is being considered as desirable.

These modes express being in general and are consequent upon every being, whether considered absolutely – thing and one; or considered in relation as distinct from each other – something; or in relation to each other – true and good. Apart from the more standard metaphysical considerations of substance, accident, essence, *esse*, etc., we can consider being as thing, one, something, true, and good. As indicated in the introduction to this chapter, the latter modes of being have come to be known as the transcendentals. Let us take a moment to reflect on this term.

What is transcendent passes over other things. This is borne out by a consideration of the term itself – '*transcendens*': *trans* = across, *scendens* = stepping. When we think of things that we typically take to be transcendent – e.g., God and angels – they go beyond material things and are situated somewhat above them. Similarly, when we think of ourselves as getting over some past situation, affliction, or malady, we typically say that we have transcended that. Even in a more technical philosophical sense, when we consider Kant's notion of a transcendental philosophy as one that seeks out the conditions for the possibility of something, we are looking past that for which we seek the conditions and focusing on the conditions themselves. In all these instances we are stepping over something and adopting a higher order perspective.[11]

In the case of the transcendentals, they are features of being that step over and thereby surpass the categorical determinations of being. Accordingly, they express general notions of being that coincide with being yet reveal something not already signified by the term 'being.' So, Parmenides notwithstanding, we can enlarge and enrich our notion of being, not only by considering the special modes of being involved in the consideration of substance and accident, but also by considering those modes that express being in general and are consequent upon all beings. Unlike the categories, the transcendentals are convertible with each other insofar as they have the same reference – i.e., being – of which they are not particular but general modes.[12] Nevertheless, they are distinct from each other insofar as they express *different* modes of being, each adding something to the notion not already signified by the term 'being.' Whatever is, then, is one, true, good, and the like, since wherever being is found it will be found to be one, true, good, etc.

The foregoing division is taken from Aquinas's disputed questions *On Truth* (*De veritate*), q.1, a.1; it offers Aquinas's fullest treatment of the transcendentals. Elsewhere, Aquinas reiterates the same teaching, but he narrows down the conceptions of being to a combination of some or all of one, true, and good.[13] This narrowing is understandable insofar as any addition that we seek to make to being will be a conceptual addition, not a real one, since being is not a genus and cannot be added to from without. Such conceptual additions are either negations or relations, in which case when we seek to enlarge our notion of being we do so through considering it negatively, and so we have being as undivided – i.e., one – or relationally – i.e., as true and good.[14] Bearing this in mind, we will narrow our focus to consider unity, truth, and goodness in themselves, but before proceeding we will consider the place of beauty or lack thereof in the transcendentals.[15]

To begin with, Aquinas never includes beauty when affirming the traditional list of transcendentals – unity, truth, and goodness – not even in the more extensive list from the *De veritate*. Yet surprisingly there has been some focus on beauty as a transcendental in the literature.[16] I do not propose to enter into this disputed area in any great amount of depth; the only thing I will say is that, given what we have seen, for something to be a transcendental it has to be convertible with being and the other transcendentals, yet it must add a distinct sense to being not already signified by the term 'being' itself. One, true, and good do this, but it seems to me that beauty does not (or at least not as Aquinas understood beauty), since for Aquinas the essence of beauty consists in integrity or completeness, proportion, and luminosity;[17] the latter are not convertible with being, nor are they convertible with the other transcendentals (unity, truth, and goodness), in which case beauty is not a transcendental. Beauty accordingly appears to signify a determinate mode of being for some beings that have it. Hence, I do not consider it to be Aquinas's position that beauty is a transcendental.[18]

Let us now turn to unity, truth, and goodness.

The essence of unity is undividedness or indivision.[19] Every being is undivided in itself, and so every being is one. This, of course, is not the numerical unity which is the principle of number, but what could be called metaphysical or ontological unity (since it pertains to being). The idea is that every being is an undivided whole in some way. This goes not only for God, who is utterly simple, but also for creatures, who are composite. Anything that is divided from the being in question is not *of* that being and so not identified with it.

Let us take the typical components of a material substance: matter and form. Despite picturesque or just false ways of thinking, the matter and the form of a thing are not divided from the thing; rather, they are united in the thing as potency and act. The matter of the thing is formed in some respect to produce an individual thing of that kind. Accordingly, while distinct, matter and form are unified in the thing; and this applies to all the thing's metaphysical compositions. Composition is of act and potency, so that the components are united in the single individual. Such composite things are actually one, and when their parts are divided up, they cease to be.[20] Hence, every such being precisely as the being that it is is one. As Norris Clarke puts it: "It coheres together within itself as a single undivided whole, but is distinct in its being from every other being: it is itself, but is not any other being. This is true even of God, even though He contains the qualitative fullness of all perfection."[21]

The foregoing reasoning also serves to account for the transcendental perfections of thing (res) and something (aliquid) left over from the *De veritate*. This is because the being in question *qua* one is one thing, and as one thing it is distinct from other things. Accordingly, *res* and *aliquid* pertain to *unum* and so can be devised from a consideration of *unum*.[22]

Now, it has been noted that the components of a thing are united as act and potency. This, then, entails that the thing's principle of unity is the principle of act which actualizes its potency. Per our focus on matter and form, there is a unified material thing because the form actualizes the potency of the matter to be an individual of that kind. It follows, then, that the fundamental principle of actuality will be the fundamental principle of unity, since any potency in the thing will be subsumed and actualized under it. For Aquinas, the most fundamental principle of actuality is the act of existence – *esse*; it is the act of all acts. Nothing would be were it not for *esse*, and everything in the substance is actual because of its *esse*.[23] Accordingly, the composition of matter and form in the thing serves to establish it as an individual thing of that kind, but the composite of matter and form itself stands in potency to the act of existence without which there would be nothing. So, the various metaphysical components of a thing are brought together in unity through their participation in the thing's *esse* without which it would not be. And so the reason why unity coincides with being becomes manifest: A thing is unified in its *esse*, and it is its *esse* by which the thing is a being at all. Hence, wherever being is found, unity is found.

Let us now consider truth.

Like unity, truth adds something to being not already signified by the term 'being.' But unlike unity, truth does not add a negation to being, but a relation. The relation pertains to intellect, so that being is true in relation to an intellect. The essence of truth then is the conformity of intellect and thing.[24] Let us consider this.

In an early text, Aquinas argues that truth is not something that has its being wholly outside of the mind, nor is it wholly intrinsic to the mind. Rather, Aquinas argues that truth is founded upon extramental being, but depends on the intellect for its realization.[25] Aquinas goes on to explain that the foundation of truth is the *esse* of a thing as opposed to its quiddity, since it is by means of its *esse* that a thing is made present to and capable of being understood by the intelligent subject. This is because the *esse* of the object by which it is in the world and present to the knower is individuated to that object; for instance, the *esse* of a dog is that of a dog and not a cat. Accordingly, the real existence of the object is revelatory of the kind of object that it is since its *esse* is individuated to the object itself. The thing's *esse*, then, is the cause of truth since it is revelatory of the nature of the thing, yet the truth is found properly in the intellect, since it is the intellect that is conformed to the reality of the thing in the act of knowing.[26]

Accordingly, there can be no truth unless there is an intellect for which something is true. Truth is simply the intellectual grasp of a thing in its being, founded upon the thing's *esse*. Once the intellect comes to grasp the thing's quiddity as revealed by its *esse*, we have the formal ratio of truth; but the cause of the intellect's so grasping the thing is the thing's actually being thus and so. Hence, unless there is conformity of intellect and thing (or mind and world), there is no truth. While this is the case for a created intellect, it is reversed for the divine intellect. All existing things depend on God for their *esse*. In creating such things, God grants an act of existence to some possibility of being, knowledge of which God has in his divine mind.[27] The truth of things in the world, then, depends on their participation in God's being, and when created intellects come to know such things, they come to know them in their being as manifesting some intelligible nature that God has granted them.

Truth is transcendental on this account because everywhere being is found it is intelligible and thus capable of being recognized as such. This notion of truth as a transcendental allows Aquinas to unify earlier accounts which stressed either the truth of being as found in the things themselves or the truth of the intellect as conformed to the nature of things; for on this account truth is found in things but properly realized in the intellect's conformity with things.[28]

When it comes to truth, then, we again see the link with Aquinas's metaphysics of *esse*. Nothing would be were it not for *esse*, which *esse* is limited or specified to the essence of the thing whose *esse* it is. Accordingly, the very intelligibility of a thing depends on its *esse*, since the thing would be nothing otherwise. Nothing is and so nothing is even intelligible without the *esse* granted to it by God. Given that the intelligibility of a thing is derived from its *esse* and that there is nothing without *esse*, truth coincides with being and so is found everywhere being is found.[29]

Let us now consider goodness.

Like truth, goodness does not add anything to being, but designates a relation. Whereas truth signifies the relation of being to an intellect, goodness signifies the relation of being to the will. In other words, the goodness of being is being considered as desirable; and this tracks the traditional Aristotelian definition of the good as that which all desire.[30]

Now, while it takes an intelligent being to understand and thereby recognize the desirability of being, Aquinas holds that desirability is not simply in the eye of the beholder but is a real feature of being itself. His reasoning for this turns on how he understands the notion of perfection.

Something is perfect when it is complete in itself. Accordingly, when something is lacking in some respect, it is perfected (in that respect) when it receives what it lacks. When such a thing receives what it lacks and is thereby perfected, what it receives is good for it. All this is to say that when the thing is perfected it is actualized in a certain respect. Now, nothing is actual unless it exists, and nothing exists unless it has *esse*. Hence, whatever is perfected and thereby actualized is only perfected through *esse*, since anything which perfects anything else will have to have *esse* in some respect. It is because of *esse*, then, that anything is perfect and thereby good, in which case *esse* is not only the act of all acts, but the perfection of all perfections.[31] *Esse* is the principle of being, without which there is nothing; and since *esse* is the perfection of all perfections, all being is good. Therefore, wherever being is found, goodness is found, with goodness representing the desirability of being.[32]

Once again, we see the connection between *esse* and the transcendentals. Once Aquinas can show that the feature of being he has in mind (e.g., goodness) is something that things have because of *esse*, he can show that it is a feature of being per se. Such a feature may not be immediately evident, but it becomes evident with some reflection on the nature of *esse* itself.

PARTICIPATION IN BEING

We have noted the correspondence of unity, truth, and goodness with *esse*. This is not surprising given that the focus of the transcendentals is on the very character of being itself. Accordingly, if we can isolate that metaphysical reality without which there is nothing and in which every being (other than God) must participate in order to be, we can elaborate the general character of being from that fundamental metaphysical reality. Hence, for Aquinas, unity, truth, and goodness will have to express some determination of *esse*, since without *esse* nothing would be. Anything, then, that participates in *esse* and is accordingly a being will have the character of unity, truth, and goodness.

One of the most significant developments in the study of Aquinas's thought which emerged in the previous century was the retrieval of his metaphysics of *esse* and the accompanying participation framework to articulate that metaphysics. The work of Cornelio Fabro and Louis-Bertrand Geiger were significant studies in the Platonic heritage of Thomism with particular reference to Aquinas's participation metaphysics.[33] Not only that, the work of Étienne Gilson and his brilliant follower Joseph Owens focusing on *esse* as the act of all acts served to pinpoint Aquinas's distinctive contribution to metaphysical thinking.[34] Current generations of Thomists have benefited from their work on the distinctive originality of Aquinas's metaphysical thought, and this originality can be seen in how the doctrine of the transcendentals is integrated with Aquinas's participation metaphysics.

The notion of participation is a familiar one in the history of philosophy. Plato often spoke about participation in the forms, but frustratingly he never gave an account of what this participation entailed; such frustration was felt keenly by Aristotle in his dismissal of the Platonic notion.[35] Aquinas himself is a little more patient with the Platonists, even going so far as to defend them against Aristotle's dismissal of participation. Indeed, Aquinas is so concerned with defending the Platonic notion of participation that he offers a definition of it that cannot be found in the writings of Plato but which is in general accord with Plato's thinking (this despite the fact that Aquinas had read very little of Plato's original work).[36]

Aquinas is the first person in the history of philosophy to offer a clear articulation of the meaning of participation. Perhaps his clearest treatment is in the relatively early commentary on the *De hebdomadibus* of Boethius. Geiger tells us that, to his knowledge, this is the only definition of participation that can be found in the writings of Aquinas.[37] I would add to the latter the commentary on the *Metaphysics*, adverted to in the previous paragraph, wherein Aquinas defends the Platonists from Aristotle's attacks and gives his own account which he takes to be in accord with that of the Platonists. Nevertheless, Aquinas's commentary on the *De hebdomadibus* offers us an important instance in which he undertakes a prolonged investigation into the nature of participation.

He begins by offering us a literal definition of what it means to participate: To participate is to take a part (*partem capere*) such that the participated characteristic will not be possessed essentially or universally by the thing, but as distinct from the essence of the thing and in a partial manner. Aquinas then goes on to outline three ways in which one thing can be said to participate in something else: (1) as something more universal is realized in something less so, e.g., as a genus is realized in a species or a species in an individual; (2) as a form is realized individually in a receiving subject; and (3) as the power of a cause is realized in an effect.[38]

Aquinas is no Platonist when it comes to the forms; he firmly sides with Aristotle in this respect, since he maintains that the Platonists have confused the mode of existence of the forms in the intellect (as universal) with their mode of existence in reality (as individual).[39] Nevertheless, Aquinas does hold that there is some real metaphysical participation that pertains to being; this is not the participation of individuals in their forms, but of an existing thing in its act of existence (its *esse*).

While Aquinas grants with Aristotle that material substances are composites of matter and form, such that matter stands in potency to the determination and thus actualization of form, he does not hold that matter is *the* principle of potency or that form is *the* principle of act. Rather, Aquinas argues that there is an even more fundamental composition, and that is of essence and *esse*. The essence of the thing stands in potency to its *esse* in order to be. Without *esse* nothing would be. Even immaterial creatures, which are not composed of matter and form, stand in potency to some principle of actuality, and that is the act of existence. Hence, for Aquinas, the most fundamental principle of actuality, the act of all acts, is *esse*.

Given that essence and *esse* are distinct, the *esse* that a thing has is limited to the confines of the essence that it actuates. Thus, the existence of a horse is not that of a cat or a dog, etc. Hence, a thing's *esse* is limited to the limitations of the essence as a distinct limiting potency.[40] Without being received in a distinct limiting potency *esse* would be unlimited; and indeed this is the case for God, who is pure *esse* itself. But insofar as *esse* is received by essence as a distinct limiting potency, *esse* is limited to the confines of the essence it actuates.

Now, reflecting on Aquinas's definition of participation, a participation relationship obtains when we have something that is in itself universal but received in a partial manner in a receiving subject. Such is the case with essence and *esse* given that *esse* is limited to the confines of the essence it actuates. It follows, then, that the essence of a thing participates in its act of existence. This is not merely logical participation of two concepts, one of which is more universal than the other, such as genus and species. Rather, what we have with essence and *esse* is real metaphysical participation, since essence and *esse* are real components of the individual that exists.

The foregoing notion of participation is found throughout Aquinas's work; for he holds that things in which essence and *esse* are distinct exist not per se, but *per participationem*. Only God exists per se because only in God are essence and *esse* identical. It is the consistent teaching, then, of Aquinas that individual creatures participate in their individual acts of existence. Taken collectively such individual acts of existence are referred to as *esse commune*, and such *esse commune* in turn participates in God's *esse* (*esse divinum*).[41]

So far so good, but how does all of this relate to Aquinas's thinking on the transcendentals?

We noted at the end of the previous section that for the transcendental properties – unity, truth, and goodness – Aquinas shows that these properties are had by a thing because it has *esse*, and since *esse* is that without which there is nothing, wherever being is found such properties will be found. Accordingly, creatures are one because their metaphysical components are brought together and held in actuality by the *esse* in which they participate. Beings are true because they are individual participants in *esse*; as such individual participants they have an intelligible character which manifests a divine idea and are present in the world to be known because of the *esse* that they have. Finally, beings are good because in participating in *esse* they have a share in that principle of actuality without which nothing can be brought to perfection. To be thus is to be good. Accordingly, a creature's participation in its *esse*, and ultimately in God's *esse*, will entail that the creature is one, true, and good. It cannot not be so since such properties are applicable to anything in which *esse* is found.

While having its roots in classical thought, the doctrine of the transcendentals did not come into its own until Philip the Chancellor wrote the *Summa de bono*. Accordingly, the whole discussion of the transcendentals in the thirteenth century of Aquinas was a relatively recent one. Nevertheless, Aquinas was able to integrate such a discussion with the more traditional metaphysical discussion of matter, form, essence, and *esse*. This not only indicates the profound depth of Aquinas's metaphysical vision insofar as it is able to integrate fairly new and not fully settled philosophical developments, but it is also an indicator of the truth of his position given that disparate discussions on the nature of being from Plato and Aristotle through to Philip the Chancellor and his contemporaries can be brought together and held in synthetic unity. Setting aside the robust (and to my mind convincing) argumentation offered in its favor, were there not something of the truth to Aquinas's metaphysical vision, the seams would quickly come apart, given the different trajectories of the metaphysical themes that he brings together.

GOODNESS AND BEING

The *De hebdomadibus* of Boethius was generally concerned with perplexities over how creatures could be said to be good, but not essentially good. As we have seen, in his commentary on this treatise Aquinas offers a sustained investigation of the nature of participation. As should be clear, Aquinas's account is that creatures are not good per se, but through participation; their goodness is a dependent goodness on God's goodness. Creatures accordingly have the character of goodness because they are appropriately related to some metaphysical reality in which they participate.

Aquinas is clear that, like truth, goodness is a real feature of being itself. While it takes an intelligent person to recognize the desirability of being in some given circumstance, being is not rendered desirable through its being recognized as such. Beings exist, they have *esse*, independent of our thinking of them, and so they are desirable independent of our desiring them on any occasion. The locus of value, then, is not situated in the eye of the beholder (or the desire of the one who desires), but in the being itself.

When it comes to truth, one can easily see that even if no (created) intelligent being recognized the truth of beings, they would still be intelligible given that they are formed in their existence through their manifesting some divine idea in the mind of God. Hence, at the limit we can say that there is always one intellect to which all beings are present and sustained in their truth. Can we say something similar about the goodness of creatures? Is there always some being to which all beings are desirable and thereby good? In what follows I shall argue that this is the case for Aquinas.

All creatures exist because they have been granted *esse* by God.[42] In granting *esse* to creatures, God envisages some possibility of being to which to grant *esse*. Accordingly, the very intelligibility of a creature is something that God sees in his own divine essence prior to his actually creating it.[43] But God is pure *esse* itself, and as such there is nothing distinct from him which would determine him to create anything. Hence, God is free to create or not to create.[44] Given that there are creatures, we must consider God's choice in creating; in doing so we will come to terms with the desirability of creatures.

As pure *esse* itself, God is the good itself. Hence, any choice that God makes through reflecting on his own divine essence will be a choice made through reflection on the good itself. Nothing necessitates God to make a choice to create, but given that he does create, that choice must be motivated out of the pure goodness that God himself is. God then undertakes to bring about creatures out of his own goodness. All of creation, then, is an expression of God's goodness willed for the good of the creature.[45]

Now, prior to their being created, creatures did not exist. Hence, creatures could do nothing to merit being brought into existence. God expresses his goodness to creatures in creating them as a wholly gratuitous act which none could merit but which all have received. Just as a creature is not intelligible except as expressing some possibility of being to which God grants existence, so too a creature is not good except as expressing something of the divine goodness. Hence, there is someone who eternally sees the goodness of every creature, and this because every creature is a manifestation of that divine goodness that God sees in himself and through which he creates. All creatures are good and loved as the goods they are precisely because God is good and permits creatures to manifest that goodness.

Given that the goodness of all creatures is found in God, the perfection of all creatures will be in God also. This perfection will not be a perfection discontinuous with the nature of a creature. A man is not made perfect in the way that a dog is made perfect. Rather, it will be a perfection proper to the creature as the kind of thing that it is. Hence, a man will be perfected as a man – i.e., a rational animal capable of knowing the truth and loving the good. But the fount of all truth and goodness is God himself. Hence, man will be perfected through coming to know God as he is in himself. At this point we begin to see a transformation of our philosophical reasoning; for at this point one must consider Christ's life, death, and resurrection and the cosmic significance these salvific events have in returning humanity to God. We thus depart from the waters of philosophy to the wine of theology. I do not wish to enter into theological reflection on such issues here, yet I think that even here philosophy has something to contribute to an understanding of the drama of salvation.[46]

Consider again the fact that God is the good itself; he loves creatures and communicates the good to them not because of what they are, but because of what he is. It follows, then, that there is nothing a creature could do for God to stop loving that creature; for that creature is a manifestation of the divine goodness. Hence, no matter what sin a creature commits, God does not cease to love it; for to do so he would have to stop loving himself. Accordingly, the mystery of the Incarnation is a rescue operation for the forgiveness of sins, and belief in the accompanying salvation that man can enjoy through Christ's merits is consistent with what we can establish philosophically about the goodness of man in his relation to God. This claim of a parallelism between philosophy and faith of course does not establish the truth of the theological doctrines in question, but it does show that the Thomistic metaphysics of *esse* and the accompanying understanding of the goodness of all creatures fit nicely with those doctrines; so that one who believes such theological truths can be assured of the metaphysical foundations that they presuppose.

Faith is a willed assent of the rational individual to those truths about God that we cannot discern by our natural reason.[47] As an assent of the individual, it cannot be coerced, but only invited. Insofar as it is about the unseen things of God, it cannot come from man, but must be granted by God's grace.[48] This grace is offered as a gift, yet it can be refused. There can be explicit refusal of grace, but there is also the lack of a proper disposition to accept grace when it is offered.[49] Not fully understanding God's love and care of creatures is one way that the rational individual can be improperly disposed to the reception of grace. Hence, good philosophy serves to dispose the mind of the individual man to the acceptance of those truths about God that are revealed, such as the fact that God loves him regardless of his sins and seeks to bring the sinner back to communion with him. As we have seen, Aquinas's metaphysical thought on the goodness of beings is fully consistent with this revealed truth, and so aids in disposing the rational individual in the acceptance thereof.

NOTES

1 For details of the emergence of the doctrine of the transcendentals in
   thirteenth-century thought prior to Aquinas, see J. Aertsen, *Medieval
   Philosophy and the Transcendentals: The Case of Thomas Aquinas*
   (Leiden, New York, and Cologne: Brill, 1996), ch. 1.

2 *Met.* II, 993b30; all references to Aristotle will be to Aristotle, *The
   Complete Works of Aristotle*, edited by J. Barnes (Princeton: Princeton
   University Press, 1984).

3 *Met.* IV, 1003b23–4.

4 See, for example, Plotinus, *The Enneads*, V, translated by S. McKenna
   (London: Penguin, 1991); Pseudo-Dionysius, "The Divine Names,"
   translated by C. Luibheid, in *The Complete Works* (Mahway, NJ: Paulist
   Press, 1987), wherein he treats of being, unity, truth, goodness, and beauty
   as co-extensive names for God.

5 Avicenna, *The Metaphysics of the Healing*, translated by M. Marmura
   (Provo, UT: Brigham Young University Press, 2003), I, ch. 5.

6 *In Meta*, Proemium; *In BDT* q.5 a.1.

7 For Aquinas's reaction to Parmenides, see *In I Meta*, lect. 9. For further
   details on the analogy of being in Aquinas's thought (including further
   details on his reaction to Parmenides), see J. F. Wippel, *The Metaphysical
   Thought of Thomas Aquinas: From Finite Being to Uncreated Being*
   (Washington, DC: The Catholic University of America Press, 2000), ch. 3.

8 See *In I Sent.*, d.8 q.1 a.3; *QDV* q.21, a.1; *QDP* q.9 a.7 ad 6 and 15; *ST* I q.5
   a.2; *ST* I q.11 a.2 ad 4; *In I Meta*, lect. 2 n.46; *In IV Meta*, lect. 6 n.605; *In
   X Meta*, lect. 4 n.1998; *In XI Meta*, lect. 5 n.2211.

9 *QDV* q.1 a.1; *QDV* q.21 a.1.

10 See Aristotle, *De anima*, Book 3, c.8, 431b21.

11 See Aertsen, *Medieval Philosophy*, pp. 91–2; W. Norris Clarke, *The One
   and the Many: A Contemporary Metaphysics* (South Bend, IN: University
   of Notre Dame Press, 2001), p. 43.

12 *In I Sent.*, d.8 q.1 a.3; *ST* I q.5 a.1; *ST* II-II q.109 a.2 ad 1.

13 See, for example, *In I Sent.*, d.8 q.1 a.3; *In II Sent.*, d.34 q.1 a.1 ad 1; *In II
   Sent.*, d.40 q.1 a.4; *QDV* q.21 a.1; *ST* I q.16 a.3; *ST* I q.93 a.9.

14 *QDV* q.21 a.1; *QDP* q.9 a.7 ad 6.

15 For a treatment of 'thing' and 'something' as transcendentals, see Aertsen,
   Medieval Philosophy, pp. 102–3, 109–10, 193–9.

16 For a summary article reflecting on (and affirming) beauty as a transcendental, see F. O'Rourke, *Ciphers of Transcendence: Essays in Philosophy of Religion in Honour of Patrick Masterson* (Newbridge: Irish Academic Press, 2019), ch. 3.

17 *ST* I q.39 a.8.

18 For further details on beauty as a transcendental, see Aertsen, *Medieval Philosophy*, ch. 8. For an interesting study of beauty as a divine name in the thought of Pseudo-Dionysius and Aquinas, see B. T. Sammon, *The God Who Is Beauty: Beauty as a Divine Name in Thomas Aquinas and Dionysius the Areopagite* (Cambridge: James Clarke & Co., 2014).

19 *QDV* q.1 a.1; *QDP* q.9 a.7; *In I Sent.*, d.24 q.1 a.3 ad 3; *ST* I q.11 a.1.

20 *ST* I q.11 a.1.

21 Norris Clarke, *The One and the Many*, p. 61.

22 *In IV Meta*, lect. 2 n.552.

23 For details of Aquinas's metaphysics of essence and *esse*, see G. Kerr, *Aquinas's Way to God: The Proof in* De Ente et Essentia (New York: Oxford University Press, 2015), chs. 1–3.

24 *In I Sent.*, d.19 q.5 a.1; *QDV* q.1 a.1; *ST* I q.16 a.1.

25 *In I Sent.*, d.19 q.5 a.1; for a discussion of this text, see J. F. Wippel, "Truth in Thomas Aquinas" in *Metaphysical Themes in Thomas Aquinas II* (Washington, DC: The Catholic University of America Press, 2007), pp. 65–72.

26 For discussion of the role of *esse* as the cause of truth, see Wippel, "Truth in Thomas Aquinas."

27 For details, see G. Kerr, *Aquinas and the Metaphysics of Creation* (New York: Oxford University Press, 2019), ch. 2.

28 For details, see Wippel, "Truth in Thomas Aquinas," pp. 109–12. See also *In I Sent.*, d.19 q.5 a.1 ad 1; *QDV* q.1 a.1.

29 For a defense of Aquinas's epistemological realism based on the revelation or disclosure of a thing's essence by means of its individual act of existence impressing itself on the receiving subject, see W. Norris Clarke, "Action as the Self-Revelation of Being: A Central Theme in the Thought of St. Thomas" in *Explorations in Metaphysics: Being – God – Person* (South Bend, IN: University of Notre Dame Press, 1994), pp. 45–65; G. Kerr, "Ontological Commitment and Thomistic Realism" in J. McEvoy, M. Dunne, and J. Hynes (eds.), *Thomas Aquinas: Teaching and Scholar* (Dublin: Four Courts Press, 2012), pp. 211–29.

30 Aristotle, *Nicomachean Ethics*, Book 1, ch. 1. Thomas endorses this definition of the good on a number of occasions: *SCG* I.37; *ST* I-II q.29 a.5; *ST* I-II q.94 a.2; *QDV* q.1 a.1; *QDV* q.21 a.1; *QDP* q.9 a.7 ad 6; *QDM* q.1 a.1.

31 *QDP* q.7 a.2 ad 9; *ST* I q.3 a.4.

32 *SCG* III.7; *ST* I q.5 a.1; *QDV* q.21 a.1.

33 See C. Fabro, *La nozione metafisica di partecipazione secondo s. Tommaso d'Aquino* (Turin: Società Editrice Internazionale, 1950); C. Fabro, *Participation et causalité selon s. Thomas d'Aquin* (Leuven and Paris: Publications Universitaires de Louvain and Béatrice-Nauwelaerts, 1961); L.-B. Geiger, *La Participation dans la Philosophie de S. Thomas d'Aquin* (Paris: Librairie Philosophique J. Vrin, 1942).

34 See É. Gilson, *Being and Some Philosophers* (Toronto: Pontifical Institute of Mediaeval Studies, 1952); É. Gilson, *L'être et l'essence* (Paris: Librairie Philosophique J. Vrin, 1994); J. Owens, *An Interpretation of Existence* (Houston, TX: Center for Thomistic Studies, University of St. Thomas, 1985).

35 *Metaphysics*, Book 1, 987b7–13.

36 *In I Meta*, lect. 10 n.154.

37 Geiger, *La Participation*, p. 48.

38 *In BDH*, lect. II, p. 271:70–83.

39 *ST* I q.84 a.1.

40 For details of Thomas's endorsement of the principle that act is limited by potency, see J. F. Wippel, "Thomas Aquinas and the Axiom 'What Is Received Is Received according to the Mode of the Receiver'" in *Metaphysical Themes in Thomas Aquinas II* (Washington, DC: The Catholic University of America Press, 2007), pp. 113–23; J. F. Wippel, "Thomas Aquinas and the Axiom that Unreceived Act Is Unlimited" in *Metaphysical Themes in Thomas Aquinas II* (Washington, DC: The Catholic University of America Press, 2007), pp. 123–52; W. Norris Clarke, "The Limitation of Act by Potency in St. Thomas: Aristotelianism or Neoplatonism?" in *Explorations in Metaphysics: Being – God – Person* (South Bend, IN: University of Notre Dame Press, 1994), pp. 89–101.

41 *Diu. nom.* c.5 lect. 2.

42 *In II Sent.*, d.1 q.1 a.2; *SCG* II.17; *QDP* q.3 a.1; *ST* I q.45 a.1; *DSS* Cap.10 n.56.

43 *ST* I q.14. For a discussion of Aquinas's thinking on the divine ideas, see
    V. Boland, *Ideas in God according to Saint Thomas Aquinas: Sources and
    Synthesis* (New York: Brill, 1996).

44 *QDP* q.1 a.5; *ST* I q.19 a.4; *SCG* I.44.

45 *ST* I q.19 a.3. For discussion, see N. Kretzmann, *The Metaphysics of
    Theism: Aquinas's Natural Theology in* Summa Contra Gentiles
    I (Oxford: Clarendon Press, 1997), pp. 199–203; J. F. Wippel, "Norman
    Kretzmann on Aquinas's Attribution of Will and Freedom to Create to
    God," *Religious Studies* 39 (2003): 287–98; J. F. Wippel, "Thomas Aquinas
    on the Ultimate Why Question: Why Is There Anything At All Rather
    Than Nothing Whatsoever" in J. Wippel (ed.), *The Ultimate Why
    Question: Why Is There Anything At All Rather Than Nothing
    Whatsoever?* (Washington, DC: The Catholic University of America
    Press, 2011), pp. 84–109; Kerr, *Aquinas and the Metaphysics of Creation*,
    ch. 2, §2.2.

46 I delve into this issue in more detail in Kerr, *Aquinas and the Metaphysics
    of Creation*, ch. 7.

47 *ST* II-II q.1 a.1; *ST* II-II q.2 a.1.

48 *ST* II-II q.6 a.1.

49 For discussion, see E. Stump, *Aquinas* (New York and London: Routledge,
    2003), ch. 12.

5   The Metaphysics of Creation
Secondary Causality, Modern Science

James Dominic Rooney, OP

When it comes to God's creation of and interaction with the universe, it has sometimes been suggested that Christian revelation tells us nothing about the world and its origins, restricting itself to questions of value and not to matters of fact.[1] Thomas Aquinas, by contrast, argued that a false account of creation implies false opinions about God.[2] Aquinas consistently held that there were a number of truths about the creation of the universe that are central to Christian revelation: first, the truth that the world causally depends on God for its existence and all of its operations. Given the way in which Aquinas conceives of this dependence, this first truth implies that the universe is guided by God's intelligent ordering or providence. The second truth is that God created the world with no constraints of any kind, including the necessity of creating from pre-existing matter, the necessity of employing causal intermediaries, or a necessity imposed by his reasons (such that he was not free to do otherwise). The third is that the universe was created in time: that is, having a definite beginning in the finite past. Of these three central truths about creation, Aquinas held that only the third is a revealed truth strictly inaccessible to human philosophical discovery, whereas the first and second are truths for which we can give conclusive, independent philosophical demonstrations even though they are also taught by Scripture. Beginning with his theological motivations, I will explain Aquinas's commitments in regard to God's creation, the universe's dependence upon God, and its beginning in time.

There is, however, an apparent problem with the coherence of Aquinas's notion of creation: God's causal role seems to render the causal activity of created entities superfluous. In my view, showing why Aquinas's account is not saddled with this problem is best done by an appeal to his understanding of God's providence. Even though God causes the being of everything, the intelligent way in which God acts allows for created entities and their actions to provide reasons in light of which he can act differently. As God's reasons for causing a given effect can be counterfactually dependent on a creature and what it does, God's causing a created effect does not require that this effect could not *also* be dependent on a creature. In the ordinary course of things, then, God is not *individually* sufficient for bringing about the created actions and effects of creatures. Thus, Aquinas holds that God and creatures jointly or concurrently bring about the same effect, each being causally necessary for the same effect in different respects or orders of causal dependence. As I intend to show, this metaphysics of the Christian doctrine of creation, in conclusion, remains compatible with contemporary science.

CREATION *EX NIHILO* AND GENESIS I

Thomas Aquinas's contemporaries were thoroughly engrossed in questions around the doctrine of creation because of the rediscovery of the writings of Aristotle and the influence of the Arabic commentary tradition through which Aristotle was filtered to the Latin West. Some thinkers at the University of Paris saw Arabic commentators, chiefly Averroes (Ibn Rushd), as holding a view of creation on which the world was demonstrably and necessarily eternal.[3] The Averroist view appeared to be in contradiction with the widely held Christian view of creation, including binding teaching proposed at the Fourth Council of the Lateran,[4] prompting both official censures directed at nascent Averroism in the Parisian academy[5] and a flurry of academic works that argued against the position. Aquinas followed suit as a professor at Paris. Aside from the summary of his views in the *Summa theologiae* and *Summa contra Gentiles*, Aquinas dedicates two significant treatises to questions of creation: one, the *De aeternitate mundi*; and the other, an extensive set of 'disputed questions,' *De potentia Dei*.[6]

A representative figure often contrasted with Aquinas on these questions was Bonaventure (Giovanni di Fidanza), who held the Franciscan chair of theology, which was the counterpart to Aquinas's Dominican chair at the University of Paris. Bonaventure and Aquinas each were inspired by the theological synthesis of Augustine, but Bonaventure's positions on creation represent an older or more traditional position among early scholastics.[7] Bonaventure opposes the claim that the world is necessary and eternal by arguing that, if one holds that everything in the universe was caused by God, then there is a contradiction in holding that the universe existed eternally: "To posit that the world is eternal or eternally produced, while positing likewise that all things have been produced from nothing, is altogether opposed to the truth and reason ... For this involves, in itself, an obvious contradiction."[8] Borrowing from Alexander of Hales, Bonaventure argues that God's creating the universe from no pre-existing matter (*ex nihilo*) requires that nothing be logically prior to the existence of the universe, so that the universe would begin to exist at a finite moment in the past.[9]

As Bonaventure's argument illustrates, the issues being discussed in connection to God's creation were ultimately *metaphysical* questions about causality and God's reasons for creating. In fact, Bonaventure, Aquinas, and many of their contemporaries inherited a reading from Augustine such that Genesis 1 was understood to teach primarily that the universe was created by God in time and without making use of any pre-existing matter – that is, from nothing. Augustine argued that Genesis should not be understood to teach that the universe was less than 6,000 years old – which would have been in contradiction to the best science of the day – and, further, that the six days of creation were a logical division of a single, simultaneous act by which God created the universe, accompanied by the gradual emergence of everything over time by means of 'rational principles' (*rationes seminales*) which God implanted in the material universe at its origin.[10] Given Augustine's proposals for accommodating different scientific accounts of the development and age of the universe, the question for Aquinas and Bonaventure was then not so much how to interpret the book of Genesis in a way compatible with natural science, but rather how to address a view on which the universe and God's actions in creating it were metaphysically necessary.

Aquinas spent much of his life addressing questions about creation, developing a position that opposed the earlier scholastic consensus represented by Bonaventure. The position he developed required Aquinas to clearly differentiate his own view from those that were dogmatically suspect.[11] On the one hand, Aquinas argued that creation can be demonstrated by reason alone, insofar as one considers the dependence of everything on God for its existence.[12] The arguments presented in *Summa theologiae* I q.3, for example, are supposed to show that various kinds of phenomena, such as change or contingency, entail the existence of a first cause, metaphysically necessary to account for the existence of the universe. On the other, Aquinas embraces an epistemic reserve about whether philosophical reasoning can show definitively that the universe existed eternally or began to exist at a finite point in the past. In his early writings, he endorses the position of Maimonides (Moses ben Maimon) that no demonstration can be given either way,[13] and, in later writing, explicitly claims that it is only known as an article of faith that the universe began to exist in time.[14] He therefore argued, as summarized in his *De aeternitate mundi*, that the existence of an eternally created universe is metaphysically possible. He shows that each of the assumptions (e.g., about causality) that are taken to show the universe must have begun to exist in time are false and so there is no contradiction in the notion of an eternally dependent universe.[15]

Aquinas has principled reasons for this position, given the way in which he understands what it is for God to create. *Pace*

Bonaventure, Aquinas thinks that the way in which God was a cause does not require that the cause temporally precede the effect – cause and effect can be simultaneous since God does not act successively in creating.[16] Further, since creation *ex nihilo* does not require a 'sub-stratum' on which God is operating, creation is not a change *in* but the *coming to be* of what is created.[17] God's act is to bring about the 'whole being' of what is created immediately and directly; creation is thus "to produce a thing in being in respect to its whole substance."[18] Aquinas here borrows the notion from Avicenna (Ibn Sina) of a *contingent* being as one that is constantly dependent upon a necessary being for its existence.[19] Aquinas adopts this into the notion of a being whose essence is 'really distinct' from its existence.[20] As all of creation is contingent, what is created depends on God at every time it exists.[21] Consequently, even if the universe did not originate at any point in the finite past, this fact would not entail that the universe (or anything in it) ceases to be contingent. There is then nothing contradictory in the possibility that the universe existed for eternity but was, for all that period, dependent on God for its existence.[22] For this same reason, speculations in modern cosmology that there was no first moment of time would be compatible with the fact of the contingent character of the material universe and the necessity of God causing it to exist.[23] Nevertheless, Aquinas elsewhere says that whether the universe is eternal or not is a contingent fact that we know via Revelation and not from general metaphysical reasoning. This is because *when* the universe (or anything in it) came into existence is not an essential feature of it. But, as scientific demonstrations begin with premises drawn from the essences of created things, we would not be able to demonstrate whether or not the universe came into existence at a particular time from facts about its essence.[24]

OCCASIONALISM, NECESSITATION, AND PROVIDENCE

Aquinas's view that creation involves causing the 'whole being' of what is created is the guiding thread for his overall doctrine of divine causality: God is an efficient cause in a radically different way from creatures. To create *ex nihilo* involves creating the whole of the being of an entity, not merely changing how things exist, and this is something only God can do. Creatures have causal powers, but they can bring into existence new entities only *from* what already exists, and thus they cannot create, properly speaking.[25] In addition, creation involves a real dependence relation of what is created on God, yet it involves no intrinsic change or property coming to exist in God – all that results on God's part is a new logical relation between him and what he creates, namely, the relation of 'being the cause' of it.[26] Finally, and more controversially, Aquinas claims that God's causality is immediately active in every created thing. God not only creates at some initial point all created entities with their properties and causal powers; rather, the powers and operations of every created entity continue to be dependent upon God for their being and exercise:

> God is the cause of the action of all things inasmuch as he gives them power to act and preserves them and applies them to action and inasmuch as by his power every other power acts. And when we add that God is his own power and that he is within each thing, not as a part of its essence, but as holding the thing in being, it follows that he operates immediately in every operation, without excluding the operation of the will and nature.[27]

These strong claims about God working within every created cause follow from his general way of understanding creation *ex nihilo* as immediate and direct causal dependence on God – as everything that exists is individually dependent on God's continuing preserving causality, so too are all of their actions and powers.

If God causes the entire being and operation of every created entity, at every point in time, does this not render the causal activity of created entities superfluous? This worry concerns metaphysical or causal *overdetermination*. Contemporary authors, such as John Polkinghorne, Philip Clayton, and Keith Ward, believe there is a dilemma for Aquinas's view: If every physical state has a physical cause, and God is also the full cause of the being of those physical states, either the physical cause is sufficient for the physical effect or God is. It does not seem coherent to say that both are individually sufficient causes of the same effect. But if God is the full cause of the effect, then the physical cause is doing no causal work, and the view is equivalent to occasionalism. Or, if the physical cause individually accomplishes the effect, and God does nothing, then the view seems to make God's causality superfluous – and, if this were true, then it is not easy to see how God can guide the course of events.[28] Some interpreters of Aquinas claim that he holds that God's causality is 'non-competitive' with creaturely causality, but without explaining how this fact avoids the overdetermination worry, or relying on religious faith to bridge the gap.[29] These interpretations make it appear as if Aquinas's position is merely that God is a special kind of cause, where divine causality alone does not result in overdetermination despite being sufficient for directly and immediately bringing about every created effect. And that would be clearly an ad hoc and unsatisfying response.

Aquinas was familiar with occasionalism from Islamic thought, and he rejects it explicitly, appealing first to a response by Averroes to other Islamic occasionalists. Contrary to a prominent school of Islamic theology beginning with al-Ashʿarī (874–936), which held that all entities other than God can exercise no real causal influence, Averroes proposed an account of divine causality that attempted to preserve the notion that creatures can exercise efficient causality.[30] Aquinas adopts parts of this response from the Islamic dialectic and incorporates it in his position.[31] Aquinas argues, for example, that the occasionalist position seems to lead to skepticism about what is otherwise evident to our senses and that it would make the whole nature of created entities useless if they did not actually exercise any of their own proper activity. In sum, he argues that nothing about the fact that God is the cause of creaturely actions requires us to think that created things exercise no real activity or causal power. Instead, he proposes that God is the cause of the natures and powers by which they operate, and that his causal agency sets them in motion, applying them to their activities.[32]

The key way, however, in which Aquinas goes beyond his Islamic interlocutors is in how he conceives of the way that God brings about creaturely actions, adopting a significantly different understanding of divine providence. Although some today dispute or qualify whether Averroes held that God creates necessarily,[33] what is uncontroversial is that, for Averroes, as it was for his predecessor Avicenna, God's causality entails that everything he creates is necessitated – that is, all that occurs is necessary.[34] Avicenna arrives at this position because he thinks God acts (in quasi-Leibnizian fashion) in light of his best reasons. Appealing to a version of the principle of sufficient reason, Avicenna reasoned that God must have a sufficient reason to bring about what he does, and so that what God does is necessitated by his reasons. Thus, God produces the first Intelligence in the Avicennan emanationist scheme by necessity, and that one produces the next ... and so on.[35] Aquinas agrees with Avicenna that, because God is an intelligent agent, God acts in light of reasons. 'Providence' is the intelligent plan or design by which God chooses to bring about what he does, existing from eternity in God's intellect, and which he executes temporally in his act of 'governing' the cosmos.[36] So, too, God's knowledge, in line with his causal role in creation, is not metaphysically dependent on what he creates. Unlike our knowledge, God's knowledge of the created world is causative of what he knows.[37]

However, Aquinas holds that God is supremely free and not constrained by reasons independent of himself. The divine ideas, on the basis of which God creates, are not metaphysically independent of God – rather, God knows what is metaphysically possible in virtue of knowing his own essence and power.[38] But, contra Avicenna (and Leibniz), Aquinas denies it is strictly true that God cannot do better than he does, denying the supposition that there is any one, unique 'best' possible world for God to create or that God's reasons would constrain his actions with strict necessity (God *always* has some other potential actions open to him).[39] Clearly, God is not metaphysically dependent on the course of events in time, or upon creaturely action, to bring about what he does. And, since God operates outside of time and is the total cause of all that exists, God choosing to do anything *on account of* something else does not imply that God needed to choose to do anything at all or to do it in the way that he chose to do, even though there was an order among the actions he (in fact) chose to perform. So, God's being a rational agent implies only a highly qualified kind of necessity in God's actions: One thing God does might be a necessary means, in his providence, to another he has freely chosen to accomplish (as, for example, choosing to redeem humanity by the Incarnation and Passion rather than in some other way).[40] Aquinas thus rejects the position that God creates necessarily, that God cannot do otherwise, or that what God chooses to create is necessitated by God's decisions.[41]

Nevertheless, what Aquinas insists upon is that God *does* act in such a way that creatures and their actions can be reasons for what he brings about – and, because he is not necessitated to do anything, everything flows from God's goodness and not from any necessity.[42] While I cannot here discuss all elements of Aquinas's view of providence, this is the basis for Aquinas's rejection of occasionalism. The very claim that God is a radically different sort of cause allows Aquinas to say that God's causal action is not in 'competition' with creaturely causality. Creaturely 'secondary' causes remain dependent on God's 'primary' causality for their efficacy, but that does not take away their causal efficacy.[43] As we see in Aquinas's account of how God responds to petitionary prayers, God can be responsive to what creatures do by taking account of their actions in his providence; he can choose to heal someone on account of the prayers of a saint, such that God's healing would be counterfactually dependent on the saint's prayer.[44] In much the same way, however, Aquinas holds that God causing everything does not remove contingency or freedom from what he causes. This is because, while God acts as the transcendental efficient cause of everything's being, *how* God brings about their actions involves, for example, having chosen to allow them to be real efficient causes, to exercise free decisions, etc. God would just be causing them, intelligently, in such a way that he is causing the very free or contingent actions the creature performs from its own powers.[45]

Aquinas's appeal to God's manner of bringing about his effects by means of his providence can, I think, adequately address the over-determination worries. Aquinas often discusses 'secondary' causality – the way creatures exercise their own causal powers even when under the influence of God's 'primary' causality – by means of an analogy with how instruments exercise causal influence even while operating under the power of an agent.[46] When a butcher cuts meat with a knife, the sharpness of the knife is precisely the means by which the action of the butcher accomplishes the goal of cutting the meat, even though the knife would not cut the meat without the action of the butcher. That is, the instrument – the knife – exercises its own causality even though it could not exercise that causality unless under the influence of the primary agent – the butcher. By analogy, there is no reason why God cannot bring about some created effects in light of created causes, as if these are instruments by which he has chosen to act, even though all of these depend on God.[47] When God brings about created effects, then, he brings about those effects *precisely by means of* their created causes, and in the way that the created things cause them to occur. This is nothing more than to say that these effects are brought about by the real causal power of the created agents, even if the whole created causal order depends on God to exist and act.

It is often overlooked too that, although everything depends on God for their existence, Aquinas holds that God ordinarily brings about effects in his government through causal intermediaries. It is not true that everything depends upon God *immediately and directly* either for their existence or for their operations. Even though every-thing about a created entity depends on God, the fact that God's power *could* be sufficient for bringing about the effect of any creature does not entail that he *is* always actually acting in a way sufficient by himself to bring about those effects *without* the creature. On the contrary, God has good reasons not to bring about every creaturely act immediately and, in how things actually operate in the universe, it is apparent to us that creatures exercise real causal activity. This points to a distinction between God's providence/creation and his government in time: "God created all things immediately, but in the creation itself He established an order among things, so that some depend on others, by which they are preserved in being, though He remains the principal cause of their preservation."[48] God is not therefore engaged in 'continual creation.'[49] God's act of creation is intelligent and involves his providential ordering of causes which, as they work out in time, involve the real causal dependence of created entities upon each other without God having to specifically intervene, even if he can exceptionally intervene in the created order of things and perform miracles.[50] The causal order by which God causes the existence of everything, consequently, is in no apparent conflict with the way in which created entities relate to each other as cause and effect. If we understand Aquinas's doctrine of creation in light of these qualifications, it seems unclear where the overdetermination worry could take hold.[51]

CONCLUSION: CONTEMPORARY SCIENCE AND GOD'S CAUSAL ACTIVITY

From the above, it should be apparent that, while revelation teaches us about the dependence of the universe on God, Aquinas does not think that the truths about creation entail much in regard to the scientific details concerning the universe's origins. That the universe began to exist in time is ultimately something Aquinas does not believe our science could demonstrate definitively, even if we could show that it was likely. Similarly, the dependence upon God's causality is not a dependence in any created causal order, but a dependence that involves all of the existence and operations of every creature – there would be *no need* for a special physical force, for example, by which God intervenes in order for God to guide the course of events.[52]

So it could seem as if Aquinas's notion of creation has no scientific implications. But this is not quite correct.

What it shows us, first, is that the revealed truth that God created the universe, and providentially disposes all creaturely activity, is compatible with a wide range of possible scientific accounts of the origins of things. Although I have already discussed cosmology, it is also typical in discussions of faith and science to highlight evolutionary biology as in conflict, or potential conflict, with belief in the existence of a provident God who created the universe. From Aquinas's perspective, however, it is hard to see where any potential conflict *could even be*. While Aquinas was not aware of any scientific evidence for the generation of new species over the course of biological history, there would not be any reason from his account of creation that he could not accept its occurrence.[53] Similarly, God's providence can guide the course of world history, including biological evolution, without any particular miraculous interventions needed over the course of the universe. It might also be thought that there is a significant problem for how non-living things could give rise to living ones, i.e., abiogenesis. Yet abiogenesis poses no unique problem for Aquinas's account. God is able to cause the existence of contingent or chance processes, and nevertheless bring about definite, foreseen, and intended outcomes by means of them. If we assume that random changes over time in material bodies are metaphysically capable of giving rise to living organisms (which I think Aquinas can accept[54]), then a random natural process is something that still falls under the direction of God's providence. When we discover that organisms were generated by natural and chance processes from non-living things, we would *ipso facto* discover that God brought about living things in this way.

The only special difficulty, which I wager underlies many worries about evolutionary biology among theists of various stripes, is that if there was a biological account which exhaustively explains the origin of human beings, on the basis of chance, this seems to entail some kind of materialism about the human person incompatible with the existence of an immortal human soul. On the one hand, it is noteworthy that this is ultimately not a question about creation, but about philosophy of mind. Aquinas has a 'hylomorphic' account of how human beings are essentially material organisms, although with a special kind of substantial form that can survive their death, and this involves a different mind–body relation from that of classical Cartesian 'substance dualism.'[55] Whether and how a hylomorphic account of the person is defensible in light of contemporary neuroscience and evolutionary biology has no direct bearing on Aquinas's account of God's causal activity, so I leave it to one side. On the other hand, Aquinas's account of creation nevertheless can be helpful in considering how God *could* use a random biological process to bring about human beings with immaterial souls. In sum, it would be possible for Aquinas to admit every biological fact about human origins, while only denying that these alone are *sufficient* to account for the existence of a human being.

This is essentially how Aquinas explains the causal role that biological parents have in producing a child: Their contributions – sexual activity, egg and sperm, etc. – are all causally necessary for producing a child, but God needs to intervene to immediately create a human soul.[56] Further, given Aquinas's hylomorphism, God's action follows immediately when the biological conditions are sufficient.[57] There is no reason Aquinas could not apply the same understanding to the random biological processes that would have been involved in human evolutionary origins: The biological process was necessary, but not sufficient, for the production of a human being, and, when evolutionary history made it such that there were biological conditions that would potentially produce a human being, God's action followed immediately, leading to the production of the first human being in much the same way as every human being is produced by their parents.[58] We can note that, as with the cosmological story, this tells us essentially nothing about what actually occurred biologically; instead, this is a metaphysical description of what steps in the biological process *depend upon* God's causal activity. Although this story is conditional on Aquinas's hylomorphic account of the human soul being correct (which *does* have implications for neuroscience and biology), the parts of the causal story that deal with what God would have to do to bring about a human being otherwise posit no scientific facts over and above those already known in biology or neuroscience. For this reason, it is hard to see how Aquinas's metaphysics could conflict with contemporary science.

Yet there is a principled reason for Aquinas's metaphysical reserve in regard to natural science; the goal was not to insulate Christian doctrine against science, but to defend the autonomy of the natural sciences and other related modes of investigation against overreach from theology or metaphysics. God has so set up the world that it operates according to intelligible natural laws, knowable *sans* revelation, and the way that he governs the world does not undermine the ability of these creatures to exercise their own natural modes of activity. Much can be gained in understanding God's intentions, then, by exploring the natures of these creatures via scientific means. Aquinas holds this to be true of normative facts as well. A well-known tradition of *natural law* ethics and politics holds that human nature is what accounts for the normative facts about what human beings ought to do. While it is certainly possible for God to create special positive laws,[59] God does not need to do anything more than create human beings in order to establish a moral law.[60] This is because, as rational creatures, humans can discern how their natures participate in his eternal law, the design he has in his providence.[61]

Even more strongly, the formal autonomy of scientific investigation, Aquinas thinks, has theological import. The conclusions of natural inquiry, whether in philosophy or in the natural sciences, are the starting points for knowledge we can have of God's existence and his nature, and Aquinas thinks this is a revealed fact (referencing Rom. 1:20).[62] Certainly, Aquinas thinks, the truth of revelation could not *contradict* the results of the natural sciences, as truth cannot contradict truth.[63] But Aquinas thinks it would be equally difficult to see how human beings could see the gospel message as *intelligible* if there was no ground for natural knowledge of God or morality, even though he readily admits that Christianity requires belief in revealed truths that cannot be established by natural reason alone.[64] That is, it seems to be the case that Christian revelation presupposes that we do have *natural knowledge* of these things because "faith presupposes natural knowledge, even as grace presupposes nature."[65]

Finally, that everything is not immediately caused by God as if by miracle, and that God has reasons to allow creatures to exercise their own kinds of causality, is also important to preserve the responsibility of human beings within a providentially guided universe. Because God can guide the course of history in a way that respects and is compatible with human free decisions, Aquinas can affirm classical Christian doctrines about the necessity of grace for supernatural conversion, coming to faith in and love of God, as a special instance of his general approach to God's causality.[66] This, too, set Aquinas apart from his Islamic interlocutors, who often proposed a deterministic theory of causality that implied either a denial of or a compatibilist understanding of human free agency.[67] In the end, Aquinas's account of divine causality remains a plausible and attractive way to explain the nature of God's causal activity, given the way that his understanding God's providence provides unified solutions, by appeal to a few metaphysical principles, to many apparent puzzles or difficulties with theism.

NOTES

1 See F. J. Ayala, *Darwin's Gift to Science and Religion* (Washington, DC: Joseph Henry Press, 2007), p. ix; S. J. Gould, "Nonoverlapping Magisteria," *Natural History* 106 (1997): 16–22.

2 *SCG* II.3.

3 See L. X. López-Farjeat, "Avicenna's Influence on Aquinas Early Doctrine of Creation in 'In Sent.', D. 1, Q. 1, A. 2," *Recherches de Théologie et Philosophie médiévales* 79 (2012): 307–37, especially p. 315, fn. 19, for references to texts by Averroes on the eternity of time and motion.

4 Lateran IV, Canon 1.

5 See, for example, local Parisian censures of 1215 and 1231.

6 J. F. Wippel, "The Condemnations of 1270 and 1277 at Paris," *Journal of Medieval and Renaissance Studies* 7 (1977): 169–201; J. F. Wippel, "Thomas Aquinas and the Condemnation of 1277," *The Modern Schoolman* 72 (1995): 233–72.

7 J. Wawrykow, "Aquinas and Bonaventure on Creation" in G. Anderson and M. Bockmuehl (eds.), *Creation* ex nihilo: *Origins, Development, Contemporary Challenges* (Notre Dame, IN: University of Notre Dame Press, 2018), pp. 173–94, here pp. 174–80.

8 Bonaventure, *In II Sent.*, d.1 p.1 a.1 q.2 (ed. Quaracchi, II: 22a–b). Translation from T. Noone and R. E. Hauser, "Saint Bonaventure" in E. N. Zalta (ed.), *The Stanford Encyclopedia of Philosophy* (2020) [online], https://plato.stanford.edu/archives/win2020/entries/bonaventure/.

9 Ibid., sec. 3.2.

10 See Augustine, *The Literal Meaning of Genesis*, 2 vols., translated and annotated by J. H. Taylor (New York: Newman Press, 1982), especially Vol. 1, p. 36.

11 For an itinerary of Aquinas's thought and writings on creation, see W. A. Wallace, "Aquinas on Creation: Science, Theology, and Matters of Fact," *The Thomist* 38 (1974): 485–523, especially pp. 503–4.

12 *In II Sent.*, d.1 q.1 a.2.

13 *In II Sent.*, d.1 q.1 a.5, co. See López-Farjeat, "Avicenna's Influence," pp. 317–18.

14 *Quodl* XII q.5 a.1.

15 *De aeternitate mundi.*

16 *ST* I q.46 a.2 ad 1.

17 *QDP* a.2 Resp.; *ST* I q.46 a.1 ad 1.

18 *In II Sent.*, d.1 q.1 a.2, co. (my translation).

19 López-Farjeat, "Avicenna's Influence," pp. 330–1.

20 G. Kerr, *Aquinas and the Metaphysics of Creation* (New York: Oxford University Press, 2019), pp. 49–51.

21 See *ST* I q.104 a.1.

22 See further Kerr, *Aquinas and the Metaphysics of Creation*, pp. 159–73.

23 G. Kerr, "A Thomistic Metaphysics of Creation," *Religious Studies* 48 (2012): 337–56, especially pp. 338–50.

24 *QDP* q.3 a.17; *ST* I q.46 a.2.

25 *QDP* a.1, Resp. and a.4.

26 *QDP* a.3.

27 *QDP* a.7. T. Aquinas, "On Creation: *Quaestiones disputatae De potentia dei*, Q.3″ in *Thomas Aquinas in Translation*, translated by S. Selner-Wright (Washington, DC: The Catholic University of America Press, 2011).

28 I. Silva, "Thomas Aquinas Holds Fast: Objections to Aquinas within Today's Debate on Divine Action," *Heythrop Journal* 48 (2013): 658–67, here pp. 659–60.

29 See A. Farrer, *Faith and Speculation: An Essay in Philosophical Theology* (London: Adam and Charles Black, 1967), especially p. 62, 110. (Polkinghorne, Clayton, and Ward were largely responding to Farrer.)

30 K. Richardson, "Causation in Arabic and Islamic Thought," sec.1.2, in E. N. Zalta (ed.), *The Stanford Encyclopedia of Philosophy* (2020) [online] https://plato.stanford.edu/archives/win2020/entries/arabic-islamic-causation/.

31 See M. Fakhry, *Islamic Occasionalism and Its Critique by Averroes and Aquinas* (Abingdon and New York: Routledge, 2008 [1958]).

32 *QDP* a.7 co.

33 R. Acar, *Talking about God and Talking about Creation: Avicenna's and Thomas Aquinas' Positions*. Islamic Philosophy, Theology and Science. Texts and Studies 58 (Leiden and Boston: Brill, 2005), pp. 146–9.

34 Richardson, "Causation in Arabic and Islamic Thought," sec.3.1, 3.3; Acar, *Talking about God and Talking about Creation*, pp. 132–46.

35 See Avicenna, *The Metaphysics of the Healing*, translated by M. Marmura (Provo, UT: Brigham Young University Press, 2005), pp. 126–7; cited in Richardson, "Causation in Arabic and Islamic Thought."

36 *ST* I q.22 a.1.

37 *ST* I q.14 a.8.

38 *SCG* I.46; *ST* I q.14 a.9; *ST* I q.15 a.1.

39 For example, he rejects Avicenna's reasoning explicitly at *QDP* q.3 a.15; *QDP* q.3 a.17 ad 4.

40 See *ST* I q.19 a.3.

41 Pace N. Kretzmann, *The Metaphysics of Theism: Aquinas's Natural Theology in* Summa Contra Gentiles I (Oxford: Clarendon Press, 1997), pp. 224–5, God is not necessitated either in deciding whether to create or what to create – see Kerr, *Aquinas and the Metaphysics of Creation*, pp. 62–7.

42 See T. R. Wittman, *God and Creation in the Theology of Thomas Aquinas and Karl Barth* (Cambridge: Cambridge University Press, 2019), pp. 57–65.

43 See *ST* I q.105 a.5; *SCG* III.109.

44 *SCG* III.96.

45 See *ST* I q.19 a.8.

46 *ST* I q.105 a.5 Resp.

47 Wittman, *God and Creation*, pp. 100–6.

48 *ST* I q.104 a.2 Resp. (Translation by the English Dominican Fathers.)

49 See, for example, J. L. Kvanvig and H. J. McCann, "Divine Conservation and the Persistence of the World" in T. V. Morris (ed.), *Divine and Human Action* (Ithaca, NY: Cornell University Press, 1988), pp. 13–49.

50 God acts on the basis of his divine ideas and his Word in creating and guiding the providential order of creation. See M. W. Levering, *Engaging the Doctrine of Creation: Cosmos, Creatures, and the Wise and Good Creator* (Grand Rapids, MI: Baker Academic, 2017), pp. 54–71; Wittman, *God and Creation*, pp. 94–5.

51 Silva, "Thomas Aquinas Holds Fast," pp. 662–4.

52 J. Polkinghorne, *Science and Providence: God's Interaction with the World* (Boston, MA: New Science Library, 1989), p. 31; J. Polkinghorne, "Chaos Theory and Divine Action" in W. M. Richardson and W. J. Wildman (eds.), *Religion and Science: History, Method and Dialogue* (New York: Routledge, 1996), pp. 247–9; P. Clayton, "Natural Law and Divine Action: The Search for an Expanded Theory of Causation," *Zygon* 39 (2004): 615–36.

53 M. J. Dodds, *Unlocking Divine Action: Contemporary Science and Thomas Aquinas* (Washington, DC: The Catholic University of America Press, 2012), pp. 221–5.

54 E. Feser, *Aristotle's Revenge: The Metaphysical Foundations of Physical and Biological Science* (Haverton, PA: Editiones Scholasticae, 2019), pp. 372–8.

55 Cf. E. Stump, "Non-Cartesian Substance Dualism and Materialism without Reductionism," *Faith and Philosophy* 12 (1995): 505–31; Chapter 6 in this volume.

56 *ST* I q.90 aa.1–2; *SCG* II.87.

57 Levering, *Engaging the Doctrine of Creation*, pp. 220–3.

58 This is essentially how the Catholic Church today explains the process; International Theological Commission, *Communion and Stewardship* (2004), https://www.vatican.va/roman_curia/congregations/cfaith/cti_documents/rc_con_cfaith_doc_20040723_communion-stewardship_en.html, paragraph 68. Also see Dodds, *Unlocking Divine Action*, pp. 203–4.

59 *ST* I-II q.91 a.4.

60 *ST* I-II q.91 a.2.

61 Also, *SCG* III.129.

62 *SCG* I.8; *SCG* I.12.

63 *SCG* I.7.

64 For a fuller defense from a Thomistic point of view, see T. J. White, *Wisdom in the Face of Modernity* (Washington, DC: The Catholic University of America Press, 2009).

65 *ST* I q.2 a.2 ad 1.

66 *SCG* III.148.

67 C. Belo, "Freedom and Determinism" in R. Taylor and L. X. López-Farjeat (eds.), *Routledge Companion to Islamic Philosophy* (New York: Routledge, 2016), pp. 325–36.

6 The Nature of Human Beings

Eleonore Stump

INTRODUCTION

On Aquinas's view, a human being is a material object, a hylomorphic compound of prime matter and the substantial form of a human being. That form is capable of existing on its own, apart from matter; and it does so in the period between the death of a human being and the resurrection of his body, when that form configures matter again. The resurrection of the body is not a reassembly of bodily bits that had previously composed the body; it is more nearly a reconstitution of the substantial form with prime matter. Finally, after death some human beings go to heaven. In heaven, a human being is perfected, so that the true nature of a human being is revealed best in the condition of human beings in heaven. A human being in heaven sees God and is united in loving relationship with God and with all others who are also united to God. In this vision and union, she has the full perfection of her human nature and also her complete beatitude.

Densely compressed, this is Aquinas's view of the nature of human beings. It can conveniently be divided into four parts:

(1) A human being as a material object
(2) The soul of a human being
(3) The separated soul and the resurrection of the body
(4) The perfection of a human being

In what follows, I will consider each part in turn.[1]

A HUMAN BEING AS A MATERIAL OBJECT

Aquinas's view of the nature of human beings is situated within his general metaphysics, about which a little needs to be said here, although earlier chapters in this volume explore some of the relevant issues in more depth.

Aquinas's metaphysics is in many respects Aristotelian. For Aquinas, some things are made out of matter and other things (such as angels) are not. Like Aristotle, Aquinas thinks that a macro-level material thing is matter organized or configured in some way, where the organization or configuration is dynamic rather than static. That is, the organization of the matter includes causal relations among the material components of the thing as well as such static features as shape and spatial location. This dynamic configuration or organization, which unifies the whole composite, is what Aquinas calls 'form.'

Also like Aristotle, Aquinas recognizes levels of organization. What counts as matter for a macro-level object may itself be organized or configured in a certain way. A material object may also have integral parts, which are themselves constituted of matter and form.[2] But if we conceptually strip away every form or configuration of a material substance, all that remains is prime matter, matter which cannot itself be decomposed further into matter and form.

Prime matter is thus matter without any form at all, "materiality" apart from configuration. When it is a component in a matter–form composite, prime matter is the component of the configured composite which makes it the case that the configured thing is extended in three dimensions and occupies a particular place at a particular time.[3] But by itself, apart from form, prime matter exists just potentially; it exists in actuality only as an ingredient in something configured.[4] So we can remove form from prime matter only in thought; everything which exists in reality is configured in some way. Configuration or organization is necessary for the existence of anything at all; without form, nothing is actual.

This last point holds also for immaterial things. For Aquinas, there are things that exist and are organized in a certain way, but the organization is not an organization of matter. An angel – that is, a certain kind of subsistent immaterial intelligence – is an example. An angel has no matter to configure, but it is nonetheless configured in a certain way; that is, it has certain characteristics and not others, certain capacities and not others, and so on. Consequently, although matter is not necessary for the existence of a thing, on Aquinas's view form is. For Aquinas, to be is to be configured.

The metaphysical parts of a material thing therefore include form as well as matter. It is not true on Aquinas's account that a material whole is nothing but its material parts or is identical to its material components.[5] The highlighting of the role of the form or configuration of a whole gives Aquinas's metaphysics one of its distinctive characteristics and makes it anti-reductionistic.[6] So, for example, expounding a view of Aristotle's, Aquinas says,

> sometimes a composite takes its species from something one, which is a form ... or a composition ... or an organization ... In all such cases, it cannot be that the composite itself is those things out of which it is composed ... And [Aristotle] proves this in the following way. If those things out of which the composition is formed are dissociated or separated from one another ... the whole does not remain after the dissolution, just as flesh does not remain once [its] elements are separated [from each other] ... [But] fire and earth remain after the dissolution of the flesh.[7]

Aquinas takes it that the forms of material objects can be divided into two sorts: substantial forms and accidental forms. One way of distinguishing the two is by what they configure. A substantial form of a material substance configures prime matter, and it is the form in virtue of which the composite whole is a member of the species to which it belongs. By contrast, an accidental form configures something which is an actually existing matter–form composite; it is the form in virtue of whose advent the composite whole comes to be altered in some way.[8] The complete form (that is, the substantial and accidental forms taken together) of a material substance is the organization of the matter of that object in such a way that it is constituted as that object rather than some other one and has the causal powers it does. For my purposes here, we can leave accidental forms to one side and concentrate just on substantial forms.

No material thing has more than one substantial form, on Aquinas's view.[9] A composite that consists of prime matter configured by a substantial form could not itself be one component among others of a larger whole configured by yet another substantial form. That is because if a substantial form were to configure what is already configured by a substantial form, then it would be configuring a matter–form composite, not prime matter.

Elements – earth, air, fire, and water – are substances,[10] and different elements can combine to form a compound which is itself a substance.[11] But the constituent things that existed earlier cease to exist as the things that they were when they become part of the substance configured by the substantial form of the whole.[12] Instead, a new substance is generated. So, for example, earth and fire can combine to form flesh. But they can do so only in case the substantial form of each combining element is lost in the composite[13] and is replaced by the one substantial form of the whole composite.[14] On Aquinas's view, the parts of a whole are actual (rather than potential) things existing in their own right, as independent substances, only when the composite of which they are parts is decomposed and the substantial form of the whole is lost.[15] The difference between a substance and an artifact for Aquinas is precisely that in an artifact the components retain the configuration they had in isolation. Bread is a substance for Aquinas, rather than an artifact, because the configuration of the components of bread do not remain, as the things they were, when they are mixed together and baked into bread.[16]

On Aquinas's view, the substantial form of a whole confers causal powers on the whole; and the characteristic operations and functions of a substance derive from the substantial form configuring the whole.[17] In fact, Aquinas supposes, as we increase complexity in systems, even systems of inanimate things, properties arise that are properties of the whole system but not properties of the material parts of the system. For example, Aquinas says,

> to the extent to which a form is more perfect, to that extent it surpasses [its] corporeal matter ... For the form of an element does not have any operation except that which arises by means of the active and passive qualities which are the dispositions of the corporeal matter [it informs]. But the form of a mineral body has an operation that exceeds the active and passive qualities ... as, for example, that a magnet attracts iron.[18]

On Aquinas's account of form, then, even inanimate material objects can have systems-level properties; and these systems-level properties bring with them causal powers that belong to the whole but not to its parts. Aquinas is committed to the existence of top-down causation, even for inanimate objects. From his point of view, a mineral such as a magnet has a property and a causal power (to attract iron) conferred on it only by the form of the whole. None of the components of the magnet taken *singillatim* and apart from the configuration of the whole have this property or the causal power of this whole. On Aquinas's metaphysics, where the bits of iron move is determined by a causal power vested in the magnet as a whole.

This general metaphysical account of matter and form applies to human beings also. The matter of a human being is configured by the substantial form of a human being, which is the soul. The soul confers the systems-level properties, such as mental properties, on a human being. These systems-level properties are not ontologically basic; they are realized in the lower-level properties of the components of the system. Nonetheless, they emerge only at the level of the whole system, and they are or confer causal powers on the system as a whole.

On Aquinas's views, although the existence of a particular substantial form is necessary for the existence of an individual material substance, that substance is not identical to its substantial form alone. A substantial form is only one constituent of a material substance; the matter configured by the form is also a constituent.[19] Insofar as all these constituents compose a particular substance, that substance is not identical to any one of its constituents or even to the set of them. For Aquinas, constitution is not identity. He says, "a composite is not those things out of which it is composed ... [as, for example,] flesh is not identical to fire and earth [the elements of which it is composed]."[20] This part of his metaphysics makes a difference to the interpretation of his account of a human being in the period after death.

THE SOUL OF A HUMAN BEING

Many philosophers suppose that the major monotheisms, and Christianity in particular, are committed to substance dualism of a Cartesian sort. On the Cartesian view, a human being may have a body, but he is neither identical with it nor composed of it.[21] In addition, there will be causal interactions between a human being and the body that he has. Cognitive processes will have effects on the body, and bodily processes will have effects on the soul. But intellectual cognitive functions are not exercised in or by the body; they take place only in the soul that is distinct from the body. For these and other reasons, on the Cartesian view, a human being just is his soul.

As a matter of historical fact, however, Aquinas, whose views surely represent one major strand of one major monotheism, is familiar with an account very like that of Cartesian dualism, which he associates with Plato; and he rejects it emphatically.[22]

On Aquinas's own view, a human being is a material substance and so is composed of prime matter and a substantial form, which is the soul of that human being. The Latin translated 'soul' is Aquinas's generic term for the substantial form of any material object that is living. On his use of the term, then, plants have souls, too; not in the sense that they enjoy being talked to, but only in the sense that plants are living things. On his view, a plant has a soul in virtue of the fact that it has a configuration of matter which allows for nutrition, growth, reproduction, and the other sorts of activities common to living things. Non-human animals have souls, too, since they are living things; but the configuration of their matter allows them an operation not possible for plants – namely, perception. For human beings, the substantial form is the intellective soul, because it confers intellective powers on the whole composite.

Since he takes the soul to be a form, Aquinas holds that the soul is immaterial.[23] But because Aquinas sees the soul as the configuring form of prime matter, so that soul and matter together are the metaphysical constituents of a human body, he says, "[A]lthough the soul is incorruptible, it is nonetheless in no genus other than [the genus] *body*, because since it is part of human nature, it does not belong to the soul itself to be in a genus or a species."[24]

Unlike human souls, the souls of plants and non-human animals are what Aquinas thinks of as material forms. A material form is a form that goes out of existence when the material composite it configures goes out of existence.[25] By contrast, the substantial form that is the soul of a human being can exist apart from matter and does so after the death of the body. So, on the one hand, like an angel, the substantial form of a human being is able to exist and function on its own, apart from matter.[26] On the other hand, the human soul is not, as Plato thought, a spiritual substance moving a body which is also a substance in its own right. Rather, the human soul is the substantial form constituting the material substance that a human being is; and it configures prime matter, as all other substantial forms of material objects do.[27]

Aquinas takes the forms of material objects generally to come into existence with the existence of their composites; and although God is the ultimate or remote cause of the existence of non-human forms of material objects, the proximate cause is just the cause that brings about the existence of the composite that is the material object. After canvassing various opinions that he takes to be mistaken about the forms of non-human material objects, Aquinas summarizes the flaws of those opinions in this way: "All these [mistaken] opinions seem to have developed from a common root, because they were all seeking a cause for forms as if the forms themselves came into being in their own right. But, as Aristotle shows ... what comes into being, properly speaking, is the composite."[28]

Nonetheless, on Aquinas's view, in this regard the human soul is different from all other forms that configure matter. Each substantial form of a human being is created directly by God and imposed on matter.[29] This is what we might expect Aquinas to hold once we recognize that for him the soul is a subsistent form, as the angels are; the angels, too, are created directly by God. No immaterial subsistent forms can be generated by the sort of natural generation that material objects are capable of, according to Aquinas; immaterial subsistent forms can come into existence only by being handmade, as it were, by God.[30]

On the other hand, however, Aquinas rejects vehemently the notion that the soul can be created before the body and then infused into an already existent body.[31] He says,

> [I]f the soul is united to the body as its form and is naturally part of human nature, then it is completely impossible [for the soul to be created before the body] ... Since the soul is a part of human nature, it does not have its natural perfection unless it is united to the body. And so it would not have been fitting to create the soul without the body.[32]

Consequently, because the form that is the human soul is a subsistent form able to exist apart from matter but also able to configure matter, the soul has a double aspect. On the one hand, unlike the forms of other material objects, every human soul is directly created by God as an individual thing in its own right. On the other hand, like the form of any material object, the human soul exists in the composite it configures; and it comes into existence only with that composite, not before it.

On Cartesian dualism, as it is generally understood, (1) both the human soul and the body are substances in their own right. Each can engage in acts independently of the other, and each can causally affect the other. Soul and body are somehow joined together in a human being; but (2) a human being is identical with his soul, and intellective functions take place in the soul rather than the body. On Aquinas's account, both (1) and (2) are false. Although for Aquinas the separated human soul can exist on its own after death, it nonetheless is not a substance in its own right but only a metaphysical part of a substance.[33] And so Aquinas says, "[B]ody and soul are not two actually existing substances, but instead one actually existing substance arises from these two."[34] In addition, as a metaphysical part of the substance it brings into existence by configuring prime matter, the soul could not interact causally with the prime matter it informs. Prime matter is not able to exert causal influence on anything, in virtue of having no form of its own; and for the same reason it cannot receive the causal influence of anything else either.

On Aquinas's account, the substantial form that configures a human being allows for sets of operations not possible for non-human animals – namely, intellective and volitional processes. Because the human soul has this distinctive set of capacities, Aquinas tends to call it 'the intellective soul,' or 'the rational soul,' to distinguish it from the nutritive soul of plants and the sensitive (i.e., capable of perception) soul of animals generally. The intellective soul is thus that same configuration of prime matter on the basis of which something exists as a living human body. There is not one configuration of matter that makes the body a human body and then another configuration that is the intellective soul.[35] As Aquinas says: "There is no other substantial form in human beings apart from the intellective soul."[36] In virtue of this one form, a human being exists as an actual being, as a material object, as a living thing, as an animal, and as a human being with intellective cognitive capacities.[37] Even intellective function, then, is implemented in the body, on Aquinas's account.[38]

In fact, Aquinas thinks that there is something misleading about attributing cognitive functions just to the soul itself. Rather, even such higher cognitive functions as understanding are to be attributed to the whole composite that is the human being. So, for example, he says, "We can say that the soul understands in the same way that we can say that the eye sees; but it would be more appropriate to say that a human being understands by means of the soul."[39] And he specifically identifies the intellect itself with the form of the body: "[T]he intellect, which is the source of intellective function, is the form of the human body."[40]

One way to sum up the differences between Cartesian dualism and Aquinas's account is by noting that on Cartesian dualism, but not on Aquinas's account, the soul is only a configured subsistent form and not also a configurer of matter. In consequence of this difference, Aquinas's account is not vulnerable to the two main problems thought to afflict Cartesian dualism; namely, that it cannot explain the nature of the causal interaction between soul and body and that it attributes cognitive functions only to the soul. On Aquinas's account, there is no efficient causal interaction between the soul and the matter it informs, and all human cognitive functions can be implemented in the body.

That constitution is not identity on Aquinas's account helps to clarify his view that the soul can persist in a disembodied condition. Since a material substance is composed of matter and form as its constituents, if constitution were identity, then the loss of either matter or form would be enough to entail the loss of the whole substance. In that case, any substance would cease to exist when it lost either its substantial form or the matter configured by that form. But because constitution is not identity for Aquinas, it is possible for him to suppose that a substance can survive the loss of some of its constituents, provided that the remaining constituents can exist on their own and are sufficient for the existence of the substance.

THE SEPARATED SOUL AND THE RESURRECTION OF THE BODY

Since Aquinas thinks of a human being as a composite of matter and soul and since he recognizes that dead human bodies do not engage in the operations conferred by the soul, he does accept that a human being falls apart at death. On his view, the disembodied soul persists after death, but it is not the complete human being who was the composite; it is only an enduring metaphysical part of that human being. It remains in a disembodied condition until the resurrection of the body, when it will once again be part of a complete human being.

Even given Aquinas's view that there can be subsistent immaterial forms, this part of Aquinas's account has been thought to pose three major puzzles.[41]

First, what persists is the substantial form of a human being, but it seems that every human being has the same substantial form, because the substantial form is what configures matter into a human being. How, then, is the separated soul of Dominic, say, to be distinguished from the separated soul of Francis?

Second, it seems as if one and the same body of a human being could not be brought back into existence after a period of non-existence. To take just one perplexity, the atoms that composed that body will have been dispersed, if they even still exist and have not been transmuted into energy. But if the atoms that compose the resurrected body are not the same atoms as those that originally composed the body of the human being in question, then in what sense is the new body the same as the pre-mortem body of that human being?

Third, since Aquinas denies that a human being is identical to his soul, it can seem as if the separated soul is not the human being who existed before death. Rather, it can seem that a human being ceases to exist at death and does not exist again until the resurrection of the body. But is this truly Aquinas's position? As I will show below, this position has seriously problematic theological and philosophical consequences.

In what follows, I will say something very briefly about each of the first two problems in turn and then concentrate on the third.

As regards the first problem, on Aquinas's view the separated soul of a human being such as Dominic will differ from the separated soul of another human being such as Francis in multiple ways. To

begin with historical differences, the soul of Dominic will have configured the body of Dominic rather than the body of Francis. Then
there will also be intrinsic differences. The separated soul of Dominic
will have the mind of Dominic, not the mind of Francis. That is, the
intellectual faculties of the separated soul of Dominic are the intellectual faculties Dominic had during his lifetime; the intellective
memories of the separated soul of Dominic are those that Dominic
laid down during his earthly life, and so on. Finally, on Aquinas's view
of the generation of human souls, each soul is an individual particular
in virtue of being created directly by God.[42] There are, then, multiple
ways in which the separated soul of one human being is distinct from
that of another.

As regards the second problem, for Aquinas the individuation
and identity of any substance is provided by its substantial form.
Consequently, it is in fact the soul that constitutes matter into *this*
human body. In the resurrection of the body, the substantial form that
is the human soul is imposed again on prime matter; and so it makes
that matter be this human being again. The constituents of Dominic
in his resurrected state are therefore the same as those of Dominic
during his earthly life: this substantial form – the soul of Dominic,
which has been continually in existence in the period between
Dominic's death and his resurrection – and the prime matter which
is configured by the soul of Dominic into the body of Dominic. The
matter of Dominic's resurrected body is the same as the matter of
Dominic's earthly body not because it is composed of numerically the
same atoms as it had before death, but rather because it is configured
by the one individual substantial form which is the soul of Dominic.

As regards the third problem, some scholars take it as evident
that for Aquinas the separated soul is not the same human being as
the human being whose soul it was during the pre-mortem period.[43]
On their interpretation of Aquinas, Aquinas thinks that the soul of
Dominic, separated from the body of Dominic, is not a human being
at all and that, for this reason, the soul of Dominic is not Dominic. On
this interpretation, for Aquinas Dominic goes out of existence at his

death and comes back into existence only at the resurrection of his body.

This interpretation of Aquinas's view is plausible because Aquinas emphasizes that, in his view, a human being is not identical to his soul.[44] The problem with this interpretation, however, is not only that it leaves Aquinas contradicting himself, but also that it has to attribute to Aquinas theological positions that are bizarre or even heretical.

So, for example, it is Christian doctrine, explicitly accepted by Aquinas, that before the last judgment and the resurrection of the body, Christ harrowed hell. On this doctrine, the souls of those believing Jews who lived before the time of Christ and were waiting for the Messiah were sent to a particular part of hell in which there was no torment of any kind; and, in the harrowing of hell, Christ brought them out of that part of hell into heaven. But on the interpretation of Aquinas according to which the separated soul of Abraham is not Abraham, Aquinas would have to hold that Abraham himself was not in that part of hell when the separated soul of Abraham was in hell. Instead, on this interpretation of Aquinas's position, Aquinas would have to say that Abraham went out of existence with his death and that he will return to existence only when he is resurrected, at which time he will be in heaven with all the redeemed. On this interpretation, Aquinas would have to say that Christ never took Abraham from hell; in fact, Christ never took any human beings from hell.

These claims are not only heretical, so that it is historically implausible to attribute them to Aquinas, but they are also contradicted by explicit claims of Aquinas's. For example, Aquinas says,

> [T]he holy Fathers were held in hell because access to the life of glory was not available to them on account of the sin of our first parent ... When Christ descended into hell, he freed the holy Fathers from hell ... [So] it is written that "despoiling the principalities and powers", namely, of hell, by taking out Isaac and

Jacob and the other just souls, he brought them over, that is, he brought them far from the kingdom of darkness into heaven, as the gloss explains.[45]

Furthermore, Aquinas holds that Christ "is called a human being univocally with other human beings."[46] So if Aquinas must be interpreted as holding that a human being ceases to exist at death and does not come into existence again until the resurrection of the body, then for Aquinas this claim will have to apply also to Christ in his human nature. In that case, on this interpretation, Aquinas would have to hold that Christ was no longer human for the days between his bodily death and resurrection. But Aquinas maintains the orthodox doctrine that Christ is composite, fully human and fully divine.[47] So, if in the period between Christ's death and resurrection Christ was no longer a human being, then in fact in that period Christ, the composite, did not exist. Consequently, either in that period no one harrowed hell, contrary to the orthodox doctrine that Aquinas explicitly espouses; or else someone harrowed hell, but it was only the second person of the Trinity in his divine nature, a claim which is also contrary to the orthodox doctrine that Aquinas explicitly accepts. For example, in answer to the question whether the whole Christ was in hell during the days between Christ's death and resurrection, Aquinas says, "[T]he whole [Christ] was in hell because the whole person of Christ was there in virtue of the [human] soul united to him."[48] So although Aquinas accepts the truth of the claims that Christ died and that a human being is not identical to his soul, nonetheless he says, "[I]t is said of him [the composite Christ] that he descended into hell because his soul, separated from the body, descended into hell."[49]

Finally, to take one more example, Aquinas says, "[W]hen the body is destroyed, the soul is brought to an eternal and heavenly home, which is nothing other than the enjoyment of the deity, as the angels enjoy it in heaven ... And so, immediately, when the holy soul is separated from the body, it sees God by sight. And this is the final beatitude."[50] But if the separated soul of Dominic is not

Dominic, then that something-which-is-not-Dominic, with a mind and a will, loves God in heaven and is loved by him – but only for the period between the death and the resurrection of Dominic. At the point of the resurrection of Dominic, the place in the loving union with God held by the separated soul of Dominic is taken by Dominic himself.

Not only are these views theological gibberish, but they are contradicted by Aquinas's explicit claims about the nature of the separated soul's bliss. He says, for example, that

> souls immediately after their separation from the body become unchangeable as regards the will ... [B]eatitude, which consists in the vision of God, is everlasting ... But it is not possible for a soul to be blessed if its will did not have rectitude ... And so it must be that the rectitude of the will in the blessed soul is everlasting.[51]

So it is true that for Aquinas a human being Dominic is not identical to his soul. Dominic is identical to an individual in the species *rational animal*. But since what makes Dominic this individual is the substantial form which configures him, and since the substantial form can exist independently of the body, then for Aquinas the existence of the separated substantial form of Dominic is sufficient for the existence of Dominic whose substantial form it is. Dominic can continue to exist when the only metaphysical constituent that remains of him is his separated soul. But it does not follow that Dominic is identical to his soul, because for Aquinas constitution is not identity.

THE PERFECTION OF A HUMAN BEING

On Aquinas's views, the nature of a thing – that is, the nature the thing has as a member of a particular species – includes the power to engage in an operation determinative of that thing as a member of that species. So, for example, on the definition of *human being* that Aquinas inherited as part of the old logic deriving from Aristotle's work, a human being is a rational animal. On this definition, the differentia for the species *human being* is *rational*, and the intellective power conferred by the form of a human being is the species-specific potentiality of a human being.[52]

The actuality of a thing can thus be understood in two ways, according to Aquinas. On the one hand, there is the actuality which a substance has just in virtue of existing as an individual member of a species, with a particular substantial form that confers on it the species-specific potentiality characteristic of its species. On the other hand, that species-specific potentiality is part of the essence of the thing in question; and so, as that potentiality becomes actualized, there is a sense in which the thing in question becomes additionally actualized, because a part of its nature that was only potential becomes actual.

For Aquinas, being and goodness are correlative; consequently, the perfection of a thing and the actualization of its species-specific potentiality are also correlative.[53] On this way of thinking about the perfection of a substance, it is perfected when and to the extent to which it performs instances of its species-specific operation and thereby actualizes its species-specific potentiality. In the case of human beings, the perfection of a human being is also the ultimate happiness for that human being. On Aquinas's view, human beings in heaven are in a state of both perfection and beatitude.

When he is describing human happiness in heaven, in some places Aquinas seems to manifest an adherence to an apparently Aristotelian understanding of the perfection of a human being and to emphasize the impersonal and self-contained character of that condition. So, for example, he says, "the ultimate happiness of a human being consists in the contemplation of truth" in the vision of God's essence; and Aquinas seems to take it as an advantage of this view of human happiness that "for this work a human being is more self-sufficient insofar as he has little need of help from any external things for it."[54]

But if we took this picture as the complete description of Aquinas's view of perfection and beatitude in heaven, it would be a misimpression. Another side of Aquinas's position can be seen readily in his biblical commentaries. For example, when Aquinas is commenting on Christ's saying to the Father, "This is eternal life, that they may know you, the only true God" (John 17:3), he says,

> [O]ur Lord says that eternal life lies in vision, in seeing; that is, basically, in its whole substance, it consists in this. But it is love that moves to this vision and is in a certain way its fulfillment: for the fulfillment and ornament of beatitude is the delight experienced in the enjoyment of God, and this is caused by love. Still, the substance of beatitude consists in vision ... [as it says in] 1 John 3.2: *we will see him as he is.*[55]

Here, beatitude, which is also the fulfillment of human nature, consists in seeing God as God is. But the God who is seen is properly referred to by a personal pronoun: We will see *him* as *he* is. And this vision of God will unite a human being to God in love with delight.

Elsewhere in his commentary on the Gospel of John, when he is describing the perfection of human nature in its connection to truth, Aquinas's emphasis is decidedly on the second-personal relationships among persons. There he says, "If you ask where to go, cling to Christ, for he is the truth, which we desire to reach."[56] Here, Aquinas is identifying the perfection of human beings in the contemplation of truth with a personal relationship to Christ; and he is emphasizing a human being's need for that relationship by exhorting him to *cling* to Christ. And in the same commentary, expounding Christ's prayer in the Gospel of John that his disciples might be one as he and the Father are one, Aquinas says,

> [W]e read: *God is love, and he who abides in love abides in God, and God abides in him* ... God loves absolutely those to whom he wills all good, that is, that they have God himself. And to have God is to have truth, for God is truth. But truth is had or possessed when it is known. So God, who is truth, truly and absolutely loves those to whom he manifests himself.[57]

In his commentary on Galatians, in the context of a discussion of the fruits of the Holy Spirit, Aquinas describes the perfection of a human being not only as a matter of a first-personal experience of a vision of God's essence, but also as a decidedly second-personal relationship with God. He says,

> [T]he ultimate perfection, by which a person is made perfect inwardly, is joy, which stems from the presence of what is loved. Whoever has the love of God, however, already has what he loves, as is said in 1 John 4:16: "whoever abides in the love of God abides in God, and God abides in him." And joy wells up from this.[58]

In fact, on Aquinas's view, the Holy Spirit unites a human being in grace with God in a relationship personal enough to count as friendship with God. Aquinas says,

> In the first place, it is proper to friendship to converse with one's friend ... It is also a property of friendship that one take delight in a friend's presence, that one rejoice in his words and deeds ... and it is especially in our sorrows that we hasten to our friends for consolation. Since then the Holy Spirit constitutes us God's friends and makes God dwell in us and us dwell in God, it follows that through the Holy Spirit we have joy in God.[59]

And when in connection with the fruits of the Holy Spirit Aquinas describes the fulfillment of human nature, he also emphasizes the second-personal character of that fulfillment. He says,

> [God] himself is love. Hence it is written (Rom. v.5): "The love of God is poured forth in our hearts by the Holy Spirit who is given to us." The necessary result of this love is joy, because every lover rejoices at being united to the beloved. Now love has always the actual presence of God whom it loves. So the consequence of this love is joy. And the perfection of joy is peace ... because our desires rest altogether in [God].[60]

Aquinas generalizes this account of human perfection and beatitude in his view of the nature of all created things. For Aquinas, the perfection of *any* created thing is a matter of relationship to the creator. He says, "[T]he perfection of each thing is nothing but sharing a likeness to God; for we are good to the extent that we resemble God."[61] For human beings, a resemblance to God in fact amounts to an image of God; and, on Aquinas's account of human nature, that image includes the intellective capacities that are distinctive of human nature.

As the preceding texts show, for Aquinas the actualization of these capacities fulfills the image of God in human beings in two ways, both by facilitating the fulfillment of human intellective capacities in the vision of the divine essence and by enabling second-personal relationship with God in love with joy. As Aquinas puts it, in a line that combines both ways into one: "Perfect beatitude requires that the intellect attains the very essence of the first cause, and so it will have its perfection through union with God as the object in which alone the beatitude of a human being consists."[62]

It makes a difference here that on Christian doctrine God is triune: one and only one God in three persons. For Aquinas, a human being in heaven sees the one divine essence as it is but is also united with the three divine persons in the love they share with each other. The fulfillment of the image of God in human beings and the perfection of a human being in heaven therefore brings a human being to resemble the triune God. The pure *esse* that is the deity and the three divine persons who are united in mutual love in the Trinity are mirrored in the condition of a human being who sees God in heaven and is united to God in mutual indwelling and love.

For Aquinas, then, the ultimate perfection of any human being is her union with God. That is because in being united to God in love she both actualizes the species-specific potentiality for human beings and also most fulfills the image of God in human nature.

CONCLUSION

Clearly, Aquinas's account of the nature of a human being appropri-
ates a great deal that is recognizably Aristotelian: A human being is a
rational animal, a material substance composed of substantial form
and prime matter, with a species-specific capacity for reason whose
actualization perfects a human being. But it should also be clear that
in the end there is a significant difference between an Aristotelian
understanding of human nature and Aquinas's Christian account.

As Aquinas's account of the perfection of a human being shows,
for Aquinas a human being is a relational entity: the creature of a
creator. Although Aquinas does espouse the categorization of a
human being as a rational animal, still there is a way in which his
account of human nature is understood more aptly if we think of the
genus for human beings on Aquinas's account as *subsistent creature*.
For Aquinas, a creature that is both subsistent and also relational is a
creaturely image of the subsistent relation that a divine person of the
Trinity is. Aquinas's account of human nature thus in effect fleshes
out Augustine's famous line: Augustine says to God, "You have made
us for yourself, and our hearts are restless till they rest in you."[63]

It remains true that, on the Thomistic account, a human being
is a rational animal; the soul of a human being is the intellective form
conferring the power of rationality. But the pagan taxonomy of
Aristotle does not exhaust the Thomistic account of the nature of a
human being. For Aquinas, as for Aristotle, the rational functions of
mind and will are the species-specific capacity of a human being. But,
unlike Aristotle, Aquinas thought that the human species-specific
capacity is that capacity of intellect and will whose ultimate actualization is the intellect's vision of the essence of God and the joy of the
will in union with God.

That union in effect deifies a human being – but by perfecting
human nature and not by destroying it. That is why, although the
separated soul is subsistent and capable of union with God, Aquinas
espouses the Christian doctrine that the body of a human being must

be resurrected for the final perfection of a human being. On his view, although the soul is a subsistent form, and Dominic continues to exist even if only his soul persists after death, nonetheless a human being is a material substance. Unlike Plato, Aquinas did not think that the body is a hindrance to the perfection of a human being. For Aquinas, a human being has her final perfection and full beatitude in union with God in heaven when the body is resurrected.

Finally, for Aquinas, a human being in perfection is not solitary or self-sufficient. On the contrary, in the perfected state, each human being in heaven will also be united with each of the others united with God, not because a perfected human being has need of those others but because there is more joy in union that is shared. This shared love and joy is itself the fulfillment of the image of God that is imprinted in the nature of human beings.[64]

NOTES

1 For detailed discussions of some of these topics, see E. Stump, *Aquinas* (New York and London: Routledge, 2003), chs. 1 and 6; E. Stump, "Emergence, Causal Powers, and Aristotelianism in Metaphysics" in R. Groff and J. Greco (eds.), *Powers and Capacities in Philosophy: The New Aristotelianism* (New York and Oxford: Routledge, 2013), pp. 48–68; E. Stump, "Resurrection, Reassembly, and Reconstitution: Aquinas on the Soul" in B. Niederbacher and E. Runggaldier (eds.), *Die menschliche Seele: Brauchen wir den Dualismus?* (Frankfurt: Ontos Verlag, 2006), pp. 151–71. Some parts of this essay are taken from those texts. In the interest of brevity, I will omit here some of the detailed discussion and scholarly controversy surrounding some of the claims made in this chapter, since they can be found in this previous work of mine.

2 See, for example, *DPN* 2 (346).

3 *DPN* 1 (340).

4 *DPN* 2 (349); see also *In VII Meta* 2.1289–92.

5 For a contemporary argument against the reduction of wholes to their parts, see P. van Inwagen, "Composition as Identity" in J. Tomberlin (ed.), *Philosophical Perspectives 8* (Altascadero, CA: Ridgeview Publishing Co., 1994), pp. 207–19.

6 For discussion of the general problem of reductionism relevant to the issues considered here, see A. Garfinkel, "Reductionism" in R. Boyd, P. Gasper, and J. D. Trout (eds.), *The Philosophy of Science* (Cambridge, MA: MIT Press, 1993), pp. 443–59. See also P. Kitcher, "1953 and All That: A Tale of Two Sciences," *The Philosophical Review* 93 (1984): 335–73.

7 *In VII Meta* 17.1673–4. (Although I regularly consult already available translations of the works of Aquinas, which influence my translations to a greater or lesser degree, the translation in this and the other quotations from Aquinas in this chapter are my own.) Someone might suppose that on this argument a heap is something more than the sum of its parts. For a detailed explanation of the parts of Aquinas's metaphysics that block this apparent implication, see Stump, *Aquinas*, ch. 1.

8 For the claims about what substantial and accidental forms configure, see, for example, *DPN* 1 (339).

9 To avoid confusion, it might be helpful here to emphasize that Aquinas's point is a point about substances. Statues are not substances but artifacts; for Aquinas there can be more than one substantial form in an artifact.

10 Cf. *DPN* 3 (354), where Aquinas talks about water being divided into water until it is divided into the smallest bits that are still water – namely, the element *water*.

11 See, for example, *CT* 211 (410), where Aquinas discusses the case in which the combination of elements constitutes a complete inanimate thing which is an individual in the genus of substance.

12 The point of saying that they go out of existence as things in their own right is to preclude the misunderstanding that these things cease to exist *simpliciter*. They continue to exist as components of the whole.

13 On Aquinas's view, flesh existing on its own does not have the same form as flesh in an animal. That is because the proper function of flesh (or any other constituent of the whole) is given by the substantial form of the whole. When it exists on its own, without being configured by the form of the whole, no part of the whole functions as it does when it is in the whole. See, for example, *ST* III q.5 a.3, where Aquinas explains that flesh which is not informed by the substantial form of a human being is called 'flesh' only equivocally, and *ST* III q.5 a.4, where he makes the more general claim that there is no true human flesh which is not completed by

a human soul. (Cf. *In II DA* 1.226 and *In VII Meta* 9.1519.) See also *In VII Meta* 11.1519 and *SCG* IV.36 (3740), where Aquinas explains that the substantial form of a thing confers on that thing operations proper to it.

14 *SCG* IV.35 (3732); cf. also *In VII Meta* 17.1680; *In VII Meta* 16.1633.

15 *In VII Meta* 16.1633.

16 For an excellent paper discussing this difference, see M. Rota, "Substance and Artifact in Thomas Aquinas," *History of Philosophy Quarterly* 21 (2004): 241–59.

17 See, for example, *SCG* IV.36 (3740).

18 *QDSC* un.2.

19 See, for example, *QDUVI* 1, where Aquinas says that a suppositum will not be the same as a nature in anything in which there is either accident or individual matter, because in that case the suppositum is related to the nature by means of an addition. See also *SCG* IV.40 (3781).

20 *In VII Meta* 17.1673–4.

21 Meditation VI, in *The Philosophical Writings of Descartes*, translated by J. Cottingham, R. Stoothoff, and D. Murdoch (Cambridge: Cambridge University Press, 1984), vol. II, p. 54. In other places, Descartes seems to hold that a complete human being is a compound of body and soul; see, for example, his reply to objections, in *The Philosophical Writings of Descartes*, vol. II, pp. 299–300. How this position is to be reconciled with the position in the quotation from Meditation VI is not entirely clear; but my interest in this chapter is only in the dualism commonly associated with Descartes, regardless of whether or not Descartes himself actually held it.

22 See, for example, *SCG* II.57.

23 *ST* I q.75 a.5.

24 *QDSC* un.2 ad 16.

25 Cf., for example, *ST* I q.75 a.3.

26 Cf., for example, *ST* I a.75 a.6.

27 Cf., for example, *ST* I q.76 a.1.

28 *ST* I q.65 a.4.

29 See, for example, *ST* I q.90 a.2.

30 See, for example, *ST* I q.118 a.2.

31 *ST* I q.118 aa.2–3.

32 *ST* I q.90 a.4.

33 *QDSC* un.2 ad 16.

34 *SCG* II.69.
35 See, for example, *QDSC* un.4.
36 *ST* I q.76 a.4.
37 *ST* I q.76 a.6 ad 1.
38 *ST* I q.75 a.1.
39 *ST* I q.75 a.2 ad 2, emphasis added.
40 *ST* I q.76 a.1.
41 For some discussion of the literature on these problems, see Stump, "Resurrection, Reassembly, and Reconstitution."
42 See, for example, *QDA* un.1 ad 2.
43 To take just one example, see P. van Inwagen, "Resurrection" in E. Craig (ed.), *Routledge Encyclopedia of Philosophy* 8 (London: Routledge, 1998). For some recent discussion of the issue in contemporary philosophy, see P. Toner, "Personhood and Death in St. Thomas Aquinas," *History of Philosophy Quarterly* 26 (2009): 121–38. For some discussion of the issue in recent Catholic theology, see A. Hofer, "Balthasar's Eschatology on the Intermediate State: The Question of Knowability," *Logos: A Journal of Catholic Thought and Culture* 12 (2009): 148–72. (I am grateful to Thomas Joseph White for calling this paper to my attention.)
44 See, for example, *In I Cor* c.15, 1.2.
45 *ST* III q.52 a.5.
46 *ST* III q.2 a.5.
47 See, for example, *ST* III q.2 a.4.
48 *ST* III q.52 a.2.
49 *ST* III q.50 a.3.
50 *SCG* IV.91.
51 *SCG* IV.92.
52 See, for example, *SCG* I.42 n.343: "The differentia that specifies a genus does not complete the nature (*rationem*) of the genus; instead, it is through the differentia that the genus acquires its being in actuality. For there is a complete nature of *animal* before the addition of *rational*, but an animal cannot be in actuality unless it is rational or irrational."
53 See, for example, *ST* I q.48 a.5.
54 *SCG* III.37.
55 *Super Johan*, c.17 l.1.
56 *Super Johan*, c.14 l.2.
57 *Super Johan*, c.14 l.5.

58 *In Gal*, c.5, 1.6.

59 *SCG* IV c.23.

60 *ST* I-II q.70 a.3.

61 *Super Johan*, c.17 1.3.

62 *ST* I-II q.3 a.8.

63 Augustine, *Confessions* I.1.

64 I am grateful to Thomas Joseph White for very helpful comments on an earlier draft of this paper.

PART III Epistemology

7 The Nature of Cognition and Knowledge

Therese Scarpelli Cory

Wherever Aquinas discusses mental life – cognition, perception, thought, knowledge, reasoning – his writing can seem like a trackless wilderness to the uninitiated. The texts overflow with technical Latin terms that come into English as impenetrable jargon: 'intellect in actuality,' 'habit of science,' 'sensible species,' 'intelligible being,' 'intellected intention,' 'estimative power,' 'word of the heart.' Even terms corresponding to familiar English terms, such as 'belief,' 'judgment,' 'experience,' 'passion,' 'intention,' or 'perception,' are used in confusing and unexpected ways.

The path through this wilderness lies in recognizing cognition and knowledge as part of the larger landscape of Aquinas's natural world. For Aquinas, being expresses itself in self-diffusing action. Substances constantly press outwards, making other beings like themselves.[1] A pumpkin vine, for instance, converts soil nutrients to pumpkin seeds and reproduces itself in more little pumpkin plants. But if the right kind of creatures wander within range, the pumpkin can also simultaneously express itself in conscious experience – that is, in *a goat's perception of a pumpkin*, or in *a farmer's thought that pumpkins are a kind of squash*.

Here, the pumpkin is reproducing itself in a mode of being different from the one that it naturally has itself: i.e. in what I will call "conscious being," which is the very stuff of conscious experience. Conscious being comes in a variety of flavors, allowing the pumpkin to express itself in different ways (visually, tactilely, imaginatively, intellectually), which together make up the passerby's experience of the pumpkin.

A *theory of conscious natures* – embedded in a broader theory of nature – thus frames both Aquinas's psychological theory of cognition and his epistemological theory of knowledge.[2] The mental world is part of the natural world. Conscious being has a nature, with its own internal dynamism and its own kind of life or characteristic activities. Epistemological questions about knowledge thus are questions about a kind of conscious life uniquely available to humans. This chapter first examines Aquinas's psychological account of *cognition*, and then shows how a epistemological theory of *knowledge* fits into that account.

THE CONSTITUTION OF COGNITIVE BEING

Form and Matter, Actuality and Action

Aquinas's psychology is often described as a prolific system of "faculties,"[3] which can comprise, on the cognitive side, as many as eleven senses and two intellects, not to mention the associated appetites. But 'faculty' is not really the best terminology here. 'Faculty' language (with associated terms like 'function' or 'processing') evokes mechanistic comparisons, as though the mind were an assemblage of devices for processing sensory input. It gives the impression of a mental Rube Goldberg machine in which raw sensory data, or "information," circulates through an elaborate series of successively refining or processing "faculties."

Aquinas himself speaks instead of cognitive "strengths" or "powers" (*vires, potentiae*) – notions drawn from his broader theory of natural action and reception. Cognitive powers are all (with one exception) what he calls "passive powers." And passive powers are nothing more than a substance's potential for some new being: For example, water's having the "passive power to be frozen" is just *water's being potentially ice*.[4] (Note: For Aquinas, a potential is not a statistical probability, but a real feature of something, an emptiness waiting to be "filled" by some actuality.)

So cognitive passive powers are *potentials in an animal for some kind of being*. What kind of being? Aquinas speaks of "sense in actuality" or "intellect in actuality."[5] I suggest that these should be understood as *kinds of conscious being, which is just the stuff of conscious experience*. The powers of vision, smell, imagination, intellect, etc., in other words, are an animal's potentials for varieties of conscious being that are varieties of conscious experience. The goat's "power of vision" is just its potential for visual being, which is visual experience.[6]

These cognitive potentials are actualized in just the same way any potential is actualized for Aquinas: through form. Water becomes hot by receiving the form of heat. Similarly, a goat acquires visual experience by receiving a visual form, or "species," as Aquinas calls cognitive forms. Conscious experience, then, is *a kind of being that is constituted in an animal*, not a product of the hidden churning of psychological mechanisms.

Here, a common confusion should be avoided. Aquinas is often said to hold the "Aristotelian" view that cognizing is *nothing more than passive reception* (seeing red is receiving the form of red), against medieval "Augustinians" who hold that cognizing is an *action* (seeing red is an action that the soul performs).[7] In reality, Aquinas holds a middle position: Just as water, having passively become cold, now performs its own action of chilling the surrounding air, so too a goat, having passively acquired visual being, *initiates its own visual actions*. The reason is that, for Aquinas, being gives rise to action. So cognitive being, once acquired, gives rise to cognitive actions.[8]

But visual being is already visual experience. So what does a visual action add to visual being? Aquinas does not say, but I suggest that the distinction represents the difference between merely *having an experience* versus *attending to something within the field of experience*. In other words, visual being is merely a (passive) visual experience, or "seeing," while visual action adds the (active) dimension of "looking at" – i.e., picking out, distinguishing. Similarly, the intellect formed by a species is able to "go forth into diverse thoughts, such that by the species 'human' one can think various things about humans."[9]

Agents and Patients

Aquinas thus explains mental life in terms of how cognitive (conscious) being comes to be in certain recipients, and the actions it enables its recipient to perform. So what are the causes of conscious being? What kinds of recipients can receive it? What kinds of agents can cause it?

To answer these questions, we must distinguish between two main genera of conscious being: bodily and non-bodily.

Bodily conscious being includes all kinds of sensory experience, both internal and external (for instance, auditory and imaginative; see below). Like any bodily reality, sensory experiences are spatially and temporally extended, divisible into parts, and localized in a body part.[10] For sensory being, then, the proper recipients are living sense organs formed by the appropriate cognitive power: eye, ear, flesh, etc., for the external senses, and various brain parts for the internal senses.

What makes a body part suited to be a sense organ, such that, for example, a hamster's flesh can take on an experience of warmth and pressure, but a stone cannot? For Aquinas, the hamster's flesh is (1) ensouled and (2) materially organized so as to have the relevant "complexion" (a harmonious biological state). Under those conditions, the soul automatically bestows on the flesh the power of touch – i.e., the potential for tactile experiences.[11]

Importantly, the fact that Aquinas insists that sensory experience is a *bodily reality* does not mean he thinks it is a *material reality*. "Every cognitive potential, insofar as it is cognitive, is immaterial."[12] In the cognitive hierarchy, sense is "in the middle" between material being and the non-bodily being of intellect:[13] Forms are received without their matter, but still in a bodily organ.[14] Such remarks are puzzling, until we realize that Aquinas does not mean what we mean by 'material.' For Aquinas, material changes play a "zero-sum game": One material form is gained only at the expense of another (e.g., heat drives out cold). In contrast, immaterial forms do not drive anything out in the receiver. So sensory experience is *bodily* in being extended in space and time, but *immaterial* in being received by a bodily organ without causing that organ to suffer any corresponding loss of its pre-existing qualities.[15] (Intellectual experience, in contrast, is both immaterial and non-bodily.)

So what kinds of agents can cause sensory experiences? Recall that agents make their patients like themselves. So one might worry that sensory being cannot be caused by non-sensate things. Aquinas holds, however, that sense objects – goats, waterfalls – are able to generate not only material changes, but also sensory experiences. Either way, they are doing the same thing as agents: communicating their own forms, without any of their own matter. The difference between material changes and sensory experiences thus originates entirely on the "patient" side, depending on the disposition of the patient. Given a certain disposition, the patient receives the agent's form in material being: For example, iron's temperature increases from a nearby fire, since iron's material structure makes it susceptible to warming. Given a different disposition, such as the bodily "complexion" making an animal's flesh suited for tactile experience, the patient will receive the agent's form in "spiritual being" – i.e., as forming a sensory experience, the feeling of warmth.[16] Sometimes both kinds of being can be acquired at once: For example, living flesh exposed to heat will acquire both elevated temperature and a tactile warming experience.[17]

It is difficult enough to explain how *bodily kinds of conscious being* are caused. But in explaining the causes of *non-bodily conscious being* – that is, intellectual experience – the difficulties for Aquinas will be even greater. At least sense objects are bodies acting on other bodies, i.e., sensory organs. But bodies cannot act on non-bodies. So what causes intellectual experience? We will return to this problem below.

A CONSCIOUS MULTITUDE: THE PATCHWORK
OF EXPERIENCE

Now let us examine the different kinds of conscious being that can be generated in us. As mentioned earlier, Aquinas describes no fewer than *eleven* cognitive powers. While he devotes more attention to some than to others – especially intellect – he provides enough detail for us to assemble the picture of what each of them contributes to our unified experience. Let us start with an animal's cognitive experience to establish a baseline, and then note what is distinctive of the human animal's experience.[18]

Engaging with the Environment: Proper Senses, Common Sense, Imagination

Imagine a crocodile basking in the Nile, observing a goat who comes to the water's edge to drink. The goat is acting through its "sensible qualities" on the crocodile's external senses. Through its color, it acts on the crocodile's vision. By splashing about and generating air vibrations, it acts on the crocodile's auditory system.[19] Through its goaty odor, it acts on the crocodile's sense of smell. The goat is thus unwittingly generating instances of "sensible being" in the crocodile's various sense organs, by bestowing on those organs forms (the "sensible species") that are propagated from forms in the goat itself.

Importantly, each sensible, as it is generated in the appropriate sense, is always conditioned by what Aquinas calls the "common sensibles": motion and rest, magnitude (which can be spatial or temporal, and includes shape), number, and unity.[20] The reason is that the goat is a body, extended in three dimensions and exhibiting motions that take up time. And thus the goat's actions on the crocodile's senses are all conditioned by *quantity* in various ways. For instance, the goat's colors have sizes and shapes ("magnitude") and are arranged into a pattern of color variation whose various parts are different from but contiguous with each other ("number"), all of which go to make up one visual whole ("unity"). Moreover, as the goat splashes this way and that, its hair moves and catches the light differently, so the goat-shaped collection of colors is itself continuously in motion, changing in size or shape or hue ("motion"). As the crocodile observes the goat, corresponding changes in sensible being occur in the crocodile's eye.

Its vision is "in motion" with the goat's motion, so to speak. Similarly, when the crocodile hears the goat splashing, it hears not just sounds, but sounds in motion, lasting a certain amount of time, with a certain loudness and pattern. The common sensibles are called "common" because they affect many senses.

Let us not forget, however, that the goat is not the only agent acting on the crocodile's senses at that moment. A whole array of substances are acting on the crocodile's senses at every moment, as long as the crocodile is awake: Nile water, sky, birds invisibly rustling about in the reeds, other crocodiles swimming nearby, etc. *All* these agents, and not just the goat, are simultaneously contributing to the sensible being of the crocodile's actualized senses. I would suggest that, for Aquinas, every substance acting on, say, the crocodile's sighted eye contributes a "part" of the visual being that actualizes the crocodile's visual potential at that moment. All these parts make up the total "visual being" in the crocodile's eye at that moment – the total "visual field," as it were. As far as the external senses are concerned, then, it is as though all things acting on sight were one visible whole, and as though all things acting on hearing were one audible whole, etc. It will be the work of the inner senses to distinguish individual substances within that whole.[21]

These five sensory "wholes," each located in its own organ, are drawn together into a single sensory experience by the common sense, which is the first of what Aquinas calls the "internal senses." Common sense is responsible for unifying the crocodile's sensory life so that the different kinds of sensory experience can appear as distinct from each other. Without common sense, Aquinas says, the five senses might just as well be five different animals – one seeing color, another hearing sound, etc. The common sense, however, brings them together into a single sensory whole in which, for example, a goaty scent appears in relation to, and as distinguishable from, a goat-shaped color pattern.[22]

How does common sense relate to the five external senses? It is not a sense for receiving the combined "input" of the five senses, as one might at first suppose.[23] Rather, Aquinas apparently views common sense and the five external senses as a single five-branched sensory unit that is affected by things in the crocodile's neighborhood in five different ways, at five locations in the crocodile's body. Insofar as this sensory unit is taken as one thing, it is "common sense," unifying the crocodile's sensory activity. But insofar as it is taken as divided into five external senses, then it is "sight," or "smell," or "taste," each with its own organ receptive to neighboring things in its own distinctive way.[24]

The multifaceted sensory experience generated in common sense through the five external senses leaves behind a "motion" in another internal sense, the crocodile's *imaginative sense*. This "motion," a likeness of the original sensory experience, can be brought to life again when the original causes are no longer acting on the crocodile.[25] The imaginative sense is also capable of recombining these impressions to form new ones (which occurs randomly in dreaming, but deliberately in human creative activities, as when a fiction author creates an imaginary scene). Hallucinations are the result of mistaking imaginative activity for sensory activity.[26]

Receiving Particular Intentions: Estimative Sense and Memory

As the crocodile silently lurks in the water, then, it is being acted upon by objects within range, which cause in the crocodile a single multidimensional conscious experience in the external senses and common sense, which reverberates in and is preserved by the imaginative sense. But the story of the crocodile's cognitive life does not stop there. Cognitive life is ordered toward the good of the cognizer – here, the crocodile's healthy flourishing. And in order to flourish (including pursuing prey), the crocodile must have a conscious life that is more complex than what we have just described. For instance, in order to attack the goat only at the right time and in the right way, it must be able to pick out the goat from its background and recognize it as edible, while simultaneously identifying and avoiding any nearby threats to itself. In addition, it must have some expectation of how the goat is likely to behave when attacked, and adjust its mode of attack in response to past failures. This additional complexity is contributed by two remaining potentials for conscious being, located in other parts of the crocodile's brain: the estimative sense and memory.

Recall that our crocodile is being acted upon by many substances at once – goat, Nile water, sky, clouds, fish, wind – whose effects in the crocodile's senses, unified by its common sense, make up one sensory "whole." At the visual level, the crocodile sees patterns of colored shapes within a horizon of vision, and visually differentiates the green parts from the brown-and-white part. But in order to isolate one part of the whole as this individual goat, and other parts as those reeds, the *estimative sense* is needed (also called the *cogitative sense* or particular reason in humans).[27]

The estimative sense is affected by certain aspects of the goat that are not sensory qualities, but that are relevant to the crocodile's flourishing, including, most fundamentally, the goat's being *this individual*. Acting through the external and common senses, the goat causes forms in the estimative sense that Aquinas calls "intentions."[28] The crocodile's formation by the particular intention for *this individual* (this goat) explains how the crocodile isolates the goat as one discrete thing within its sensory field, bearing a certain set of sensory qualities.

In appearing to the crocodile as this individual, the goat also appears as relevant to the crocodile's own flourishing – that is, as "this edible prey."[29] In return, the crocodile would appear to the goat – if the goat were lucky enough to spot it lurking there – as "this threat," i.e., something from which to flee. The estimative sense is thus intimately linked to the animal's appetites, which are grounded in its nature, with its distinctive place in its ecosystem. It is because the goat is suitable prey *for crocodiles* that it appears as "actionable" (specifically, edible) to this crocodile. And this edible appearance in turn explains why the crocodile desires to eat it and moves to attack.[30]

A thing's "actionable" appearance is thus conditioned by the perceiving animal's nature. The baby goat appears to the mother goat as "to be suckled," but, to the crocodile, an individual fitting the same pattern appears as "to be eaten." In some animals, however, these actionable appearances can be reconfigured through association with pleasure and pain.[31] For instance, if a crocodile receives an electric shock every time it attacks a goat, eventually individuals fitting goaty descriptions will appear to the crocodile as "to be avoided" rather than "to be eaten."

The reason that the estimative sense can be trained in some animals is that it is paired with *memory*, which is continuously capturing and storing estimative intentions,[32] presumably in cooperation with the imaginative sense's capturing and storing of sensory fields. As similar intentions (this brown-and-white, splashing, smelly, edible individual) repeatedly actualize the estimative sense, leaving their trace in memory, the crocodile becomes accustomed to certain recurring patterns. For instance, the mature crocodile will have expectations about how individuals that fit goaty patterns will thrash when attacked, and that smaller ones are easier prey than larger ones.[33] But again, none of this is equivalent to understanding *what a goat is*, for which intellect is required.

The crocodile's cognitive life can thus be summarized as follows: The external senses together with common sense are responsible for the "baseline" being of an animal's conscious experience, with all its colors, textures, shapes, movements, and patterns. Through the conscious being generated in those external senses (which also reverberates in imagination), the goat's causal power presses further into the crocodile's brain, generating its "particular intention" in the estimative power (which also reverberates in memory). At this new estimative level of conscious being, the crocodile now distinguishes the goat from its surroundings as *this action-relevant individual*.

In short, the goat is assimilating the crocodile to itself through a series of sensory "instruments," with each conscious "level" serving as instrument for acting on the next one up. Many goats must act on the crocodile over time in order for this assimilation to reach completeness in a mature crocodile familiar with the ways of goats.

INTELLECT

In assimilating the crocodile to itself, the goat falls short in one respect: It has not assimilated the crocodile to its own *goat essence*.[34] The crocodile remains ignorant of *what a goat is*: It perceives individual goats, not *as goats*, but only as individuals exemplifying recurring pattern of characteristics. It is the task of the cognitive potential called "intellect" to allow for that final stage of assimilation, and to explain how conscious experience can include the *kind of being* that an individual is.

Humans are the only animals with intellect. And intellect is the only cognitive potential that is "incorporeal":[35] The potential for intellectual experience is not a potential of a body part (eye, brain), but of the human soul.[36] Aquinas thus says that the human soul is on the "horizon" between bodies and pure intellects, i.e., angels.[37] Our intellectual life opens up to us realities beyond all bodily restrictions to the this-here-and-now – whether these are the essences of bodily substances, such as goatness or beauty, or non-bodily existences like angels and God and even the human soul itself.[38]

To see what intellect adds to human conscious life, imagine a human traveler, Max, observing the shoreline from a passing boat. Now Max has the same bodily cognitive potentials as the crocodile. In humans, though, Aquinas upgrades the estimative sense to a "cogitative" sense that is ordered toward the further activities of intellect and is responsive to intellectual guidance.[39] (*Cautionary note*: In discussing human cognition, Aquinas often groups the last three inner senses – imaginative, cogitative, and memory – under the label 'imagination,' whose forms he calls "phantasms."[40])

But Max's soul carries an additional, non-bodily potential: intellect. So for Max, there is the possibility of being assimilated also to the *nature* that this goat shares with other goats. And now a metaphysical problem surfaces: How can a goat actualize this intellectual potential? For Aquinas, non-bodily agents can act on bodies; an angel could whisk the goat out from the jaws of the crocodile. But the reverse is not true. Goats cannot act on angels. And similarly, since the human soul has a kind of being that is non-bodily, goats cannot act on the human soul. So the goat can cause in Max sensory being and thereby cogitative being, because the potentials it is actualizing, and the instruments whereby it acts, are all bodily. But its causal influence will run out at *non-bodily, intellectual being*.[41]

As a result, many of Aquinas's sources and contemporaries conclude that not goats, but *other intellects* – a separate cosmic intellect, or angels, or God himself, for instance – are the causes of intellectual being in us, assimilating us to the "goatness" that they already possess.[42] Aquinas, however, makes both goats and an intellectual cause responsible for our intellectual experience, while insisting that the relevant intellectual cause is *something in the human soul*. Thus, in addition to the soul's potential for intellectual being, which he calls "possible intellect," he posits an active power in the soul for causing intellectual being: the so-called agent intellect.[43]

The agent intellect must collaborate with phantasms in order to cause intellectual experience. On the one side, Max's agent intellect can bring about effects in non-bodily, intelligible, intellectual being, but it lacks any power of making something *goatlike*. On the other side, the goat can make things like itself, but it cannot have non-bodily, intelligible, intellectual effects. Working together, each supplies what is lacking in the other, to produce *intelligible goatness* in the soul, in an action Aquinas calls "abstraction."[44] (Of course, the goat's activity must be mediated through the external and internal senses, as above. Within Max's cognitive system, the last bodily "carrier" of the goat's power to make something like itself is the phantasm of the goat as "this individual exhibiting such and such a pattern."[45])

The goat phantasm and the agent intellect together produce a *new form* that is properly an *intelligible and intellectual form*, the form of universal "goatness."[46] This new form, the "intelligible species," informs Max's soul, actualizing its potential for intellectual being, and conforming it to the essence of the goat.[47] (In his technical vocabulary, Aquinas says that the agent intellect "abstracts an intelligible species from the phantasm," and this species "informs the possible intellect."[48])

With his soul formed in this way, Max now possesses *actual intellectual being, i.e., conscious intellectual experience*: that is, Max now has the thought, "goat." Crucially, this intellectual experience is equally the intellectual manifestation of goatness in him. Thus, Aquinas identifies the "intellect in actuality" with the "intelligible in actuality" – meaning simply that intellectual experience is at one and the same time both (1) the soul's acquiring intellectual being and (2) goatness's being realized in the soul.[49] This intellectual experience adds a richness to Max's total experience of the goat, which is lacking in the crocodile's parallel experience. Max grasps the goat not only as *this individual exhibiting such and such a pattern* (through his internal and external senses), but also as a *goat* (due to his intellect). In other words, Max's intellectual experience expands his awareness of the goat to include *what this thing is*.

By acknowledging that intellectual experience is *part of a unified conscious life*, we can make sense of Aquinas's famous remark that human beings know essences by "turning to" phantasms.[50] What he means is that, in this life, Max's grasp of 'goat' or 'goatness' is always the grasp of *the essence of some individual*. Even if there is no determinate individual that Max has in mind when he later ponders what a goat is and how goats are different from sheep, he cannot help conceptualizing goatness in terms of *what makes individual goats be what they are*. This is true even if he is thinking about 'goatness' in the abstract; the project is always ultimately to understand *concrete individual goats*. Human intellectual knowledge "turns to phantasms" in the sense that, in our present condition, we grasp essences only as what makes individual objects of sense be what they are.[51]

But how much do we know when we grasp goatness? At first, very little. For Aquinas, human beings start with an "indistinct" grasp of essences.[52] In order to encounter the goat *as a goat*, Max does not need to be a zoologist, capable of explaining what is distinctive of goats, or classifying them in relation to other species. Indeed, most of us probably still only understand 'goat' as "a kind of four-legged animal" fitting a certain description and/or answering to a certain name in our local language.

In short, an initial understanding of goatness may provide little more than an intellectual placeholder that makes it possible to inquire further into *what kind* of being a goat is. That further inquiry involves what Aquinas calls the "second and third intellectual operations," and finally takes us into the territory of what is now called "epistemology."

KNOWLEDGE AND UNDERSTANDING

Growing toward Truth

Aquinas does not identify a discrete domain of study that perfectly aligns with contemporary epistemology, which has historically been largely concerned with evidence for beliefs. For Aquinas, epistemological questions arise from continuing the conversation that we have been having about *acts of cognition* (itself part of a larger theory of living natures). The way he thinks about it, the causal pressure from other substances only takes us so far. When Max is attending to the goat *as goat*, he is performing a kind of act that Aquinas labels the "first intellectual operation," namely, contemplation. This grasp of goatness usually remains quite indistinct, unless Max takes steps to develop it further, so as to achieve deeper and more informed contemplative actions. This further development requires a project of forming new judgments and stabilizing them to the extent possible, through reasoning on the basis of available evidence.

The acts contributing to this project are what Aquinas calls the "second and third intellectual operations" – namely, "composition and division" and "reasoning." Since these acts can easily fail, one must learn how to perform them well. The standards they must meet, and the criteria for performing them well (which address many of the questions that we would call epistemological), are articulated in what Aquinas calls logic and rhetoric.[53]

For Aquinas, practicing the second and third intellectual operations amounts to a process of intellectual self-development, a process whereby a certain kind of living thing – the human animal – grows to intellectual maturity. This intellectual growth has as its goal the mature intellect's *truth*: that is, its conforming or measuring up to the standard set by beings.[54] In other words, truth is the teleological good of intellect,[55] and our natural tendency toward this good is what impels us to "inquire" and develop its knowledge, so as to measure up better to beings as they are. Thus, truth for Aquinas is richer than mere "truth value" – that is, the labeling of propositions as either "T" or "F." Truth as conformity is measured by a sliding scale along which the intellect approximates being to greater and lesser degrees. Similarly, intellectual perfection does not consist in having as many true beliefs and as few false beliefs as possible, but rather consists in a condition in which the intellect's own internal complexity most perfectly reflects the complexity of being itself.[56]

Judging and Forming Propositions

Most literature on Aquinas calls the second intellectual operation "judging." But Aquinas himself usually calls it "composing and dividing."[57] What, if anything, is the difference?

"Judging" in its most basic sense in Aquinas is simply a distinguishing, and it happens any time anything complex is apprehended. For instance, faced with the goat's brown-and-white pattern, Max's sight "discerns" or "judges" between brown and white, meaning that when both colors are visible at once, they show up precisely *as different* from each other. Similarly, as we saw, the common sense "judges" between colors and sounds.[58]

Judging in this broad sense of "distinguishing" is just the apprehension of a complex whole *as complex*, i.e., such that the different parts of the whole appear as different from each other (or to put it another way, so that the parts appear *as parts*, in relation to each other). Presumably the first act of intellect already involves judging in this sense of apprehending a complex. After all, in grasping some "one" that is 'goatness,' Max nonetheless grasps it as a *complex* whole (a brown-and-white, gamboling, splashing, bleating kind of being). If not, there would be no material to work with as he reflects later about what is essential to being a goat.[59]

Now the second intellectual operation, "composition and division," is a *special kind of judging or distinguishing* – i.e., special in that the intellect *creates* the relevant complex whole on its own initiative, *bringing together* single thought-parts into a thought-whole, or *dividing them* from each other.[60] These humanly constructed thought complexes are what Aquinas calls "propositions," which are expressible in spoken or written sentences in some human language.[61] Propositions produced by composition are expressible in affirmative language – "A goat is a kind of animal" – while those produced by division are expressible in negative language: "Goats do not fly."

The fact that propositions are *expressible* in human languages does not mean that they *are* linguistic entities. Of course, it is impossible to talk about propositions without expressing them in some language, such as in English sentences. Nevertheless, that should not mislead us into thinking that the activities of composing or dividing rearrange *linguistic items*, i.e., terms into sentences. Rather, they rearrange the *being of thought*, or intellectual being. Indeed, the actualized intellect is *rearranging itself*, forming itself into thought complexes. These complex structures of intellectual being can be expressed in some human language, but are not themselves linguistic entities.[62]

Degrees of Certainty in Assent

Now, Aquinas insists that truth occurs "primarily" in composing and dividing.[63] But truth is intellect's conformity to beings, and *every* instance of intellectual being can be evaluated for conformity to beings. Why, then, do truth and falsity apply "primarily" to composing and dividing?

The reason is that Aquinas construes composing and dividing as activities of *learning about the world*, i.e., something the intellect actively does to move itself from known to unknown.[64] When the intellect is initially formed through the natural causal activity of the goat and the agent intellect, there is simply *the way goatness appears*. But with composing and dividing, the intellect is beginning to re-form itself actively, taking initiative to develop what it received passively from goats. In doing so it aims at its own good – namely, to be more conformed to beings in all their complexity.

Therefore, the forming of propositions such as "goats are smaller than crocodiles" typically carries a *commitment* to goats being this way, *taking a stand* on how goats are in their own existence.[65] Aquinas describes this intellectual commitment as "judging existence,"[66] "assenting," or "terminating inquiry."[67] The intellect may be impelled to commit itself by the inexorable causal pressure of the thing it is studying. Or its commitment may be freely moved by the will.[68]

Sometimes Aquinas speaks of composing and dividing as though it always implies this commitment or assent.[69] And that is why truth and falsity "primarily" pertain to this second intellectual operation: In actively committing itself to a thought complex, the intellect is *adding* something beyond what it passively receives, opening up the possibility of its doing so wrongly (falsity).[70]

Indeed, in composing or dividing, the intellect normally does commit itself. When Max thinks that "goats are animals" or that "this crocodile aims to eat that goat," he *intends to express something about goatness as it really is*, or about *the actual threat posed by this crocodile to that goat*.

But Aquinas also recognizes that we can commit ourselves with greater or lesser degrees of certainty, or not at all (as when identifying a hypothesis for further investigation). Thus, he distinguishes various degrees of "certitude and firmness" with which one might hold a proposition.[71] In fact, he thinks that there is a degree of certitude appropriate to any given situation of assent, so that it is possible to assert a proposition with too much confidence.[72] The appropriate degree of confidence is determined by *whether the proposition itself is self-evident or not*, and *how this particular knower has arrived at the proposition* (e.g., through reasoning, testimony, etc.).

Aquinas distinguishes "per se known" (i.e., self-evident) propositions from those whose truth is evident only through something else. In self-evident propositions, the subject and predicate are essentially related in such a way that once one understands both terms, one sees that the proposition *must* be true. In other words, the truth of the proposition is evident from its own terms.

But for Aquinas, a proposition can be self-evident *in itself*, without its evidence being apparent to everyone. Some self-evident propositions, such as "Every whole is greater than its parts," are evident to everyone, because everyone understands those terms. Other self-evident propositions, however, are not evident to all knowers, because experience and education are required to understand the terms well enough to see their essential relationship. To use Aquinas's example, the proposition "Anything that is not a body is not circumscribed by place" is evident only to "the wise," because one needs a certain amount of education to see the essential relationship between place and body.[73] Another interesting example is as follows: The proposition "God exists" is self-evident in itself, but not evident to us, since we cannot conceptualize God's essence so as to *see* its identity with his existing. The truth of this proposition becomes evident to us only through reasoning.[74] The ability to recognize self-evident propositions *as* self-evident is what Aquinas calls the virtue of *intellectus* or insight.[75]

Another group of propositions, however, are not self-evident, because the terms are related only contingently. These are propositions such as "the crocodile is aiming to eat that goat" or "goats in this region are unusually small." Since there is no *essential* relationship between regional goats and smallness, the corresponding proposition does not carry its own evidence within it, and must be made evident through something else.

Now if the knower understands a proposition as self-evident, the proposition itself compels his assent, and he holds it with complete certitude. But if a proposition lacks self-evidence *to him* (whether or not the proposition is self-evident in itself), he must move himself voluntarily to assent to it, and may hold it with varying degrees of firmness.[76] The appropriate degree of firmness will depend on whatever has inclined him toward voluntary assent by lending that proposition a borrowed "evidence" – for example, sensation, testimony (human and divine), and arguments.[77] The firmness of adherence should be calibrated to the weight of this borrowed evidence.

Thus, Aquinas differentiates several degrees of "firmness" in assent. For instance, if Max is not drawn either toward "the crocodile is aiming to eat that goat" or its opposite, "the crocodile is not aiming to eat that goat," he is in a condition of suspended judgment (*dubitatio*, having an unresolved question). When he "leans toward" the former proposition for insignificant reasons (e.g., from a hunch that this crocodile looks especially mean), he is "suspecting" it to be true. But if he solidly inclines toward one proposition while retaining a "fear of the opposite" proposition, then he is "opining" it to be true.[78]

Reasoning

I have just mentioned several sources that may lend external weight, inclining Max to assent to a proposition about goats. One of these deserves special mention – namely, *a set of propositions taken together as an argument*, from which the target proposition is drawn as a conclusion. For instance, in thinking about how to classify goats relative to other animals, Max might reason: "Sheep are woolly. But goats are not woolly. Therefore goats are not sheep."

Drawing conclusions from premises is the third kind of intellectual operation, namely, reasoning. Like composition and division, reasoning is a motion of intellectual self-development, from the less distinct to the more distinct, from ignorance to familiarity, from potency to actuality – as always, with the goal of becoming more and more assimilated to being.

Now the goal of reasoning, broadly speaking, is a true conclusion: literally, the proposition that "concludes" or terminates inquiry. And we can distinguish two kinds of reasoning depending on whether its weight *inclines* the intellect to assent to the conclusion ("probable" or "dialectical" reasoning), or *compels* assent ("demonstrative" reasoning).[79]

Probable reasoning results in what was described above as "opinion."[80] The evidence in the premises lends weight to the conclusion, making it probable without compelling assent. Some examples, such as inductive predictions, are unsurprising:

(1) Crocodiles eat sheep, birds, fish, and other small- to mid-sized animals.
(2) Therefore, they also eat goats.

But other examples may surprise the modern reader. For instance, most deductive arguments are merely probable for Aquinas, because their premises, though true, do not express necessary relationships:

(1) What makes noise is liable to attract predator attention.
(2) The goat is making noise.
(3) Therefore, the goat is liable to attract predator attention.

(1) pairs two actions – noisemaking and predator attention – that often occur together, but are not necessarily related. (Consider: Some predators hunt by smell rather than hearing, and some noisemakers – e.g., lions – have no predators). Regarding (2), an individual creature's

relationship to its actions is always contingent; there is no necessary relationship between this goat and this action of noisy splashing. Now, on condition that Max assents to the premises, he will be compelled to assent to the conclusion. Nevertheless, his assent to the conclusion is not *absolutely* compelled, because it depends on premises that do not compel him to assent to them.

The stronger form of reasoning is *demonstrative,* in which the conclusion is "evident" from premises that express necessary relationships.[81] Demonstration is the highest achievement of human reasoning, for Aquinas. Demonstrative arguments must meet high standards that guarantee the necessity and evidence of the conclusion. In Aquinas's terminology, an intellect that is practiced in demonstrating has the intellectual "virtue of science" (*scientia*). To "know *p* scientifically" (*scire*) is to assent to *p*, dispositionally or actually, on the basis of demonstrative reasoning. Such assent is compelled by premises that are themselves individually compelling.[82]

Now, Aquinas distinguishes two kinds of demonstrative arguments: "*quia* demonstrations," which merely show *that* something is the case, and "*propter quid* demonstrations," which explain *why* something is the case.[83]

Quia demonstrations proceed from better-known effects to their less-known causes.[84] For instance, suppose that Max knows that there is a distinctive way in which crocodiles lunge only toward prey; and he knows that crocodiles lunge in just that way toward goats. He thus concludes: "Goats are prey for crocodiles." Here he is reasoning from an effect (the lunging) to the cause (the goat's status as crocodile-prey). The premises express necessary relationships grounded in the natures of crocodiles. So he now scientifically knows *that* goats are prey for crocodiles.

Propter quid demonstrations, however, are explanatory. Correspondingly, their premises must meet a higher bar: In addition to being necessarily true, they must also be self-evident or at least reducible to further self-evident premises.[85] For instance, Max, now wondering *why* goats are crocodile-prey, could reason as follows:

(1) Crocodiles are meat eaters.

(2) Goats are meaty.

(3) Therefore, crocodiles are goat eaters.

The reasoning does not establish any new propositions, but rather *explains* an already known proposition: Crocodiles eat goats. The premises, if not self-evident, can be deduced from self-evident propositions about the natures of goats and crocodiles. (The definition of a creature's nature will always include its material makeup, organic structures, and nutritional needs, from which it can be shown that crocodiles are by nature meat eaters, and that goats are meaty.) Someone who performs demonstrative reasoning while understanding all the premises is compelled absolutely to accept the conclusion.

Aquinas's distinction between these two goals of demonstration – showing *that* versus explaining *why* goats are prey for crocodiles – underscores something important about his theory of human reasoning. In contemporary epistemology, attaining perfection as a knower has often been equated with maximizing the number of true beliefs one holds, and minimizing the number of false ones. But, for Aquinas, the goal of assenting to true propositions, while important, takes a back seat to the greater perfection which consists in *explaining things in terms of their natures.* (Similarly, some contemporary epistemologists and philosophers of science have emphasized the importance of "understanding" in the sense of grasping "how things hang together" over "knowledge" in the narrower sense of justified true belief.[86])

In other words, *explaining why* is the most perfect way of intellectually conforming to beings as they are. Being is complex, in Aquinas's view, and true propositions assimilate us to that complexity. But that complexity is not mere static arrangement of parts in a whole; it is organized in *hierarchies of overlapping and interlocking causal dependencies.* Matter supports form, and form gives being to matter. Substances sustain their parts, and the parts constitute the whole substance; actualities are sustained by agents. Final causes (goals) draw forth actions oriented toward them. The goat's nature grounds its natural properties, including its powers and ultimately its actions. The list can be multiplied according to all the modes of dependency that Aquinas's metaphysics identifies. These manifold modes of dependency are part of the very fabric of complex beings themselves. That is why the perfection of "science" requires the ability to demonstrate the *why*. We are not assimilated to complex beings as they really are, unless we are assimilated to the *hierarchies of dependency* weaving through that complexity. To be intellectually assimilated to hierarchies of dependency *just is* what it means to *have an explanation*, for Aquinas.

For Aquinas, then, perceiving, imagining, wondering, contemplating, abstracting, inquiring, composing, judging, assenting, and reasoning are part of the *life of embodied cognitive natures*. His theory of cognition and his epistemology must both be understood in light of how such natures are moved, or move themselves, from potency to actuality and from imperfection to perfection. Human and non-human animals are surrounded by beings that are constantly pressing in, assimilating this special cognitive nature to themselves by generating conscious experiences. We humans – endowed with agent intellects – have the special task of collaborating with these external causes to generate non-bodily intellectual experiences in ourselves, whereby we understand the *whatness* of beings. Thus formed, we can embark on a program of self-improvement by rearranging our own intellectual being into complexes that better "measure up" to the structure and complexity of created being. The epistemological and logical norms that these self-rearranging activities should follow, therefore, are simply rules for vital well-functioning: the self-development of an intelligent organism.

NOTES

1   *ST* I q.4 a.3: "Every agent makes something like itself"; J. F. Wippel, "Thomas Aquinas on Our Knowledge of God and the Axiom that Every Agent Produces Something Like Itself" in *Metaphysical Themes in Thomas Aquinas II* (Washington, DC: The Catholic University of America Press, 2007), pp. 152–71.

2 In the first *Cambridge Companion to Aquinas*, MacDonald contends that Aquinas's epistemology is rooted in his cognition theory and metaphysics. See S. MacDonald, "Theory of Knowledge" in N. Kretzmann and E. Stump (eds.), *The Cambridge Companion to Aquinas* (Cambridge and New York: Cambridge University Press, 1993), p. 160. Taking this thought a step further, I suggest that the reason for this cognition–epistemology relationship is Aquinas's notion of mind as a *nature* tending toward certain acts, a subset of which are of interest to epistemologists.

3 See examples in R. Pasnau and C. Shields, *The Philosophy of Aquinas* (Boulder, CO: Westview Press, 2004), pp. 177–9; P. Porro, *Thomas Aquinas: A Historical and Philosophical Profile*, translated by J. G. Trabbic and R. W. Nutt (Washington, DC: The Catholic University of America Press, 2016), pp. 229–35; A. Lisska, *Aquinas's Theory of Perception: An Analytic Reconstruction* (Oxford: Oxford University Press, 2016), p. 194, despite earlier using 'potency' and 'disposition' language on pp. 95–103.

4 *QDA* q.12; *ST* I q.77 a.3; G. Frost, "Aquinas on Passive Powers," *Vivarium* 59 (2021): 33–51, here, pp. 44–9, showing that Aquinas's "potency for being heated" is identical with a "potency to be hot," even if they conceptually differ.

5 For these labels, see, for example, *QDSC* q.10, ad 3. For "imagination existing in actuality," see *In IV Sent.*, d.17 q.1 a.3 ad qc.3 ad 1. The "in actuality (*in actu*)" phrase is his standard label for actual being, as distinct from the corresponding potential: For example, "water that is hot in actuality" is just hot water; K. Fisher, "Thomas Aquinas on Hylomorphism and the In-Act Principle," *British Journal for the History of Philosophy* 25 (2017): 1053–72.

6 *QDSC* q.10, a.3, equating the actuality of the sight-potential (*visus in actu*) with actual seeing (*videre in actu*).

7 See, for example, J. F. Silva, "Medieval Theories of Active Perception: An Overview" in J. F. Silva and M. Yrjönsuuri (eds.), *Active Perception in the History of Philosophy* (Cham: Springer, 2014), p. 118. This standard reading of Aquinas arises from texts such as *ST* I q.79 a.2 s.c., identifying *intelligere* (intellectual contemplation) with *pati* (being affected).

8 *In I Sent.*, d.40 q.1 a.1 ad qc. 1, distinguishing sensing *qua* species-reception, from sensing *qua* "act following upon sense perfected by a species"; *Quodl* VIII q.2 a.1, making sense-action ("judging") follow from

a sense "already formed"; *In II DA* c.26, distinguishing sight as "being immuted" from sight as "judging"; *QDV* q.8 a.6: "Intellection follows upon the passion [species-reception] and action [abstraction of the species] as an effect upon a cause." See Porro, *Thomas Aquinas*, p. 233.

9   *QDV* q.8 a.13 ad 2. Aquinas's theory of attention is underdeveloped, but see his treatment of prayer (*In IV Sent.*, d.15, q.4, a.2, ad qc.4–5; *ST* II-II q.83 a.13); and his account of "reading someone's thoughts" (*QDV* q.8 a.13; *QDM* q.16 a.8), discussed in T. S. Cory, "Attention, Intentionality, and Mind-Reading in Aquinas's De malo 16.8" in M. V. Dougherty (ed.), *Aquinas's Disputed Questions on Evil: A Critical Guide* (Cambridge: Cambridge University Press, 2016), pp. 164–91, here pp. 164–6.

10 See *In II DA* c.24, describing sensory potentials as forms of a "magnitude," i.e., the spatially extended sense organ; *In DS*, proem.; *ST* I q.54 a.5.

11 See *In II DA* c.24, on the organ's form as its power, and the "complexion" required for touch.

12 *SCG* 2.62.

13 *In II DA* c.5.

14 *In DS* c.1.

15 This "non-competitive" acquisition of a bodily quality is just what Aquinas means by the "spiritual immutation" of the organ in sensation (see *In II DA* c.14; *ST* I q.78 a.3). I owe this interpretation to D. Cory, "Agency and Materiality in Aquinas's Soul Theory," PhD thesis, The Catholic University of America (2018), pp. 95–120. On the physical non-materiality of sense, see also P. Hoffman, "St. Thomas Aquinas on the Halfway State of Sensible Being," *Philosophical Review* 99 (1990): 73–92; M. Burnyeat, "Aquinas on Spiritual Change" in D. Perler (ed.), *Ancient and Medieval Theories of Intentionality* (Leiden: Brill, 2001), pp. 129–53.

16 See the "dubitatio" in *In II DA* c.24. He clarifies that the agent is not the form of the sense object, but rather the substance so formed, for example, the "colored stone" acting in virtue of color. Thus, we see *something colored*, not *color*, which helps Aquinas explain why it is ultimately possible for intellect to abstract a concept of substance from sensory experience.

17 *ST* I q.78 a.3.

18 In discussing animal experience in Aquinas, I am indebted especially to D. De Haan, "Perception and the *Vis Cogitativa*: A Thomistic Analysis of

Aspectual, Actional, and Affectional Percepts," *American Catholic Philosophical Quarterly* 88 (2014): 397–437; D. De Haan, "Approaching Other Animals with Caution: Exploring Insights from Aquinas's Psychology," *New Blackfriars* 100 (2019): 715–37; D. De Haan, "Aquinas on Sensing, Perceiving, Thinking, Understanding, and Cognizing Individuals" in E. Baltuta (ed.), *Medieval Perceptual Puzzles: Theories of Sense-Perception in the 13th and 14th Centuries* (Leiden: Brill, 2019), pp. 238–68. See also Lisska, *Aquinas's Theory of Perception.*

19 Sight and sound are the most important because they "show forth many differences among things" and hence facilitate "prudent" judgments in higher animals; see *In DS* c.1.

20 See *In II DA* c.25. It is important to emphasize that the common sensibles are not objects of sensation independent of the proper sensibles such as color and sound. Rather, the eye sees movement and shape insofar as *a colored thing* is moving and shaped.

21 Aquinas says very little about unified sensory fields, but the account seems to demand them, and he seems to acknowledge them in a few scattered remarks. For example, someone high up "sees all at once" everyone traveling on a road (*ST* I q.14 a.13 ad 3); and sight can be carried to many "as one, so that they are seen all at once," or "as many, that is, considering each part in itself, in which way they are not all seen at once" (*QDV* q.8 a.14). On the potential divisibility of what is visually continuous, see *In DS* c.14, 17.

22 *In II DA* c.27.

23 In *In DS* c.18, Aquinas denies that common sense is a single receiver for all sensations, as though all sensible forms were combined stereoscopically into a single form to be received by common sense. Such a combination is "impossible" for reasons unstated, but he probably means that it is impossible for a single physical organ to be structured for susceptibility to all sensibles. The physical makeup necessary for an organ to receive one sensible would be at odds with those necessary to receive another sensible. That is why the eye and nose must be different body parts in the first place.

24 For the analogy of a single point as the termination of multiple lines, which can be considered differently as one versus as many, see *In II DA* c.27; *In DS* c.18. Aquinas also says that common sense is the "root" of the external senses, and that they "participate" in its power (*In II DA* c.27), or

that they are its "instruments" (*In DS* c.18), or that its "one power extends itself to all the objects of the five senses" (*ST* I q.1 a.3 ad 2).

25 See *In III Sent.*, d.27 q.3 a.1; *SCG* 2 c.67; *SCG* 2 c.73; *ST* I q.17 a.2 ad 2.

26 *SCG* 3 c.104; *ST* I q.17 a.2 ad 2; *ST* I q.54 a.5 ad 1.

27 See *ST* I, q.78 a.4; *SCG* 2 c.60, and for discussion of the cogitative, De Haan, "Perception and the *Vis Cogitativa*"; G. Klubertanz, *The Discursive Power: Sources and Doctrine of the* Vis Cogitativa *according to St. Thomas Aquinas* (Saint Louis: The Modern Schoolman, 1952). A. Oelze, *Animal Rationality: Later Medieval Theories 1250–1350* (Leiden: Brill, 2018), pp. 57–69, makes a case for reading Aquinas's animal estimation as mere stimulus and response. I take estimation instead to be a kind of *conscious being*, and hold (with De Haan, "Perception and the *Vis Cogitativa*") that animals grasp individuals as exemplifying *recurring patterns*, i.e., as falling under a composite notion (one could here use the language of "sortal") applicable to many individuals. This "sortal" enables the animal to "sort" (or in Aquinas's language "collate") individuals according to pattern, despite not being able to conceptualize the *essence* of those individuals.

28 *In II DA* c.13; De Haan, "Aquinas on Sensing, Perceiving, Thinking, Understanding, and Cognizing Individuals," §3, notes that the animal discerns *only* the particular intentions of neighboring substances that are relevant to its flourishing. The point is that the crocodile *sees* whatever is in its visual field (i.e., acting on its vision), but only *picks out as individuals from that field* what is relevant to its flourishing. Note that the goat is sensible (i.e., capable of acting on a perceiver) only through the agency of its sensible qualities. But through that agency, it can communicate more of itself than just its own sensible qualities. This "more of itself" (e.g., its individuality, threat level, essence) is communicated to the estimative/cogitative power or intellect. When these are detected instantly upon sensing the goat, Aquinas says that they are "sensed *per accidens*." See again De Haan, "Aquinas on Sensing, Perceiving, Thinking, Understanding, and Cognizing Individuals."

29 *In II DA* c.13; *In DS* c.1.

30 See *ST* Ia-IIa q.29 a.1; *In II Sent.*, d.24 q.2 a.1; *In I Met.*, lect. 1.

31 *QDV* q.24 a.2 ad 7.

32 For Aquinas's theory of memory, see *QDV* q.10 aa.1–3; *ST* Ia q.78 a.4; *In DM* c.1.

33   In humans, this is called *experientia* (familiarity), but the phenomenon in humans is different, because familiarization is also guided by intellect through rational inquiry (*In I Met.* c.15; *In II PA* lect. 20). See M. Barker, "Experience and Experimentation: The Meaning of *Experimentum* in Aquinas," *The Thomist* 76 (2012): 37–71, here pp. 57–71.

34   See *Quodl* VIII q.2 a.1.

35   See *SCG* 2 cc.49–51; A. Wood, *Thomas Aquinas on the Immateriality of the Human Intellect* (Washington, DC: The Catholic University of America Press, 2020). Only incorporeal being can be assimilated to essences in a properly *universal* way, because only incorporeal being can be related indifferently to many individuals (*ST* I q.76 a.2 ad 3).

36   *DUI* c.3.

37   *SCG* 2 c.68.

38   Indeed, in grasping abstracted essences, the soul already is grasping itself; see *ST* I q.89 a.1.

39   See, for example, *QDV* q.14 a.1 ad 9; *ST* I q.78 a.4; *QDA* q.13; discussed in De Haan, "Perception and the *Vis Cogitativa.*"

40   See, for example, texts contrasting sense, imagination, and intellect, as the three main cognitive divisions (*Quodl.* VIII q.2 a.1 s.c.; *ST* I q.84 a.7). For "phantasms" as the material for intellectual abstraction, see, for example, *ST* I q.76 a.1; "phantasm" in this sense presumably incorporates both imaginative forms and cogitative intentions.

41   See *Quodl* VIII q.2 a.1.

42   *QDA* q.5.

43   *ST* I q.79 aa.1–5; *QDA* aa.3–5; *QDSC* aa.9–10.

44   *Quodl* VIII q.2 a.1.

45   *QDV* q.8 a.9; *ST* I q.55 a.2 ad 2.

46   See T. S. Cory, "Rethinking Abstractionism: Aquinas's Intellectual Light and Some Arabic Sources," *Journal of the History of Philosophy* 53 (2015): 607–46, against the standard reading of Aquinas's abstraction as stripping out content (as in N. Kretzmann, "Philosophy of Mind" in Kretzmann and Stump (eds.), *The Cambridge Companion to Aquinas*, p. 142).

47   For literature and controversies about Aquinas's intelligible species, see T. S. Cory, "Aquinas's Intelligible Species as Formal Constituents," *Documenti e studi sulla tradizione filosofica medievale* 31 (2020): 261–309.

48   *ST* I qq.84–5.

49 *In IV Sent.*, d.49 q.2 a.1 ad 10; *SCG* 1 c.51.

50 *ST* I q.84 a.7; *In II Sent.*, d.20 q.2 a.2 ad 3. For the soul's cognitive state while separated from the body, see *ST* I q.89.

51 T. S. Cory, "What Is an Intellectual Turn? The *Liber de Causis*, Avicenna, and Aquinas's Turn to Phantasms," *Tópicos* 45 (2013): 129–62; Kretzmann, "Philosophy of Mind," p. 142; G. P. Klubertanz, "St. Thomas and the Knowledge of the Singular," *New Scholasticism* 26 (1952): 135–66, here pp. 164–5; R. Pasnau, *Thomas Aquinas on Human Nature* (Cambridge: Cambridge University Press, 2002), pp. 289–95.

52 *ST* I, q.85 a.3.

53 *In PA*, prologue; see also *In Peri herm.*, Prologue; *In DC*, Prologue. See MacDonald, "Theory of Knowledge," p. 162. On Aquinas's logic, see R. W. Schmidt, *The Domain of Logic according to St. Thomas Aquinas* (The Hague: Martinus Nijhoff, 1966).

54 *QDV* q.1 outlines Aquinas's truth theory; see J. F. Wippel, "Truth in Thomas Aquinas: Part 1," *Review of Metaphysics* 43 (1989): 295–326; J. F. Wippel, "Truth in Thomas Aquinas: Part 2," *Review of Metaphysics* 43 (1990): 543–67.

55 *In III Sent.*, d.23 q.2 a.3 ad qc.3; *SCG* 1 c.61.

56 Our focus here is created being; for intellectual assimilation to the divine essence, see, for example, K. Krause, *Thomas Aquinas on Seeing God: The Beatific Vision in His Commentary on Peter Lombard's Sentences IV.49.2* (Milwaukee: Marquette University Press, 2020).

57 *QDSC* a.9 ad 6. The closest Aquinas comes is to describe what follows upon acts of contemplation as "judging"; in *QDV* q.1 a.3 he uses "composing" and "judging" almost interchangeably, but not quite.

58 *In DS* c.18; *ST* I, q.78 a 4 ad 2. *Quodl.* VIII q.2 a.1 equates sense-judging with sense-action; *ST* I-II q.45 a.4 attributes to sense "instantaneous" judgment without inquiry. For estimative judging, see *ST* I, q.83 a.1; *In II NE* c.11 n.13.

59 See *In I PA* lect. 2, for how inquiry can begin from knowing that a name ('goat') refers to "this."

60 *ST* I q.16 a.2.

61 *ST* I q.85 a.2 ad 3.

62 On the non-linguistic character of thought in Aquinas, see J. O'Callaghan, *Thomist Realism and the Linguistic Turn* (South Bend, IN: University of Notre Dame Press, 2003).

63   *QDV* q.1 a.3.

64   *ST* I q.58 a.4, explaining that angels do not compose and divide because they already "instantly see" in a nature whatever is contained in it.

65   The copula "is" signifies a thing's being (*In I Sent.*, d.33 q.1 a.1).

66   Note that Aquinas associates judging (broadly) with apprehending a thing as existing, probably because judging is (broadly) a discernment of distinctness, and existing implies being distinct from other things. On the relationship between discerning and apprehending a thing as existing, see J. Owens, "Judgment and Truth in Aquinas," *Mediaeval Studies* 32 (1970): 138–58, here pp. 145–6.

67   *QDV* q.14 a.1.

68   *QDV* q.14 a. 1; *ST* II-II q.1 a.4; *ST* II-II q.2 a.9.

69   *In Peri herm.*, Prologue, no. 1.

70   In judging how things really are, intellect is *adding* something from itself (*QDV* q.1 a.3).

71   *ST* II-II q.5 a.4.

72   Overstepping the bounds of evidence to opine falsely is the only way that demonic intellects can be false; see *QDM* q.16 a.6.

73   See *In IV Met.*, lect. 5 n.8; *QDV* q.10 a.12; *ST* I-II q.94 a.2.

74   *ST* I q.2 a.1.

75   *In VI Ethic.*, lect. 5.

76   See *In III Sent.*, d.23 q.2 a.2 ad qc.2. This notion is related to what is now loosely called "strength" or "degree" of belief. Aquinas discusses this aspect of belief usually in connection with a special kind of belief that is faith (*credere*) in divinely revealed truths (see, e.g., *QDV* q.14; *ST* II-II, qq.1–7). Not everything he says about faith applies to all beliefs, but in the course of the discussion he makes known various conditions that govern firmness of assent generally.

77   See, for example, *QDV* q.14, aa.9–10.

78   See *ST* II-II q.1 a.4; *ST* II-II q.2 a.1.

79   See Schmidt, *The Domain of Logic according to St. Thomas Aquinas*, pp. 31–5.

80   See *In PA*, prologue; *In I PA* c.6, c.31.

81   *In I PA*, lect. 13, 16.

82   For Aquinas's theory of demonstration and *scientia* in detail, see J. Jenkins, *Knowledge and Faith in Thomas Aquinas* (Cambridge: Cambridge University Press, 1997), pp. 11–50.

83 For an overview, see *In II DA* c.3.

84 See *In I PA*, lect. 23–5.

85 On the criteria for *propter quid* demonstrations, see *In I PA* lect. 4–20. Such demonstrating is what MacDonald, "Theory of Knowledge," p. 174, associates with "paradigm" *scientia*.

86 See, for example, S. Grimm, "Understanding" in E. N. Zalta (ed.), *The Stanford Encyclopedia of Philosophy* [online] (2021), https://plato .stanford.edu/archives/sum2021/entries/understanding/.

8 Intellectual Virtues
Acquiring Understanding

Angela Knobel

Following Aristotle, Aquinas posited three virtues of the speculative intellect: science, wisdom, and understanding. Aquinas's accounts of the virtues of science and wisdom have received a great deal of attention, as has his notion of intellectual virtue in general. But understanding as an intellectual *virtue* has received almost no attention at all. Part of the difficulty stems from Aquinas himself: Aquinas uses *intellectus* broadly, and typically without specifying whether he means to refer to our natural habitual knowledge of first principles, the act of understanding, or a developed virtue. At the same time, however, Aquinas clearly considers the virtue of understanding to be both important in its own right and fundamental to the virtues of science and wisdom. This chapter seeks to examine understanding as an intellectual virtue in Aquinas and to propose a hypothesis about what, given Aquinas's account, it would mean to develop the intellectual virtue of understanding. I will argue that Aquinas's account implies that we can develop the virtue of understanding only insofar as we can come to increase what we habitually know and thereby pave the way for our understanding to operate more readily and more effectively. In this way, the virtue of understanding is importantly different from the other intellectual virtues.

In what follows, I will first briefly outline Aquinas's account of the intellectual virtues and of the distinctions between them. With that background in place, I will then turn to a more detailed examination of understanding. If we want to examine understanding as a virtue, we first need to examine understanding as an *act*: to examine what happens when we understand. In any act of understanding, no matter how basic, we grasp something of the essence of a thing. It is merely that we grasp that essence more or less distinctly: less distinctly in our initial, imperfect acts of understanding and more distinctly in the more perfect ones. Since the virtues are habitual perfections that enable the powers of the soul to function at their utmost, a virtue of understanding would arguably perfect this process: It would enable its possessor to grasp the essences of things more easily, more readily, and more distinctly. Can we, then, develop habits that enable us to understand more easily, more readily, and more distinctly? I will argue that Aquinas's answer is both yes and no. The act most central to understanding – the intellect's ability to ascend to fuller knowledge of a thing – is not something we cultivate. What we *can* cultivate, however, are the habits that pave the way for the moment of understanding.

INTELLECTUAL VIRTUE IN GENERAL

In his *Sentences* commentary, Aquinas tells us that "a virtue is a habit perfecting a power for a good act."[1] Because there are different ways in which it can be correct to call an act good, we can mean different things when we call the habits that dispose to those acts virtuous. The distinction that is fundamental to understanding Aquinas's account of intellectual virtue is the distinction between those habits that dispose to *materially* good acts and those habits that dispose to *formally* good acts.[2]

We call something good "formally and *per se*," says Aquinas, when its object is good.[3] This is the sense in which goodness is attributed to the desiring parts of the soul: "[Good] is attributed to the desiring part in a *formal* sense, in that the good itself is the object at which this part aims."[4] Since goodness is the object of the will, Aquinas maintains that "only an act of the will or of the appetitive part can be called good in this way."[5] Nonetheless, "something of the formal goodness of the will" can "reach" the acts the will commands "as when someone of a right intention thinks or walks."[6]

An act is good "materially and *per accidens*," by contrast, when it is "fitting to the acting power."[7] An act is *materially* good, that is, when it exhibits the well-functioning of the power that produced it, "as when someone rightly understands and when an eye can clearly see."[8] Material goodness does involve a genuine perfection. It simply involves a perfection that (at least in the case of four of the five intellectual virtues) is independent of the goodness of the will. When we call an act good *materially*, we are saying that it exhibits the perfection of the power that produced it. Our intellect is functioning well *qua* intellect when we rightly understand, just as our eye is functioning well *qua* eye when it sees clearly. Like clear sight, right understanding can be ordered to an evil end, and like unclear sight, deficient understanding can be ordered to a good end. But it will still be true that in the former case our eyes and intellect are functioning well and in the latter case they are functioning poorly: "[T]he act of a non-appetitive power may be good with the goodness of the will, though not with the goodness of its own genus, as when someone walks with a limp for the sake of God, or out of a right intention thinks about things in which he is mentally dull."[9]

To speak of virtues in the intellect, then, is to speak of habits that dispose the intellect to *materially* good acts: habits that dispose the intellect to do the work proper to it in an excellent way. Since the intellect is ordered to the knowledge of truth, the intellectual virtues will be habits that "perfect the intellect for knowing the truth."[10] Since such habits are good materially but not formally, to have an intellectual virtue is to have a habit that makes one capable of finding truth. At the same time, it is important to be precise about what we mean when we say that the intellectual virtues *perfect* the intellect for knowing the truth. To say that a habit *perfects* the intellect implies that that habit gives the intellect something it does not already possess. In some sense it is true that any unimpaired, uneducated mind is able to learn a language, or begin to study a science, or learn a craft. But that sense of able is clearly not what is meant when we speak of the ability the intellectual virtues provide. The person who possesses the relevant intellectual virtues is able, *right now*, to engage in the intellectual activity in question *well*: to readily and easily perform some craft, or readily and easily engage in a science, or readily and easily "rightly understand," etc. I will return to this point in what follows.

The various intellectual virtues are distinguished according to the different ways in which the intellect can be perfected for knowing the truth. As we have seen, the intellectual virtues "complete the cognitive part for knowing the truth."[11] But because different truths are known in different ways, the intellect will need to be perfected in different kinds of ways in order to know different kinds of truths. The first and broadest division that Aquinas offers is between speculative and practical knowledge: the habits that perfect the intellect for knowing necessary truths on the one hand and "contingent practical truths" on the other. Within necessary truths, Aquinas further distinguishes "necessary truths known in themselves" from "necessary truths known from something else." Within "contingent practical truths," Aquinas distinguishes "knowing how to do things ... that are *in us*" from knowing how to do things that are *outside us*.[12]

These divisions correspond to the five intellectual virtues. The virtue of *understanding*, says Aquinas, perfects the intellect for the knowledge of "necessary truths known in themselves," while the virtues of *science* and *wisdom* perfect the intellect for the knowledge of "necessary truths known from something else."[13] *Prudence* perfects the intellect for knowledge of contingent truths "that are in us," while *skill* perfects the intellect for knowledge of contingent truths that are outside us.

The trio of speculative intellectual virtues – science, wisdom, and understanding – are interdependent. Understanding perfects the intellect for knowledge of "necessary truths." But knowledge does not stop, of course, at knowledge of necessary truths: We must move from truths known "in themselves" to knowledge of other things. Aquinas tells us that these latter truths, truths perceived "through reason's inquiry," have "the status of an endpoint or terminus."[14] Science and wisdom each perfect reason's ability to reach a different kind of terminus. The virtue of science "perfects the intellect with respect to what is ultimate in this or that genus of knowable things," while the virtue of wisdom perfects the intellect with respect to what is "first and maximally knowable by its nature."[15]

Although we cannot offer a full account of the virtues of science and wisdom here, it is nonetheless important to make a few remarks by way of clarification. First, it is important to note that science is a broad term that could potentially refer to a variety of different habitual intellectual perfections. That is to say, I could have a habit of science with respect to biology, or chemistry, or any number of other subsets of the genus of knowable things; a habit of science does not at once perfect the intellect with respect to all such subsets. Gregory Reichberg has pointed out that a habit of science perfects the intellect's ability to deduce conclusions from principles in two ways. First, it serves "as an intellectual memory from which a demonstrative inference can be recalled at will"; and second, "it then enables its possessors to *extend* their knowledge to new conclusions."[16] The intellectual memory that Reichberg refers to is *of some subset* of the genus of knowable things: of classifications of living things, say, or elements in the periodic table, etc. As one develops a habit of, say, zoology, one would simultaneously extend that knowledge and increase one's intellectual memory, but one would not typically be cultivating other scientific habits: To increase a habit of science with respect to one genus of knowable things does not necessarily mean that other scientific habits are cultivated at all, let alone increased.

The specialized nature of the sciences underscores an important difference between science and wisdom. Since both science and wisdom have to do with the ability to derive conclusions from starting points, it might seem that there is not an important difference between them, or even that wisdom is just one of the many different types of science. Aquinas even partially concedes this, saying that wisdom "is a certain sort of scientific knowledge (*sapientia est quae-dam scientia*), since it has what is common to all types of scientific knowledge, viz., that it demonstrates conclusions from principles."[17] At the same time, however, wisdom involves a different kind of knowledge and hence requires a different kind of habitual perfection than the other sciences do. Wisdom, says Aquinas, "passes judgment" on all the other sciences, "not only with respect to their conclusions but with respect to their first principles."[18]

Aquinas is also clear, finally, that science and wisdom not only take their departure from but also culminate in understanding.[19] The end result of reason's inquiry, that is to say, is in part that we attain a deeper understanding of our starting points. Part of the task of this chapter will be to unpack this claim.

It seems relatively clear that the successful practice of science or wisdom would require the cultivation of a habit. But Aquinas also believes that we need to cultivate a virtue of understanding: a habit regarding the very principles from which science and wisdom take their departure, one which enables us to readily and easily grasp "necessary truths known in themselves." Almost no scholarly litera-ture addresses the question of what such a habit would be, let alone what it would mean to cultivate it. At least some scholars imply that the virtue of understanding is identical to our natural habitual know-ledge of first principles, the knowledge that Aquinas says all human beings possess from their very first interactions with the world.[20] Other scholars assert that the virtue of understanding develops over time, but do not offer any details about how that development occurs or what it would mean to possess understanding as an intellectual virtue.[21] My goal in the remainder of this chapter will be to shed some light on these questions, and specifically to offer a hypothesis – a hypothesis which I will argue finds support in Aquinas's text – about what the cultivation of the intellectual virtue of understanding does (and does not) entail. First, however, it will be important to clarify what "necessary truths known in themselves" *are* – that is, what kind of truth it is that the virtue of understanding will enable us to grasp. In what follows, I will show that the knowledge of the *per se notum* has primarily to do with the knowledge of essences, and thus that the virtue of understanding will be the habit or habits that enable us to quickly and readily grasp the essences of things.

WHAT HAPPENS WHEN WE UNDERSTAND?

Particularly in broad overviews of Aquinas's account of the intellectual virtues, the virtue of understanding is sometimes described as a habit that enables one to grasp "first principles."[22] This claim is correct, but it can also be confusing. First, we need to be clear on what "first principles" means. Are the principles that the virtue of understanding enables us to grasp first insofar as they are foundational, or first insofar as they are the first principles we know? Are they first insofar as everything else is derived from them, or first insofar as their truth is presupposed by other truths? Most importantly, why do we need to cultivate a virtue in order to know them? In what follows, I will show that Aquinas holds that we understand a range of truths. Some truths are understood immediately, as a result of our first interactions with the world. Other truths are understood only after a process that includes reason, experience, and intellectual training. In all its instances, Aquinas thinks that understanding provides quidditative knowledge: It gives us insight into the essence of a thing. It is merely that not all instances of understanding provide equal degrees of essential insight. The essential knowledge we acquire immediately, as a result of our very first interactions with the world and without any intellectual training or development, is indistinct: Even those first interactions give us some knowledge of the essences of things, but the essential knowledge they give us is vague and unclear.[23] The essential knowledge that is made possible through reason, experience, and intellectual training, by contrast, is increasingly distinct: It enables us to grasp the essences of things more and more distinctly. Given all of this, it is reasonable to conclude that we will possess a *virtue* of understanding when we possess the habit or habits that enable us to more quickly, readily, and easily arrive at a *distinct* knowledge of the essences of things.

Aquinas says that the virtue of understanding perfects the intellect with respect to "necessary truths known in themselves" (with respect to what is *per se notum*). These truths, he says, "have the status of a starting point or principle" and are "perceived immediately by the intellect."[24] If we wish to unpack the kinds of truths the virtue of understanding enables us to know, we can begin by examining what it means for a truth to "have the status of a starting point or principle" and by examining what it means for a truth to be "perceived immediately by the intellect."

The most universally known "starting points or principles" are, of course, the first speculative principles, the principles which Aquinas says that we know from our very first interactions with the world. Aquinas says that these truths – which include propositions such as "every whole is greater than its part" and "things equal to one and the same thing are equal to each other," and the principle of non-contradiction, are known "*per se* in general to everyone."[25] But the principles that we all know from our very first interactions with the world are not and cannot be the only principles that Aquinas has in mind when he says that the virtue of understanding perfects the intellect with respect to truths that "have the status of a starting point or principle." A principle that is known "*per se* in general to everyone" from their very first interactions with the world does not require a virtue to be known: We know these truths and know them habitually *before* any further habitual perfections are present in our intellect.[26] So when Aquinas says that the virtue of understanding perfects our intellect with respect to truths that have the status of a starting point or principle, he must have truths other than the first speculative principles (i.e., the truths known *per se* in general to all) in mind.

In Aquinas's commentary on the *Posterior Analytics*, he describes a way in which one might arrive at a rather different "starting point or principle," one which we do not know directly, but only as a result of reason and experience. Specifically, Aquinas contrasts what is known by experience with what we come to understand as a result of experience. "When someone remembers that such an herb has healed from a fever many times," says Aquinas, "there is said to be experience that such an herb can heal a fever."[27] But, says Aquinas,

> reason does not stop in the experience of particulars, but from many particulars in which it has experience, it receives one common thing, which is established in the soul, and it considers that thing without consideration of anything of singulars, and this common thing it receives as a principle of art and science. For example, so long as a doctor has considered this herb to have healed Socrates of fever and Plato of fever and many other individual men of fever, this is experience. But when in his consideration he ascends to this, that such a species of herb heals fever simply, this is received as a certain rule of the art of medicine.[28]

The quote above includes a number of important claims which merit our careful consideration.

First, Aquinas says that from many particulars, reason "receives one common thing, which is established in the soul" and that it receives this common thing *as a principle of art and science*. In grasping the healing properties of the herb, we move beyond mere experience: beyond grasping various instances in which various individuals have recovered from fever after consuming the herb. We grasp instead something about the nature of the herb *as such*: that this kind of herb heals fever. We grasp, that is to say, something about the essence of the thing in question.

Second, in the example above, it is knowledge of the herb's essence (the common thing that all herbs of this kind share) that provides the rule, the "principle of art and science." Aquinas describes reason's move from knowledge of the particular to knowledge of the principle as an *ascent*: We move from our knowledge of many particular things to knowledge of a rule of the art of medicine. It is because we come to know something about the essence of a certain kind of herb that we are able to grasp a principle of medicine. The knowledge that this particular kind of herb heals is indeed a starting point, but not because our reason *starts there*: Our reason starts in a much different place, namely in experience. The knowledge is a starting point insofar as it is foundational: It is something upon which we can build in developing our knowledge of the art of medicine.

Aquinas recognizes the kind of knowledge described above as a kind of *per se* knowledge: as a kind of necessary truth "known in itself." The difference between this and *per se notum* principles like the principle of non-contradiction is that the former kind of necessary truth, while true in virtue of itself, is not necessarily known to all. Aquinas distinguishes two kinds of *per se notum* truths: those that are *per se notum* "to us" and those that are *per se notum* "in themselves." Into the latter category falls every proposition that "is such that its predicate is part of the notion of its subject."[29] But while such propositions are both necessarily true and true in virtue of themselves, their truth is not obvious to everyone, because not everyone has the requisite knowledge. "Man is rational," for instance, "is known *per se* given its own nature, since anyone who expresses man expresses rational," but, says Aquinas, "this proposition is not known *per se* to someone who does not know the real definition of man."[30] But other truths – namely, those *per se* truths whose terms are known to everyone – "are known *per se* in general to everyone."[31]

When, having experienced various instances of its healing properties, we ascend to the knowledge that a certain type of herb heals, we gain knowledge of a *per se notum* truth: To know (enough) about what this herb is is to know that it heals fever. But such a truth, while *per se notum*, is clearly not known to all.

When we keep in mind that the *per se notum* (and hence the range of truths we can come to understand) includes not merely the first speculative principles but also truths that are *per se notum* in themselves but not to all, we are better able to understand Aquinas's claim that *per se notum* truths are known "immediately" and "in virtue of themselves." The healing properties of an herb, when known as "common," are known "*per se*," and hence our knowledge of them must be "immediate." But truths like this are also arrived at only through a process: a process that includes experience, discursive reason, and (sometimes) intellectual training. It is important to clarify, then, the sense in which such truths are immediate.

Truths are "immediate," says Aquinas, when they are "not demonstrated by any other middle, but are clear in virtue of themselves."[32] It is the lack of a "middle" that makes the truth of a principle immediate: the fact that its predicate "is included in the notion of the subject."[33] As Gregory Reichberg notes, "the *immediacy* of this apprehension must be taken formally: the negation in question bears only on the mediation exercised by the middle term in a syllogistic deduction."[34] Thomas Hibbs, making the same point, says that "the accent is upon the translucency of these principles, and on their apparent analyticity."[35] One does not need to look outside the principle to see the truth of it in this sense: To know all of the terms contained in it is to immediately apprehend its truth. But this kind of immediacy does not remove the need for experience and other kinds of mental preparation. "Other forms of cognitive mediation," Reichberg explains, "are fully compatible with and even necessary to the act of intuitive insight: prior reflection upon sensory data, conceptual analysis, and even dialectical inductive reasoning."[36] Indeed, as Thomas Hibbs has pointed out, Aquinas's claim that the principles are known "in themselves" should not be mistaken for a "covert espousal of intuitionism."[37] Aquinas holds that the truth of the principle is grasped as soon as the terms are known, but – as we have already noted – he also holds that the knowledge of the terms themselves arises from reason and experience. This means that: (1) even this kind of knowledge is not separate from experience; and (2) we might need to undergo intellectual training before we can "immediately apprehend" what is *per se notum*.[38]

When we appreciate the full scope of what understanding can apply to – that we understand not merely first speculative principles but also whatever is *per se notum* – two things fall into place. First, we are better able to make sense of Aquinas's repeated claim that understanding has to do with the knowledge of the essences of things. Second, we can begin to make sense of why a *virtue* (in the robust sense of the term) might be necessary for understanding. In what follows I will address each of these points in turn.

So far I have focused on the claim that Aquinas makes when he refers directly to understanding as a virtue – namely, his claim that the virtue of understanding enables us to know "necessary truths known in themselves." But Aquinas more consistently describes understanding as what it is that enables us to know the essences of things.[39] By implication, then, to know what is *per se notum* is to know something about the essence of a thing. The text considered above is consistent with that implication, for what the intellect "ascended" to when it moved beyond its experience was clearly a fuller essential knowledge of the herb, specifically knowledge of the herb's curative properties. By implication, then, in coming to know what is *per se notum* in itself but not to all, we acquire essential knowledge. If knowledge of the *per se notum* is really quidditative knowledge, however, then it should also be the case that the more basic kind of understanding – our knowledge of what is *per se notum* in general to everyone – is *also* a kind of quidditative knowledge. As I will show in what follows, this is indeed the case. It is merely that our more basic quidditative knowledge is, in Aquinas's words, "indistinct." Our knowledge of the first principles is a kind of knowledge of the essences of things, but it is only the most vague and indistinct essential knowledge, and greatly in need of refinement. To see this, it will be necessary to say something about what Aquinas believes occurs in the most basic of our acts of understanding, or in what he calls acts of "simple apprehension."

Knowledge of What Is Per Se in General to Everyone as Essential Knowledge

Aquinas holds that all human knowledge begins in the senses. He also holds that the object of the intellect, what the intellect most properly knows, is the essence of a thing.[40] This presents a problem, because what we receive in sensation is material, and what our intellect knows is immaterial: What the intellect knows is not delivered through the senses, but we somehow know what we know on the basis of what we receive through senses. Somehow, then, what we receive materially through the senses is the source of what is known, immaterially, in the intellect. Aquinas's account of how this occurs is detailed and complicated. My goal here is to describe only as much of his account as will be necessary (1) to offer an overview of his view and (2) to make sense of some of the claims he makes about understanding.

Aquinas maintains that what we receive materially through the senses comes to be known immaterially in the intellect through abstraction. We receive sensory data through the five senses. That data is then "bundled by the common sense and organized into a phantasm, that is, a form in the imagination that is a likeness" of the object of sensation.[41] The phantasms that come to exist in our imagination are still material: They are present in the "neurophysical power of imagination whose organ is a part of the brain."[42] According to Aquinas, the agent intellect then abstracts the "impressed intelligible species" from the phantasm.[43]

Therese Cory has convincingly argued that in abstraction the agent intellect makes an intelligible version of the phantasm.[44] This is what the "impressed intelligible species" is: It is not the phantasm itself, and it does not transform the phantasm. In abstraction the agent intellect rather makes an intelligible version of the phantasm – that is, a version of the phantasm that has been stripped of everything material.[45] The impressed intelligible species is immaterial, but has the "determinacy of content" of the phantasm.

The most basic act of understanding occurs when the possible intellect, having received (thanks to the agent intellect) that impressed intelligible species, forms a concept.[46] This might seem to imply that our initial concept will be rather precise: a concept of whatever is contained in the intelligible species. But Aquinas holds only that our first concept is formed on the basis of what we receive in the impressed intelligible species: that concept does not itself have the determinacy of the intelligible species.[47] The implication is not that there is something inadequate about what is received in the intelligible species. Rather, the implication is that the receiver, the one forming the concept, does not yet have the tools to form a precise concept of what is received.

According to Aquinas, the first concept we form, what we grasp in the very first act of simple apprehension, is a confused, indistinct concept of "being."[48] This point is worth dwelling on. No matter what the content of the impressed intelligible species, if my act of simple apprehension is genuinely my *first* act of simple apprehension, then according to Aquinas, I will apprehend *something* of the essence of the thing. But if it is genuinely my first apprehension, I will grasp only that it is a being. So, if I encounter an elephant, and if it is genuinely my first apprehension of anything at all in the world, then no matter what is conveyed (by means of abstraction) in the impressed intelligible species, I will apprehend the elephant only as something that is – I will apprehend only a being. Not until I also apprehend other things can that initial, indistinct apprehension begin to be refined.

Benjamin Block, explaining this point, notes that Aquinas compares what the intellect first understands to the ear's first experience of sound. Whatever we initially hear will be some particular sound, just as whatever we initially understand will be drawn from some particular impressed intelligible species. At the same time, however, we cannot distinguish anything particular to that sound *until we hear other sounds*. In the same way, our initial concept of a thing, drawn from the impressed intelligible species, cannot have any determinate content; it cannot be distinguished from other things, *until we apprehend other beings.*[49] Thus, "the first concept will simply be that of *being,* until other concepts are produced by which one kind of being can be distinguished from another."[50] Thus, the imperfection of our first concept is due not to a deficiency in the impressed intelligible species, but to a deficiency in us: We initially lack the tools to adequately grasp the reality that we experience. As we apprehend other things, we become able to compare the objects of our experience and thus form more accurate concepts of them.

Aquinas's account of what occurs in our very first act of apprehension helps to underline the fact that all understanding has to do with our knowledge of the essences of things. Even in our first act of apprehension, we apprehend something of the essence of whatever it is we apprehend. It is merely that we grasp that essence imperfectly – in Aquinas's terms, "indistinctly": We grasp of the thing only that it is a being. As we apprehend other things, it becomes possible for us to refine that vague initial concept.[51]

Aquinas's view of how our vague and indistinct first concept is refined is complicated, and I will not attempt to give a thorough account of it here. But I do wish to emphasize the central feature of that process, because it is pertinent to the question at hand. Aquinas claims that human beings can only gain access to the essences of things indirectly, through a process of discursive reason.

Angels know essences directly. We, by contrast, at first have only the most vague and indistinct conceptions of the essences of things, conceptions that can be made more precise only through a process of reasoning. This is the case, Aquinas tells us, with everything except the first principles, which we know directly.[52] How, then, does the process of discursive reason enable us to attain a clearer grasp of the essences of things? Aquinas tells us that while angels can perceive essences directly, human beings do "not attain to the innermost of a thing except through the things placed about it, as through doors."[53] Because of this, human beings "proceed to the knowledge of a thing's essence from its effects and properties."[54] Aquinas says that this process "is called reason, although it ends in understanding inasmuch as inquiry leads to a thing's essence."[55]

Just how it is that reasoning about a thing's "effects and properties" enables us to more clearly grasp its essence is an important question, but it is also one that exceeds the scope of the present discussion.[56] What is relevant for present purposes is this: Aquinas clearly believes that, in order for our understanding to increase, we must engage in something *other than* acts of understanding. Angels understand essences completely from the beginning. But humans apprehend essences unclearly and indistinctly, and can gain a clearer apprehension only through "composing and dividing and reasoning discursively."[57] In the human case, deeper insight into the essence of a thing – a deeper act of understanding – can occur only after discursive reason has, so to speak, cleared the way: insofar as discursive reason helps to uncover some essential difference.

The picture offered above helps to illuminate why understanding might require the cultivation of a virtue. Clearly, no virtue is needed for the most basic acts of simple apprehension, the acts through which we know the first speculative principles. But if we are to understand those things that are *per se notum* "in general but not to all," we must move beyond that first, indistinct essential knowledge. It is plausible that the cultivation of a habit could help us to more quickly, readily, and easily attain that latter kind of knowledge. In Aquinas's example, understanding occurs when an individual grasps that an herb is curative and thus arrives at a principle of the art of medicine. One person can surely be better disposed to grasp the healing properties of an herb than another. Someone who has engaged in a systematic study of the healing properties of herbs in general, for instance, will be better suited to discover the healing properties of a newly encountered herb. Similarly, someone who has encountered many different kinds of animals will be in a better position to grasp the essence of a newly encountered species than will someone who has not. The same will be true, though in a different way, of someone who has engaged in an extensive study of zoology but who has encountered relatively few animals. And someone who has *both* engaged in an extensive study of zoology *and* encountered many different kinds of animals will be in a still better position to grasp the essence of a newly encountered species. So, it is plausible that understanding – at least understanding what is *per se notum* in general but not to all – is something that we can *become proficient* at. And if we can become proficient in understanding, then it is plausible to think that the process of becoming proficient involves the cultivation of habits. But what would such habits be? What would they perfect? We will address these questions in the next section.

CULTIVATING UNDERSTANDING

We have seen that the *per se notum* includes a range of truths. Some *per se notum* truths are understood immediately, in and through our first interactions with the world. Others are understood only gradually, through a process that involves reason, experience, and intellectual training. A virtue, Aquinas tells us, is an "utmost" of a power: It enables the power in which it inheres to function at its optimum level. It follows that a *virtue* of understanding should make its possessor adept at grasping the *per se notum*. Since no particular aptitude is required in order to grasp what is *per se notum* to everyone, it would also seem to follow that a virtue of understanding would primarily concern what is *per se notum* in itself but not to all. My goal in this section is to examine what sort of habits could confer that aptitude. In what follows I will first argue that it is plausible that such an aptitude could be acquired. Then I will distinguish two ways in which that aptitude might be understood. A virtue of understanding, I will argue, would seem to involve both sorts of aptitude. However, Aquinas seems to believe that one kind of aptitude is much more amenable to development than the other.

In the example we considered previously, an individual ascends from the experiential knowledge that a given herb has cured the fever of several different individuals to knowledge of something about the essence of that herb as such. But it is plausible that some individuals could make this ascent more easily than others, and it is equally plausible that, through training, one could become *better* at making that ascent. If I have practiced medicine for a long time, for instance, and have become familiar with both fevers (how they arise, what occurs as they run their course, what are the signs that a fever has begun to improve, and so forth) as well as with the use of herbs, then I will be in a much better position to grasp that a given herb heals. Cultivating the virtue of understanding would arguably mean cultivating the qualities, whatever they are, that cause one to become better at understanding. But what would those qualities be?

In the example of the herb, we can distinguish two distinct factors, both of which contribute in a fundamental way to the understanding that eventually occurs. First, there are the factors that prepare the ground, as it were, for the act of understanding that occurs: the things that make the ascent possible. In the example that Aquinas offers, experience plays a key role: It is on the basis of experiencing several instances of it that the ascent to our understanding of the herb's curative power is made possible. Experience is not, of course, the only thing that enables this ascent. Other (relevant) things I already understand surely also prepare the ground for acts of deeper understanding. Someone who already understands a great deal about how the body functions, or who has made an extensive study of the curative properties of herbs in general, is surely in a better position to grasp the curative properties of an herb than someone who lacks that understanding. Even beyond what we have experienced and what we know, our ability to understand, to make the ascent to essential knowledge, will be impacted by capacities such as memory and imagination.[58] My ability to grasp that an herb is curative will be impacted by my ability to recall the various instances in which I have experienced it to cure. And so on.

The factors described above are clearly crucial to understanding those truths that are *per se notum* in themselves but not to all. After all, Aquinas is clear that, with the exception of the first speculative principles, we cannot arrive at understanding except through a process of discursive reason. But none of these factors, important as they may be, can stand in for the act of understanding itself: They merely facilitate it. To put the same point differently: Even given all of our past experience and everything else we understand, a new act of understanding still requires an ascent. The important point for present purposes is this: We can distinguish our capacity to ascend to a new and fuller understanding from the various preparatory factors that make the ascent possible. An extensive experience, a detailed understanding of the workings of the human body, and a previous study of the curative properties of herbs all make it easier for a given act of understanding to occur. But one individual could still make that ascent on the basis of less experience, or on the basis of a much more minimal understanding of medicine, than another. The capacity to *have* the insight, to engage in the actual act of understanding, is not reducible to the preparatory factors that make those acts possible, and it is not possessed equally by all. When we speak about whether and how a virtue of understanding can be cultivated, then, it is important to be clear about what we are claiming can be cultivated. Are we referring to habits that make it *easier* for new acts of understanding to occur – habits that, so to speak, set the stage for deeper acts of understanding to occur? Or are we referring to a habit that somehow increases our ability to *understand* in and of itself – a habit that directly facilitates our ability to make the ascending act itself? While it would be natural to assume that a virtue of understanding would involve the cultivation of this latter ability, Aquinas seems to deny that such an ability can be cultivated.

In the seventh article of question 85 of the *ST* I-II, Aquinas asks whether one person can "understand one and the same thing more than someone else does."[59] Aquinas first responds by distinguishing between the thing that is understood and the act of understanding in the one who understands. If by "more" we mean that the thing is understood to be other than it actually is, then that is impossible: To understand a thing to be other than it is would be not to understand at all, but to fall short of understanding. But, says Aquinas, "more" can also refer to "the act of intellective understanding *on the part of the one who is engaged in understanding.*"[60] If this is what is meant, then, says Aquinas, it certainly can be the case that one person understands a thing *more* than another, because one person can have "more power of understanding" than another.[61] Aquinas compares differences in the power of understanding to differences in sight: "[S]omeone can understand the same thing better than someone else, in virtue of having more power of understanding – in the same way that someone who has a more perfect power and in whom the visual power is more perfect sees a given thing better by a corporeal act of seeing than someone else does."[62]

That one person has a more perfect power of understanding than another occurs, says Aquinas, "in one of two ways." First, some people have a "more perfect" intellect than others do. This is because "actuality and form are received into matter in accord with the matter's capacity."[63] Just as animals of different species have souls that correspond to their bodily capacities, so too do different men, thanks to differences in their bodily composition, have a greater or lesser power of understanding. Second, the "lower powers the intellect needs for its own operation" can be better disposed in one individual than in another: "those in whom the power of imagining and the cogitative power and the power of remembering are better disposed for intellective understanding."[64]

Although Aquinas clearly asserts that one individual can have a greater understanding than another, his answer implies serious restrictions on the degree to which we might cultivate a virtue of understanding in ourselves: that is, habits that enable us to understand more quickly, readily, and easily. Some people, Aquinas tells us, are simply smarter than other people, just as some people have better sight than others do. In others, the capacities that make understanding possible – imagination, memory, and the cogitative power – are "better disposed." But the first of these factors – the factor most closely tied to our ability to make the ascent itself – is something we can do nothing about: The power of our intellect depends on the way our form is individuated in matter. The ability that enables us to actually ascend – to actually perform the act whereby we move to a fuller understanding – seems relatively fixed.

Where does this leave us with respect to the question of this chapter? If we take seriously Aquinas's claim above, we are left with a positive and a negative conclusion about the possibility of cultivating a virtue of understanding. The negative conclusion is that, if by understanding we mean the ability itself, considered apart from all else we bring to bear, to ascend to a fuller understanding of the essence of a thing, then understanding is not something that can be increased or cultivated. The positive conclusion is that, if by under-standing we mean not only that ability but everything we bring to bear in a given act of understanding, then we can indeed cultivate habits that increase our ability to understand. If I commit a great number of phylum and species classifications to memory, for instance, I will be in a much better position to grasp the nature of an unfamiliar animal, even though I have not increased the ability to ascend in and of itself. The habit created in the preceding example, of course, is a habit of memory, and hence cannot even be said to be part of a virtue of understanding properly speaking. But I certainly will grow in understanding as I come to understand more things, as the amount and depth of my understanding increases. And it certainly is true that the greater my understanding already is, the more quickly, readily, and easily I will understand. The positive conclusion, then, is this: I can cultivate understanding insofar as I can come to understand more things. Doing so will not increase my ability to ascend as such, but it will pave the way for that ascent to occur.

If the account offered above is correct, then the virtue of under-standing is dramatically different from other virtues. Typically, we think of the cultivation of a virtue primarily in terms of the cultiva-tion of an *ability*: as involving something akin to a skill. If the account offered above is correct, there is a skill-like ability involved in understanding, but it is also not something that can be cultivated. This may seem counterintuitive. I will conclude with some reflections about what my account means for our notion of understanding as a virtue.

First, on the account offered above, the habits that together constitute the virtue of understanding will differ in important ways from the habits that constitute the other virtues, but it is still reasonable to speak of a *virtue* of understanding. Even if we cannot cultivate the ability to have the moment of insight itself, we can nonetheless pave the way for those insights, and those insights, once had, increase the body of truths which we habitually know. Even if we do not typically think of our body of habitual knowledge as a *virtue*, it does function as one in the case of understanding. The truths we already habitually know make it possible for us to more quickly, readily, and easily understand: They set the stage for still deeper insights into the essences of things, as, or more importantly, the increase in this ability corresponds to our own efforts to cultivate understanding. Even if the flash of insight itself is not something we control, even if the ability to have those insights is not something we can cultivate, the content of our knowledge – the body of truths that we understand – *does* grow in parallel with our efforts. In that sense, we very much can cultivate a virtue of understanding in ourselves, because we can cultivate habits that enable us to more quickly, readily, and easily understand. An account like this also underscores the mutual interplay of science and understanding mentioned earlier in this chapter. Aquinas tells us, as we saw above, that science and wisdom culminate in understanding. One way of understanding what Aquinas means by this is to say that the very process of broadening our knowledge disposes us to the deepening of it: The more we understand where our principles lead, the better we understand the principles themselves.

Second, the account of understanding offered above accommodates the cyclic nature of understanding. Aquinas repeatedly describes understanding as something that is present at both the beginning and the end of the intellectual process: It is both what makes science and wisdom possible and what science and wisdom ultimate culminate in. On the account offered here, we understand something of the thing we seek to understand at the beginning of the intellectual process; it is merely that we understand it indistinctly. An increase in understanding does not mean, then, that we come to know something utterly new, but merely that we grasp more clearly what we already knew – albeit in a much more unclear and imperfect fashion.

Finally, the account I have offered here helps to explain a further feature of understanding; namely, the fact that growth in understanding is typically domain specific. When someone's understanding progresses a great deal, that is to say, that progress typically tends to occur within an increasingly narrow domain of study. Someone who devotes himself to the study of zoology and who comes to understand a great deal about animals does not, in virtue of that study, become better able to understand music or physics. This is consistent with the picture offered above, for the following reason. If it were possible to cultivate the ability to have the actual moments of insight themselves, then in developing the ability to understand one thing, I would develop the ability to understand all things. If, by contrast, I can cultivate understanding only to the extent that I can come to understand more things, then it would follow as a natural consequence that my understanding would become deep in some areas and remain shallow in others. Aquinas's account of understanding underscores the all too human elements of the pursuit of knowledge. We can make real progress in our understanding, but that progress necessarily occurs slowly; it requires time and teachers and specialization.

We have been speaking in this chapter of a thoroughly human understanding: one that we acquire through our own efforts and which leads to a purely human kind of knowledge. Aquinas, of course, also recognizes another understanding, one which is directly bestowed by God and which provides a more than human knowledge of more than human things. That kind of understanding is discussed elsewhere in this volume.

NOTES

1 *In III Sent.*, d.23 q.1 a.4 qa.1. Aquinas defines virtue in different (albeit compatible) ways throughout his corpus. See, for instance, Aquinas, *QDVCom* a.7 and a.12. *Disputed Questions on the Virtues*, edited and translated by E. M. Atkins and T. Williams (Cambridge: Cambridge University Press, 2005). In his *Sentences* commentary, Aquinas says that a virtue "is a habit perfecting a power for a good act" (*In III Sent.*, d.23 q.1 a.4 qa.1). In the *Summa*, he says that a virtue is a habit "by which someone operates well" (*ST* I-II q.56 a.3).

2 Although Aquinas appeals to this distinction to explain the difference between intellectual and moral virtue in both the *Sentences* and in his *Disputed Questions on Virtue*, in the *ST* I-II Aquinas instead appeals to the distinction between habits that give "facility" for good action and those that give "right use." See *In III Sent.*, d.23 q.1 a.4 qa.1; see also *QDVCom* a.7; *ST* I-II q.56 a.3.

3 *In III Sent.*, d.23 q.1 a.4 qa.1; see also *QDVCom* a.7.

4 *QDVCom* a.12.

5 *In III Sent.*, d.23 q.1 a.4 qa.1; see also *QDVCom* a.7.

6 Ibid.

7 Ibid.

8 Ibid.

9 Ibid.

10 *QDVCom* a.7.

11 *QDVCom* a.12.

12 Ibid.

13 Ibid.

14 Ibid.

15 Ibid.

16 G. Reichberg, "The Intellectual Virtues" in S. Pope (ed.), *The Ethics of Aquinas* (Washington, DC: Georgetown University Press, 2002), p. 137.

17 *ST* I-II q.57 a.2 ad 1.

18 Ibid.

19 *In III Sent.*, d.35 q.2 a.2 qa.1.

20 In his "Aquinas: The Necessity and Some Characteristics of the Habit of First Indemonstrable (Speculative) Principles," Joseph Christianson raises the question of whether the first speculative principles are virtues and argues that they are virtues in a sense, though not completely, since they

do not provide right use. Similarly, in her *Knowledge of the First Principles in Saint Thomas Aquinas*, Mary Ugobi-Onyemere lists *intellectus* as an intellectual virtue, but in describing it, describes only the natural habitual knowledge of the first speculative principles, thus implying that the two are one and the same. See J. Christianson, "Aquinas: The Necessity and Some Characteristics of the Habit of First Indemonstrable (Speculative) Principles," *New Scholasticism* 62 (1988): 249–96, here pp. 283–5; M. Ugobi-Onyemere, *Knowledge of the First Principles in Saint Thomas Aquinas* (Oxford: Peter Lang, 2015), ch. 4.

21   In his "The Intellectual Virtues," for instance, Gregory Reichberg says the following about the virtue of understanding: "[W]hile acknowledging that the 'habit of principles' arises naturally in the mind ... Thomas nevertheless maintains that mental application of a special sort is needed if this habit is to develop aright." Reichberg does not, however, explain what it means for the "habit to develop aright" or cite text in defense of the claim that Aquinas believes "mental application of a special sort" is needed. Thomas Hibbs, similarly, says of understanding that, "as is the case with every virtue, its development requires training and experience." Like Reichberg, Hibbs neither offers details about that development nor cites supporting text in Aquinas. See G. Reichberg, "The Intellectual Virtues," p. 137; T. Hibbs, "Against a Cartesian Reading of *Intellectus* in Aquinas," *The Modern Schoolman* 66 (1988): 55–69, here p. 63.

22   See, for instance, E. Stump, *Aquinas* (New York and London: Routledge, 2003), p. 349: "[U]nderstanding is a habit that enables us to grasp first principles, the starting points of the sciences."

23   T. S. Cory, *Aquinas on Human Self-Knowledge* (Cambridge: Cambridge University Press, 2015), p. 84: Cory refers to this kind of cognition, helpfully, as "maximally indistinct."

24   *ST* I-II q.57 a.2.

25   Ibid.

26   This should not be taken to imply, of course, that these truths are innate or infused: Our habitual knowledge of them arises pre-reflectively, in our first interactions with the world. That knowledge is genuinely a development and perfection of the mind that makes its further perfection possible.

27   *In PA* Lib. 2, c.19, lect. 20 (translation by Benjamin Block: see B. Block, "Thomas Aquinas on How We Know Essences: The Formation and

Perfection of Concepts in the Human Intellect," Dissertation, The Catholic University of America (2019), p. 274).

28 Ibid.

29 *ST* I-II q.94 a.2.

30 Ibid.

31 Ibid.

32 *In I PA*, lect. 1, n.4.

33 *In I PA*, lect. 1, n.5.

34 Reichberg, "The Intellectual Virtues," p. 137.

35 Hibbs, "Against a Cartesian Reading of *Intellectus* in Aquinas," p. 56.

36 Reichberg, "The Intellectual Virtues," p. 137.

37 Hibbs, "Against a Cartesian Reading of *Intellectus* in Aquinas," p. 57.

38 We will return to this point in what follows, but it is worth pointing out that grasping the way in which understanding can rely on intellectual training is illustrative of the intimate connection between science and understanding, and particularly of how the activity of science might culminate in a deeper understanding of one's starting points.

39 See, for instance, *In III Sent.*, d.35 q.2 a.2 qa.3; *ST* II q.8 a.1; *ST* I q.85.

40 *ST* I q.85 a.6.

41 T. Cory, "Rethinking Abstractionism: Aquinas's Intellectual Light and Some Arabic Sources," *Journal of the History of Philosophy* 53 (2015): 607–46, here p. 609.

42 Ibid.

43 To make sense of this claim, it is important to understand Aquinas's distinction between the agent intellect and the possible intellect. Aquinas claims that the intellective "part" contains both the "possible" and the "agent" intellect. The possible intellect "has the capacity to receive any intelligible thing," while the agent intellect provides the light by which "things actually become intelligible." The act of the agent intellect is to "abstract intelligibles," while the act of the possible intellect "is to receive intelligibles." See *QDVCom* a.8; *ST* I q.79 a.3.

44 Cory, "Rethinking Abstractionism," p. 618.

45 Cory, "Rethinking Abstractionism," p. 621.

46 J. F. Peifer, *The Concept in Thomism* (New York: Bookman Associates, 1952), p. 145.

47 Block, "Thomas Aquinas on How We Know Essences," p. 240.

48 *ST* I q.85 a.3. Block, "Thomas Aquinas on How We Know Essences," p. 228.

49 Block, "Thomas Aquinas on How We Know Essences," p. 240.

50 Ibid.

51 *ST* I q.85 a.3.

52 *Super Johan*, c.1, lect. 1 (translation by Benjamin Block: see Block, "Thomas Aquinas on How We Know Essences," p. 61): "When I wish to conceive the ratio of a stone, I must arrive at this through reasoning. And it is thus with everything that is understood by us, except perhaps in the case of first principles, which since they are simply known, are known at once without the discourse of reason."

53 *In III Sent.*, d.35 q.2 a.2 qa.1.

54 Ibid.

55 Ibid.

56 For a thorough discussion of this question, see Block, "Thomas Aquinas on How We Know Essences," ch. 4.

57 *In III Sent.*, d.35 q.2 a.2 qa.1.

58 *ST* I q.85 a.7.

59 Ibid.

60 Ibid.

61 Ibid.

62 Ibid.

63 Ibid.

64 Ibid.

9 Intellect and Will
Free Will and Free Choice
Michael Gorman

INTRODUCTION

Freedom is, without a doubt, an important component of Aquinas's worldview. The drama of salvation, in which humans respond to God's offer to redeem them from sin and give them everlasting happiness, would make no sense if humans were not free.[1] But commentators have found it difficult to agree on the details of Aquinas's views.

In this chapter I focus mostly on one key element of Aquinas's understanding of freedom – namely, free choice or free decision. I will not aim to settle all of the disputes, but rather only to explain central aspects of Aquinas's thinking and clarify the nature of some of the controversies over it, with the goal of facilitating further study and reflection on the part of the reader.

FREE WILL AND FREE CHOICE

For Aquinas, the topic of free will (*libera voluntas*) is wider than the topic of free choice. The former can be found even in cases when the agent cannot choose among alternatives. For example, if we consider happiness at all, then we want to be happy, and we cannot will not to be happy, but this fact, for Aquinas, does not take away our freedom. Something similar applies to the blessed in heaven: Confronted with an object that contains all possible goodness, namely God, they are unable to will anything else, and yet Aquinas sees no need to deny that they have freedom.[2] In such cases, he says, even though the will cannot will otherwise, it is not being coerced against its own natural inclination, and for that reason, it is still free.[3]

Aquinas does not think, however, that free *choice* can be understood in this fashion. As he emphasizes in *QDM* q.6, choice must be free in a sense that goes beyond saying that it is not coerced contrary to natural inclination: What is needed for free choice is that the will, faced with a number of options, not be necessitated to choose in any one way. When one exercises one's power of free choice by choosing something, one could, in some sense, have chosen otherwise.[4]

It will help to put this in the broader context of Aquinas's understanding of how human choice arises.[5] The unavoidable starting point is that humans will happiness as their final end. This end is only to be arrived at through action, which means that intermediate ends must be sought, the attaining of which will facilitate reaching the final end. Let us take going to the train station as an example. One grasps (*apprehensio*) that it would be good to travel to the train station, whereupon one intends to reach this end by some means or other (*intentio*). One deliberates about various possible methods (*consilium*) – driving, taking the bus, calling a taxi – and, if appropriate, accepts them as suitable (*consensus*). One then judges (*iudicium*) that one of them is best, at which point one chooses it (*electio*).[6] Choice is followed by execution – in this case, actually going to the train station – which, for Aquinas, is a matter of *imperium* and *usus*, but since our topic here is choice, we need look no farther than *electio*.

Electio, choice or selection, is an act, and the corresponding power of free choice is often called *liberum arbitrium* by Aquinas.[7] As noted already, Aquinas is clear enough that human choice is free, and that this freedom is bound up with the fact that it is not made by necessity: One necessarily desires happiness, but one does not necessarily choose to take a taxi as a means (ultimately) to be happy – one could have chosen to strive for happiness in some other way. (One can take the situation mentioned in note 6 as a limit case where necessity is compatible with free choice, or one can say that even when there is only one rational choice to make, the choice is still non-necessitated insofar as the agent is free not to choose at all.[8]) As we shall see, for Aquinas the freedom of this choice is bound up with the fact that the judgment (iudicium) that is prior to it is free: Not only could one have decided differently, but also one's deliberation could have reached a different conclusion, and the latter may explain the former.

Now there are a number of ways in which one might worry that free choice, as Aquinas understands it, is impossible. Some of these worries are based on factors not mentioned in the schema just laid out. For example, one might worry that humans are subject to a sort of physical determinism; or that their choices and actions are governed solely by passions such as desire and anger; or that God's foreknowledge means that our choices and actions are all already in the cards; or that God's status as omnipotent ruler of the universe means that whatever we do is ultimately up to him and not to us. Alternatively, one might point to the most important element of the schema, the idea that choice flows from rational judgment, and say that if our choices must always follow our judgments, then they are determined and not free after all.

As we go along, it will become clear – using language that has become commonplace in recent philosophy – that Aquinas explains free choice sometimes in a way that has a libertarian feel, by denying that factors that might appear to remove free choice are causally decisive, and sometimes (perhaps) in a way that has a compatibilist feel, by allowing that the factors are determining but denying that they remove free choice. I will nonetheless avoid putting great emphasis on the compatibilist–libertarian divide, if only because one encounters enough variety in the definitions of these approaches that it is not always illuminating to say whether Aquinas is or is not a compatibilist or a libertarian.

One last introductory remark: It can be dangerous to speak, as I have already done, as if intellect and will themselves do things, such as judging and willing and choosing. Intellect and will should not be thought of as little inner agents competing to control human actions.

Such language can be hard to avoid, but the danger of it must be kept firmly in mind. It is agents, not powers, that reason and choose.

FREE CHOICE AND PHYSICAL DETERMINISM

Philosophers nowadays are greatly interested in the question of whether physical causes determine human choices in such a way that we cannot be said to choose freely. For example, perhaps our choices are determined by brain events – perhaps, indeed, they simply *are* brain events – and perhaps also these brain events are, ultimately, traceable to causes outside of us. Aquinas does not share our neurological concerns, but he does say enough to make it clear how he would handle this sort of issue.

Aquinas asks whether, and how, celestial bodies influence human affairs. (Before we laugh, we should remember that they most certainly do: The sun regularly leads people to don floppy hats, and the moon regularly leads sailors to adjust their plans.) Focusing on what is most relevant here, we can note that, for Aquinas, celestial bodies cannot eliminate the freedom of human choice, because the rational operations of the human mind – which include both *iudicium* and the *electio* that follows upon it – are incorporeal and thus immune to direct physical influence. Celestial bodies do indeed influence our bodies, Aquinas says, and in this way they can affect our emotions, our imaginings, and so forth (no doubt Aquinas overestimates the extent to which this is true). They might thereby have an indirect effect on our judging and choosing, but our intellect and will can pass judgment on our emotions and imaginings, so this indirect influence is subject to being overridden. In short, even if the celestial bodies can affect those aspects of our mental life that are bound up with our bodies, the celestial bodies cannot determine the choices made through our rational, immaterial mind and will.[9]

Whatever one thinks of medieval astrological theories, the relevance of these considerations is clear enough for our purposes. If the moon, which is physical, cannot determine the operations of our immaterial reason, then neither can our terrestrial environment, or even our brains, and for the very same reason. They may, to be sure, determine certain of our perceptual or emotional states, but these states will not in their turn determine particular states of our immaterial intellect and will. Here, at least, Aquinas's analysis has something of a libertarian feel: We are free not because physical causal influences determine our choices in a way that is compatible with freedom, but because they simply do not determine our judgments and choices at all.

FREE CHOICE AND THE PASSIONS

Now let us turn to another possible obstacle to free choice – namely, the passions. Aren't our choices driven by our desires and therefore not really free? One version of this thought might see passion as affecting choice directly: Our desires make us want to choose something. For Aquinas, however, passion affects choice indirectly, by influencing judgment: When we are affected by a passion, different things appear true than when we are not so affected. When we are angry, noses look punchable even when they aren't. Sometimes, Aquinas says, this happens so thoroughly that we lose the use of reason altogether and are reduced to the state of brute animals. But most of the time, we retain the use of reason and free judgment, and this enables us to make a choice about what to do, even against the way passion might be inclining us. Here too, then, Aquinas's approach has a libertarian feel: Passions may influence our choices, but they do not determine them.[10]

Now for a complication. In a discussion of whether someone in a state of mortal sin can, by free choice, avoid mortal sin without the help of grace, Aquinas says that a bad passion can catch us by surprise, leaving us unable to exercise free choice, but in such a way that the resultant movement of the will is nonetheless sinful. Here we have a human, responsible movement of the will, without free choice, but concerning an object that usually is the object of free choice. Does this count as a case of free will (and therefore responsibility) without free choice? Or is the point that we are responsible, despite our inability to exercise free choice in this particular moment, because we did exercise it earlier, in ways that left us vulnerable to an attack of passion?[11]

FREE CHOICE AND DIVINE FOREKNOWLEDGE

Another worry about human freedom has to do with divine foreknowledge of human choices and actions. Aquinas says that God's knowledge of creatures is both speculative and practical. Oversimplifying a bit, God knows things for the sake of knowing the truth about them but also for the sake of producing them.[12] Focusing for the moment on only the first of these (leaving the second for the next section), if the omniscient God already knows what I am going to do, then surely that's what I am going to do, and no alternative outcome is possible! From Aquinas's point of view, this doubt can be settled on the basis of reasoning that extends to all contingent events, not just free human actions. God does not really have *fore*-knowledge of contingent events, including our free choices and actions; instead, he simply *knows* everything that happens, because all of it is present to him in his own eternal presence. Furthermore, even though it is true that, necessarily, whatever God knows will happen *will* happen, it does not follow that whatever God knows will happen will happen *necessarily*.[13] Here again we see Aquinas operating in what we might think of as a libertarian fashion: God's foreknowledge (taken as speculative) leaves our choices free because it doesn't determine them.

FREE CHOICE AND DIVINE CAUSATION

A further difficulty for free choice arises as follows. On Aquinas's account, God not only knows what will happen, but also he is, in some way, causally responsible for it. On one level, it is unsurprising that Aquinas would say at least something along these lines. God, as creator of all, must *in some sense* be responsible for everything that happens; if God had not created the universe, then nothing would ever happen in the first place. But the question is how far this goes. Aquinas holds that God did not merely create the universe and then step back to let it run on its own; instead, God conserves it in being and continually works so as to draw actuality out of potentiality. Might this pose difficulties for the notion of free choice?

As noted earlier, God for Aquinas has not only speculative but also practical knowledge of creatures – he knows creatures in a way that is somehow productive of them. That means that the question we are discussing now, God's causation, is not entirely separable from the question discussed in the previous section – namely God's knowledge. Nonetheless, for ease of presentation, I will discuss the causal issue without reference to knowledge. Regardless of how God's causation of creatures is related to his knowledge of them, he does cause them, and that is enough to raise the difficulty I am concerned with here.[14]

The difficulty about divine causation takes two main forms. One is rooted in sacred theology – i.e., in thinking about God that takes revelation as an authority. This form of the difficulty grows out of the idea, central to Christian theology, that the will requires a supernatural influx of grace if humans are to act well, and especially if they are to merit eternal life.[15] Would such divine assistance undercut freedom? This is the main subject of Chapter 10 of this volume, and so I pass over it here.

The second version of the difficulty grows out of reflection about God and creation that is not based on revelation. Setting aside the question of grace, if God is the first cause of everything other than himself, and if 'everything' includes our acts of choosing, then it might seem that God causes our choices, in which case, it is not obvious how they can be free. What does Aquinas have to say about this?

On one line of interpretation, while Aquinas certainly thinks that God is responsible for the fact that humans exist with their natures and powers, he does not think that their individual free choices can be traced outside of themselves to God as efficient cause, because that would remove free choice.[16] And there are places where Aquinas speaks in ways that lend themselves to this interpretation.

For example, in *ST* I-II, q.9 a.6 ad 3, he notes that God gives humans a general inclination toward the good, and then he says that humans, by their reason, determine themselves to will in this or that particular direction. He adds that God sometimes (*interdum*) moves people to will something specific, giving as an example the way God moves the will by grace; but to say that God does this 'sometimes' gives the strong impression that, most of the time, God does not bring it about that people make the specific choices that they make.

On the other hand, there are texts that suggest a second line of interpretation. To begin with, Aquinas in a number of places states that everything other than God is caused by God, not only in the sense that God brings things into existence with their powers, and also conserves them in existence, but also in the sense that he moves or applies them to their actions in such a way that they act, not only by their own power, but also, and ultimately, in virtue of the divine power.[17] What's more, Aquinas sometimes states specifically that God causes movements of the will,[18] and, even more specifically, that God causes acts of choice.[19] Finally, in at least some of these texts, he seems to be speaking about all acts of will or choice. For reasons like these, some interpret Aquinas to hold, quite generally, and independently of any questions about grace, that God causes humans to make the choices that they make – that he causes them to make those choices freely.[20]

The first line of interpretation seems more libertarian in spirit, while the second has a somewhat compatibilist feel. On the other hand, I would again caution against making too much of this dichotomy. At least some commentators in the second camp would resist the compatibilist label, on the grounds that even if God causes our free choices in a way that cannot fail to bring them about, our choices are still, in some sense, not determined.[21]

The second line of interpretation seems easier to square with Aquinas's overall views on God and creation. God is the cause of every creature, and human choices are creatures, and Aquinas does explicitly say that God causes free movements of the will, including acts of choosing. On the other hand, one can be forgiven for finding this idea puzzling: That our choices are caused, and caused by an external agent, and even caused infallibly – all this can seem hard to square with their being free. Further, there is also a more specific difficulty: If God causes our choices, then how can we sin?[22]

If we do side with the second line of interpretation, we will at least have to admit that Aquinas does not provide a clear and detailed account of how divine causation is consistent with free choice. It may well turn out that the solution lies in the special nature of God's transcendent power; if so, it may even be that the details of the solution are inaccessible to us.[23] In any event, the question does not seem to have been pressing for Aquinas in such a way that he was driven to work it all out.[24]

FREE CHOICE AND PRACTICAL JUDGMENT

Now we come to one last difficulty for free choice, one derived from within Aquinas's own schema of decision making. Recall the crucial juncture between judgment and choice, *iudicium* and *electio*: Having deliberated, I conclude that such and such an action is the best one to perform, and, on that basis, I choose to perform it. One might now ask: Is my choice to perform this action controlled or determined by my having judged that it was the action to perform? For example, if I judge it best to take a taxi, is it therefore, on Aquinas's account, determined that I will do so?[25]

Those who say yes fall into the intellectualist camp: Choice is controlled by the intellect's practical judgment. Those who say no fall into the voluntarist camp: Choice is not controlled by the intellect's judgment. Here again, as with libertarianism and compatibilism, we have a distinction that is thought-provoking and helpful to a certain extent; on the other hand, different commentators interpret the distinction in different ways, so assigning Aquinas to one camp is of limited value.

Before going on, it is important to clear away a possible distraction. It is a common human experience that we think something is good or bad to do, and yet we act otherwise: We think, for example, that it would be unwise to eat that fourth slice of cake, but we eat it nonetheless. This is called 'weakness of the will' or '*akrasia.*' Weakness of the will is an important philosophical topic, but it is not the question under consideration here. As Aquinas understands it, weakness of the will happens when we choose in a way that is inconsistent with our habitual judgment about what should be done, but that does not mean it is independent of judgment altogether: At the moment at which we make our poor choice, we make it in accord with a different and erroneous judgment that has arisen and somehow managed to stand in for our habitual judgment, which has, as it were, gone dormant. I possess habitual knowledge that eating four slices of cake is bad for me, but when the moment of temptation comes, my passions overwhelm me, and that habitual knowledge does not serve to guide my choice: Instead, I reason in accord with a different judgment – namely, that it's good to eat tasty things. (Later, when my passion subsides, my habitual judgment recovers its earlier strength, and I regret my intemperate act.) Weakness of will, then, is not, on Aquinas's account, a case of choosing against judgment; on the contrary, it is a case of choosing with judgment (with a judgment that has momentarily overridden habitual judgment). So the question of *akrasia* is not relevant to the question at issue here.[26]

With the question of weakness of will set to one side, let us return to the question we are addressing in this section: How, for Aquinas, is choice's relation to practical judgment consistent with choice's freedom?

If Aquinas held that humans can just choose, regardless of their judgments about what to do, then the answer would be easy: Judgment could not possibly be seen as restricting choice at all. But this cannot be his view. He thinks of the will as a rational power, in such a way that whenever one chooses to perform some action, one so chooses on the basis of a judgment of reason.[27] This points strongly in the intellectualist direction. Such a reading of Aquinas can be pursued in either one of two main ways. One can think of Aquinas as an intellectualist of a compatibilist sort: Choice is determined by the intellect, and the intellect's operations are themselves determined, and yet this sort of causal determination is compatible with freedom.[28] Or one can think of Aquinas as an intellectualist of a libertarian sort: For example, one can hold that choice is determined by the intellect, but that the operations of the intellect are themselves undetermined.[29]

Other interpretations of Aquinas have, however, been offered, interpretations that see Aquinas as assigning a certain limited independence to the will. We can approach such voluntarist interpretations as follows. Recall that, for Aquinas, actions can typically be thought of in a variety of ways, some of which make them seem choiceworthy while others not. I can think of taking the taxi to the train station as quicker and more convenient, which makes it seem choiceworthy, or I can think of it as expensive, which makes it seem not choiceworthy. Likewise, I can think of taking the bus as cheaper, which makes it seem choiceworthy, or I can think of it as slow and inconvenient, which makes it seem not choiceworthy. It may be hard to arrive at a definitive judgment about what to do, and the more nearly balanced my options are, the harder it becomes to arrive at a final judgment. Now, on the one hand, this might make the thought that I have free choice seem more plausible – if I cannot make up my mind, there is no danger of my intellect constraining my choice. Yet the more true this is, the harder it becomes to understand how I ever do choose.

What this means is that our question – how, for Aquinas, freedom of choice is related to the intellect's judgment – is bound up with the question of how deliberation ends. Why does deliberation end at one point rather than another? Why do I end up taking the bus rather than the taxi? Some see Aquinas as holding that it is not the intellect but instead the will that closes the deal. The intellect plays an important role, to be sure: It specifies what the will chooses when it does choose. But the will itself, not the intellect, explains the exercise of the power of choice.[30] This means that the judgment whose proposed action gets chosen is not the judgment that wins the debate, so to speak, but the judgment that is being entertained when the will intervenes. Perhaps the intervention takes the form of a positive choice for the option currently presented by the intellect; perhaps it takes the form of a cessation of the will to deliberate.[31]

Any voluntarist interpretation would seem to face the following difficulty: If choice, for Aquinas, is rational by definition, then choosing must be choosing *for a reason*. Of course, I have a reason to go by taxi and a reason to go by bus, but to finally decide, I must have a reason to choose one over the other (or a reason to cease deliberating now rather than continue deliberating).[32] Such an intellectualist objection, however, leaves unaddressed its opponent's concern: Since, for Aquinas, many options can be understood as choiceworthy, it is unclear how deliberation could ever come to a conclusion without outside intervention.

Up until now, we have been approaching our question while taking, as the paradigm situation of choosing, a situation in which the chooser is facing a number of options, each of which has a pretty good case to be choiceworthy. As we all know from experience, choosing is very difficult in situations like these. But consider a different sort of situation. Suppose I am diagnosed with a strep infection, and suppose my doctor prescribes amoxicillin. If I think of taking amoxicillin as a low-cost way of eliminating a potentially serious infection, then taking it seems choiceworthy, but if I think of it as visually repellant and nasty-tasting, then it seems the opposite of choiceworthy. I am not *determined* to think of taking the amoxicillin as good or bad, choiceworthy or unchoiceworthy: I *could* think of it in either way. And yet, to a rational adult with even a modicum of temperance, this is, in fact, a very easy choice to make, and there is only a very weak sense in which I could decide that the medicine is just too yucky to take.

A late discussion by Aquinas seems to frame the issue in more or less this way.[33] In addressing the question of why the will is drawn one way rather than the other, Aquinas notes three possibilities: First, one option has more weight, and in this case the will follows reason; second, the agent may think of one thing rather than another, as happens when one is caught by surprise; third, the agent has some disposition that makes things look a certain way – Aquinas gives, as an example, the fact that things look differently to someone who is angry and to someone who is not. It strikes me as significant that Aquinas seems to think of the first possibility as the one in which the will is moved as it ought to be – it is moved "according to reason." Also significant is the way Aquinas ends these remarks. He notes that, if one's judgment is affected by one's disposition, one can often (though perhaps with difficulty) remove this disposition, and he gives as an example the fact that one can quiet one's anger. Aquinas seems to be portraying the agent not as choosing among more or less equally good options, but instead as choosing among a good option and some inferior options. A chooser who chooses the good option does so in virtue of judging correctly, in accord with reason; a chooser who chooses a bad option does so in virtue of judging incorrectly as a result of some defect.

When we think of the situation this way, then there is less temptation to go in a voluntarist direction. There's no need for a more or less arbitrary choice that would cut off otherwise endless deliberation. Either we correctly grasp that we should take our medicine, and then we do; or, perhaps, overcome by our inability to tolerate a brief but horrible taste, we assess the situation incorrectly and refuse the medicine.

It seems plausible to me that when Aquinas thinks about free choice, his paradigm for the situation in which choice is exercised is the sort of situation we have just been considering: a situation in which the right choice is clear, and in which deviations would be accounted for by pointing to some defect in the agent. On this reading, freedom of choice is more about the possibility of going right or wrong than it is about the possibility of creatively choosing among options that, in themselves, don't require one choice rather than another. If we think about the issue in this normatively loaded way, the general question of how deliberation ends becomes less troublesome. Agents who are in the right frame of mind settle on the right answer; the fact that other answers are available, and that they are not *entirely* irrational, will still not make choosing difficult for such agents. Agents who are not in the right frame of mind – who lack time to deliberate, or who are suffering from momentary passion or settled vice – will easily settle on the wrong answer. The right answer is available to such agents in principle, and it is not, even from their distorted perspective, *entirely* irrational, but again there is no difficulty in understanding why they go in the direction that they do. Of course, not all situations are so clear-cut. There will always be situations in which any agent will be flummoxed by a variety of apparently equal choices. But if we do not think of such cases as our paradigm situation of choice, we will not be puzzled about how choice ever happens at all, and we will be less inclined to suppose that it just happens in some mysterious way.[34] As for the situations in which deliberation seems endless and fruitless (as when there are 500 items on the takeout menu), we can see such situations merely as what happens to human beings when they land in situations for which their psychological system for choice is not well-suited. (Think of this analogy: Our color acuity is greatly diminished in low-light conditions, but this is no reason to wonder how it ever happens that we distinguish colors.)

To the extent that we allow ourselves to see the paradigm of choice as being one in which deviations from the right answer are examples of defect on the part of the agent, we must now face the following deep question: Why do agents go wrong, and how can wrongdoing be free? If, with Aquinas, we accept the Christian doctrine of the fall, wrongdoing might seem unsurprising, but that addresses only the general state of things. It does not explain why this agent goes wrong in this way at this time. And however illuminating one might find Aquinas's analysis of why people choose as they do in particular situations, one might worry that his analysis leaves us with no explanation of how choice is free. If I am in a mental state in which

I prefer health to momentary sensory displeasure, and if I have time to think, and so on, I will choose to drink my medicine. If I am not in such a state, I won't drink it. But is it up to me what sort of state I am in?

Aquinas is aware of this concern. He says that our character is, to a significant extent, the result of our free choices, and (as we saw earlier) he says the same thing about our ability to respond well to surprises or upsurges of passion.[35] All this seems promising as an explanation of why people choose as they choose, but it does not answer, but only defers, the problem of freedom: We can't ultimately explain the freedom of our choices now by saying that they result from earlier free choices, unless we have an independent account of what made those earlier choices free.

Much of the discussion in this section has been dominated, or at any rate influenced, by the thought that a good interpretation of Aquinas must decide between two options: Judgment controls choice or choice controls itself. But perhaps it is a mistake to approach things in this way. Perhaps choice is something that happens through the interaction of intellect and will, in such a way that the question of whether intellect or will has the last word is somehow not the right question in the first place.[36] This is an interesting and promising way to think about free choice, but Aquinas does not say it clearly, and so it would be difficult to confidently attribute it to him.

To conclude this section, the question of how will and intellect interact to bring about truly free choices has led to enormous controversy among Aquinas's commentators. It may be that the deepest reason for this is simply that, despite the great interest of the many things he says on the topic, Aquinas never provides a detailed account that shows how it all fits together.

CONCLUSION

Aquinas clearly believes that humans have freedom of will and freedom of decision or choice. His defense of choice's freedom is libertarian in style with respect to some potential freedom-blockers: for example, physical determinants, or the passions. With respect to some others, however – here I am thinking of divine causation and of the intellect's judgment – it is hard to be sure whether to go in a libertarian or a compatibilist direction. Some of these issues have been sources of disagreement among students of Aquinas for a very long time. It's worth considering the possibility that the works Aquinas left us allow for more than one reading in a way that cannot really be overcome.[37]

NOTES

1 See, for example, *ST* I q.83 a.1.

2 See *ST* I q.82 a.2. For extended discussion of the distinction between free will and free choice, see T. Hoffmann and C. Michon, "Aquinas on Free Will and Intellectual Determinism," *Philosophers' Imprint* 17 (2017): 1–36, here pp. 3–8. For a more general look at the elusiveness of the concept of freedom in Aquinas, see J. A. Spiering, "'What Is Freedom?': An Instance of the Silence of St. Thomas," *American Catholic Philosophical Quarterly* 89 (2015): 27–46.

3 See *ST* I q.82 a.1 ad 1; *QDV* q.24 a.1 ad 20.

4 For a good recent discussion of Aquinas on the "principle of alternative possibilities," see P. Furlong, "Aquinas, the Principle of Alternative Possibilities, and Augustine's Axiom," *International Philosophical Quarterly* 55 (2015): 179–96.

5 Here I have followed the schema as laid out by D. Westberg in *Right Practical Reason: Aristotle, Action, and Prudence in Aquinas* (New York: Oxford University Press, 1994), ch. 8. As Westberg explains, other readings of Aquinas have been offered. I do not think the discrepancies matter for present purposes.

6 Aquinas notes that sometimes, only one option is worth considering, in which case deliberation is passed over (*ST* I-II q.14 a.4) and consent and choice amount to the same thing (*ST* I-II q.15 a3 ad 3).

7 *ST* I q.83 a.3. I say "often" because in some important texts, for example, *QDM* q.6, the expression *liberum arbitrium* appears infrequently.

8 See *ST* I-II q.10 a.2.

9 See, for example, *ST* I q.115 a.4; *SCG* III.84–5.

10 See, for example, *ST* I-II q.10 a.3; *ST* I-II q.77 a.7.

11 *QDV* q.24 a.12. On this issue, compare E. Stump, *Aquinas* (New York and London: Routledge, 2003), pp. 297–8 with Hoffmann and Michon, "Aquinas on Free Will and Intellectual Determinism," pp. 8–10.

12 *ST* I q.14 a.16.

13 For both of these considerations, see *ST* I q.14 a.13; *SCG* I.67. For discussion, see J. F. Wippel, "Divine Knowledge, Divine Power, and Human Freedom in Thomas Aquinas and Henry of Ghent" in *Metaphysical Themes in Thomas Aquinas* (Washington, DC: The Catholic University of America Press, 1995), pp. 244–55; Stump, *Aquinas*, ch. 4.

14 For an exchange where the issue of causation is treated closely together with the issue of knowledge, see E. Stump and N. Kretzmann, "Eternity and God's Knowledge: A Reply to Shanley," *American Catholic Philosophical Quarterly* 72 (1998): 439–45; B. J. Shanley, "Aquinas on God's Causal Knowledge: A Reply to Stump and Kretzmann," *American Catholic Philosophical Quarterly* 72 (1998): 447–57.

15 See, for example, *ST* I-II q.109.

16 For a particularly clear statement of this line of thought, see Stump and Kretzmann, "Eternity and God's Knowledge," especially p. 441, note 8.

17 See, for example, *QDP* q.3 a.7; *ST* I q.105 a.5.

18 See, for example, *QDV* q.22 a.8; *SCG* III.89; *ST* I. q.105 a.4; *QDM* q.3 a.3. At ad 14, Aquinas interestingly contrasts God's interior movement of the will with the fact that the devil can move us only from the outside, by persuasion (a persuasion we can refuse to accept).

19 See, for example, *ST* I q.22 a.2 ad 4; *ST* I q.83 a.1 ad 3; *QDM* q.3 a.2 ad 4.

20 See, for example, Wippel, "Divine Knowledge, Divine Power, and Human Freedom," pp. 255–63; B. J. Shanley, "Divine Causation and Human Freedom in Aquinas," *American Catholic Philosophical Quarterly* 72 (1998): 99–122; W. M. Grant, "Aquinas among Libertarians and Compatibilists: Breaking the Logic of Theological Determinism," *Proceedings of the American Catholic Philosophical Association* 75 (2001): 221–35; F. J. Matava, *Divine Causality and Human Free Choice: Domingo Báñez, Physical Premotion and the Controversy de Auxiliis Revisited* (Leiden: Brill, 2016), ch. 6.

21 Loughran sees Aquinas as a compatibilist (but note that he discusses the philosophical and the theological problems together); Grant denies that Aquinas is a compatibilist; for Shanley, neither label is appropriate. See S. Loughran, "Aquinas, Compatibilist" in F. W. McLain and W. M. Richardson

(eds.), *Human and Divine Agency: Anglican, Catholic, and Lutheran Perspectives* (Lanham, MD: University Press of America, 1999), pp. 1–39; Grant, "Aquinas among Libertarians and Compatibilists"; B. J. Shanley, "Beyond Libertarianism and Compatibilism: Thomas Aquinas on Created Freedom" in R. Velkley (ed.), *Freedom and the Human Person* (Washington, DC: The Catholic University of America Press, 2008), pp. 70–89.

22   Aquinas discusses this question in, among other places, *ST* I-II q.79 and *QDM* q.3 aa.1–2.

23   See Matava, *Divine Causality and Human Free Choice*, pp. 292–5.

24   As Matava, *Divine Causality and Human Free Choice*, pp. 243–5 explains, it was not until the Reformation that such problems took center stage.

25   For discussion of the question whether Aquinas's views on this question changed or developed, see D. Westberg, "Did Aquinas Change His Mind about the Will?," *The Thomist* 58 (1994): 41–60.

26   For one of Aquinas's discussions of weakness of will, see *ST* I-II q.77 a.2.

27   See, for example, *ST* I-II q.13 aa.1–3.

28   Hause and Williams take Aquinas to be an intellectualist, and they are at least open to seeing this in a compatibilist way. See J. Hause, "Thomas Aquinas and the Voluntarists," *Medieval Philosophy and Theology* 6 (1997): 167–82; T. Williams, "Human Freedom and Agency" in B. Davies and E. Stump (eds.), *The Oxford Handbook of Aquinas* (New York: Oxford University Press, 2012), pp. 199–208.

29   MacDonald and McCluskey develop understandings of Aquinas that run along intellectualist-libertarian lines. See S. MacDonald, "Aquinas's Libertarian Account of Free Choice," *Revue Internationale de Philosophie* 52 (1998): 309–28; C. McCluskey, "Intellective Appetite and the Freedom of Human Action," *The Thomist* 66 (2002): 421–56.

30   The distinction between the specification and exercise of the will's act, crucial for some commentators, is found in texts such as *ST* I-II q.10 a.2 and *QDM* q.6.

31   For the former idea, see D. Gallagher, "Free Choice and Free Judgment in Thomas Aquinas," *Archiv für Geschichte der Philosophie* 76 (1994): 247–77; for the latter, see S. Jensen, "Libertarian Free Choice: A Thomistic Account," *The Thomist* 81 (2017): 315–43.

32   Or must I? For discussions of Aquinas that explicitly raise the possibility that such "contrastive reasons" are not necessary, see Hoffmann and

Michon, "Aquinas on Free Will and Intellectual Determinism," pp. 29–30;
also T. Hoffmann and P. Furlong, "Free Choice" in M. V. Dougherty (ed.),
Aquinas's Disputed Questions on Evil: A Critical Guide (Cambridge:
Cambridge University Press, 2016), pp. 64–5.

33 *QDM* q.6. My reading of this passage is, to some extent, influenced by
L. Dewan, "St. Thomas and the Causes of Free Choice," *Acta
Philosophica* 8 (1999): 87–96.

34 Gallagher, "Free Choice and Free Judgment in Thomas Aquinas," p. 277:
"We cannot give a reason[,] other than the will itself, why the will acts
according to this particular reason ... We can find no reason that
eliminates the radical contingency of freedom, but rather we can only
acknowledge its character as a mystery."

35 See, for example, *ST* I q.83, a.1 ad 5 and the texts cited in note 10.

36 For an approach like this, see D. Westberg, *Right Practical Reason*, ch. 6.
Stump, *Aquinas*, while exhibiting some voluntarist tendencies (e.g.,
p. 105) strikes me overall as tending in this direction (e.g., pp. 278–97).

37 I am grateful to Miriam Pritschet for research assistance, and to Peter
Furlong for detailed advice (no doubt insufficiently heeded) on an
earlier draft.

PART IV **Ethics**

10 Grace and Free Will

Tobias Hoffmann

Grace is a gratuitous divine gift that exceeds our human nature and allows us to obtain a supernatural, eternal good. Thomas Aquinas, who attempts to formulate the orthodox Christian teaching on grace, understands by it in one sense a stable disposition (*habitus*) infused by God into the soul that lifts human nature so as to partake in the divine nature. It is thus a created reality, not simply the fact of enjoying God's favor. In a second sense, he understands by grace an aid (*auxilium*) of God moving us to know, will, or do something. While Aquinas's terminology varies, scholars call the first kind 'habitual grace' and the second 'actual grace.'[1]

Grace connects God's free will with ours. God grants it or not, as he likes. His grace does not eliminate our free will, but rather enhances our entire soul beyond its natural limitations and inclines us to do what is right. We remain free, however, to resist grace. Only when grace is consummated, in the beatific vision of God, do we become unable to resist God's goodness. We will still be free, but unable to do evil.

In Aquinas we do not find a systematic discussion of the relation of grace and free will, but his various remarks on this topic form a coherent theory which is deeply rooted in Holy Scripture. After his first Parisian teaching period, he obtained increased direct knowledge of Augustine's writings on grace, making him revise key aspects of his

Research for this chapter was made possible through a fellowship from the Centre of Advanced Studies, Human Abilities (Berlin). I am grateful for the invitation and for helpful comments received during a colloquium at the Centre.

233

earlier teaching on grace and free will. This chapter focuses on his mature theory.[2]

Given the importance of the topic to the Christian faith and its centrality to the Reformation and the Counter-Reformation as crucial developments in Western culture, the position of Aquinas, as one of Christianity's finest and most influential theologians, is of great significance.

DIFFERENT MEANINGS OF FREEDOM

In his discussions of grace, Aquinas speaks of freedom in different senses. Three meanings stand out: one is freedom from sin, the opposite of slavery to sin (cf. John 8:31–6; Rom. 6:17–22). A second meaning is free will, or freedom of the will (*libertas voluntatis*), which can be enjoyed even apart from the ability to will (or act) otherwise, since it involves only acting of one's own accord. Hence it is also called freedom from coercion. Coercion imposes necessity, but not all necessity is coercive. Hence free will, broadly conceived, is compatible with what the medievals call necessity of immutability, as when a person in the final perfection cannot help but love God. A third meaning of free will is free choice (*liberum arbitrium*), which is incompatible with necessity of immutability, for it implies the ability to will otherwise. Free choice relates to free will broadly conceived like a species to a genus.[3] While free choice implies alternative possibilities, according to Aquinas we do not always have access to both alternatives, for God can move our free choice to one alternative. Aquinas speaks of free choice in two senses. One is a situational sense: Someone may have free choice under determinate conditions, but not under others.[4] But predominantly he understands it as the *power* to make free choices. This power coincides with the will itself and is therefore permanent.[5] While this chapter is about the relation of grace to all three notions of freedom, the focus will be on its relation to free choice.

GRACE AND THE LIMITS OF FREE WILL

In Aquinas's Christian vision of reality, God is not only the beginning (*principium*) of all that is, but also the end (*finis*), and in a special way of the rational creature – that is, of human beings and angels.[6] God orders human beings (and angels) to beatitude, that is, perfect happiness, obtained in the beatific vision of God's essence.[7] It is by God's generosity that he orders us to this end, for the beatific vision is not owed to us according to our nature.[8] Within the limits of our own nature – in other words, by our own power – we can only obtain imperfect happiness, which consists in the contemplative life of study and wisdom and the active life of the exercise of the moral virtues. Only God enjoys beatitude by nature; for us, beatitude is supernatural and can only be attained through God's action – that is, by grace – although not without our good works.[9]

Our existential situation in this life is marked by a condition that is a further reason why we need grace. According to Christian teaching, human nature, and hence every individual human being, is in a morally degraded condition because of original sin. As Aquinas explains, Adam and Eve, the first human beings, received from God the grace of original justice, which made reason and will subject to God, the lower powers to reason, and the body to the soul. Through Adam, original justice was meant to be given to all of human nature. Through Adam's personal sin, he lost original justice for himself and for all of his descendants. Original sin is the existential condition in which we lack original justice and consequently experience concupiscence – that is, the disorder of the lower powers, which are not fully in the control of reason.[10]

Original sin, just like personal sin, stains us, corrupts our natural goodness and hence our ability to do good, and puts us in a state of guilt that deserves punishment. To free us from sin and its effects, we need a supernatural dispositional gift of God.[11] Aquinas calls it variably sanctifying grace (gratia gratum faciens, literally grace that makes cherished or acceptable), justifying grace (gratia iustificans), and healing grace (gratia sanans).[12]

Aquinas asks a series of questions about what we are able to accomplish without grace. For anything that exceeds the ability of human nature, habitual grace was necessary already prior to original sin, for example, to will a supernatural good, to observe the divine precepts from charity, and to do so-called meritorious works that earn eternal life. But it was possible without habitual grace to do everything that is connatural to human nature: to avoid sin, to live perfectly virtuous lives, to love God above all things, to observe all the divine precepts (although not from charity). In our present condition marked by original sin, we can accomplish even what is connatural to us only if the weakness of our human nature is remedied by habitual grace. Before and after original si, the aid of God moving our will is necessary to act perfectly.[13] Without habitual grace, we have a limited ability to avoid sin, as Aquinas shows distinctly regarding mortal sins (sins against charity, which separate us from God, our ultimate end) and venial sin (deficiencies that do not separate us from God). We can avoid individual mortal sins, but not for a long time, for avoiding each particular mortal sin requires an amount of attention that we are unable to uphold for long. When endowed with habitual grace, we can abstain from mortal sin, although in order to persevere – to avoid mortal sin permanently – we need additional, actual graces that remedy our ignorance and the corruption of our flesh, that is, the disorder of our sensory appetite. Aquinas remarks that, for this reason, we need to pray to avoid sin and to receive the gift of perseverance. But even endowed with habitual and actual grace, we cannot for long avoid all venial sins.[14]

Without grace, then, our will has significant limitations. Is it at least up to us to prepare ourselves for grace – in other words, to convert ourselves to God and so to dispose ourselves to his grace? According to Aquinas, everyone desires happiness as the ultimate end, but not everyone desires God as that in which our happiness consists.[15] Only God himself, by actual grace, can convert us to intend him as our end; that is, to wish to adhere to him as our good. By attracting us to him as our end, God does not bypass our will, specifically our free choice (*liberum arbitrium*), but rather acts through it.[16]

In his early writings, Aquinas considered the natural capacities of the will to be greater. While he denied the Pelagian view that without grace we can do meritorious works – those acts that earn eternal life – he thought that without grace we are able to avoid permanently all mortal sins, to fulfill all the divine precepts, and even to prepare ourselves for grace by doing what lies in our power, upon which God would grant us his grace.[17] His early view about the preparation for grace thus assigns to our free will a certain control over the gift of grace. He later learned that the view that the beginning of justification requires no grace, only its full achievement (consummatio) – known in modern theology as semi-Pelagianism – is heterodox. So he revised his earlier position, because it came too close to semi-Pelagianism.[18]

PREDESTINATION

The bestowal of grace belongs to providence, the divine plan for leading all things to their final end, which is God's own goodness. The part of providence that concerns rational creatures is called predestination, a concept rooted in the Pauline epistles.[19] Among the effects of predestination is not only eternal salvation or glory – that is, the grace of the beatific vision – but also the graces necessary to attain it.[20] Aquinas's account of predestination is therefore central to comprehending his theory of grace.

Predestination presupposes God's election, which in turn is rooted in his love. Yet God elects only a determinate number for salvation, not everyone, for some fall short of attaining their final end because of their sin, whom God therefore reprobates.[21] God does not, however, predestine the elect because he foresees their merits. Quite the opposite: Whichever merits we may have are the effect of predestination, as is everything we do that orders us to salvation, including preparing ourselves for grace and using the grace we have received.[22] If predestined, the elect will attain salvation "most certainly and infallibly."[23] They are predestined to be saved through Christ's redemption,[24] which was itself achieved through free action, as we will see later in the chapter.

Predestination and reprobation are asymmetrical: While predestination is the cause of grace in this life and of glory in the next, reprobation is not the cause of fault in this life, only of eternal punishment thereafter. The fault comes from the individuals' own free choice; God does not cause but only permits their fault, which means that he does not prevent it. God offers his grace to all; some accept it, others do not. Those who close themselves to grace do so of their own fault and are therefore justly condemned. Aquinas compares them to those who cannot see sunlight because they shut their eyes.[25] Reprobation, then, has its root in a free decision by those who refute God's grace.

Aquinas finds the asymmetry of predestination and reprobation expressed in Hosea 13:9, which he quotes as follows: "Your ruin is from yourself, Israel; and only from me is your help." Thus, Aquinas does not adopt a theory of double predestination, as though God predestined not only to salvation but also to damnation.[26]

The theory of selective predestination, while claiming the authority of St. Paul (especially Rom. 8:28–30, 9:6–29), is in tension with the Apostle's assurance that God wants all human beings to be saved (1 Tim 2:4). To solve the tension, Aquinas adopts John of Damascus's distinction between God's antecedent and consequent will and illustrates it with this example: A just judge wants antecedently that every human being live; but upon full consideration, he wants a particular person to be hanged – not insofar as he is a human being, but as he is a murderer. So, too, God wants antecedently all to be saved, but his all-things-considered will is to damn the reprobate because of their sin.[27]

What is the role of our free choice with regard to predestination, since it is not based on our merits? Aquinas attributes a great role to free choice; for, in his view, there is no distinction between what comes from predestination and grace, on the one hand, and from our free choice, on the other, for they relate like the primary cause to the secondary cause. As we will see in more detail in the next section, God as primary cause is actively contributing to every effect of a secondary cause (i.e., created cause). Hence, what is done by free choice comes also from predestination.[28] For this reason, even though predestination reaches its effect unfailingly, it does so contingently, for it happens through our free choice.[29] This is also the reason why

Aquinas can exclude two opposite errors regarding the efficacy of prayer: the idea that our prayers and whatever we do for our salvation are irrelevant; and the idea that our prayers might change divine predestination. Instead, while our prayers do not alter predestination, they belong to its effect. God's general providence achieves its effect not apart from, but through, secondary causes. So, too, predestination, as part of providence, achieves its effect through the prayers or other good things we do. Hence, Aquinas urges us to make the effort of prayer and good works so that predestination may attain its effect.[30] Based on a story transmitted by John of Damascus, Aquinas gives the example that Trajan was predestined to be saved by the prayers of a certain Gregory, without whose prayers he would have been damned.[31] Unfortunately, however, our prayers are heard only for the predestined, not for the reprobate.[32]

According to Aquinas, then, free choice badly used is the cause of reprobation, while a good use of free choice is not the cause of predestination, but only the cause of its effects. Nevertheless, we may wonder why God does not predestine all to salvation, given that on Aquinas's view predestination is a guarantee of salvation. God attracts to himself even some who are averse to him, so why does he not attract all?[33] According to Aquinas, the acceptance of grace is itself a gift of grace and the effect of predestination,[34] so why does God permit some to resist his grace, while he moves others to accept it?

Aquinas can make only the general terms of God's election intelligible, not the particular preference of one person over another. God's purpose is that the universe may represent the divine goodness in different ways. The predestination of the elect represents God's goodness as mercy, whereas reprobation represents his goodness as justice. "But why he elects these to glory, and why he reprobates those, has no reason, except the divine will."[35] Aquinas compares it to building a house: There is a reason why there must be bricks in each wall, but not why this brick ought to be here and that brick there. To counter the appearance of injustice, Aquinas remarks that predestination is not due to anyone. When someone encounters two beggars and gives money only to one, the benefactor thereby does no injustice to the other.[36] According to this teaching, those who miss out on salvation did not find God's mercy.

There is an uncomfortable implication in Aquinas's account of predestination. As we have seen, he traces reprobation not to a divine choice, but to human sin, which God does not cause or want, only permits. Those who are not part of the elect may well receive grace, but not the grace of perseverance in the good until the end of their lives, or the grace of accepting grace. Because of original sin, they will sooner or later sin mortally, and so they will be punished with eternal damnation for their personal sin, or even for original sin itself.[37] Salvation is undeserved, and the election and predestination for salvation depend on God, not the individual. Reprobation is deserved; yet whether an individual ends up deserving reprobation follows inevitably from being left out from God's election and predestination. On the other hand, Aquinas holds that we are free to accept or refute God's grace, and it is up to us whether we pray for God's grace. And when discussing the certitude of hope, Aquinas denies that the failure of some to attain beatitude is due to God's lack of mercy; he attributes it not to the divine will, but entirely to their own free choice posing the obstacle of sin.[38] So Aquinas seems to hold that it is ultimately up to the individual whether he or she belongs to the reprobate. Given this tension, it is not surprising that his theory of predestination has been subject to quite different interpretations.[39] A similar tension is found in Augustine's account, after which Aquinas's is largely modeled.[40]

An indication that for Aquinas reprobation is not in the last analysis the outcome of a divine choice is found in his theory of angelic sin. The angels lack original sin, and, according to Aquinas, those who sinned did not do so necessarily, even when left without grace.[41] He also accepts, at least implicitly, Anselm of Canterbury's claim that the devil sinned not because God did not want to offer him grace, but because he did not want to accept it.[42]

GOD'S MOTION OF OUR WILL

Aquinas holds, as we have seen, that God causing our acts leaves our free choice intact. To understand the relation between the causality of grace and our will, we need to turn to the general relation between God as primary cause and creatures as secondary causes.

For Aquinas, this relation is largely similar regarding natural causes and the will. Using the example of fire causing heat, he wants to avoid two extremes: to say that God, not fire, causes heat (a view he attributes to Islamic theologians called *mutakallimūn*), and, conversely, to say that fire, not God, causes heat. Rather, both God and fire produce the same effect, but at different levels. God is not a cause like other causes, for he acts as the creator and thus in a way that is beyond our experience of how a cause acts. Aquinas mentions four dimensions of God's activity as primary cause: He gives a secondary cause its power to act; he conserves this power in being; he applies this power to the action, thus allowing it to employ its own force, such as when a knife's cutting power is applied to an object; and he is that by virtue of which the secondary cause acts, just as a pickaxe acts by virtue of a person swinging it. He clarifies that God sustains the action of the secondary cause by acting not externally but directly within the secondary cause, since by giving each thing its existence, he is present in it. Thereby God does not eliminate the operation of the secondary cause – whether it be the will or a natural cause – but rather makes its operation possible.[43] So in Aquinas's view, God's contribution does not limit itself to giving things the powers to act, but rather he is causally active in the very exercise of those powers.

Nevertheless, God does not degrade us to his puppets, but rather leaves room for free choice. God's primary causality in everything that happens does not mean that everything happens by necessity. Rather, God makes it so that some things happen necessarily, others contingently, because God prepared necessary secondary causes for necessary effects and contingent secondary causes for contingent effects.[44] In moving the will, God makes it so that we control our acts – in other words, that we determine ourselves to alternative outcomes. Natural causes lack such control. A falling stone cannot help but fall down; all swallows make similar nests and all spiders similar webs.[45] What is special about the will is that it is a moved self-mover. In fact, instruments are moved in different ways: A saw is moved by the artisan in a purely corporeal way; a horse is moved by the rider through its sensory appetite; a slave is moved by the master through his or her will.[46] Accordingly, when we are moved by God as an instrument, this does not exclude that we move ourselves by our free choice.[47] So God moves our will to its act not by necessity or force, but "in the mode of free will" – by making it so that we act voluntarily.[48] In sum, God as the author of our being moves us in a unique way, not only respecting our freedom, but actually causing it.[49]

Since we are not only moved, but also move ourselves in our choicemaking, we are responsible for our actions.[50] In our sinful acts, what belongs to their perfection (especially their existence as acts) is mainly from God, but what belongs to their deficiency is from us.[51]

God's causation of our willing is also unique in another way. Created things can cause our willing only by formal causality (giving content to our willing) or final causality (being the reason for our willing something).[52] But God can cause our willing by efficient causality (from not willing something to willing it). Willing is an inner inclination; it cannot be imposed from without. We can be forced to do something, but not to will something – no more than a stone can be forced to move upward by its own inclination. Only God, from whom all things have their inclinations, can change a natural inclination or the inclination of the will. And so he can move us by grace to will a determinate thing.[53]

Aquinas sees an important confirmation for the rootedness of our willing in God in the following reflection. What grounds the control of our acts is that we act upon deliberation – that is, upon reasoning about which means are best to achieve a particular end. But what grounds the control of our deliberation? If it could come only from prior deliberation, we would have an infinite regress. Instead, following Aristotle's *Eudemian Ethics* (VII.14, 1248a15–29), Aquinas traces it to God, who moves our will while leaving it indeterminate regarding alternatives.[54]

We will consider in the next three sections how God's grace and human free choice act together.

CHRIST'S AND THE VIRGIN MARY'S FREE WILL

We have seen that divine predestination leaves room for human free choice insofar as its realization happens through our free choice. This does not mean that our salvation depends on one or the other particular choice of ours, for there are many acts through which we can merit eternal life, as we will see in the following section. But our salvation depended upon two particular human acts: on Christ's acceptance of his passion and the Virgin Mary's consent to become his mother. For God's plan to succeed, Christ and Mary had to act as they did.

Through his passion, which Christ underwent voluntarily, he freed us from sin and fault, reconciled us with God, and "opened for us the door of heaven."[55] Christ is in fact the mediator of all grace.[56] Christ himself, according to his human nature, was predestined to be the cause of our predestination, in that God arranged from eternity that through him we may be saved.[57]

Christ's human will is a distinct power from his divine will, with distinct acts of willing. Even so, Aquinas writes that God's will moved Christ's human will from within to will in conformity with it, just as it does regarding the will of other saints, "which operates in them to will and to carry out" (Phil. 2:13). Christ's human nature was an instrument of his divine nature, but one that moves by free will, unlike lifeless tools or work animals.[58] Christ's human will was naturally inclined to avoid pain and was thus averse to undergoing the passion that God wanted him to suffer. But by his considered will, Christ always willed the same as God.[59] This does not mean that he lacked free choice in his human nature; his will was fixed on the good, but not determined to will this or that good.[60]

Mary, too, had a unique role in the accomplishment of God's plan; and, as being closest to Christ, who has the fullness of all graces, she participated most in his grace. By giving birth to Christ, she was instrumental in grace reaching everyone else.[61] According to Aquinas, at the annunciation her consent was expected as a proxy for all humanity. He all but writes that, although she consented freely – that is, without being coerced – she could not have done otherwise.[62] She is like the proverbial mother who could not help but save her child from drowning. As we will see in the next section, Aquinas writes explicitly that grace can infallibly move us to give our free consent.

OPERATIVE AND COOPERATIVE GRACE

Grace never operates without or even against our free will, but it does not always produce its effect in cooperation with our will. When God's grace moves our mind – that is, our intellect and will – to produce its effect without our collaboration, it is called operative grace; when it does so with our cooperation, it is called cooperative grace. Aquinas makes this conceptual distinction regarding both actual grace and habitual grace.[63]

By operative actual grace, God causes our justification by efficient causality, moving us to will the good – especially after willing evil – and to have an act of faith, by which we believe that God brings about our justification through Christ.[64] Once our will is thus fixed on the good end, we can collaborate with cooperative actual grace to do good deeds in view of this end, and thereby we can accomplish God's precepts and counsels.[65] God does not justify us without us, because we consent to our justification, but this consent is itself an effect of grace, and if God so wants, it comes about infallibly, albeit without coercion.[66] Justification can happen instantaneously, as in the conversion of St. Paul, but usually it progresses in stages: At first there is imperfect conversion and nascent charity, both of which gradually grow through further grace and our collaboration with it.[67]

Operative habitual grace, too, accomplishes our justification, yet not by acting directly on our will, but by transforming our very being, making us participate in the divine nature. It does so not as an efficient cause, but as a formal cause: Just as whiteness makes a surface white, so too operative habitual grace heals us, justifies us, and makes us acceptable to God. Habitual grace lays the foundation for our ability to do meritorious actions; in this respect, it is cooperative habitual grace.[68] What disposes us to receive habitual grace is not an effort we make, but operative actual grace, moving our soul and inspiring in us a good purpose.[69]

Aquinas's teaching on merit illustrates in a special way the relation between free will and grace. Merit is a notion that belongs to justice, whereas grace is gratuitous. Nevertheless, we can merit to receive grace. Because of a divine arrangement, God commits himself to grant eternal life and other graces as a reward for actions done freely out of charity. And so "every human act that is in the power of free choice, if related to God, can be meritorious."[70] The possibility of doing such meritorious actions presupposes habitual grace, which reconciles us with God. Insofar as our acts come from our free choice, they are not proportioned to any divine reward, and so they merit only by some fittingness (ex congruo), because it is fitting that God rewards those who do what they can. But insofar as our acts have God as their principle, there is a relation among equals. In fact, by making us adopted sons and daughters, we become God's rightful heirs and able to merit in a way that is wholly deserving (ex condigno).[71]

Since merit presupposes habitual grace, one cannot merit for oneself the first grace – the grace of conversion or justification; nor can one merit the forgiveness of sin, since sin is an impediment to merit. Even when endowed with habitual grace, one can attain perseverance only through unmerited actual graces. Fortunately, God gives graces not only as merited and hence out of justice, but also out of mercy. We can obtain many unmerited graces in response to our prayers.[72]

Fundamentally, what the relation between grace and our free will amounts to is the relationship between God's gratuitous love and our response. While our response is free, regarding both operative and cooperative grace, it is in our control only with regard to cooperative grace.

It is also possible that we obstruct God's grace. We cannot block God's first initiative; that is, his directing us by actual grace to the good in preparation for habitual grace. But, thereafter, we can resist the further bestowal of grace.[73] Worse, through mortal sin, we entirely lose charity and all grace.[74]

INFUSED VIRTUES, GIFTS, AND SACRAMENTS

Insofar as habitual grace makes the soul a new creation – that is, a participation in divine being – it perfects the essence of our soul.[75] It perfects the soul's powers (especially intellect and will) only indirectly: "Just as its powers flow from the essence of the soul, so too certain perfections flow from grace into the powers of the soul, which perfections are called virtues and the gifts [of the Holy Spirit], by which the powers are perfected with regard to their acts."[76] While habitual grace achieves some of the things ordered to our beatitude directly, especially making us acceptable to God, it achieves other things ordered to our beatitude – above all our collaboration with grace in meritorious action – through the mediation of the virtues and gifts.[77] The virtues that flow from grace, it is implied, are the infused virtues, the most important of which are the so-called theological virtues of faith, hope, and charity.[78]

Free will plays a particularly important role with regard to faith and charity. Faith – whether theological or not – is by nature voluntary, for it is assent to something not evident, and thus to something underdetermined. It therefore requires a choice to make the intellect affirm one alternative rather than another.[79] What is peculiar to theological faith is that when the will makes the intellect assent to the divine truth, it does so not only because there are reasons for believing, but above all "because of an interior instinct of God" inviting to the faith. Aquinas uses the word 'instinct' deliberately, for it is the word that Aristotle employs to explain the divine origin of the start of deliberation. Recall that Aquinas does not see in its divine origin an interference with our free agency, but rather its foundation (see 'God's Motion of Our Will' above). Precisely insofar as the act of Christian faith proceeds from our free choice, albeit as moved by God through grace, it is meritorious.[80] While the good use of our free choice is foundational for faith, its bad use – namely, our refusal to assent to the true Christian faith – results in unbelief or heresy.[81]

Acts of charity, too, originate in a divine motion of our mind. But Aquinas insists that our mind not only is moved, but also is itself the source of its acts, for love implies by definition voluntariness, and voluntariness implies that one is the source of one's acts.[82] The infusion of charity depends above all on the free will of the Holy Spirit, "who distributes his gifts as he wills," but also on our free choice in accepting the gift of grace. Its intensity depends in part on our free choice: through acts of charity we grow in charity, and through lack of such acts or through venial sin, our charity diminishes, while through mortal sin, it is lost.[83]

The gifts of the Holy Spirit are perfections that dispose us to follow well a divine instinct or inspiration, analogous to the virtues (whether naturally acquired or infused) that dispose us to follow our reason. Aquinas explains the divine instinct with reference to Isaiah 50:5 – "the Lord opened my ear; I do not contradict, I did not go away" – and to Aristotle's theory of the start of deliberation as originating in a divine instinct.[84] Thus, spiritual human beings are mainly moved not by their own will, but by the instinct of the Holy Spirit inclining them to action. This does not mean that they do not act by their free choice, for the very motion of their free choice is caused by the Holy Spirit.[85] It is not caused in the manner of a lifeless tool, however, but by leaving free choice intact. Since we remain free self-movers even when moved by the Holy Spirit, we need the gifts to respond well to his motions.[86]

While the infused virtues and the gifts perfect the powers of our soul regarding our actions at a general level, the sacraments are needed for certain special effects that belong to the Christian life; for example, baptism makes us members of Christ.[87] The sacraments not only signify but also cause grace, yet not through their own force, but as instruments of God.[88] Here, it is not grace that moves us to act; it is rather the case that the acts of the dispensers of the sacraments "somehow lead to grace."[89] As goes without saying, the dispensers and recipients of the sacraments are free to give and receive them.

THE LAW OF FREEDOM

Not only is our free will involved in the reception and use of grace, but our freedom is also an effect of grace. A common thread in Aquinas's various explanations of this idea is the citation of II Cor. 3:17: "Where the spirit of the Lord is, there is freedom."

Aquinas makes a connection between grace, the New Law of the New Testament, and freedom. He holds that "the New Law is chiefly the grace of the Holy Spirit"[90] and explains why St. James calls the New Law the law of freedom (James 1:25): It asks of us only those things that are necessary for our salvation (as opposed to the Law of the Old Testament, it is implied), and it makes us observe the precepts and prohibitions freely, insofar as we observe them from an "inner instinct of grace." What we do from an inner instinct, and hence on our own accord, we do freely, as Aquinas explains with reference to Aristotle's statement that "the human being is free who is for his or her own sake," rather than for the sake of some master, as is the slave.[91] The grace of the Holy Spirit inclines us so because it renders us lovers of God, and thus makes us tend out of love to the true good and to what God's law commands.[92] We thus gain freedom from sin, which Aquinas also calls 'true freedom,' for it connects us to justice and makes us tend to what is truly suitable (conveniens) to us, and 'spiritual freedom,' for it comes about through charity, an effect of the Holy Spirit.[93]

FREE WILL IN HEAVEN

The full accomplishment of our free will is when we are completely fixed on the good and no longer able to sin.[94] This is the effect of consummated grace, which is called 'glory.'[95] It will be obtained through the beatific vision of God. When seeing God – that is, when we have a direct intellectual grasp of God's nature – we will see that in him there is every aspect of goodness, and hence of desirability. Nothing that would distance us from God will be attractive to us, precisely because we will see that it conflicts with our beatitude.[96] So we will no longer have free choice to love God or not. While our sinful choices will disappear, our free choice will remain. In fact, what is detrimental to freedom is to be able to sin – that is, to divert from our final end – but it belongs to the perfection of our freedom to be able to choose without diverting from our final end.[97] Accordingly, just as Christ, in his earthly life, had free choice regarding this or that particular good, although he was fixed on the good in general, so also we will keep free choice in heaven.[98] What further sustains the blessed in making good choices is the gift of counsel, which assists them, for example, in choices relating to the praise of God and to prayers of intercession.[99]

DIVINE DETERMINISM?

A question lurking in the background throughout this chapter is to what extent, on Aquinas's theory, grace leaves us control of our acts. In his view, the most important choice is made by God, not us; he decides whether we are predestined to eternal salvation or not. Yet God does not micromanage our choices to lead us to the intended end. Rather, if we are predestined, God accomplishes our salvation by means of the free choices we make in our lives. While our choices imply by definition alternative possibilities, not all alternatives are accessible to us. Christ, who enjoys the fullness of grace and thereby is made perfectly obedient to God, could not in fact refuse to accept his passion. Mary was moved by grace in such a way that she could not but consent to becoming Christ's mother. When by actual operative grace God turns our soul to him, we cannot help but be attracted to God. Nevertheless, these acts are eminently free. After the reception of operative grace, however, we can collaborate with grace or not, or posit an obstacle to grace, or even act directly against it. Our charity grows or diminishes in proportion to our collaboration with grace.

In this life, then, our will is only occasionally determined, in the reception of operative grace. Only in the beatific vision will our response to God be determined completely and permanently, making us unable not to love him, although leaving us free to express our love differently. The determination to love God is not achieved through operative grace, however, but through our full realization that every aspect of goodness is in God and that everything else is good only in relation to God.

NOTES

1 For definitions of grace, see *ST* I-II q.110 a.2; *ST* I-II q.112 a.1; *SCG* III.150. For a rich introduction to Aquinas's teaching on grace, see J.-P. Torrell, *Saint Thomas d'Aquin, maître spirituel*, 3rd edn. (Paris: Les Éditions du Cerf, 2017), chs. 5–8; for an English translation of an earlier version of these chapters, see J.-P. Torrell, *Saint Thomas Aquinas. Volume 2: Spiritual Master*, translated by R. Royal (Washington, DC: The Catholic University of America Press, 2003), chs. 6–9. Valuet offers a comprehensive and detailed account of Aquinas's theory of grace and free will; see B. Valuet, *Dieu joueur d'échecs? Prédestination, grâce et libre arbitre. Volume 2: Relecture de saint Thomas d'Aquin* (Le Barroux: Éditions Sainte-Madeleine, 2018). The conclusion of this monumental work is summarized in B. Valuet, "Prédestination, grâce et libre arbitre, tentative de synthèse personnelle," *Revue thomiste* 119 (2019): 67–90, 299–322. For a philosophical reflection on Aquinas's theory of grace and free will, see E. Stump, *Atonement* (Oxford: Oxford University Press, 2018), ch. 7.

2 Regarding the development of Aquinas's teaching on grace, see the summary account in J. M. Anderson, *Virtue and Grace in the Theology of Thomas Aquinas* (Cambridge: Cambridge University Press, 2020), pp. 82–107 and the more detailed treatments in B. J. F. Lonergan, *Grace and Freedom: Operative Grace in the Thought of St. Thomas Aquinas. Collected Works of Bernard Lonergan, vol. 1* (Toronto: University of Toronto Press, 2000) (first published in four articles in 1941–2); H. Bouillard, *Conversion et grâce chez S. Thomas d'Aquin* (Paris: Éditions Aubier-Montaigne, 1944); J. P. Wawrykow, *God's Grace and Human*

Action: "Merit" in the Theology of Thomas Aquinas (Notre Dame, IN: University of Notre Dame Press, 1995). See also note 18. Aquinas's discussions of grace in *In Sent.* and *QDV* reflect his early view, while those in *SCG*, *ST* and his commentaries on the Pauline epistles and the Gospel of John reflect his revised view.

3 For the distinction between free will in a broad sense (*libertas voluntatis*), as compatible with necessity, and free choice (*liberum arbitrium*), as implying alternative possibilities, see T. Hoffmann and C. Michon, "Aquinas on Free Will and Intellectual Determinism," *Philosophers' Imprint* 17 (2017): 1–36, here pp. 3–8; Chapter 9 in this volume.

4 See, for example, *QDM* q.16 a.5 s.c.3.

5 *ST* I q.83 aa.2–4.

6 *ST* I q.2 intr.

7 *ST* I q.12 a.1; *ST* I-II q.3 a.8.

8 *QDV* q.14 a.10 ad 2.

9 *ST* I-II q.3 a.3; *ST* I-II q.4 a.7; *ST* I-II q.5 aa.5–7.

10 On the cause of original sin, see *ST* I-II q.81 a.1, a.3; on its essence, see *ST* I-II q.82 a.1, a.3; on original justice, see *ST* I q.95 a.1; *ST* I-II q.81 a.2; *ST* I-II q.82 a.3. According to Aquinas, only Christ was spared original sin, while Mary was cleansed of it before her birth; see *ST* I-II q.81 a.3; *ST* III q.27. See also Chapter 13 in this volume.

11 *ST* I-II q.109 a.7.

12 For the identity of the grace signified by these different expressions, see *ST* I-II q.111 a.2.

13 *ST* I-II q.109 aa.2–5, a.8.

14 *ST* I-II q.109 aa.8–10; see also *SCG* III.155, 160. For the distinction between mortal and venial sin, see *ST* I-II q.72 a.5; *ST* I-II q.88.

15 *ST* I-II q.5 a.8.

16 *ST* I-II q.109 a.6.

17 *In II Sent.*, d.28 q.1 aa.1–4. See also *QDV* q.24 aa.12–15, where he holds essentially the same view, only with more nuance.

18 For Aquinas's discovery of semi-Pelagianism, which he must have made in 1259 or 1260, see Bouillard, *Conversion et Grâce*, pp. 92–115. As Bouillard points out (pp. 105–6), in *Quodl* I q.4 a.2 (of 1269), Aquinas shows clear awareness of the difference between the original heresy by Pelagius and the more moderate one of the semi-Pelagians, whom he simply calls Pelagians. For a helpful summary and discussion of

Bouillard's book, see Wawrykow, *God's Grace and Human Action*, pp. 34–42.

19   For the definitions of providence and predestination, see *ST* I q.22 a.1 and *ST* I q.23 a.1, respectively. For comprehensive investigations of Aquinas's theory of predestination and its chronological development, see M. Paluch, *La profondeur de l'amour divin: La prédestination dans l'œuvre de saint Thomas d'Aquin* (Paris: Librairie Philosophique J. Vrin, 2004); Valuet, *Dieu joueur d'échecs?* Useful studies of more particular scope are contained in S. A. Long, R. W. Nutt, and T. J. White (eds.), *Thomism and Predestination: Principles and Disputations* (Ave Maria, FL: Sapientia Press, 2016).

20   *ST* I q.23 a.3 ad 2; *ST* I q.23 a.5.

21   *ST* I q.23 aa.2–3, a.7.

22   *ST* I q.23 a.5; *In Rom* 8, lect. 6, n.703; *In Rom* 9, lect. 2, nn.760–4; *In Rom* 9, lect. 3, nn.771–3; *In Eph* 1, lect. 4, n.34. Even Christ, who in his human nature is predestined to be the Son of God (*ST* III q.24 aa.1–2), is predestined to this apart from his merits; see *In Rom* 1, lect. 3, n.48.

23   *ST* I q.23 a.6.

24   *ST* III q.24 a.4.

25   *Super Johan* 6, lect. 5, n.937, n.943; *Super Johan* 10, lect. 5 n.1447; *Super Johan* 12, lect. 7 n.1698.

26   *ST* I q.23 a.3 ad 2; *ST* I-II q.112 a.3 ad 2; *Super Johan* 17, lect. 3, n.2218; *In Rom* 9, lect. 2, n.764; *In Rom* 9, lect. 3, nn.781–4. Note that in the Marietti edition, *In Rom* 9, lect. 2, n.764 omits a 'non' (not), thus significantly altering the sense; for the text according to the soon to be published critical edition, see Paluch, *La profondeur de l'amour divin*, p. 262, note 1.

27   *ST* I q.19 a.6 ad 1; *ST* I q.23 a.4 ad 3; *In I Tim* 2, lect. 1, n.62. See also Paluch, *La profondeur de l'amour divin*, pp. 273–308.

28   *ST* I q.23 a.5.

29   *ST* I q.23 a.6.

30   *QDV* q.6 a.6; *ST* I q.23 a.8; *ST* II-II q.83 a.2; cf. *SCG* III.95.

31   *QDV* q.6 a.6 ad s.c.4.

32   *ST* II-II q.83 a.7 ad 3.

33   *Super Johan* 6, lect. 5, n.938.

34   *ST* I-II q.113 a.3; *QDV* 6.2 ad 11; *In Rom* 9, lect. 3, n.772.

35   *ST* I q.23 a.5 ad 3.

36 *ST* I q.23 a.5 ad 3; *In Rom* 9, lect. 3–4, especially n.773, nn.788–91, nn.792–5; *Super Johan* 6, lect. 5, n.938. Although God's election comes from his pure will, it is not irrational; see *In Eph* 1, lect. 4, n.34.

37 Regarding original sin as the reason for reprobation, see *QDV* q.6 a.2 ad 9; *In Rom* 9, lect. 3, n.773.

38 *ST* II-II q.18 a.4 ad 3.

39 T. P. O'Neill, *Grace, Predestination, and the Permission of Sin: A Thomistic Analysis* (Washington, DC: The Catholic University of America Press, 2019) presents interpretations of Aquinas's theory from Domingo Báñez to twentieth-century Thomists.

40 For an overview of discussions of Augustine's theory of predestination, see P. Rigby, *The Theology of Augustine's Confessions* (Cambridge: Cambridge University Press, 2015), pp. 134–41.

41 *QDM* q.16 a.4 ad 22.

42 *Quodl.* I q.4 a.2 obj.2 and ad 2. On Aquinas's theory of angelic sin, see T. Hoffmann, *Free Will and the Rebel Angels in Medieval Philosophy* (Cambridge: Cambridge University Press, 2021), pp. 204–14.

43 *QDP* q.3 a.7. See also, very concisely, *ST* I q.83 a.1 ad 3. Regarding Aquinas's theory of God's primary causality in our free actions, see D. B. Burrell, *Freedom and Creation in Three Traditions* (South Bend, IN: University of Notre Dame Press, 1993), pp. 95–139; B. J. Shanley, "Divine Causation and Human Freedom in Aquinas," *American Catholic Philosophical Quarterly* 72 (1998): 99–122; F. J. Matava, *Divine Causality and Human Free Choice: Domingo Báñez, Physical Premotion and the Controversy de Auxiliis Revisited* (Leiden: Brill, 2016), chs. 6–7. For God's primary causality in general, see Chapter 5 in this volume.

44 *ST* I q.19 a.8; *ST* I q.22 a.4; *ST* I-II q.10 a.4.

45 *QDP* q.3 a.7 ad 13. For the example of the stone, cf. *QDV* q.24 a.1; for that of swallows and spiders, see *SCG* II.82.

46 *ST* III q.18 a.1 ad 2.

47 *ST* I-II q.21 a.4 ad 2.

48 *In Rom* 9, lect. 3, n.778; *SCG* III.148 n.3212.

49 *ST* I q.83 a.1 ad 3.

50 *ST* I q.105 a.4 ad 3.

51 *QDP* q.3 a.7 ad 15; *SCG* III.161 n.3327.

52 For Aquinas's theory of formal and final causality in willing, see C. L. Löwe, *Thomas Aquinas on the Metaphysics of the Human Act* (Cambridge: Cambridge University Press, 2021), pp. 86–9.

53 *ST* I q.106 a.2; *ST* I-II q.6 a.4; *ST* I-II q.9 a.6, especially ad 3, where Aquinas mentions God moving our will through grace.

54 *ST* I-II q.109 a.2 ad 1; *QDM* 6; *In II Cor* 3, lect. 1, n.87.

55 *ST* III q.49 aa.1–5.

56 *ST* III q.7 a.1, a.9; *ST* III q.8 a.1, a.5; *ST* III q.26 a.1. See also Chapter 15 in this volume.

57 *ST* III q.24 a.4.

58 *ST* III q.18 a.1, especially ad 1 and ad 2.

59 *ST* III q.18 a.5; *ST* III q.21 a.4.

60 *ST* III q.18 a.4 ad 3.

61 *ST* III q.27 a.5 ad 1.

62 *ST* III q.30 a.1, especially ad 1; *In III Sent.*, d.3 q.3 ql.1. For a slightly different approach, see *QDV* q.12 a.10 ad 6.

63 For the definitions of actual and habitual grace, see the references in note 1; for the division of each into operative and cooperative grace, see *ST* I-II q.111 a.2. Lonergan, *Grace and Freedom* and L. Feingold, "God's Movement of the Soul Through Operative and Cooperative Grace" in Long, Nutt, and White (eds.), *Thomism and Predestination*, pp. 166–91 give nuanced accounts of Aquinas's theory of operative and cooperative grace. The difficulty of reconciling actual grace with human free will culminated in the so-called *De Auxiliis* controversy of the late sixteenth and early seventeenth centuries, whose main protagonists, Domingo Báñez and Luis de Molina, both claimed to be followers of Aquinas. The two aforementioned studies and Matava, *Divine Causality and Human Free Choice*, ch. 7, suggest different ways to overcome the theoretical difficulties underlying the controversy.

64 *ST* I-II q.111 a.2; *ST* I-II q.112 a.2; *ST* I-II q.113 aa.3–4.

65 *ST* I-II q.111 a.2, especially ad 3; for grace prompting us to accomplish the precepts and counsels, see *ST* I-II q.108 a.1, a.4.

66 *ST* I-II q.111 a.2 ad 2; *ST* I-II q.112 a.3; cf. *ST* I-II q.113 a.7 ad 1.

67 *ST* I-II q.113 q.10. For various stages in conversion, see *ST* III q.85 a.5.

68 *ST* I-II q.111 a.2. For grace as making us a new creation and participants in the divine nature, see *ST* I-II q.110 a.4; *ST* I-II q.112 a.1.

69 *ST* I-II q.109 a.6.

70 *ST* II-II q.2 a.9.

71 *ST* I-II q.114 aa.1–4, a.6. For Aquinas's teaching on merit, see Wawrykow, *God's Grace and Human Action*.

72 *ST* I-II q.114 aa.5–9; *ST* II-II q.83 q.16.

73 *ST* I-II q.112 aa.2–3; *Quodl.* I q.4 a.3 ad 2; cf. *ST* I q.62 a.3; *SCG* III.159 n.3313. E. Stump, *Aquinas* (New York and London: Routledge, 2003), ch. 13 proposes a detailed hypothesis, consistent with Aquinas and lacking any taint of Pelagianism, of how we control in some way the bestowal of grace upon us by ceasing to resist grace.

74 *ST* II-II q.24 a.12; *ST* I-II q.85 a.4.

75 *ST* I-II q.110 a.4. For an explanation of why the soul's essence, and not only its powers, can be the subject of a *habitus*, namely of habitual grace, see *ST* I-II q.50 a.2.

76 *ST* III q.62 a.2. For the relation of the soul to its powers, see *ST* I q.77 a.6.

77 *ST* I-II q.110 a.4 ad 2; *ST* III q.7 a.2 ad 1. While Aquinas mentions here only the virtues, the gifts are implied.

78 Aquinas gives a more simple account of charity, faith, and hope being caused by grace in *SCG* III.151–3. For the nature of the infused virtues in general and of the theological virtues in particular, see *ST* I-II q.63 aa.3–4 and q.62, respectively. See also Chapter 12 in this volume; Anderson, *Virtue and Grace*; A. M. Knobel, *Aquinas and the Infused Moral Virtues* (Notre Dame, IN: University of Notre Dame Press, 2021).

79 *ST* II-II q.1 a.4; *ST* II-II q.2 a.1 ad 3.

80 *ST* II-II q.2 aa.9–10; *Super Johan* 6, lect. 4, n.935. For Aquinas's use of the word 'instinct,' especially regarding faith, see M. S. Sherwin, *By Knowledge and by Love: Charity and Knowledge in the Moral Theology of St. Thomas Aquinas* (Washington, DC: The Catholic University of America Press, 2005), pp. 139–46, and the literature he refers to.

81 *ST* II-II q.11 a.1.

82 *ST* II-II q.23 a.2; *QDC* a.1. The divine precept to love God and neighbor (Mt 22:37–9) can therefore only be fulfilled by one's own free will; see *ST* II-II q.44 a.1 ad 2.

83 *ST* II-II q.24 a.3, a.6, a.10, a.12.

84 *ST* I-II q.68 aa.1–2. See also Chapter 12 in this volume.

85 *In Rom* 8, lect. 3, n.635.

86 *ST* I-II q.68 a.3 ad 2; *ST* II-II q.52 a.1 ad 3.

87 *ST* III q.62 a.2.

88 *ST* III q.62 a.1.

89 *ST* I-II q.108 a.1.

90 *ST* I-II q.106 a.1.

91 *ST* I-II q.108 a.1 obj.2 and ad 2; cf. *Metaphysics* I.2, 982b26.

92 *SCG* IV.22 nn.3588–9; *In II Cor* 3, lect. 3, nn.111–12.

93 *ST* II-II q.183 a.4. See also *In Rom* 6, lect. 4, nn.508–13.

94 *SCG* III.138 n.3120; *ST* II-II q.88 a.4 ad 1.

95 *ST* I-II q.114 a.9; cf. *ST* I-II q.111 a.3 ad 2; *ST* II-II q.24 a.3 ad 2.

96 *ST* I q.82 a.2.

97 *ST* I q.62 a.8 ad 3.

98 *ST* III q.18 a.4 ad 3.

99 *ST* II-II q.52 a.3 ad 1. For Aquinas's theory of free will in heaven, see in more detail S. F. Gaine, *Will There Be Free Will in Heaven? Freedom, Impeccability, and Beatitude* (London: T&T Clark, 2003).

11 From Metaethics to Normative Ethics

Colleen McCluskey

The nature of Aquinas's ethical theory has often been the subject of debate among scholars. During much of the twentieth century, he was regarded as holding a natural law theory. In more recent years, recognition of his extensive discussion on virtue has led scholars to argue for a virtue-based account. Currently, an important debate centers on what counts as genuine virtues for Aquinas.

In this chapter, I provide a description of the basic structure of Aquinas's moral theory. I touch on disputes of interest to scholars but largely refer the interested reader to relevant secondary literature. Aquinas's account rests on his theory of human psychology and especially his position on *eudaimonia* (commonly translated as happiness). This, therefore, is my starting point.[1]

THE FOUNDATION FOR THE VIRTUE ACCOUNT:
HUMAN NATURE AND THE ULTIMATE END

Aquinas's account of human nature grounds his ethics. His account is teleologically based, structured around an ultimate end for human life, which he identifies as happiness. The ultimate end is defined by what satisfies completely all human desires. Only a perfect good, lacking nothing of goodness, is capable of this level of satisfaction. This is because the ultimate source of desire in human beings is the will, which Aquinas argues is a desire or inclination toward the good.[2] If an object is not perfectly good, then the will need not incline toward it. If the will does incline toward it, its inclination or desire will be satisfied only temporarily. If our desires are not satisfied completely, then we desire something more, and we are not entirely happy.

Aquinas acknowledges that human beings can desire many things that they mistakenly think will make them happy; happiness in what he calls the general sense is just the satisfaction of our desires. It is a further question, what instantiates this general concept; that is, it is a further question, what in fact satisfies completely all of our desires. On Aquinas's theological worldview, only the vision of and union with God, the perfect being, fits the bill, whether we recognize this or not.[3] This is because everything else is less than fully perfect, and its attainment ultimately will leave us dissatisfied. Thus, on Aquinas's view, what instantiates the general concept of happiness is a relationship with the divine being.[4]

Nevertheless, Aquinas argues for a twofold conception of happiness: what he calls perfect happiness and imperfect happiness.[5] He follows Aristotle in maintaining that imperfect happiness is achieved through activities perfected by virtue.[6] This is the kind of happiness that can be attained in the present life on the basis of our own efforts, insofar as we are able to acquire virtues.[7] Perfect happiness, however, involves our relationship with God, which will not be realized completely until the next life. The attainment of this end is not possible on the basis of our efforts alone.[8] It requires supernatural aid, as I discuss later.

The specification of this end follows from human nature. Human beings possess the rational capacities of intellect and will. The intellect enables us to cognize the world and identify ends worth pursuing, while the will is an appetitive capacity that inclines toward those objects the intellect has identified as good and to be pursued.[9] Thus, the will is a rational appetite, an inclination toward the good as conceived by intellect. Because ultimately all action comes about from the inclination of the will, it follows that all human action is goal-directed. Aquinas argues that there must be an ultimate end, toward which attainment all actions are directed.[10] Since the will is an appetite for the good, something's being at least perceived as good is a necessary condition for the will's inclining toward it, although it is not a sufficient condition. This is because the intellect is able to identify reasons not to pursue any particular good with the exception of the perfect good.[11] This view grounds human freedom of action. Nevertheless, it also entails that human beings cannot fail to will happiness if they are convinced that a particular object will make them happy. Furthermore, they are unable to will misery for its own sake.

Human nature includes a further power that factors into the performance of actions and plays a significant role in Aquinas's ethics. This power is the sensory appetite, the source of the passions. The medieval notion of a passion has no direct analogue in current philosophy. It is closest to our concept of emotion, and many readers of medieval philosophy translate the Latin *'passio'* as 'emotion.' In my view, this is misleading, since many philosophers today argue that emotions are rational in nature, whereas Aquinas locates the passions in what he calls the sensory appetite, which is an appetitive power responsive to sensory apprehension.[12] Thus, the passions, strictly speaking, are associated with sensory perception, which is part of a human being's material nature and therefore not a rational power. The stimulation of a passion produces a corresponding corporal reaction.[13] Nevertheless, Aquinas argues that the passions are responsive to the judgment and control of the rational powers of intellect and will.[14] As such, he argues that the passions are indirectly rational. He identifies eleven passions: pleasure, sadness, love, hatred, desire, aversion, fear, daring, hope, despair, and anger.[15]

In and of themselves, passions are involuntary. They arise in response to our interpretations of sense perception. If I see a bear in the woods, I am likely to experience the passion of fear. If I see a bear in the zoo, I am likely to feel pleasure. As such, passions are morally neutral because they are involuntary.[16] I cannot help but feel such passions under these circumstances. But insofar as I can control my subsequent response to these feelings, Aquinas thinks that the passions are subject to and controllable by the powers that enable me to control my response. I can judge that fleeing the bear in the woods would be harmful to me so that even though I feel fear at the sight of it, I calmly and slowly edge away from it. I can judge that although it would be fun to watch the bear at the zoo all afternoon, it is time to leave for home. Thus, I need not act on the promptings of a passion but instead control my feelings and act in what I judge to be a more appropriate manner. I do this voluntarily by virtue of my intellect and will. Aquinas argues that passions are good when they are under the control of the intellect and will and bad when they are not so controlled.[17] As I discuss later in this chapter, the passions too have a role to play in Aquinas's account of ethics.[18]

In summary, ultimately human actions aim at achieving the final goal of human life, namely happiness.[19] Although Aquinas grants that human beings can have different conceptions of what happiness comprises, he regards it as entirely uncontroversial that all desire happiness. On his view, human action is produced and guided by what he calls internal principles and external principles.[20] Powers internal to the human agent are one of two internal principles. These powers are comprised of the intellect, the will, and the passions of the sensory appetite. The powers of the soul are a necessary condition for the attainment of happiness, but they are not sufficient. This is because intellect, will, and passion can go wrong in the pursuit of happiness; we can think that something not conducive to our happiness will make us happy and pursue it. Therefore, we need a second internal principle to help direct us toward our authentic end; these are habits, the most important of which for his moral theory are the virtues and the gifts of the Holy Spirit.[21] As we shall see, virtues perfect human action, which directs us to our ultimate end, while vices, which are bad habits, incline agents away from that end. Furthermore, as we shall see, the operation of the virtues (as well as gifts, beatitudes, and fruits) requires two principles external to human psychology; these principles are law and grace.[22] I examine each of these factors in turn, beginning with Aquinas's account of the virtues.

THE ROLE OF THE VIRTUES

Aquinas describes habits as the second internal principle of human action. Appealing to Aristotle's account in *Metaphysics*, he characterizes habits as dispositions that incline us well or badly.[23] When we are inclined toward what is suitable for our nature, we are disposed well; if we are attracted toward what is not so suitable, we are disposed badly. Virtues incline us toward what is suitable while vices incline us toward the unsuitable. Suitability is determined by those things conducive toward realizing the ultimate end (or those things that do not contravene our progress toward that end). Aquinas says that the virtues both dispose us to act well and in fact move us to act well.[24] Nevertheless, virtues do not determine our actions; we always retain the freedom not to act on the basis of a virtue.

According to Aquinas, a good human life consists of good deeds.[25] This involves not only what one does but also how one performs those actions. The latter involves choosing the right action because it is the right action and not merely out of impulses stirred by passion. The (direct, internal) principles of human action are intellect, will, and the passions because they are the powers by which we deliberate, choose, and are moved to act. Virtues affect these powers.

Aquinas accepts Aristotle's distinction between intellectual and moral virtues.[26] The various intellectual virtues perfect the speculative and practical parts of the intellect; they help us arrive at correct judgments about the way the world is and about what we ought to do. The moral virtues perfect the appetitive parts of the soul – that is, the will and the passions. We cannot act well unless our intellects are well disposed by the habits that are the intellectual virtues and our appetites (both rational and sensory) are well disposed by the habits that are the moral virtues.[27]

Given that our nature as human beings is fulfilled in a particular end (union with God), it is rational for human beings to pursue what enables us to attain that end; thus, Aquinas defines actions good in species as those in accordance with right reason and actions bad in species as those that violate right reason.[28] Virtues also conform to right reason insofar as they move us to perform the right action. Therefore, virtues are in accordance with human nature, while vices, which are not in conformity with right reason, are contrary to human nature.[29]

Although it is obvious that virtues play important roles in the attainment of the ultimate end, exactly how they do so is a matter of some dispute. The question is whether they are merely instrumental to the good life or are also constitutive of the good life.[30] Do the virtues simply "make possible the activity that *is* happiness: intimately knowing and enjoying God" (as Stenberg argues) or are they *also* a constitutive part of what makes a life truly fulfilling for human beings?[31] I shall not adjudicate this debate, since it strikes me as obvious that, on Aquinas's account, virtues are required for attaining the ultimate end, and it also seems to me that a virtuous individual engages in a form of life valuable in its own right.[32]

Aquinas describes virtues as perfective of the powers in which they inhere. Powers are perfected insofar as they are determined to their appropriate actions.[33] But as I discussed earlier, all action is performed for the sake of an end, and in due course for the sake of the ultimate end. Thus, virtues play an essential role in the attainment of ends, including the ultimate end. Aquinas accepts the following definition of virtue: "a good quality of the mind, by which we will rightly, which no one uses badly, which God works in us without us."[34] Strictly speaking, this definition applies to what the tradition calls infused virtues. These include the theological virtues of faith, hope, and charity, which are present in us because of activity on the part of God. Although we do not obtain these virtues through our own efforts, we must consent to their reception; God does not infuse them within us against our wills.[35] By contrast, we acquire the cardinal virtues of prudence, justice, fortitude, and temperance by our own efforts.[36] Aquinas argues that his definition applies to the acquired virtues as well if we omit the final qualification (i.e., "which God works in us without us").[37]

Aquinas accepts the traditional identification of four virtues as cardinal (or principle): prudence, justice, temperance, and fortitude.[38] Since practical reason is the intellective power that enables our judgments about what action to take, prudence is the intellectual virtue that perfects practical reason. Aquinas defines prudence as right reasoning about what to do.[39] It is not sufficient to possess prudence; in order to make correct judgments about action, one must be oriented properly both toward the end (i.e., one must have correct goals) and toward what is required to achieve this end. This orientation is carried out by the appetitive parts of the soul (i.e., the will and the sensory appetite). Without the proper orientation, practical intellect is likely to go in a wrong direction under the influence of disordered passions and/or a disordered will. In order for prudence to be operative, one must also possess the moral virtues, which perfect the appetitive parts.[40]

Aquinas also argues that one cannot possess the moral virtues unless one possesses prudence as well. This is because the moral virtues perfect powers that require the direction of reason.[41] Recall that the object of the will is the good as conceived by reason, while the good of the sensory appetite (the seat of the passions) is to obey the dictates of reason.[42] The moral virtues cannot move us correctly unless we are able to judge correctly what we ought to do, which requires prudence.[43]

Justice is the cardinal virtue associated with the will.[44] This virtue regulates our relationships with one another. Aquinas defines it as that habit by which one gives to others what is due to them.[45] Justice is particularly concerned with regulating relationships within a community in light of the common good.[46] It has two main parts or species: commutative justice and distributive justice. Commutative justice regulates relationships between individuals within a given society, while distributive justice deals with relationships between the community and its members, specifically in the distribution of common goods to individuals within the community.[47]

Fortitude and temperance regulate the passions of the sensory appetite so that they do not interfere with the judgments of reason about what to do. Passions can move us to act against our own interests. They can incite action that is contrary to our better judgments. Thus, Aquinas argues that we need temperance to restrain those passions that would distract us away from what we ought to do.[48] But passions can also move us to withdraw from those actions we ought to perform. Aquinas argues that we need fortitude in order to strengthen our resolve to do the right thing.[49]

As noted earlier, Aquinas argues for two kinds of happiness: imperfect and perfect happiness. The acquired virtues enable us to pursue and achieve imperfect happiness. Perfect happiness requires infused virtues, among other things. This is because the attainment of perfect happiness goes beyond our natural capacities.[50] The object of perfect happiness is God, who is beyond our capacity to comprehend, and whose assistance we require in order to establish the kind of relationship that instantiates our ultimate end. Therefore, in order to achieve perfect happiness (a relationship with the divine being), we require divine assistance.[51]

This assistance takes different forms, including the infused virtues. The primary infused virtues are the theological virtues of faith, hope, and charity.[52] These three virtues work together to direct us to our supernatural ultimate end.[53] Although faith affects the intellect primarily, Aquinas argues for a concurrent act of the will. Faith involves assent, which makes it a function of the intellect.[54] In the act of faith, we assent to what exceeds our natural comprehension, namely God and much of what is associated with God.[55] This means that the intellect's natural powers of comprehension are not sufficient for assent, since we lack the kind of certainty that can be generated with objects of natural knowledge. Therefore, the assent to faith requires a movement of the will.[56] But this is not a blind movement, for Aquinas argues that the one who is moved to assent recognizes that it is reasonable to do so in virtue of what he calls the light of faith.[57]

Hope and charity are both virtues of the will.[58] Hope as a passion has as its object a future good that is difficult but possible to attain.[59] Hope as a theological virtue retains this basic idea. It is directed toward a future supernatural good – i.e., our relationship with God – which is challenging insofar as it exceeds our natural capacities but is possible with God's assistance. Infusion with this theological virtue gives us hope that we will enjoy such a relationship fully in the next life.[60] Aquinas describes charity as love of or friendship with God.[61] The infusion of charity enables human beings to engage in a relationship with God, a relationship that will be perfected in the next life. Thus, charity provides the possibility of and basis for our ultimate end.[62] Love for God also moves us to love what God cares about. This includes care and concern for other human beings, since God loves them just as he loves us. Thus, love for God motivates love of neighbor.[63]

Aquinas's discussion of acquired and infused virtues raises questions about their relationship more generally.[64] There is a debate in the secondary literature over whether acquired virtues are genuine virtues.[65] I would argue that Aquinas regards acquired virtues as genuine virtues; as we saw earlier, Aquinas maintains that, by removing the qualifier that governs infused virtue (i.e., "which God works in us without us"), the same definition of virtue applies to acquired virtues. Nevertheless, he qualifies this claim, arguing that the infused virtues are perfect virtues insofar as they order human beings to their (supernatural) ultimate end directly (*simpliciter*). The acquired virtues are virtues in a qualified sense (*secundum quid*) because they are concerned with matters in this life.[66]

Some commentators infer from this position that imperfect virtues cannot be genuine virtues. It is not clear to me that this conclusion follows. Aquinas regards the acquired virtues as imperfect, not because they fail to do what they are intended to do – that is, perfect the natural human capacities of intellect, will, and the sensory appetite in order to bring about good action. He regards them as imperfect because, by themselves, they are insufficient to direct us toward our supernatural ultimate end. But I see no reason to think that this fact, in and of itself, means that acquired virtues are not genuine virtues. It is also true that Aquinas believes the infused virtues to be superior to the acquired virtues.[67] But once again this fact by itself does not entail that acquired virtues are not virtues.

Nevertheless, this debate raises questions about the role of acquired virtues in human life. Aquinas distinguishes between two principles that govern human life and determine the goodness of individual actions: human reason and divine law.[68] The acquired virtues move us to act under the guidance of (right) reason, using our natural capacities. They govern our ways of living in this life and contribute to the achievement of imperfect happiness. Along with the gifts and fruits of the Holy Spirit (which will be the subject of the following section), the infused virtues are necessary for us to pursue our ultimate end, which is our relationship with God, since it surpasses our natural capacities.[69] Divine law directs the workings of the infused virtues. Nevertheless, this explanation raises the question of why acquired virtues are valuable on Aquinas's account if what actually enables us to pursue our ultimate end are the infused virtues.

Although the divine law – or, alternatively, the divine object – is a superior object to our natural rational capacities, the latter are still good in Aquinas's eyes. For one thing, the infused virtues work with our natural capacities to direct us to the ultimate end. Nevertheless, imperfect happiness remains a good worth pursuing, and the acquired virtues enable us to achieve it. But one might think that infused moral and intellectual virtues also could enable us to achieve the good of imperfect happiness. Imperfect happiness consists primarily of the activity of contemplation and secondarily of the practical intellect's activity regulating our actions and passions.[70] Certainly, God could infuse virtues in us by which we would engage in these activities. But I would argue that a great good would be missing if God did so directly. There is value in the activities by which we acquire moral and intellectual virtue and pursue imperfect happiness.

Ultimately, the question consists of what is the relationship between the earthly life (and its related goods) and our supernatural ultimate end. For the theist (specifically a Christian theist in the state of grace on Aquinas's view), one's judgments and actions will be directed by charity; by virtue of this direction, Aquinas calls charity the form of all the other virtues.[71] This means that, for the Christian, her actions will be motivated and guided by her love for God. Of course, this explains why she goes to church on Sunday and gives alms to the poor. But it also affects what we might think of as secular activities. Using one of Aquinas's own examples, it affects her relationship with food. The non-Christian with the acquired virtue of temperance chooses healthy foods in the right proportions in order to safeguard his health and not impede his cognitive capacity. The Christian with infused temperance abstains from food and drink in order to chastise the body. The Christian and the non-Christian arrive at different actions because the virtues that regulate their conduct are directed by separate principles of operation: the rule of natural reason in the case of the acquired virtues and divine law in the case of the infused virtues.[72]

These two principles of operation need not contradict one another; they might also work together. The Christian does not abstain from food at all times, but only when doing so is in accordance with a religious goal (e.g., during Lent). Otherwise, she, too, follows the practices of good nutrition. Her ultimate motivation for doing so includes her realization that her body is a gift from God, a temple of the Holy Spirit, which behooves her to maintain it in good health. Nevertheless, understanding and applying the practices of good health are functions of natural reason. Thus, she has a different incentive for eating properly, but acquired virtues assist her in achieving that goal.

Furthermore, as Dahm has argued, the acquired virtues play a role in preparing human capacities to receive the infused virtues.[73] As I pointed out earlier, God does not infuse virtue against our wills; we have the freedom to accept the gift of virtue or reject it. Acquiring virtues and perfecting our rational capacities of intellect and will provide the orientation that makes it more likely that we accept God's help. Thus, both acquired and infused virtues have roles to play in the integrated life of the Christian.

THE GIFTS, BEATITUDES, AND FRUITS OF THE HOLY SPIRIT

In addition to acquired and infused virtues, Aquinas incorporates what the tradition calls the gifts, beatitudes, and fruits into his account of ethics, all of which have their source in the Holy Spirit.

Aquinas's account of them is grounded in biblical sources and religious authorities, especially Ambrose, Augustine, and Gregory.

Aquinas describes the gifts as habits that are infused along with the theological virtues (in particular, charity) and infused forms of the moral virtues.[74] The gifts number seven in total and include the following: understanding, counsel, wisdom, knowledge, piety, fortitude, and fear of the Lord.[75] They are required because of the supernatural nature of the ultimate end, which, as we have seen, we cannot achieve on the basis of our own efforts.[76] Aquinas compares the gifts to the workings of the acquired virtues, which are also habits, but which move human beings to act in accordance with natural reason. The gifts perfect human beings for activities that have to do with the higher end, for which acquired virtue is insufficient. In particular, they prompt us to respond to divine inspiration.[77]

One might wonder why the theological virtues and infused moral virtues are not sufficient for this task. Aquinas argues that human beings only imperfectly possess the infused virtues, since, as he puts it, "we love and know God imperfectly."[78] He adds that whatever possesses virtue imperfectly cannot function by itself, unless it is moved by another. He provides an analogy with a physician and his student; the physician is able to work independently because he has mastered the art of medicine, but the student requires the direction of the physician in order to proceed. Thus, we require the direction of the Holy Spirit, who dwells in us through charity and who guides us to the ultimate end by giving us these habits that enable us to obey divine commands promptly.[79]

The gifts have their effects on our rational and appetitive capacities. The speculative powers of the intellect are perfected by understanding and wisdom, while counsel and knowledge perfect the practical part of the intellect. The appetitive powers are perfected by piety (with respect to our relationships with others), fortitude (to guard against fear in the face of danger), and fear of the Lord (which regulates our desires for pleasure).[80] Aquinas compares their effects with that of the acquired virtues. Just as the moral virtues perfect the appetitive powers so that they follow the direction of reason and the intellectual virtues perfect reason so that it might arrive at correct judgment, so too the gifts perfect these capacities in order to be suitably directed toward God.[81] Aquinas summarizes the function of all three types of habits: the moral virtues perfect the appetites to keep them in line with the directives of reason; the intellectual virtues perfect reason itself; the theological virtues act to unite the human mind (*mens*) to God; and the gifts dispose the powers of the soul to be subject (*subdantur*) to divine prompting.[82] In other words, the gifts help us to respond to the movement of God within us. Just as virtues play their roles in the perfection of an agent's goodness, so too Aquinas states that the gifts are part of a good human life.[83]

The beatitudes are another part of Aquinas's religious commitment for which he makes room in his moral theory.[84] There is a natural connection in the Latin between the beatitudes (*beatitudines*) and Aquinas's usual word for what is most often translated as 'happiness' (*beatitudo*).[85] The beatitudes have the general form of "happy are those who do φ, for they will receive ψ"; for example, happy are those who mourn, for they will be comforted. The content of the first part specifies what Aquinas calls a merit, while the second part describes a reward for that merit. Merit has a very specific technical meaning; Aquinas says that what are mentioned as merits in the beatitudes are a preparation for or a disposition to happiness, whether that be the perfect happiness of the future life or a kind of inchoate or incipient happiness under development by the saintly in this life. The rewards themselves either are a constitutive part of the perfect happiness in the next life, or they constitute the initiation of happiness in this life.[86]

The beatitudes describe actions or activities (*actus*), according to Aquinas. To put it rather crudely (and misleadingly), the point is this: If the agent engages in a particular activity, the agent will receive a reward that constitutes some form of happiness. This is misleading because it implies an instrumentalist interpretation, which Aquinas does not intend. Rather, the possession of the virtues and gifts disposes an agent to engage in the kind of activities described by the beatitudes.[87] As a result, she attains what she is aiming at, that is, the reward. The reward is not her direct motivation for engaging in these activities.[88]

Aquinas also argues that the beatitudes have a particular relationship with three common conceptions of happiness: the life of (sensual) pleasure, the active life, and the life of contemplation.[89] The pursuit of mere sensual pleasure for its own sake is an obstacle to our future happiness; some of the beatitudes direct us away from the attraction of such pleasure so that we are unaffected by its allure. These beatitudes have as their reward what we are trying to acquire in the misguided pursuit of physical pleasure. The active life concerns our duties toward and relationships with others. Some of the beatitudes help us to focus our attention wholeheartedly toward our neighbor, going above and beyond what acquired virtue would specify, and rewarding us accordingly. The active life can also dispose us toward the pursuit of the contemplative life, so some of the beatitudes direct us in this regard. Finally, there are beatitudes with a connection to the contemplative life itself, either the inchoate form in this life or the happiness in the next life. Aquinas says that those with clean hearts have the reward of seeing God, and those who work for peace demonstrate that they are God's followers and have the reward of being adopted children of God.[90]

The notion of fruit has both a natural meaning and a supernatural meaning. In his discussion of action, Aquinas argues that *fruitio* (often translated as 'enjoyment') is the final step in the process of action. It is an activity of the will upon the attainment of an end.[91] Once we achieve a particular end, we experience satisfaction and enjoyment, although we will not achieve complete enjoyment until the next life when we attain perfect happiness. At that point, there will be nothing further that we desire, and our wills will be completely satisfied.

Enjoyment or satisfaction might imply that the fruits represent a passive state. In fact, Aquinas describes this state as a kind of quiescence.[92] But as Ten Klooster points out, this is misleading.[93] Aquinas clearly identities them as *actus* – that is, actions, activities, or works. Attainment of an end generates an activity of the will. To enjoy something, for Aquinas, is not something that happens to one; it is something that stimulates movement in the will. One way to see what Aquinas has in mind is to consider an individual who takes no satisfaction or joy in accomplishing his goals. Such a case is often puzzling, but I think it demonstrates that taking joy in our accomplishments is something that we do, which, on Aquinas's theory of action, involves the will.

Fruits can be considered from the standpoint of our natural capacities or from the standpoint of divine activity. Actions in accordance with (right) reason generate fruits of reason, *fruitio* in its natural sense.[94] Actions that proceed from the power of the Holy Spirit constitute the fruits of the Holy Spirit, *fruitio* in its supernatural sense.[95] There are twelve fruits of the Holy Spirit: charity, joy, peace, patience, forbearance, goodness, kindness (*benignitas*), meekness, faith, modesty, self-control, and chastity.[96] A number of these fruits share common names with virtues, but the fruits operate differently than the virtues. For example, as we saw above, faith as a theological virtue has to do with our belief in God. Faith as a fruit of the Holy Spirit is expressed as an unwillingness to harm other human beings through anger, fraud, or deceit and is a form of fidelity to our neighbor.[97] Chastity as a fruit regulates all of our desires so that we are not bothered by them.[98] Chastity as a virtue regulates sexual desire, ensuring that one engages in appropriate sexual activity.[99]

Both the beatitudes and the fruits are associated with actions or activities. According to Aquinas, all beatitudes are fruits, but not all fruits are beatitudes. This is because any good or virtuous actions, including those prompted by acquired virtues, result in fruition (enjoyment or delight), but this is not sufficient for beatitude. Beatitudes involve fruition over what is perfect and excellent.[100] Therefore, although related, the notion of a fruit is broader than that of beatitude.

Ten Klooster identifies another way in which the beatitudes and the fruits might be distinguished. Although both denote activities, he argues that beatitudes specify direct actions while the fruits designate interior activities.[101] Drawing on one of his examples, peace is mentioned both in the beatitudes (blessed are the peacemakers) and as one of the fruits.[102] If one is a peacemaker, one engages in activities intended to bring about peace (e.g., negotiations and other activities of diplomacy). In contrast, peace as a fruit has two senses: first, as quiescence in the face of external disruptions; and second, as focused undisturbed attention on one object, regarding all other objects as insignificant.[103] Both of these activities of peace as a fruit have an interior focus.

In summary, then, virtues, gifts, beatitudes, and fruits all work together to orient human beings toward their authentic ultimate end, enabling them to attain this relationship with God. As Ten Klooster puts it,

> The infused virtues and the gifts of the Holy Spirit are the infused *habitus* that allow the believer to act toward the final end of eternal happiness. Beatitudes and fruits are the *actus* that spring forth from them.[104]

The virtues and gifts orient one toward the authentic ultimate end. As a result of this orientation, one engages in both interior activities (fruits) and exterior actions (beatitudes) appropriate for the attainment of this end.

So far in this chapter, I have discussed what Aquinas calls interior principles of action that play important roles in Aquinas's moral theory. Next, I consider the external principles of action (grace and law) and discuss their roles in his ethics.

GRACE AND LAW

The fundamental extrinsic principle that moves human beings toward the good is God. God does this in two ways: He instructs us by virtue of law and assists us by virtue of grace.[105] As we have seen, the ultimate end of human life is beyond natural human capacities to obtain. Thus, human beings have need of infused virtues and gifts, beatitudes and fruits in order to incline toward and attain this end. Grace is a highly technical matter in Aquinas's writings, and I will not be able to do it justice here.[106] In its essence, grace is a gratuitous gift from God infused into the souls of human beings out of God's great love for them.[107] Aquinas calls grace a habitual gift by which our souls are moved to participate in God's goodness.[108] Grace is given (at least logically) prior to the infused virtues and gifts. It facilitates the movement of the infused virtues and gifts into the soul's powers.[109] Thus, grace is both a necessary and a sufficient condition for the infused virtues and gifts. Nevertheless, because human beings retain freedom of action, they can lose virtues and gifts by their own free choices if they commit grave and serious sin.[110] The activities of grace are not coercive.

Law is the second external principle of action that plays a role in Aquinas's moral theory. By definition, a law is an ordinance of reason promulgated by the individual responsible for the wellbeing of the community.[111] Aquinas recognizes several types of laws, including what he calls eternal law, natural law, human law, and divine law. Eternal law expresses God's providence by which he governs the entirety of creation.[112] This includes the natural functioning of the universe, governed by what we would call laws of nature.[113] Aquinas defines natural law as human participation in the eternal law. Because of their rational capacities, human beings are able to comprehend the order and governance of the created realm and to understand the basic distinction between what is good and what is bad.[114]

Aquinas identifies three fundamental inclinations that help define what is good and worth pursuing for human beings: self-preservation (which human beings share with all of creation); preservation of the species, which includes not only reproductive acts, but also the raising and education of subsequent offspring (which human beings have in common with all other sentient life); and finally, the desire for social activities such as the acquisition of knowledge, particularly of God, and community life (both of which are unique to human beings).[115] These inclinations provide the basis for the first precept of the natural law, namely that good is to be done and evil avoided. Subsequent precepts are derived as instantiations that regulate the natural inclinations just described.[116] Although Aquinas derives the natural law from basic inclinations, rationality enables human beings to recognize (at least in some basic way) what promotes wellbeing and what does not. This understanding is the reason why Aquinas argues that human beings participate in God's plan.

Natural law provides a general blueprint for good human actions, but it does not set down specific rules that regulate human activities in particular communities that exist under different circumstances. Thus, Aquinas argues that there is need for human law.[117] Human beings naturally incline toward the good, but they can be mistaken about what is truly good and require guidance by which they can acquire and can be perfected in the virtues. Aquinas observes that not all human beings are trained adequately by their parents to be virtuous and engage in good action.[118] Therefore, human law is required in order to promulgate regulations by which wrongdoers may be held accountable and by which they might acquire virtue.[119] On Aquinas's view, law serves to specify what is in fact virtuous and rule out unvirtuous actions. One purpose of human law for Aquinas is instruction on what are good and bad actions.[120]

Human law, however, is not sufficient to guide our actions. Aquinas provides several reasons why we also require divine law.[121] Divine law directs us to our supernatural ultimate end by providing principles to guide the function of the infused virtues, as we saw earlier. Divine law helps to direct deliberations regarding the development and enactment of human laws. Divine law regulates interior dispositions, which human law cannot discern. And finally, Aquinas observes that human law cannot prohibit every bad action without sacrificing some great goods that protect the community's wellbeing. Therefore, there is need of a higher standard by which such evildoing is addressed eventually. He gives no example, but self-defense might be such a case. Strictly speaking, killing another individual is morally wrong, but Aquinas allows that one might be required to do so in order to save one's own life or the life of an innocent person.[122] Human law could permit self-defense, although charity under the direction of divine law might rule it out. Divine law is made known to us through the Hebrew (the Old Law) and the Christian (the New Law) Scriptures.[123]

The question arises: What is the relationship between virtue and law on Aquinas's account? As we have seen, Aquinas argues that the aim of law is to lead the governed to virtue. Those who have the virtues are good so it follows that the effect of law is to make us good.[124] Both law and virtue work together in directing good human lives. The natural law describes the acts of virtue.[125] Virtues move us to perform good actions, but they do so under the direction of law, which reflects the rule of reason, whether human or divine. The acquired virtues move us under the direction of law that has its origin in human reason – that is, the natural law and human law. Promptings by infused virtues are guided by law that originates in God – that is, eternal and divine law.[126] Thus, law informs virtue while virtue move us to achieve good actions. Law and virtue work together in Aquinas's account.

So far I have been discussing Aquinas's account of virtue and good action. But Aquinas's moral theory also includes vices and bad actions (i.e., sin). I turn to this topic next.

THE ROLE OF VICE AND SIN

Aquinas's account of wrongdoing and vice is nuanced and complex. I will be able to sketch only its basic framework.[127] Aquinas defines sin as a bad action performed voluntarily.[128] Vice is a bad habit that can move one to perform bad actions.[129] Vice and sin have their origins in Aquinas's basic moral psychology. All human action originates by virtue of the activities generated by intellect, will, and the passions of the sensory appetite, while habits originate by virtue of repeated actions. Wrongdoing has its source in a defect in one or more of these capacities.[130] Describing the mechanism of wrongdoing as a defect might imply something involuntary, but Aquinas would deny this. As we shall see, the defect involved is always within the agent's voluntary control. If it were not, then the resulting action would not be a sin.

Sins of ignorance originate in the intellect.[131] Ignorance implies a lack of knowledge, which is sinful only if the missing knowledge could have been obtained. Thus, the ignorance is voluntary. Furthermore, in order to be a sin, it must be the case that acquisition of this knowledge is obligatory; on Aquinas's view, this includes knowledge of faith and morals. Aquinas identifies a third condition for a sin of ignorance; it must be the case that, had the agent possessed that knowledge, the agent would have acted differently. If the missing knowledge would not have affected what the agent did, then the sin has a different origin because it has a different cause; its cause in this case is not the lack of knowledge.[132] The origin of this sin would be in the will.[133]

What about cases where one has the requisite knowledge but fails to call it to mind? These are cases of negligence and can also be considered sins of ignorance.[134] Rather than a simple absence of knowledge, these cases involve dispositional knowledge. Since the knowledge is not occurrent and hence plays no role in the performance of the action, the knowledge is missing from the agent's deliberation. Since it is within the agent's power to call to mind the missing knowledge, such cases are voluntary and still fit the basic model.

Sins of passion arise from a defect in the sensory appetite. The heart of this sin is the failure of an agent to control her passions. On Aquinas's view, passions are subject to intellect and will; he argues that fully functional rational capacities cannot be overcome by passion. Therefore, if an agent acts on the basis of passion, she does so voluntarily, unless her intellect and will are impaired.[135] Since the action is voluntary, the agent is blameworthy. Aquinas's description might suggest that the sin has its source in intellect or will, since ultimately the action comes about because of their activities.

Nevertheless, the initial impulse comes from the sensory appetite, so Aquinas classifies it as a sin of passion.

Aquinas identifies two ways in which passions can move an agent to sin.[136] First, passions can distract agents so that they do not consider what they ought to consider when deciding what to do. My passion for sweets can distract me from the fact that eating another piece of cake will make me feel sick. Second, passions can make actions that ordinarily would not look good to an agent appear attractive. Road rage is an obvious example. Nevertheless, a fully functional agent retains the capacity to resist these mechanisms; choosing to act on the basis of passion remains voluntary and therefore blameworthy.

A defect in the will causes a sin of deliberate wrongdoing.[137] Such sins involve cases where an agent recognizes the better good but chooses the lesser good, which Aquinas describes as something bad in and of itself. The agent does so because her will has become so disordered that she prefers the lesser good and is willing to forego a greater good rather than be deprived of the lesser good.[138] Her deformed character moves her to choose what is bad, knowing that it is bad. Her object of choice is a good in and of itself; what makes it bad is the fact that it is preferred to a greater good that the agent ought to choose. Aquinas gives the example of one who pursues pleasure or riches to the neglect of his spiritual life, which he ought to prioritize. An agent under the influence of passion could also choose pleasure over, say, attending church, but the difference between these agents is that once the passion has subsided, the agent who acted out of passion feels bad. His will retains its proper orientation. The agent who acted on the basis of his disordered character doesn't care; he is perfectly content to pursue the pleasure and forego his spiritual obligations.[139]

On Aquinas's theological perspective, sins interfere with our pursuit of the ultimate end because they harm or even destroy our relationship with God, if the sin is grave.[140] But God's great love for us provides a remedy for sin, and that is grace. Grace restores us from sin and puts us back on the path to our ultimate end.[141]

CONCLUSION

Aquinas's ethical theory is comprehensive and complex. It is also grounded in a theistic commitment to a supernatural ultimate end. One might wonder whether his account should be of interest to those who do not share his theological worldview. Whether one can separate a purely secular ethics from Aquinas's moral theory is a controversial matter.[142] Nevertheless, even if the content of the moral theory cannot be separated from Aquinas's theistic commitment, I see no reason why scholars of ethics would not find the framework of his account useful. Furthermore, much of his moral psychology remains helpful in understanding human life in this world. His account of the virtues and vices contains many resources for serious thought on what constitutes a good human life, including in our current situation.[143]

NOTES

1   I have consulted both Latin texts (accessed at www.corpusthomisticum
    .org/iopera.html) and English translations (including those of the English
    Dominican Fathers, John Oesterle, and Richard Regan), although
    translations of the Latin are my own unless otherwise noted.
2   Aquinas makes this claim in many places, but, for example, see *ST* I-II
    q.10 a.1.
3   Aquinas's account of the ultimate end and its instantiation is found in *ST*
    I-II qq.1–5. For this claim, see *ST* I-II q.2 a.8; *ST* I-II q.3 a.8. For a thorough
    discussion of how to interpret Aquinas's definition of happiness, see
    J. Stenberg, "'*Considerandum est quid sit beatitudo*': Aquinas on What
    Happiness Really is," *Res Philosophica* 93 (2016): 161–84.
4   Stump and Pinsent characterize this friendship as a second-personal
    relationship with God: see Chapter 12 in this volume; E. Stump, "The
    Non-Aristotelian Character of Aquinas's Ethics: Aquinas on the
    Passions," *Faith and Philosophy* 28 (2011): 29–43.
5   *ST* I-II q.3 a.2 ad 4, a.3; *ST* I-II q.3 a.6; *ST* I-II q.4 a.5; *ST* I-II q.62 a.1. For a
    thorough discussion of this point, see D. Bradley, *Aquinas on the Twofold
    Human Good: Reason and Human Happiness in Aquinas's Moral Science*
    (Washington, DC: The Catholic University of America Press, 1997).

6 *ST* I-II q.4 a.6.

7 *ST* I-II q.5 a.5; *ST* I-II q.63 a.2.

8 *ST* I-II q.5 a.5.

9 Aquinas's account of human nature is found in *ST* I qq.75–83. His discussion of the roles played by intellect and will in the pursuit of happiness is found in *ST* I-II qq.6–17.

10 *ST* I-II q.1 aa.3–6. For a discussion of some of the issues surrounding this topic, see S. MacDonald, "Ultimate Ends in Practical Reasoning: Aquinas's Aristotelian Moral Psychology and Anscombe's Fallacy," *Philosophical Review* 100 (1991): 31–66.

11 *ST* I-II q.10 a.2; *ST* I-II q.13 a.6.

12 *ST* I-II q.22 a.2.

13 *ST* I-II q.22 a.3.

14 See *ST* I-II q.24 aa.1–2.

15 *ST* I-II q.23 a.4.

16 *ST* I-II q.24 a.1.

17 *ST* I-II q.24 a.2.

18 For a comprehensive discussion of Aquinas's theory of the passions, see R. Miner, *Thomas Aquinas on the Passions* (Cambridge: Cambridge University Press, 2009).

19 The secondary literature on Aquinas's account of action is enormous, but for some recent discussions, see R. DeYoung, C. McCluskey, and C. Van Dyke, *Aquinas's Ethics: Metaphysical Foundations, Moral Theory, and Theological Context* (South Bend, IN: University of Notre Dame Press, 2009); C. L. Löwe, *Thomas Aquinas on the Metaphysics of the Human Act* (Cambridge: Cambridge University Press, 2021).

20 Aquinas introduces this distinction in the prologue to *ST* I-II q.49.

21 Along with gifts, Aquinas includes the beatitudes and the fruits of the Holy Spirit, but these are not habits; they are actions or activities. I discuss them in more detail later in this chapter.

22 One form of law is internal to human beings, i.e., the natural law. I discuss this further in the fourth section of this chapter.

23 *ST* I-II q.49 a.1.

24 *ST* I-II q.56 a.3.

25 *ST* I-II q.57 a.5.

26 See *ST* I-II q.58.

27 *ST* I-II q.58 a.2.

28 *ST* I-II q.18 a.5.

29 *ST* I-II q.61 a.3.

30 Stenberg argues for the former position, which he thinks follows from Aquinas's final definition of happiness (Stenberg, "'*Considerandum est quid sit beatitudo*,'" p. 182) but other commentators argue for the latter. For example, Stenberg cites Jean Porter as well as DeYoung, McCluskey, and Van Dyke, *Aquinas's Ethics*; see Stenberg, "'*Considerandum est quid sit beatitudo*,'" p. 181.

31 See Stenberg, "'*Considerandum est quid sit beatitudo*,'" 182, emphasis in original.

32 Aquinas implies agreement with this view insofar as he calls virtue a perfection of a power. As such, virtues help to constitute the goodness of the agent; see *ST* I-II q.55 a.3 s.c.

33 *ST* I-II q.55 a.1, 3.

34 *ST* I-II q.55 a.4. The definition comes from Peter Lombard's *Sentences*, although commentators often attribute the definition directly to Augustine.

35 *ST* I-II q.55 a.4 ad 6.

36 There are also infused versions of the cardinal virtues; see *ST* I-II q.63 a.3. As infused virtues, we acquire them through God's activity.

37 *ST* I-II q.55 a.4.

38 *ST* I-II q.61.

39 *ST* I-II q.56 a.3.

40 *ST* I-II q.57 a.4; *ST* I-II q.58 a.5; *ST* I-II q.65 a.1. Each of the cardinal virtues has associated with it other virtues, which Aquinas describes as its integral parts, subjective parts, and potential parts. It is beyond the scope of this chapter to discuss these technical notions, but Aquinas defines and illustrates them in his more detailed discussion of individual cardinal virtues, e.g., prudence in *ST* II-II q.48. *ST* II-II is an extensive examination of individual virtues and the vices associated with them.

41 In *ST* I-II q.60 a.5, following Aristotle, Aquinas lists eleven virtues as moral virtues: fortitude, temperance, liberality, magnificence, magnanimity, love of honors (*philotimia*), gentleness, friendliness, truthfulness, virtuous entertainment (*eutrapelia*) – all of which perfect the sensory appetite; and justice, which perfects the will.

42 *ST* I-II q.56 a.4, 6.

43 See *ST* I-II q.57 a.5; *ST* I-II q.58 a.4; *ST* I-II q.59 aa.3–4; *ST* I-II q.65 a.1.

44   *ST* I-II q.61 a.2.

45   *ST* II-II q.58 a.1, 11.

46   *ST* II-II q.58 a.5.

47   *ST* II-II q.61 a.1.

48   *ST* I-II q.61 a.2.

49   *ST* I-II q.61 a.2.

50   *ST* I-II q.62 a.1.

51   *ST* I-II q.63 a.2.

52   *ST* I-II q.62 a.1, 3. Each of these virtues has a natural analogue. For example, we speak of having faith in individuals to fulfill their promises, and, for Aquinas, the passions include both hope and love.

53   *ST* I-II q.62 a.3.

54   *ST* II-II q.4 a.2, 4.

55   Aquinas does think that human beings are capable of understanding some theological facts on the basis of reason alone; see *ST* I q.1 a.1.

56   *ST* II-II q.1 a.4; *ST* II-II q.2 a.1 ad 3.

57   *ST* II-II q.1 a.4 ad 2 and ad 3.

58   *ST* I-II q.62 a.3; *ST* II-II q.18 a.1; *ST* II-II q.24 a.1.

59   *ST* I-II q.40 a.1.

60   *ST* II-II q.17 a.1.

61   *ST* I-II q.65 a.5; *ST* II-II q.23 a.1.

62   See *ST* II-II q.23 a.6 ad 3.

63   See *ST* II-II q.23 a.5 ad 1.

64   J. Porter, "Moral Virtues, Charity, and Grace: Why the Infused and Acquired Virtues Cannot Co-Exist," *Journal of Moral Theology* 8 (2019): 40–66 addresses this topic and also cites relevant literature.

65   On this topic, see Chapter 12 in this volume; Stump, "The Non-Aristotelian Character of Aquinas's Ethics"; B. Dahm, "The Acquired Virtues Are Real Virtues: A Response to Stump," *Faith and Philosophy* 32 (2015): 453–70.

66   See *ST* I-II q.65 a.2.

67   See *ST* II-II q.23 a.6.

68   *ST* I-II q.63 a.2.

69   But see J. Hause, "Aquinas on the Function of Moral Virtue," *American Catholic Philosophical Quarterly* 81 (2007): 1–20, here pp. 18–20, for an objection to this view.

70   *ST* I-II q.3 a.5.

71 *ST* II-II q.23 a.8.

72 *ST* I-II q.63 a.4.

73 See Dahm, "The Acquired Virtues Are Real Virtues," pp. 464–6.

74 *ST* I-II q.68 a.5, where Aquinas argues that whoever has charity has the gifts of the Holy Spirit. Charity is infused along with the other infused virtues, so it follows that whoever has charity has the other infused items; see *ST* I-II q.65 a.3, 5. For more detailed discussion on these elements of Aquinas's theory, see Chapter 12 in this volume; E. Stump, "Aquinas's Ethics: The Infused Virtues and the Indwelling of the Holy Spirit," *Ephemerides Theologicae Lovanienses* 95 (2019): 269–81; A. ten Klooster, "Aquinas on the Fruits of the Holy Spirit as the Delight of the Christian Life," *Journal of Moral Theology* 8 (2019): 80–94.

75 *ST* I-II q.68 a.4.

76 *ST* I-II q.68 a.2.

77 *ST* I-II q.68 a.1.

78 Both the quotation and the subsequent paraphrase and analogy can be found in *ST* I-II q.68 a.2.

79 *ST* I-II q.68 a.5, 3.

80 *ST* I-II q.68 a.4. Aquinas leaves open whether the appetitive powers being perfected include the sensory appetite.

81 *ST* I-II q.68 a.4.

82 *ST* I-II q.68 a.8.

83 *ST* I-II q.55 a.3 s.c.; *ST* I-II q.68 a.4 ad 1.

84 For a detailed discussion of Aquinas's thought on the beatitudes, see Ten Klooster, "Aquinas on the Fruits of the Holy Spirit."

85 Aquinas sometimes uses the Latin *felicitas* but more often uses *beatitudo*.

86 *ST* I-II q.69 a.2.

87 *ST* I-II q.69 a.1.

88 See *ST* I-II q.69 aa.3–4.

89 See *ST* I-II q.69 a.3.

90 *ST* I-II q.69 aa.3–4.

91 *ST* I-II q.11 a.1, 3.

92 *ST* I-II q.11 a.3; *ST* I-II q.11 a.4 ad 2.

93 Ten Klooster, "Aquinas on the Fruits of the Holy Spirit," pp. 82–3.

94 See *ST* I-II q.70 a.4 ad 1.

95 *ST* I-II q.70 a.1.

96 *ST* I-II q.70 a.3.

97 *ST* I-II q.70 a.3.

98 *ST* I-II q.70 a.3.

99 See *ST* I-II q.143 a.1; *ST* I-II q.151 a.1 ad 1. See also R. Colton, "Two Rival Versions of Sexual Virtue: Simon Blackburn and John Paul II on Lust and Chastity," *The Thomist* 70 (2006): 71–101, here p. 75. Aquinas restricts appropriate sexual activity to marriage between a man and a woman; see *ST* II-II q.154 a.2; *ST* III q.41 a.1; *SCG* III.122. One can say something analogous about the fruits that share names with passions; on this topic, see Ten Klooster, "Aquinas on the Fruits of the Holy Spirit," pp. 82–3.

100 *ST* I-II q.70 a.2.

101 Ten Klooster, "Aquinas on the Fruits of the Holy Spirit," p. 90.

102 Ten Klooster, "Aquinas on the Fruits of the Holy Spirit," p. 91.

103 *ST* I-II q.70 a.3.

104 Ten Klooster, "Aquinas on the Fruits of the Holy Spirit," p. 90.

105 In the prologue to *ST* I-II q.90.

106 Aquinas's discussion of grace can be found in *ST* I-II qq.109–14.

107 *ST* I-II q.110 a.2; *ST* I-II q.112 a.1.

108 *ST* I-II q.110 a.2.

109 *ST* I-II q.110 a.3; *ST* I-II q.110 a.4 ad 1. Grace also plays a role in the remission of sin, which I discuss briefly in the next section. For Aquinas's discussion of this topic, see *ST* I-II q.113.

110 See *ST* I-II q.63 a.2 ad 2; *ST* I-II q.71 a.4.

111 *ST* I-II q.90 a.4.

112 *ST* I-II q.91 a.1.

113 *ST* I-II q.93 aa.4–5.

114 *ST* I-II q.91 a.2.

115 *ST* I-II q.94 a.2.

116 *ST* I-II q.94 a.2.

117 *ST* I-II q.91 a.3; *ST* I-II q.95 a.2.

118 Strictly speaking, Aquinas argues that the father is assigned the task of instructing his children on virtuous behavior as the mother does not possess adequate rationality to be a moral authority for her children. On this issue, see *SCG* III.122; *ST* II-II q.154 a.2.

119 *ST* I-II q.95 a.1.

120 *ST* I-II q.90 prologue. See also M. Carl, "Law, Virtue, and Happiness in Aquinas's Moral Theory," *The Thomist* 61 (1997): 425–47, here p. 428.

121 He presents these reasons in *ST* I-II q.91 a.4.

122 Aquinas's account of self-defense is complex; for his discussion, see *ST* II-II q.64 a.7.

123 *ST* I-II q.91 a.5.

124 *ST* I-II q.92 a.1. See also Carl, "Law, Virtue, and Happiness," pp. 441–4.

125 *ST* I-II q.94 a.3.

126 *ST* I-II q.63 a.2; *ST* I-II q.71 a.6.

127 For a fuller discussion of these topics, see C. McCluskey, *Thomas Aquinas on Moral Wrongdoing* (Cambridge: Cambridge University Press, 2017).

128 *ST* I-II q.71 a.1, 6; *QDM* 2.2. Strictly speaking, this is the philosophical definition. The theological definition of sin is an offense against God; see *ST* I-II q.71 a.6 ad 5.

129 *ST* I-II q.71 a.3. Of course, we always retain the freedom not to act on a vice.

130 *ST* I-II q.75 a.2.

131 *ST* I-II q.76; *QDM* 3.7.

132 *ST* I-II q.76 a.1; *ST* I-II q.6 a.8.

133 See *QDM* 3.8.

134 *QDM* 3.8; *ST* I-II q.77 a.2.

135 *ST* I-II q.77 a.7. Aquinas recognizes that this can be on a continuum.

136 *ST* I-II q.77 aa.1–2.

137 *ST* I-II q.78 a.1. The Latin is *certa malitia*, which is often translated as 'deliberate malice.' But this is misleading since the term 'malice' denotes particularly heinous acts, which would be too restrictive. Aquinas's word here is the abstract form of the Latin word for 'bad' (literally, 'badness') and is intended as a technical term to describe sins whose origin is the will.

138 *ST* I-II q.78 a.1.

139 *ST* I-II q.78 a.4.

140 *QDM* 7.1.

141 *ST* I-II q.113 a.2.

142 See, for example, D. Bradley, *Aquinas on the Twofold Human Good* C. McCluskey, "Thomism" in R. Crisp (ed.), *Oxford Handbook of the History of Ethics* (Oxford: Oxford University Press, 2013), pp. 147–66.

143 I am grateful to Eleonore Stump for her help with this project.

12 Infused Virtues, Gifts, and Fruits

Andrew Pinsent

INTRODUCTION

Aquinas's writings on normative ethics are vast, with 1,004 articles on virtue ethics and related matters in the *Summa theologiae* (*ST*) alone. These writings constitute an extraordinarily intricate picture of the kind of human life that Aquinas considers normative, but they also contain plenty of surprises, especially for those who assume that Aquinas is guided principally by the virtue ethics of Aristotle. Arguably the greatest of these surprises is that Aquinas's writings on virtue ethics are not, in fact, simply about virtues. Instead, Aquinas's virtues in the *ST* are integrated into a fourfold system of perfective attributes, namely virtues, gifts, beatitudes, and fruits (VGBF). In this chapter, I present a brief summary of this system and my interpretation of its meaning in the light of recent research.

This VGBF structure should not be surprising to anyone who has read Aquinas's own claim in his preamble to the study of virtue in the *ST* (*ST* I-II q.2 pr.) – namely, that "We must speak in the first place of the good dispositions, which are virtues, and of other matters connected with them, namely the gifts, beatitudes and fruits."[1] By 'gifts,' he means here the seven gifts of the Holy Spirit, the listing being drawn from patristic interpretations of Isaiah 11:1–2. By 'beatitudes,' he means the seven initial statements of blessedness made by Jesus Christ during the Sermon on the Mount, as described in Matthew 5:3–9. By 'fruits,' he means the twelve fruits of the Holy

Spirit, identified principally in the Vulgate version of Galatians chapter 5 and also hallowed by patristic commentaries.

This structure is also well known to anyone who studies the actual orders of questions and articles in Aquinas's texts. In *ST* I-II, in which he deals with perfective attributes in general, qq.55–67 are devoted to virtues, q.68 to gifts, q.69 to beatitudes, and q.70 to fruits. He follows the same sequence explicitly, with minor variations, in *ST* II-II qq.1–170, which address the three theological virtues of faith, hope, and love, and then the cardinal virtues of prudence, justice, and courage. The structure of the subsequent and final virtue, that of temperance, is a little different from the others, although Aquinas still devotes an article to arguing that temperance shares a gift with another virtue (*ST* II-II q.141 a.1), consistent with his expectation that all seven major virtues are linked with one or more gifts.

Despite its consistency, however, the majority of books and papers in recent decades have made little or no reference to the VGBF structure but instead focus almost exclusively on the peculiarities of Aquinas's virtues treated in isolation. If the gifts, beatitudes, and fruits are acknowledged, they tend to be treated as an afterthought, like the epicycles added to Ptolemaic orbits in pre-Copernican accounts of the solar system. In particular, the VGBF structure has rarely been treated as having anything to contribute to addressing the difficulties of Aquinas's account of virtue ethics, which has remained surprisingly intractable. In the sense of its possible significance, therefore, the VGBF structure remains largely unexplored by commentators even if its existence is acknowledged.

In this chapter, I address this challenge. My thesis is that one can draw ideas from the gifts, beatitudes, and fruits that help to provide a coherent account of Aquinas's virtue ethics as a whole.[2]

THE ROOT METAPHOR OF THE VGBF STRUCTURE

What exactly is Aquinas's account of virtue as a whole? What is it for and what is it meant to represent? The notion of a work that outlines all of the virtues systematically has its most influential precedent, of course, in Aristotle's *Nicomachean Ethics*, the aim of which is to describe what is needed for a good human life. In the broadest terms, Aquinas seems to be engaged in a similar project in *ST* I-II qq.55–70 and *ST* II-II qq.1–170, outlining the dispositions and associated attributes that are needed for human flourishing. Given the immense influence of Aristotelian virtue ethics in the High Middle Ages, Aquinas's obvious appreciation of Aristotle's work, and the many parallels in particular details, it has often been assumed that Aquinas's virtue ethics *must* somehow be based on the *Ethics*. There may, for example, be an Aristotelian core to Aquinas's work, or perhaps Aquinas's claims about the virtues can be related in a relatively straightforward manner to their counterparts in the *Ethics*.

The problem, however, which has puzzled commentators for a very long time, is that the structures of *ST* I-II qq.55–70 and *ST* II-II qq.1–170 are nothing like the *Nicomachean Ethics*. As noted above, Aquinas's virtue ethics in the *ST* is organized around seven principal virtues, the first three of which have no counterparts in Aristotle's work at all, with the remaining four diverging from their Aristotelian counterparts in many details. In particular, as noted above, all seven virtues are connected to additional non-Aristotelian perfective attributes, notably the gifts, beatitudes, and fruits.

Aquinas's VGBF structure, therefore, rapidly presents problems if one tries to relate his claims to the *Nicomachean Ethics*, but the challenge is even greater when one questions what, precisely, Aquinas means by a virtue. Aquinas does not deny that there are virtues based on habituation in the Aristotelian manner, virtues that he calls *acquired virtues*.[3] Yet Aristotle's central idea of habituation is impossible to reconcile with many of Aquinas's claims about what he calls the true virtues, without qualification, which he describes as *infused* by God and not acquired.[4] These infused virtues are not just the Christian theological virtues but include counterparts of the acquired moral virtues. So, for example, as well as acquired justice, there is perfect infused justice, Similarly, besides acquired prudence, there is perfect infused prudence, and so on for the other moral virtues described in *ST* II-II qq.1–170.[5]

As well as their source in purported divine infusion, many of the characteristics of these perfect infused virtues are radically different from their homonymous acquired counterparts. Perhaps the most important difference is Aquinas's claim that an infused virtue can be gained, cut off, or regained by a *single action* (*ST* I-II q.71 a.4), a claim that is incompatible with Aristotle's account based on habituation, according to which no virtue can be gained or lost by a single action. Whatever else may be said, one point at least should be clear: habituation cannot be the root metaphor for the infused virtues.[6] The Aristotelian acquired virtues and Aquinas's infused virtues are different in kind from one another.[7]

The presence of infused virtues severely complicates the problem of interpreting Aquinas's VGBF structure. This structure includes seven gifts, seven beatitudes, and twelve fruits, which are divided up and appended to seven major virtues, the accounts of which also encompass a further thirty associated virtues. There has, historically, been some doubt about whether some or all of these virtues in Aquinas's work should be treated as acquired or infused. Some of them – namely the theological virtues – are definitely infused. Nevertheless, I think that there is quite persuasive evidence for all the virtues that Aquinas describes in these accounts as being infused, unless stated otherwise. First, according to Aquinas, all perfect virtues are infused, which suggests that the infused option should be given the benefit of the doubt in cases of ambiguity. Second, all seven major virtues are linked to gifts of the Spirit, which are definitely infused. Third, Aquinas frequently opposes these virtues explicitly to sin.[8] Apart from being a notion that is absent from the *Nicomachean Ethics*, individual sins can, in a Christian understanding, destroy virtue by a single action, which is a characteristic of infused rather than acquired virtues. On this basis, I judge that all thirty-seven virtues in this vast structure of 815 articles should ordinarily be treated as infused unless explicitly stated otherwise.[9]

What, then, is one to do with the sixty-three perfective attributes of Aquinas's account, probably the largest purportedly systematic account of virtue ethics ever attempted? Collectively, they seem to form an account of human flourishing, but it is an account that is nothing like that of the *Nicomachean Ethics*, the foundational document of virtue ethics in the Western tradition. Given this tension, it is easy to find instances of the most obviously non-Aristotelian aspects of Aquinas's work being filtered out of consideration across the long history of commentary.[10] Additionally, in Neo-Thomist commentaries, a common approach was to claim that the Aristotelian virtues and their Thomistic counterparts must be proportionally equivalent, an interpretation that also ultimately failed, given the radical qualitative differences.[11] In more recent times, some very respected commentators have warned that Aquinas's virtue ethics may not be entirely coherent and should be treated with caution.[12]

What happens, however, if one attempts to interpret the structure as a whole, without trying to relate it to the *Nicomachean Ethics* as a starting point? To return to the original questions at the start of this section, this structure does comprise an account of human flourishing, insofar as Aquinas clearly believes that a human being with all the attributes he describes will be a truly flourishing human being. The kind of flourishing, however, is clearly not that of the *Nicomachean Ethics*, so what is it?

One can at least provide a label for this flourishing if one recalls that, according to Aquinas, the Christian life is meant to be different to that with which human beings are generally born. This Christian life begins with the grace of baptism, with the goal of union with the Most Holy Trinity. Traditional commentaries have typically called this life "the supernatural life," and Eleonore Stump, in her recent book *Atonement*, calls it "life in grace."[13] At least some of the dispositions Aquinas describes in his account of virtue clearly belong to this supernatural life, notably the three theological virtues and the seven gifts of the Holy Spirit, and the other dispositions, if they are infused, also belong to this life. So the most straightforward answer to the question of the kind of flourishing to which Aquinas's account is directed is that this is the flourishing of the supernatural life of grace. On this interpretation, *ST* I-II qq.55–70 and *ST* II-II qq.1–170 form a giant analytic map of the life of grace, the Christian counterpart of the

Nicomachean Ethics, which is about flourishing without the gifts associated with Christian grace. As I shall argue later, this interpretation does not mean that Aquinas's account lacks relevance for life outside of a Christian context, but this context is what is needed initially to understand the meaning.

Additional understanding of this life of grace can be drawn from Aquinas's claims about its ultimate goal. In his account of the virtue of love (*caritas*), *ST* II-II q.23, he not only claims that this theological virtue is the greatest virtue (a.6) but that it is the form of all the virtues (a.8) and that no other true virtue is possible without it (a.7). Moreover, he argues that this love is friendship, putting friendship rather than one of the intellectual virtues at the apex of his entire account of virtue, and placing friendship with God at the apex of his account of love (*ST* II-II q.26 a.2). These claims reinforce a non-Aristotelian interpretation, given that Aristotle argues that friendship with any god is impossible.[14] In addition, given that friendship is between persons, it should be expected that Aquinas's accounts of all the virtues will be interpreted fittingly in terms of the flourishing of the relations of persons.

This understanding can be refined still further by examining those dispositions (*habitus*) that are not virtues but are appended to the virtues, namely the seven gifts of the Holy Spirit. Like the perfect virtues, the gifts are also described as being infused by God, and it is also clear that the gifts are important for Aquinas. In *ST* I-II q.68 a.8, he argues that the gifts are more important than any virtues except the three theological virtues. In other words, the gifts are more important than thirty-four out of the thirty-seven virtues described in *ST* II-II qq.1–170. In *ST* II-II q.19 a.9 ad 4, Aquinas further adds that the gifts are the *principia* of the intellectual and moral virtues, a word that translates as 'origins,' 'principles,' or 'foundations.' Furthermore, in *ST* I-II q.68 a.2, he claims that they are essential to salvation. Whatever else may be inferred, these claims alone should lay to rest any expectation of success in trying to understand Aquinas's virtue ethics without taking the gifts of the Spirit into account.

Aquinas assigns fundamentally different modes of operation to gifts and to virtues. The distinction is not in terms of their source – namely, divine infusion – or their matters. In *ST* I-II q.68 a.4, for example, he argues that the gifts extend to all those things to which the virtues, both intellectual and moral, extend, and that whatever powers in a person can be the principles of human actions – namely, reason and appetite – can be the subjects of gifts as well as virtues. Instead, the principle of their diverse operation is set out in *ST* I-II q.68 a.1 as follows:

> Now it is manifest that human virtues perfect a human being according as it is natural for him to be moved by his reason in his interior and exterior actions. Consequently, a human being needs yet higher perfections, whereby to be disposed to be moved by God. These perfections are called gifts, not only because they are infused by God, but also because by them a human being is disposed to become amenable to divine inspiration.[15]

In this passage, Aquinas claims that what is specific about a gift is not that it is infused, since virtues are also infused, but that, by means of a gift, a person is disposed to become 'amenable' or 'readily movable' by divine inspiration. In other words, Aquinas is describing a *triadic* person–God–object scenario in which one's stance toward the object is 'moved' by God, in some sense yet to be understood. According to other statements by Aquinas, this movement is not coercive or comparable to a mechanical force, like the strings that move a puppet. Nor is this movement reducible to the mere communication of information, such as a command via stone tablets or text messages to do or avoid something.[16]

At this point, references to being "moved by God," as well as infused dispositions that enable such movement, might seem like pixie dust or unexplorable skyhooks to some readers, but it is important to understand the task of interpretation. The goal is to understand Aquinas on his own terms, which requires relating his claims to ordinary embodied experience to which human beings in general can relate regardless of their theological commitments. To make progress toward this goal, it is therefore helpful to re-express Aquinas's claims in less overtly theological terms, in which case the situation is as follows. A first person, who is the possessor of various *habitus*, is 'moved' in some way by another personal agent with respect to some object of attention. But in what does this movement consist?

Progress can be made by examining some of Aquinas's statements about specific gifts, such as the following text, in which Aquinas contrasts the intellectual virtue and the gift of knowledge:

> Human knowledge is acquired by means of demonstrative
> reasoning. On the other hand, in God, there is a sure judgment of
> truth, without any discursive process, by simple intuition ...
> wherefore God's knowledge is not discursive, or argumentative, but
> absolute and simple, to which that knowledge is likened which is a
> gift of the Holy Spirit, since it is a participated likeness
> (*participativa similitudo*) thereof.[17]

What is significant here is Aquinas's claim in the second part of the passage, that the knowledge which is a gift of the Holy Spirit is like God's knowledge. This *habitus* is not that of reasoning well from premises to conclusions, as in the case of the homonymous intellectual virtue. Nor is this knowledge reducible to the communication of new facts. Instead, Aquinas describes the gift as participating in the divine judgment of created things, a judgment that can be described as a divine *stance* or attitude consequent upon shared divine understanding.[18] By implication, by means of the gift of knowledge, at least in a small way, one begins to love created things *with God* as God loves them.

Another important aspect of gift-based movement can be found in Aquinas's description of the gift of wisdom. The following passage, from *ST* II-II q.45 a.2, once again contrasts the gift with its homonymous counterpart among the intellectual virtues:

> Accordingly it belongs to the wisdom that is an intellectual virtue
> to pronounce right judgment about divine things after reason has

made its inquiry, but it belongs to wisdom as a gift of the Holy
Spirit to judge aright about them on account of connaturality with
them ... Now this sympathy or connaturality for divine things is
the result of love, which unites us to God, according to 1 Cor. 6:17,
"The one who is joined to the Lord, is one spirit." Consequently,
wisdom which is a gift has its cause in the will, which cause is love,
but it has its essence in the intellect, whose act is to judge aright, as
stated above.

In the passage above, Aquinas observes that the intellectual virtue of
wisdom involves a judgment being made after reason has made its
inquiry, underlining how the virtue of wisdom has a discursive and
demonstrative aspect.[19] The gift of wisdom, by contrast, enables judgments of divine things on account of a 'sympathy' or 'connaturality'
for them. This notion of connaturality is clearly akin to the notion of a
'participated likeness' in the case of the gift of knowledge. In the
passage above, however, Aquinas also highlights how this connaturality is a result of love, which unites us to God. In other words, this
likeness is not a mere imitation of God, but results from a kind of
union with God.

Aquinas goes on to illustrate this union by citing 1 Cor. 6:17,
"The one who is joined to the Lord, is one spirit," and he expresses it
again in the subsequent article (ST II-II q.45 a.3) as follows:

Wisdom as a gift is more excellent than wisdom as an intellectual
virtue, since it attains to God more intimately by a kind of union of
the soul with God.

Aquinas therefore refers to the direction given by means of the gift of
wisdom as arising from an intimate attainment to God, a kind of union
or oneness of the soul with God. Due to its more intimate attainment
to God, Aquinas rates the gift higher than the virtue, a point that is
especially significant given that even little children and others who
lack the use of reason and wisdom in the ordinary human sense can
possess this gift, along with all the other gifts and infused virtues.[20]

To sum up these observations about gift-based movement, Aquinas posits a triad of two personal agents, in which the second person shares a stance with the first person, with respect to some object of attention. This sharing also involves a sense of interpersonal union of the soul of the first with the second personal agent. Considered in these terms, the operation of the gifts resembles very commonplace interactions in daily life, most evidently in the shared interactions of young children with their parents or caregivers. Young children naturally love to interact with other persons, in such a way as to share awareness of shared focus with others.[21] Common examples include recognizing faces and smiling back, raising hands to be lifted up, pointing, gaze following, and reciprocal turn taking. All these interactions invite or directly involve someone sharing a stance toward a concrete or abstract object, a sharing that also involves an experience of interpersonal union. For instance, a child pointing in a supermarket is inviting someone else, normally a harassed parent, to share the child's interest in some object, a sharing that also offers a very natural metaphor for infusion.[22] The collective name for these phenomena is 'shared attention' or 'joint attention,'[23] and they are correlated or even equivalent to instances of *second-person relatedness*, of the kind to which Martin Buber famously drew attention.[24] On this account, the special work of the gifts of the Holy Spirit is to enable second-person relatedness to God, a mode of relating that brings about an interpersonal union with God that involves a sharing in God's stance to persons and things.

Combining these insights into the gifts of the Spirit, together with Aquinas's observations on the role of divine friendship as the apex and form of the virtues, it would be unsurprising to find that second-person relatedness shapes the form of all the virtues described in the *ST*. A couple of examples will serve as illustrations.

Consider, as a first example, virtue and vice with respect to money, the latter being the deadly sin of avarice.[25] The sheer range of permutations involved in financial matters – including acquiring money, spending money, accumulating and dissipating assets, future contingencies, and lending and borrowing at interest – quickly overwhelms any attempt to treat the virtuous use of money as an Aristotelian mean between two extremes. Moreover, it is relatively easy to find counterexamples to any quantitative rule, such as exceptionally poor or wealthy persons who have led saintly lives.[26] In the *ST*, however, Aquinas hints at a different approach with his list of the 'daughters of avarice' in *ST* II-II q.118 a.8 – namely, treachery, fraud, falsehood, perjury, restlessness, violence, and insensibility to mercy. All of these actions are, of course, deadly to second-person relatedness oriented toward friendship. The implication is that the standard by which the use of money should be regarded as evil is not the violation of an Aristotelian mean but the trading away or destruction of second-person relatedness. Dante's *Divine Comedy* hints at the same insight, since the face is a privileged channel of second-person relatedness, and nowhere in the *Divine Comedy* does one ever see the face of the avaricious.[27]

As another example, consider some of the details of the virtue of temperance with respect to food and drink. As is well known, temperance in the *Nicomachean Ethics* is guided by the principle of a rational mean between the two vices of consuming too little and consuming too much. By contrast, many additional issues are folded into Aquinas's account, such as the various species of gluttony (*ST* II-II q.148 a.4). These species include improper consumption, such as eating ahead of time or consuming too much at once, and desires for improper consumables, such as foods that are overly sumptuous or prepared in excessively elaborate ways. None of these species of gluttony necessarily violate the principles of Aristotelian temperance, but they would be harmful to the wellbeing of a family or community in the context of shared meals. The suggestion is that what is being harmed is not so much human beings considered as rational animals, but human beings as persons in relation.

The root metaphor of second-person relatedness also suggests a way of resolving one of the most challenging of Aquinas's claims, namely, as noted previously, that infused virtues can be gained or lost by a single action. This claim is incompatible with Aristotelian virtue ethics, also as noted previously, but can make sense of it if one reframes the notion of flourishing in terms of personal relationship. In particular, consider the situation of a long-married couple and one of the spouses betraying the other secretly by some single action. Even if the betrayer keeps the action secret, that person cannot be wholly open with the other and may also suffer from guilt and shame, impeding and preventing friendship. The betraying spouse cannot then have dispositions oriented to second-personal flourishing. In other words, these dispositions have indeed been 'cut off' (excluduntur) by a single action, which is exactly what Aquinas claims about the infused virtues in *ST* I-II q.71 a.4. Nevertheless, the secret loss of these dispositions does not mean that the betraying spouse loses all the acquired habits of daily shared life, but these acquired habits are no longer conducive to the flourishing of the relationship until or unless there is some act of reconciliation. Hence, on this second-person account, virtues are not synonymous with habits, and habits can remain even if the infused dispositions are lost.[28]

THE FRUITION OF THE VIRTUES AND GIFTS

The final two perfective attributes in the VGBF structure – namely the beatitudes and fruits – are both described as consequences of the virtues and gifts, specifically their acts or actualizations. There is a good deal to say about how the beatitudes link with the theme of second-person relatedness.[29] Nevertheless, although, in practice, human persons will tend to pass through the narratives of the beatitudes in attaining the fruits, they are not strictly a precondition of having the fruits.[30] In this chapter, I focus therefore on the fruits, since they are most obviously the culmination and characterization of personal success of the VGBF structure as a whole.

To explain what a 'fruit' means, Aquinas draws on the metaphor of its material counterpart in *ST* I-II q.11 a.3:

> The notion of fruit implies two things: first that it should come last; second, that it should calm the appetite with a certain sweetness and delight ... that which is last simply, and in which one delights

as in the last end, is properly called a fruit; and this it is that one is properly said to enjoy.

In this passage, Aquinas draws attention to two characteristics of the fruits. First, a fruit is something that is produced last, like the product of a plant when it has come to perfection.[31] Second, a fruit is something in which one delights as in the last end.[32] These explanations, combined with the fact that many particular fruits, such as love, joy, and peace, convey a sense of the finality associated with genuine happiness, and the fact that they are usually treated last in Aquinas's accounts of the VGBF structure, strongly suggest that they should be treated as the proper culmination of the structure.

What relation, if any, do these fruits have to second-person relatedness? For the most part, Aquinas does not do much more than list the names of most of the fruits at particular points in the VGBF structure, but he describes the fruits of love, joy, and peace in some detail (ST II-II qq.27–9) within his account of the virtue of love.

With regard to the fruit of peace being an actualization or effect of love, in ST II-II q.29 a.3, Aquinas associates this fruit closely with friendship as follows:

> Peace implies a twofold union ... The first is the result of one's own desires being directed towards one thing; while the other results from one's own desire being united with the desire of another: and each of these unions is effected by love ... hence it is reckoned a sign of friendship if people "make choice of the same things" (Ethic. ix, 4), and Cicero says (De amicitia) that friends "like and dislike the same things."

In this passage, Aquinas refers to peace implying a twofold union: The first is that one's own desires are directed toward one single object, implying an internal harmony of one's desires; the second kind of union is that of one's desires being united to the desires of another person, a harmony that is a special mark of friendship.[33] Since Aquinas here describes peace as consisting in a harmony of desires with another person, with respect to some object, he appears to follow once again the triadic person–person–world scenario, but in a mode in which perfect harmony has been attained.

Aquinas's description of the fruit of joy also focuses strongly on the principle of an interpersonal relationship between a human person and God, to the point that the presence of God which must accompany the gifts is expressed in terms of God abiding *in* a person (*ST* II-II q.28 a.1, cf. 1 John 4:16 [*Super Johan*, 4:2]). This notion of union with God is emphasized still further by Aquinas's description of the fruit of love in *ST* II-II q.27 a.2. In a.4 of the same question, Aquinas also claims that this *operatio* unites the soul *immediately* to God with a bond of spiritual union.[34] So the description of the fruit of love corroborates what Aquinas claims about joy – namely, that these fruits involve a certain sense of being united with God and even united *immediately* with God.

As I have argued elsewhere, I believe that a good metaphor to unite these descriptions is the notion of *resonance*, a very common phenomenon in physics involving the result of the harmonization of two interconnected systems.[35] As the harmonization approaches perfection, there is a disproportionate intensification of joint action. In particle physics, resonances are often equivalently described as particles themselves, implying that resonances have a reified characteristic, evocative of fruits. But persons can also resonate with other persons, especially in the kind of actions associated with singing or dancing together, which specifically involve joint attention. Those who have experienced near perfect harmony in such actions will know that one can suddenly have the experience of flying along, of the whole being more than the sum of the parts, as well as a sense of intense union between or among the persons involved. This union is experienced as immediate, consistent with Aquinas's claims.

Aquinas's description of one of the fruits, benignity, also hints that resonance is an appropriate metaphor. He twice explains that 'benignity' means 'good fire' (*bonus ignis*), one by which a person 'melts' to relieve the needs of others.[36] But, of course, fire is also one of the privileged metaphors for the Holy Spirit in the Judeo-Christian Scriptures (e.g., Acts 2:3). By drawing attention to this image, Aquinas seems to suggest that the person loving with God becomes *like* God, corresponding to the notion of a resonance between a human person and God in a state of near perfect harmonization. This description is also consistent with the notion of the supernatural life of grace being one of deification, of participating in the divine life by means of, and for the sake of, friendship with God.[37]

APPLICATIONS TO A NON-THEOLOGICAL CONTEXT

The principle of second-person relatedness with God, culminating in divine friendship characterized by the fruits, underlines that the key principles of Aquinas's virtue ethics in the *ST* are theological. What relevance then, if any, does this massive volume of work have to broader and non-theological contexts? On the thesis outlined above, the form of Aquinas's virtues will follow that of God's stance in situations of second-person relatedness. Nevertheless, also on Aquinas's account, human persons are meant to have a similar kind of love for other human persons (*ST* II-II q.25 a.1), and so it is probable that shared awareness of shared focus is not wholly limited to the special case of God. It is not, therefore, a surprise to discover that second-person relatedness does in fact play an important role in shaping the forms and cultivation of many virtues, even outside of an explicitly theological context.

As an example, consider again the example of avarice and my argument that the implied evil in Aquinas's account of avarice is that of trading away or destroying second-person relatedness. This principle retains considerable explanatory power even beyond a theological context. Consider, as an illustration, the death of Mr. Jdimytai Damour, a Walmart service worker, who died after he was knocked to the ground and trampled by a crowd of around 2,000 shoppers surging into his store for a sale.[38] The fact that a person, capable of second-person relatedness with other persons, was killed as a result of material greed enables this action to be classified not only as evil but also as a consequence of the specific evil of avarice. The violation of second-person relatedness therefore assists in clarifying the complex ways in which whatever is valued in monetary terms can be misused.

As another example, consider again the example of temperance. I argued earlier that an important underlying principle in Aquinas's account is that human beings are not simply rational animals but persons in relation. The same principle can be extended, even outside of a theological context, to create much richer and more comprehensive accounts of temperance than can be drawn from the *Nicomachean Ethics*. As I have argued elsewhere in detail, once the principle of second-person relatedness is recognized, then expanded accounts of temperance easily encompass manners, which are so important for persons to flourish in society and play an important role in a child's development. Although the details of manners vary across cultures, the very fact that cultures do tend to have manners underlines that eating and drinking are not simply about consumption but second-person relatedness with other persons.[39]

Hence, although Aquinas's virtue ethics is developed organically around the root metaphor of second-person relatedness with God, the scope is not limited to an explicitly theological worldview, requiring special divine gifts. On the contrary, this account corresponds to all kinds of daily experience of second-person relatedness, in which human persons relate by sharing awareness of shared focus, as well as to recent research in experimental psychology that links aspects of second-person relatedness, such as cognition of the human face, with changes to a person's moral stance.[40] Moreover, neuroscience is uncovering neural conditions and concomitants that support such relations, such as specialized faculties for face cognition.[41] This new appreciation of Aquinas's VGBF ethics may therefore help stimulate an important and timely new approach to virtue ethics at the beginning of the third millennium.

NOTES

1 Virtues are *habitus*, which have traditionally been translated as 'habits.' To avoid associating this term with habituation in modern English, thereby almost forcing an Aristotelian interpretation, in this chapter *habitus* are translated as 'dispositions.'

2 I draw principally from research published in A. Pinsent, *The Second-Person Perspective in Aquinas's Ethics: Virtues and Gifts* (New York and Abingdon: Routledge, 2012), together with subsequent and more detailed explorations of some of the key dispositions.

3 According to Aristotle, it is from playing the lyre that good lyre players are produced, and by building well that good builders are made (cf. *NE* II.1.1103b6–22). In other words, the formation of virtue is associated with habituation to actions chosen by practical wisdom. This habituation can be likened to learning to play a musical instrument or any craft, the practice of which begins slowly and with difficulty and gradually becomes easy to perform.

4 As a preliminary indication of the distinction, in *ST* I-II q.63 a.2, Aquinas argues that human virtue directed to the good which is defined according to the rule of human reason can be caused by human acts (that is, by habitual operation, *ex assuetudine operum*), but virtue which directs a person to the good as defined by the divine law, and not by human reason, is produced in us by the divine operation alone (*causatur solum in nobis per operationem divinam*). See also QDVCom q.1 a.2 ad 18 on the distinction of acquired and infused virtues. See also *ST* II-II q.23 a.7, in which Aquinas claims that no strictly true virtue is possible without the (infused) theological virtue of *caritas*.

5 Aquinas differentiates acquired and infused justice in *ST* I-II q.100 a.12, claiming that only the latter is true justice. In *ST* I-II q.47 a.14, he distinguishes acquired and infused prudence. In *ST* I-II q.63 a.4 he describes acquired and infused temperance as distinct species of temperance. Acquired and infused courage are mentioned as distinct virtues in QDVCom a.10, ad 10.

6 The term 'metaphor,' like the term 'analogy,' is apt to be interpreted in a diversity of ways. In this chapter, I refer to metaphor in the sense used by Iain McGilchrist – namely, something that carries us out of the web of language to the world of embodied experience, thereby conveying understanding – "There is nothing more fundamental in relation to which

we can understand *that*." See I. McGilchrist, *The Master and His Emissary: The Divided Brain and the Making of the Western World* (New Haven, CT and London: Yale University Press, 2009), p. 116.

7   The same point is also underlined, for example, in J. Porter, "The Subversion of Virtue: Acquired and Infused Virtues in the 'Summa Theologiae,'" *Annual of the Society of Christian Ethics* 12 (1992): 19–41, here p. 20.

8   For example, in *ST* II-II, q.107, when Aquinas discusses vices opposed to gratitude, and in qq.110–13, when he discusses vices opposed to truth, he in fact discusses this opposition in terms of sins.

9   See A. Pinsent, "Who's Afraid of the Infused Virtues? Dispositional Infusion, Human and Divine" in H. Goris and H. Schoot (eds.), *The Virtuous Life: Thomas Aquinas on the Theological Nature of Moral Virtues* (Leuven, Paris, and Bristol, CT: Peeters, 2017), pp. 73–96, here pp. 73–4, note 2.

10 Some of the most influential historical commentators on Aquinas have filtered at least some of the non-Aristotelian attributes out of consideration. For example, in the fourteenth century, John Capreolus, later acclaimed as the 'Prince of Thomists,' correctly defended the principle that the gifts are distinct from the virtues, but he only mentioned the beatitudes in a single article of his *Defensiones Theologiae Divi Thomae Aquinatis* and did not discuss the fruits at all. In the seventeenth century, João Poinsot, also known as John of St. Thomas, wrote the most famous historical commentary on the gifts, *De donis Spiritus sancti*, but was unable to complete his planned work on the beatitudes and fruits. One result is that the VGBF structure has rarely been appreciated as forming an 'organic whole,' to use a phrase from S. Pinckaers, *Morality: The Catholic View*, translated by M. Sherwin (South Bend, IN: St. Augustine's Press, 2001), p. 87.

11 See R. Garrigou-Lagrange, *La synthèse thomiste*, Bibliothèque Française de Philosophie (Paris: Desclée de Brouwer, 1946). When describing prudence, for example, he states that the same definition is proportionally true of acquired prudence, illuminated by the natural light of reason, and of infused prudence, illuminated by the infused light of faith (p. 529). See also p. 442, 529, 534, 536 for many metaphors of proportional difference of infused and acquired virtues, such as two notes on a keyboard played an octave apart (p. 442).

INFUSED VIRTUES, GIFTS, AND FRUITS 303

12 For example, Aquinas is described as an "unexpectedly marginal figure," with an approach to the virtues that is "questionable" in A. MacIntyre, *After Virtue: A Study in Moral Theory*, 3rd edn. (Notre Dame, IN: University of Notre Dame Press, 2007), p. 178. This section has remained unchanged in chapter 13 of this edition, the most recent edition of *After Virtue*. Jean Porter, as another example, claims that Aquinas "does not completely escape from the dichotomies set by his Christian and non-Christian sources," even though he "allows his diverse sources to speak to and correct one another." Porter, "The Subversion of Virtue," p. 40.

13 E. Stump, *Atonement* (Oxford: Oxford University Press, 2018), p. 197.

14 *Nicomachean Ethics (NE)* 8.7.1158b36–1159a8.

15 In this chapter, with very minor modifications, I use the translation Thomas Aquinas, *The "Summa Theologica" of St. Thomas Aquinas, Literally Translated by the Fathers of the English Dominican Province* (London: Burns, Oates and Washbourne, 1911). This translation has become standard and there are not many places where I could improve on it significantly.

16 Cf. *ST* I-II q.68 a.3 ad 2; Pinsent, *The Second-Person Perspective*, pp. 34–8.

17 *ST* II-II q.9 a.1 ad 1.

18 Stump has described this kind of intuitive judgment as "a conative attitude prompted by the mind's understanding." See E. Stump, "The Non-Aristotelian Character of Aquinas's Ethics: Aquinas on the Passions," *Faith and Philosophy* 28 (2011): 29–43, here p. 41.

19 Aquinas makes clear, in *ST* I-II q.57, a.2, ad 1, that the intellectual virtue of wisdom, by contrast, is a kind of *scientia*, in that it enables the demonstration of conclusions from principles as well as judgment about first principles.

20 Cf. *ST* II-II q.47 a.14 ad 3 with regard to infused prudence.

21 Such interactions are especially clear in interactions between parents and very young children, but they extend to all ages, even if they are sometimes less evident as people get older and their modes of communication become more complex. A famous instance among adults that has been studied extensively is that of *mirroring*, in which one person unconsciously imitates the gestures, speech patterns, or attitudes of another, an imitation that can build rapport.

22 Pinsent, "Who's Afraid of the Infused Virtues?"

23 See P. Hobson, "What Puts Jointness into Joint Attention?" in N. Eilan,
    C. Hoerl, T. McCormack, and J. Roessler (eds.), *Joint Attention:
    Communication and Other Minds: Issues in Philosophy and Psychology*
    (Oxford: Oxford University Press, 2005), pp. 185–204, here pp. 200–1. Joint
    attention is sometimes best appreciated when it is missing, reduced, or
    atypical, as is the case of those with autistic spectrum disorder. For
    example, in Peter Hobson's account of a study of children with autism,
    the children were able to perceive and copy the strategies of a
    demonstrator to achieve the goals of each demonstration, but they did not
    adopt his style, "nor did they identify with him and copy his self-
    orientated actions so that these actions became orientated towards
    themselves." In Hobson's words: "[W]hat they learned seemed to be
    available from their position as a kind of detached observer of actions and
    goals. They were not 'moved.'"

24 M. Buber, *Ich und Du*, 1st edn. (Leipzig: Insel-Verlag, 1923). For an
    overview of the connection between joint attention and second-person
    relatedness, see Pinsent, *The Second-Person Perspective*, pp. 47–9.

25 For my complete book chapter on this topic, see A. Pinsent, "Avarice
    and Liberality" in K. Timpe and C. A. Boyd (eds.), *Virtues and
    Their Vices* (Oxford and New York: Oxford University Press, 2014),
    pp. 157–76.

26 Dante's treatment of the circle of the avaricious in his *Inferno*, with the
    avaricious and prodigal rolling and smashing weights against each other,
    shouting "Why do you hoard?" and "Why do you waste?," plausibly
    expresses the impossibility of finding a stable and rational mean between
    two extremes with regard to money (Canto VII ll.22–36).

27 For example, in the circle of the avaricious in the *Inferno*, the souls have
    lost their faces (Canto VII ll.49–54) while, in the equivalent circle of the
    Purgatorio, their faces are turned to the ground (Canto XIX ll.70–2). This
    loss suggests the notion of a diabolical transaction in which these souls
    have traded second-person relatedness in some way for monetary benefit,
    down to and including the soul of Judas, who sold Jesus for thirty pieces of
    silver, and who is portrayed as being consumed head-first inside Satan's
    jaw (*Inferno*, Canto XXXIV, ll.61–3).

28 On the night of the betrayal of Jesus Christ to death, his betrayer, Judas
    Iscariot, has not obviously stood out from the other apostles as being
    capable of betrayal (cf. John 13:25). This example also illustrates that it is

possible for someone to lose the infused virtues of a holy life and yet retain the habits associated with such a life, remaining undetected except by Jesus himself (cf. John 6:70).

29 Pinsent, *The Second-Person Perspective*, pp. 85–91.

30 In *ST* II-II q.139 a.2, Aquinas states, and does not subsequently deny, that, "The fruits are consequent upon the beatitudes, since delight is essential to beatitude." *In Gal* 5, 1.6 also includes the claim that the fruits have sweetness and delight in themselves and are "the ultimate and congruous products of the gifts." Nevertheless, other texts imply that the beatitudes are not strictly a prerequisite of the fruits, an argument made by A. ten Klooster, "Aquinas on the Fruits of the Holy Spirit as the Delight of the Christian Life," *Journal of Moral Theology* 8 (2019): 80–94.

31 In *ST* II-II q.8 a.8 ad 3, Aquinas claims that the reason why almost all the fruits pertain to the appetitive gifts is precisely because the character of end, which the word fruit implies, pertains to the appetitive rather than to the intellective faculty.

32 Aquinas repeats this observation in *ST* I-II q.70 a.1.

33 On this point, Aquinas argues this internal harmony of one's desires is only possible if the object is good: the wicked cannot have peace, because every evil that appears good to them nevertheless has many defects, which cause the appetite to remain restless and disturbed. See *ST* II-II q.29 a.2 ad 3.

34 In *ST* II-II q.27, a.4, ad 3.

35 Pinsent, *The Second-Person Perspective*, pp. 95–8.

36 *ST* I-II, q.70, a.3; *In Gal* 5.6.

37 This theme of deification has been highlighted in recent works, such as C. E. Olson and D. Meconi, *Called To Be the Children of God: The Catholic Theology of Human Deification*, annotated edn. (San Francisco: Ignatius Press, 2016). See also J. Ortiz, *Deification in the Latin Patristic Tradition* (Washington, DC: The Catholic University of America Press, 2019).

38 R. D. McFadden and A. Macropoulos, "Wal-Mart Employee Trampled to Death," *New York Times*, 28 November 2008, www.nytimes.com/2008/11/29/business/29walmart.html [accessed February 9, 2012].

39 A. Pinsent, "Temperance and the Second-Person Perspective," *European Journal for Philosophy of Religion* 12 (2020): 101–15.

40 M. Bateson, D. Nettle, and G. Roberts, "Cues of Being Watched Enhance Cooperation in a Real-World Setting," *Biology Letters* 2 (2006): 412–14, https://doi.org/10.1098/rsbl.2006.0509.

41 See A. Pinsent, "Neurotheological Eudaimonia" in N. Levy and J. Clausen (eds.), *Handbook of Neuroethics* (Dordrecht: Springer, 2014).

PART V   **Philosophical Theology**

I3   **Original Sin**

Brian Leftow

Western thinking about original sin gets its gravity from Augustine. Some orbit him. Others blast against him till they achieve escape velocity. Aquinas was in orbit, but in a distinctive path. I now explore Aquinas's views. Aquinas believed in a historical Adam and Eve, and treated the Genesis account of the fall as literal, fly-on-the-wall, accurate history. To ease exposition, I speak within these assumptions.

Aquinas held the following:

1. Adam and Eve were created good.
2. They committed a first sin.
3. Though this sin was theirs, it is also ours.
4. As it is ours, we are guilty of it.
5. Therefore, we suffer and deserve its penalties.
6. These include death.
7. These include disease.
8. These include some degree of moral ignorance.
9. These include a nature prone to disordered love, of lower rather than higher goods.
10. These include limits on our ability to do good.

The penalties in (8)–(10) produce subsequent sin, and so all other sin traces back to the first. I now flesh these out.

AQUINAS ON OUR ORIGINAL CONDITION

For Aquinas, the ultimate end for which God made us is to see God.[1] We cannot manage this by our own natural resources.[2] Thus we are paradoxical, natural things made for an end we cannot naturally achieve. We were made to receive supernatural help to get where we cannot naturally go[3] – made for grace as kittens are made for milk. As Aquinas sees it, we were first in a supernatural state, "original justice." This disposed us optimally to attain our supernatural end. Being in a purely natural condition is thus in a sense unnatural for us. It is not how we were originally made, and it deprives us of an end we were made for.

Our original justice consisted in certain things being as they should be.[4] First, we were originally in submission to God. This led God to grant three supernatural blessings.

The soul, being immortal, deserves an immortal body.[5] This is how things should be. But (leaving aside Aristotle's supposed heavenly spheres) all that is made of matter tends naturally to break down, dissolve, decay, etc. Our bodies are naturally mortal, just because they are material.[6] Thus in our initial state, God graciously made the body what it should be to "fit" the soul. God blocked its natural tendency to die. Adam and Eve, Aquinas thinks, were naturally mortal, but by grace immortal as long as they did not sin. (Of this more anon.)

God also blocked the body's tendencies to disease, decay, disorder, etc. Finally, in our original state, God subjected our lower powers to our reason. Thus reason was not troubled by passion. This too was a good our material constitution does not naturally provide. The senses of themselves bring in sensations naturally able to trouble reason and lead it astray.[7]

God decreed that these goods would be ours so long as we remained in submission to him.[8]

For Aquinas, then, we were created on a knife edge. If we rebelled, God would withdraw his supernatural blessings. We would then be left in a purely natural condition.

AQUINAS ON OUR SHARE IN THE FIRST SIN

For Aquinas, death and disease are consequences of the first sin. They are natural conditions it left us in. Since they are bad consequences, they count as penalties. Thus, for Aquinas, we all suffer the penalties of the first sin.[9] As Aquinas sees it, if we suffer a penalty for a sin, it had better be our own, not someone else's.[10] This is particularly true given the way the first sin's penalties influence subsequent sinning.

As Aquinas sees it, post-fall, we cannot avoid all sin or merit salvation. This is due to the condition the first sin left us in – the penalties for it. If some of us then wind up damned, it is hard to see how this could be fair, if the penalties are not penalties for our own sin. Suppose that I am a pagan, without even the "implicit faith" Thomas ascribes to the Roman centurion Cornelius.[11] I am not against Christianity. My unbelief is "according to pure negation": I simply haven't heard of it.[12] But I am as virtuous as a pagan can be. My intentions are as good as a pagan's can be. I do as much good as a pagan can. Due to the first sin and my ignorance, my options do not include any which avoid hell, but I consistently pick the morally best option available to me. I may even be so disposed that I would pick the best option if it were much better than the best I actually have. Despite all this, I wind up damned, simply because – due ultimately to the first sin – I have no better options to pick. If all this is so, it is hard to see how it is fair to damn me.

The problem goes away if I participate somehow in the first sin – if it is somehow my sin. For we can be responsible for things we cannot avoid if we make ourselves unable to avoid them. A drunk enough driver may run over a child because the driver is literally unable to control the car well enough to avoid it. The driver is guilty for doing so despite his or her inability to control the car, because he or she is responsible for that inability. Thus, Aquinas is under real pressure to make the first sin somehow ours.

Aquinas's thinking about this centers on a concrete whole composed of all humans descended from Adam. In *QDM* 4, 1 and *ST* I-II 81, 1, this whole is a community. Aquinas often thinks of this as a political community, a polity, as it were a city or kingdom. He suggests that the community (sometimes) does what its ruler does,[13] and he treats Adam as somehow its ruler. He suggests, too, that the polity can bear responsibility as if it were one person. As the polity is unified by physical descent from Adam and Eve, it is equally a family. Thomas sometimes draws on this too.[14] There are three linked moves here: treating the human race as one person, as a polity, and as a family. Only the third draws on something which (granted Adam and Eve) is literally true. The third is also (I will suggest) the best move.

Aquinas thinks that this concrete whole becomes guilty in the first sin. A sin originating in one part of it makes the whole guilty. Because the whole is guilty, every part of it acquires some share in the whole's guilt which is appropriate to its parthood. We are not guilty of it *qua* individuals. It is not our personal sin. But we are guilty of it *qua* members of the community.[15] We all have an individual share of a collective responsibility and guilt for this sin. Thus, "the sin of the first human is ... common to the whole ... [P]ersons punished for [it] are punished for their own sin, not the sin of another."[16]

Aquinas suggests that the human race is relevantly as if we were all one human, and Adam's will moves that mass to sin.[17] Aquinas sees us as executing Adam's sinful will, as a hand might execute a murderer's will.[18] Perhaps the picture is that Adam put the sinful impetus into our natures, and with that impetus inherited, all we do is direct it in various ways, as a hand directs the intent to commit murder toward its victim. This doesn't really work on its own. In us, while the hand executes sin, still only the will or the person is really sinful. The parallel here would be that all guilt for subsequent sin goes to Adam, not us. To get something helpful, Thomas has to flesh it out, by the polity or family moves.

Let's first think about polities. Germany in the 1930s was intensely anti-Semitic as a country. This was a communal sin. It originated in Hitler's will, but affected his entire nation. Imagine that you are a German living in Germany. You are not personally an anti-Semite. You have never been unkind to a Jew. But you are part of a country that is being extremely unkind to Jews. Some would say that you have some share of the country's guilt just because you are part of it. You might well feel soiled to be part of such a country, even though you yourself do not personally add to its anti-Semitism. This might be a perception of your individual share of a collective responsibility.[19] "Soiled" is a metaphor Aquinas takes seriously. As he sees it, sin stains the soul, be the sin original or personal.[20] For sin parts us from God, and that parting causes a sort of spiritual darkness.[21] According to Aquinas, baptism reunites us with God. This removes the stain, as removing an object interposed between us and the sun removes its shadow. But it leaves behind any bad habits our sins caused or consisted in.

Back to politics. Imagine that a rebel launches an unjust rebellion, and you fight in the rebel army. You take rebel orders. Imagine, too, that you are excusable for this as an individual: maybe the rebels hold your family hostage for your behavior. Then you might bear no individual blame for your role in the war. In a relevant sense, your actions do not originate in your will. But you might still be blameworthy *qua* a member of the army, because you are implementing the rebel's unjust will. The community does what the ruler does: the rebel forms the intention to rebel, and the community (army) executes it as your arm executes your intention. You are blameworthy as an instrument in executing the rebel commander's will, not for your own will. To use another of Aquinas's analogies, you are tainted as an arm might be tainted by committing a crime. Your arm is not a sinner if you murder someone with it. But your murder makes you as a whole guilty, and so your arm has some participation in guilt, some moral taint.[22] Your arm acquires this taint by being the instrument of the will which is the first source of the sin, i.e., your will.

The rub here is that Aquinas nowhere explains just how Adam counts as the ruler of the human race. There is no literal way we execute his orders. This is at best an analogy. It gets the idea of corporate responsibility before our minds, but it can't tell us why we are corporately responsible for the first sin. So let's switch to talk of families.

Suppose that we are responsible only for what we could have prevented – a thesis Aquinas endorses.[23] Then it can seem that we cannot be responsible for the first sin, because we came along too late to prevent it. But consider again the role of the human community or family. Families can be agents: they can corporately make charitable gifts. Suppose that the family including all humans committed the first sin. This is not a stretch. For perhaps the fall was complete only when both parties had bitten the apple. At the time, that family consisted only of Adam and Eve. It committed the first sin. Then this whole could have prevented the first sin, for at the time, Adam and Eve were its only parts, and they could have prevented it.

Note that if the first sin was a family sin, it does not matter how many members the family had at the time. Suddenly, whether Adam and Eve were historical becomes irrelevant. What matters is only that there was a sin attributable to the whole. If there was, it remains true of the whole later that it did the deed and could have prevented it, even though it now contains new parts. The new parts partake in a way of this sin even though they were not parts of it when the sin was committed. In the same way, my current atoms make up something which sinned eight years ago and could have prevented that sin, and so they partake of that taint even though they were not parts when it happened. They are tainted *qua* parts of me, not *qua* individual atoms – and in the same way, Aquinas says, each new human's original sin is sin *qua* member of the human family, not *qua* individual. So, it's not that we individually could have prevented the sin, but that a thing of which we are part could have. The thing gets the blame, and its later parts retain it, derivatively and in the way appropriate to parts. When Aquinas writes that "a man may from birth be under a family disgrace on account of a crime committed by one of his forebears,"[24] he may have exactly this sort of participated responsibility in mind. A further dimension of this "family disgrace" emerges shortly.

If there can be family guilt, there can also be guilt passed on through the generations, family penalties, and desert of those penalties *qua* member of a family. The only way to levy a penalty on a family is to penalize its members. If later generations of the family do not clear themselves or the family of the family guilt, they remain liable for the penalty. If the first sin was a family sin, that the guilt be transmitted by physical descent suddenly, shockingly, makes sense. For physical descent transmits membership in the family.

For Aquinas's idea to work, he needs families to have a particular ontological "thickness." They must be real enough to bear responsibility and guilt, and to deserve penalties. Yet they must depend on their parts in such a way that at least some of the guilt they bear exists in their members. Today's version of Western individualism jibs at this. But this is just cultural parochialism. Some cultures – traditional China comes to mind – have been built on such a conception of families. Nor is it implausible that family guilt would inhere at least partly in family members. For families can act only in and through their members.

AQUINAS ON OUR DESERT OF THE PENALTIES

As Aquinas sees it, the justice of passing on the fall's penalties follows from the following claims:

- The original pair's supernatural blessings were given by God to be passed on.[25]
- They were so given that later generations would have them only if they were passed on.
- Later generations had no right to them save insofar as they were passed on that way.
- The penalties are just what follows necessarily from the withdrawing of an unmerited gift.[26]

As Aquinas sees it, we are justly dispossessed. What seems like punishment is just the natural consequence of that dispossession. If the four claims just listed are true, it might even not be quite right to say that we suffer penalties due to the fall. Rather, we suffer the sort of hard luck one has if one happens to be born to a father who gambles away the family farm. Lacking the farm is not a penalty on us, although it was one for our feckless father. If we ask why God wouldn't rescue us in such a case, the Christian reply is that he has, and is still working at it. He does not get the farm back for us. Instead, he provides a down payment on a still better place. In the meanwhile, though, we are born under "family disgrace" in the following sense. The original pair were in a supernatural, graced state. They lost it. Because they did, the nature the family passes down does not bring grace with it. It is a dis-graced nature.

THE DEATH PENALTY

Genesis depicts God telling Adam and Eve that if they eat the fruit, they will "surely die." (Thomas reads this as: death became necessary for them.[27]) Paul comments on this in Romans 5:12 when he says that death entered the world through sin. Now, Paul might not mean ordinary physical death. "Death" has at least two other biblical meanings. Ephesians 2:1 speaks of being "dead in your sins." And in Revelation we hear of the second death.[28] But suppose we take "death" here as common, garden-variety death. There are three possibilities. Perhaps Adam and Eve were naturally immortal, and mortality was a radical change. Perhaps they were naturally mortal. They might also have been naturally indeterminate between mortality and immortality, with the determination to come after the garden trial period.

In Genesis, after the pair eat the forbidden fruit, God worries lest they eat from the Tree of Life and live forever. On the first possibility, the story would be that they were initially immortal, became mortal as soon as they ate, and then God worried that the tree would change them back. The text gives no hint of this dramatic change. So it favors the second or third options.

As Thomas sees it, in the original state, we were immortal as long as we did not sin.[29] But we had the power to sin, and if we sinned, we would become mortal.[30] Since we were able to sin, we were able to be able to die. But we were not then able to die. This is a coherent claim. So, too, I am able to be able to play the piano well – I can move my fingers, etc. – but I am not actually able to play well, having never practiced. Thus, for Thomas, we were originally immortal. Thomas adds a gloss: changing from immortality to mortality did not require any change in our physical makeup. Our initial immortality was a gift of grace that took us beyond the fate our physical makeup would naturally dictate. Becoming mortal was merely God withdrawing the gift and leaving us only what we naturally were. Thomas treats disease in parallel.[31] Here again, the "penalty" is merely our natural condition.

AQUINAS ON MORAL IGNORANCE

Aquinas holds that sin "wounds" reason, particularly in practical matters.[32] To follow this thought further, we would have to delve into his "natural law" account of morality and moral knowledge, and perhaps his account of weakness of will. I have no space to do this here.

AQUINAS ON DISORDERED LOVE

Adam and Eve disordered their love, preferring the lower to the higher. They wanted to do so and did. Here, the "penalty" is having what they wanted, permanently. Augustine often calls such disordered love concupiscence. Aquinas adopts this usage.[33] To Augustine, disordered love is the main driver of sinfulness:

> Man's first ruin was caused by love of self ... if he had not loved himself, and had instead put God before himself, he would have wanted always to be subject to God, and he would not have turned away to disregarding God's will and doing his own. That, after all, is what loving oneself means: wanting to do one's own will.[34]

"The first ruin of man" is the first sin.

For Aquinas, Adam's descendants inherit the condition of original sin. This is partly original sinfulness, proneness to sin communicated in our origin (i.e., by physical descent). But it comes with a share of corporate guilt, and so includes an original guilt. The sinfulness – that about us which makes us prone to sin – consists in the inordinate condition(s) of the soul which result from the absence of original justice.[35] In the reason there is the darkness to which I just briefly alluded. In the will there is malice, a proneness to evil in choice.[36] In the desires there is a proneness to disordered desire – habitual concupiscence.[37] This is what the desires are naturally like without original justice.[38]

The lack of original justice is what makes us concupiscent. It is what leaves our powers to be what they naturally are, and so (says Thomas) constitutes the powers' being in this condition.[39] Aquinas also adds an "amen" to Augustine's tracing concupiscence to self-love.[40] Again, we are in this state solely because of a lack of original justice[41] – that is, special divine grace. So concupiscence, too, is a matter of being left with only the resources of human nature to work with. Yet, in a different sense, concupiscence is unnatural. We are rational animals. So, in a different sense, it is natural to us for reason to order our desires properly. In this sense, our actual condition, in which this is not so, is unnatural.[42] In this sense of 'nature,' original sin leaves us in a less than natural condition.

That original sinfulness consists in a lack need not imply that we are any less positively corrupt than even Calvin would hold. Calvin seems to see this: "those who have defined original sin as the want of the original righteousness which we ought to have had, though they substantially comprehend the whole case, do not significantly enough express its power and energy. For our nature is not only utterly devoid of goodness, but so prolific in all kinds of evil that it can never be idle."[43] Calvin's dissatisfaction is with a lack of emphasis on the consequences of this loss, not with a treatment of original sin as a lack.

AQUINAS ON HOW CORRUPT WE NATURALLY ARE

Still, Aquinas did see the consequences as less severe than Calvin did. How morally good one thinks a non-Christian can be in principle tells us how deeply one thinks original sin corrupts us, for non-Christian virtue is as far as we can get given only our purely natural resources. In Augustine's eyes, the answer to "how good can a non-Christian get" is: not very. According to Augustine, even the best non-Christian virtue is pursued out of pride or a desire for one's own good opinion of oneself.[44] So it is just a subtle form of vice.[45] It fails to be genuine virtue because the actions it produces are improperly motivated and so are not truly good. They stem ultimately from a love of self above all else, even God. Genuine virtue requires love of God more than self.[46] For Augustine, even outwardly meritorious works, apart from faith, are just a different sort of sin. Augustine writes that "if [the] commandment is kept from the fear of punishment and not from the love of righteousness, it is kept servilely, not freely, and therefore it is not kept at all"[47] – and we are incapable of loving righteousness in our fallen state.

Aquinas's view of non-Christian goodness is subtle and capable of more than one interpretation. As Aquinas sees it, we do retain post-fall a natural inclination to virtue.[48] But original sin entails that we all lack a natural direction to virtue, having instead some degree of moral ignorance, malice, weakness, and disordered desire.[49] We are able naturally to develop virtues of a sort. These virtues are genuine even though imperfect as long as the goods they direct us to are able to be oriented to God. They are not true virtues insofar as they pursue goods which cannot be so ordered.[50] Even though genuine, they are virtues only in a restricted sense, since they do not direct us to our true last end, God.[51] *Contra* Augustine, then, Aquinas holds that there can be genuine moral virtues even without love of God.[52] Pagan virtues, for Aquinas, are not merely splendid vices. Further, for Aquinas, we are naturally capable of actions which are good insofar as they conduce to our natural end, even though they do not produce merit toward salvation[53] and they do not suffice even for our full natural good.[54] We cannot fulfill all the commandments, or fulfill any of them in the fully right way.[55] But we can take what are genuinely steps in the right direction.

NOTES

1 See, for example, *QDV* 14, 2.
2 *ST* I q.12 a.4.
3 *QDM* 4, 5.
4 *SCG* IV 52.
5 *In V Rom*, 1.3; *SCG* IV 52.
6 *SCG* IV 52; *CT* 186.
7 *SCG* IV52; *CT* 186.
8 *CT* 186.
9 *SCG* IV 51, 52.
10 *SCG* IV, 50.
11 *ST* II-II q.10 a.4.
12 *ST* II-II q.10 a.1.
13 *QDM* 4, 1.
14 *ST* I-II q.81, a.1 ad 5.
15 *QDM* 4, 1.
16 *QDM* 4, 1 ad 19.
17 *SCG* IV 52.
18 *ST* I-II q.81 a.1.
19 There is a large literature on collective responsibility. For a bibliography, see M. Smiley, "Collective Responsibility" in E. N. Zalta (ed.), *The Stanford Encyclopedia of Philosophy* [online] (2020), https://plato .stanford.edu/entries/collective-responsibility/.
20 *ST* I-II q.86.
21 *ST* I-II q.86 a.2 ad 2.
22 *SCG* IV 52.
23 *CT* 196.
24 *ST* I-II q.81 a.1 ad 5.
25 *CT* 187.
26 *CT* 195; *SCG* IV 52.
27 *SCG* IV, 50.
28 Revelation 2:11, 20:6, 20:14, and 21:8.
29 *ST* I q.97 a.1.
30 *CT* 186.
31 *CT* 186.
32 *ST* I-II q.85 a.3.
33 *ST* I-II q.82 a.3.

34 Augustine, *Sermons*, vol. 4, translated by E. Hill (Brooklyn: New City Press, 1992), 96.2, pp. 29–30.

35 *ST* I-II q.82, a.1 ad 1 and ad 3.

36 *QDM* 4, 2 ad 7.

37 These are distinguished into three kinds at *ST* I-II q.77 a.5.

38 *QDM* 4, 2 ad 4.

39 *QDM* 4, 2 ad 7.

40 *ST* I-II q.77 a.4.

41 *QDM* 4, 2 ad 7.

42 *QDM* 4, 2 ad 1.

43 J. Calvin, *Institutes of the Christian Religion*, translated by H. Beveridge (Grand Rapids, MI: William B. Eerdmans, 1989), p. 218.

44 Augustine, *The City of God*, translated by M. Dods (New York: Random House, 1950), V 13, pp. 163–4, V 20, pp. 173–4.

45 Augustine, *The City of God*, XIX 25, pp. 706–7.

46 Augustine, *The City of God*, V 19, pp. 171–2, XIX 25, pp. 706–7.

47 Augustine, "The Spirit and the Letter," translated by P. Holmes and R. Wallis, in P. Schaff (ed.), *The Nicene and Post-Nicene Fathers*, vol. 5 (Peabody, MA: Hendrickson Publishers, 1994), p. 94.

48 *ST* I-II q.85, a.2 ad 3.

49 *ST* I-II q.85 a.3.

50 *ST* II-II q.23 a.7.

51 *ST* I-II q.65 a.2; *ST* II-II q.23 a.7.

52 *ST* I-II q.65 a.2.

53 *ST* II-II q.10 a.4.

54 *ST* I-II q.109 a.2.

55 *ST* I-II q.109 a.4.

14 The Incarnation

Timothy Pawl

INTRODUCTION

The doctrine of the Incarnation is the Christian teaching that Jesus Christ, the man who was born of Mary and crucified under Pontius Pilate, was not merely a human, but was God incarnate – one person of the Holy Trinity. Retaining his divine nature, the Son of God took on, or *assumed*, in the technical language, a human nature, and thus became a real human, no less a human than you or I. Jesus Christ, then, on the traditional view that Aquinas inherited and defended, is one divine person with two complete natures. This chapter will focus on Aquinas's metaphysical understanding of the Incarnation. For a discussion of the goal of the Incarnation – the regeneration of humans to right relationship with God – see Chapter 15 in this volume, by Thomas Williams.[1]

Aquinas's most extensive and mature discussion of the Incarnation is in the Third Part of his *Summa theologica*. That said, one can find substantive discussions of the Incarnation in his *Summa contra Gentiles*; his commentaries on Scripture, especially the commentary on the Gospel of John and the commentaries on Paul's epistles to the Romans and the Philippians; his *Compendium of Theology*; his *Disputed Question on the Union of the Incarnate Word*; his commentary on Lombard's *Sentences*; and various *Quodlibetal Questions*.[2]

This chapter explains Aquinas's view of personhood, his view of natures, his understanding of the hypostatic union, the fittingness of the Son's becoming incarnate, Christ's human intellect, will, and passions, and the main philosophical problem for the Incarnation.

PERSON

Aquinas follows Boethius's analysis of personhood found in *De persona et duabus naturis*.[3] There, Boethius defines a person as an individual substance with a rational nature. As Aquinas writes, using the synonymous Greek and Latin technical terms, *hypostasis* and *suppositum*, for an individual substance: "[A] person is nothing other than a hypostasis or *suppositum* of a rational nature."[4] We might define a person, then, by saying that persons are in the genus of *supposita*, with a specific difference of having a rational nature. To explicate the notion of *person*, then, one must first analyze the concepts of a *suppositum* and *nature*. The remainder of this section discusses *suppositum*; the next section focuses on nature.

Concerning a *suppositum*, Aquinas says the following:

> The "individual substance," which is included in the definition of a person, implies a complete substance subsisting of itself and separate from all else; otherwise, a man's hand might be called a person, since it is an individual substance; nevertheless, because it is an individual substance existing in something else, it cannot be called a person; nor, for the same reason, can the human nature in Christ, although it may be called something individual and singular.[5]

We will return to the final point concerning Christ's human nature in the next section. For now, note that the *suppositum* must be a complete, individual, singular substance, subsisting of itself, and separate from all else. No accidental form is a substance, complete or otherwise, and so no accidental form is a *suppositum*. Additionally, a mere component part, like a hand, exists in another, in the whole human whose hand it is, and so is not a *suppositum*. Not all *supposita* will be persons, on this definition, since some individual, singular substances exist separate from all else, and so fulfill the conditions for being a *suppositum*, yet are not rational, and so fail to fulfill the specific difference of a person: for instance, a worm or a tree, or, to use Aquinas's example, a stone.[6]

One final important point concerning Aquinas on personhood: A contemporary notion of personhood, often attributed to Locke as its chief exponent in the theological discussions of the Incarnation, understands *person* in a psychological sense as a thing which has psychological states or powers, such as consciousness.[7] As we will see in the next section on natures, the assumed human nature of Christ, on Aquinas's view, had a rational soul with psychological powers. As such, were this psychological sense of *person* the sense used in the doctrine of the Incarnation, the view that there is only one person in Christ would be inconsistent.

NATURE

Aquinas followed Boethius's lead on natures as well as persons.[8] On Aquinas's view, the assumed human nature of Christ was not something common to all humans, such as a Platonic form of humanity;[9] rather, it was something concrete, composed of a created body and a created rational soul.[10] It was something of which Aquinas was not reticent to apply predicates such as *visible, passable, having corporeal defects*, and so on.[11] It had an intellect and a will.[12] Aquinas claimed, following the texts of Conciliar Christology, especially Leo's Tome, that

> in Christ the human nature has its proper form and power whereby it acts; and so has the Divine. Hence the human nature has its proper operation distinct from the Divine, and conversely.[13]

There is a sense in which the human nature did things. For instance, it weighed down the boat in the sea of Galilei. As Aquinas says in his *Compendium of Theology*,

> in Christ the human nature is held to be, as it were, the organ of His divine nature ... When Christ touched a leper, the action belonged to His human nature, but the fact that the touch cured the man of his leprosy, is owing to the power of the divine nature.[14]

The human nature has real causal powers that it enacts. The Word uses those powers as an instrument in activity as an organ of action.[15] In the same passage, Aquinas notes that an axe makes a chest, but does so only as directed by a carpenter. In such a case, the axe does have real causal powers, which powers are employed by the person using it – so, likewise, on Aquinas's view, for the assumed human nature of Christ.

As we see, the human nature of Christ is an individual, singular substance. It is composed of body and soul. It has a will, an intellect, its own set of causal powers, and its own activity which employs those powers. We might rightly ask at this point: How is such a being *not* a person?

In response, return to the quotation in the previous section concerning Aquinas's understanding of an individual substance. There, he gives the answer. To be a person, a thing must be an individual substance (a *suppositum*; a hypostasis). Being an individual substance requires as a necessary condition *not* subsisting in another – an individual substance must *not* exist in another, as a part of a larger whole. Now, Christ's human nature *does* subsist in another. Thus, it fails to fulfill the conditions for being an individual substance. As a consequence, it fails to fulfill the conditions for being a person.

Christ's human nature, as we have seen, is not a person in the traditional sense of *person* that Aquinas is using. Its lack of personhood is not due, on Aquinas's view, to its lacking anything essential to being a human being in the same sense as you or I am. In fact, Aquinas is clear on this point. He writes:

> As long as the human nature is united to the Word of God, it does not have its own suppositum or hypostasis beyond the person of the Word, because it does not exist in itself. But if it were separated from the Word, it would have, not only its own hypostasis or suppositum, but also its own person; because it would now exist per se. Just as also a part of a composite body, as long as it is undivided from the whole, is [i.e., exists per se] only potentially, not actually; but this is only brought about by separation.[16]

Here we see that, for Aquinas, the lack of personhood of the human nature is not due to something it fails to have, some ontological tidbit

necessary for personizing the nature. Rather, it lacks personhood due
to its having something additional. It is united to the divine nature
through the hypostatic union. It fails to be a person not by subtraction
but by addition – in particular, addition to the person of Christ
through the hypostatic union. To that hypostatic union and
Aquinas's understanding of it we now turn.

HYPOSTATIC UNION

Although the hypostatic union and the assumption are related and
essential elements for understanding the Incarnation, they are not
exactly the same thing. As Aquinas notes, the relata of these two
relations are different.[17] A divine *person* assumes a human nature; a
divine *nature* is hypostatically united to a human nature. The hypostatic union is itself a created thing.[18] It exists in the created human
nature of Christ. While the union, when linguistically expressed,
takes as one of its relata the divine nature, on Aquinas's view, the
union is not ontologically *in* the divine nature. That is, the divine
nature does not metaphysically bear or include the union.[19] The
relation is a relation of reason with respect to the divine nature, but
a real relation with respect to the assumed human nature. As Aquinas
says in his Commentary on Paul's Letter to the Romans, just as
something is newly said of someone in virtue of the change of position
of another without change in the subject of the predication (e.g., he is
now to the right of the other because the other has moved), so likewise in the Incarnation something new is truly said of the Word
without there being any change in the divine nature of the Word.[20]

The hypostatic union came into existence at the same time as the
human nature did. The human nature did not exist prior to being hypostatically united to the Son. For if it had done, it would have satisfied the
conditions for being a person, and, in such a case, it would have been a
man that was assumed, not merely a human nature. Aquinas explicitly
rejects the view that a man was assumed as heretical.[21]

The hypostatic union is the grounding for an important teaching
in Christology: the communication of idioms (*communicatio*

idiomatum).[22] On this teaching, a term predicable of Christ because of one nature can be said of him truthfully when using a subject term drawn from the other nature.[23] For instance, one can say, with Aquinas, that "a man created the stars" and "God has suffered" are both true.[24] In these cases, the ontological foundation for the subject term is a different nature than the foundation for the predicate term. A 'man' (because of his human nature) 'created the stars' (because of his divine nature). Aquinas gives the reasoning for the communication of idioms as follows:

> Since, however, we can predicate of a suppositum of any nature all that is proper to that nature to which the suppositum pertains, and since in Christ the suppositum of the human nature is the same as the suppositum of the divine nature, it is evident that everything belonging to the divine nature and everything belonging to the human nature can be predicated indifferently of this suppositum which pertains to both natures.[25]

The communication of idioms is a linguistic phenomenon. Aquinas is not affirming that the accidental forms which inhere in the assumed human nature somehow migrate to the divine nature. On Aquinas's view of divine simplicity, the divine nature cannot have accidents.[26] This union between the divine nature and the component parts of the human nature remains even during Christ's three days of death, even though Christ was not a man during those three days, on Aquinas's view.[27]

The hypostatic union undergirds the Incarnation and the communication of idioms. Aquinas considered whether the other divine persons could possibly become incarnate, and, if so, whether there was a certain fittingness to the Son's having been the one to become incarnate. To these questions I now turn.

THE FITTINGNESS OF THE INCARNATION OF THE SON

While in the actual creation, only the Son assumed a human nature, and that only once, on Aquinas's view of the metaphysics of the Incarnation, the other two divine persons could become incarnate as well.[28] Given that each could have become incarnate, a reasonable question is why it was that only the Son in fact did. In what follows I discuss Aquinas's reasons for thinking that the Father and Holy Spirit could have become incarnate, then his reasons for thinking that there is a special fittingness to the Son's having been the one to become incarnate.

Concerning who can assume a human nature, Aquinas argues that all three divine persons can;[29] for the divine persons, having one nature, have one and the same power. By that one power, each is omnipotent. So if one divine person can do something with respect to creation, the others can, too. After all, if one had a power with respect to creation that the others lacked, those others would, in lacking that power, not be omnipotent. Moreover, the Son can become incarnate. Thus, he concludes, the Father and Holy Spirit can, too. His argumentation is not about what God would will, but rather about the limits of divine power.

Given that each divine person could have become incarnate on Aquinas's view, why is it that the Son is the one who became incarnate? For Aquinas, it is due to a special fittingness in the Son's becoming incarnate.[30] Aquinas argues that we can see the fittingness of the Son uniting to humanity in at least three ways: on the part of the similarity of the things united; on the part of the goal of the union; and on the part of the remedy had through the union.

First, consider the likeness between the Word and humanity, which can be seen in two ways. The first way concerns how humans restore their works. When a human creation falls into ruin, a craftsperson uses his knowledge and understanding of the craft to restore it. So, likewise, when a divine creation, humanity, falls into ruin, the divine craftsperson, the Father, fittingly uses his knowledge and understanding, the Word, to restore it. The second way concerns the essence of humans. We humans, for Aquinas, are rational animals. Our proper perfection is found in our rationality, and wisdom is the highest activity of that rationality. Now, the Word is the wisdom of God (cf. 1 Cor. 1:24, which Aquinas cites in the *sed contra*, following

St. John Damascene). So it is fitting that the Word be the one to bring humans to our supernatural perfection.

Second, consider the goal of the union. The goal of the Incarnation is the bestowal of the heavenly inheritance on humans. Now, it is the children of a person who naturally inherit. So it is fitting that *God the Son* be the one to become incarnate, for in joining with humanity he makes humans heirs and adopted children as well.

Finally, consider the remedy being supplied. Humans first fell into sin in the book of Genesis by seeking knowledge of good and evil. It is fitting, then, that the person most associated with the fullness of knowledge, the Word, be the one through whom humans are restored to right relation with God. God offers sinful humanity the fulfillment of their desire, and they come to see that the culmination of their desire was found in God all along.

CHRIST'S HUMAN INTELLECT

One emphasis found across Aquinas's later writings is on the proper activities of Christ with respect to his humanity. As noted above, on orthodox Christology, Christ had a real human nature with a human soul, just as you or I do. That nature was not there for show. Christ *did* things with and through it. In this and the following two sections on Christ's will and passions, I discuss the integrity of Christ's human nature alongside the prerogatives that Christ had in virtue of his divinity.

Because of Aquinas's emphasis on the proper activities of the human nature, Aquinas taught that Christ acquired knowledge through his assumed human nature.[31] Christ's intellect was *online*, doing things, just as yours or mine is. For instance, Christ reasoned discursively with his human intellect.[32] Christ had eyes to see, ears to hear, and a mind to reason, and by means of each of these activities he had real, acquired knowledge.

With the genuineness of Christ's human intellectual activities firmly in place, Aquinas does not shy away from predicating divine prerogatives of Christ as well. On Aquinas's view, due to the hypostatic union, Christ, even in his human nature, had an impressive array of knowledge.[33] Aquinas writes that Christ, in his human intellect, by means of infused knowledge, "knew all singular truths – present, past, and future."[34] The infused knowledge whereby he knew all things past, present, and future was habitual, not perpetually occurrent.[35] These knowledge claims might be surprising to contemporary readers, but on this point Aquinas stood in the mainstream of theological reflection.[36]

Why would Aquinas affirm such knowledge in the human intellect? He gives various reasons. One reason is that the blessed in heaven have the beatific knowledge of God through their participation in the divine light. But Christ's human nature, through the hypostatic union, participates in that light more fully than any other created thing. Thus, his human nature would have the beatific knowledge to the highest degree.[37] In the same passage, Aquinas notes that the Gospel of John (1:14) states that Christ had the fullness of grace and truth. But if he were ignorant of what could be known, he would lack the fullness of truth. Thus, he had to know all that a created thing could know. Elsewhere he argues from Christ's role as author of salvation or as judge of all human actions to this impressive knowledge.[38]

CHRIST'S HUMAN WILL

Aquinas's insistence on safeguarding the integrity of the humanity of Christ while affirming divine prerogatives of the person comes out just as clearly in his discussion of Christ's human will. Aquinas held Christ's human will, or Christ in virtue of his human will, to be temptable, free, yet impeccable.[39]

Concerning the temptation of Christ, Aquinas follows the clear scriptural teaching that Jesus was tempted in the wilderness by the devil.[40] For Aquinas, it is important that the source of the temptation was the devil, something external to Christ, not something internal to Christ, such as a disordered appetite.[41] On Aquinas's view, an internal source of temptation is evidence of concupiscence – inordinate desire for the pleasurable. Since Christ lacked such inordinate desires, he could not be tempted in that sense.[42]

Concerning Christ's freedom, Aquinas follows Christian tradition in asserting that Christ had two wills, one divine and one human.[43] While the human will is subjugated to the divine will, it is nevertheless free.[44] Aquinas writes:

> [T]he perfection of the divine nature includes having will … similarly, also, the perfection of human nature includes having a will by which a man has free choice.[45]

Here again we see the genuine activities of the human nature of Christ emphasized by Aquinas.

Even while safeguarding the integrity of the human nature, Aquinas affirms the impeccability of Christ. Aquinas follows the traditional view that Christ was without sin.[46] Aquinas also thought that Christ is impeccable.[47] While Christ is impeccable, and so unable to sin even by his human nature, that impeccability is not owed to the nature in itself. This is clear since the nature is of the very same type as yours and mine, and a person with my nature is, sadly, readily able to sin. Rather, the impeccability of Christ's human nature derives from the features that nature has in virtue of the hypostatic union. It is the sort of thing that in itself has the features required for sin, but its ability to activate them for the sake of sinning is contextually precluded. Oliver Crisp provides an example to illustrate the state of Christ's human nature.[48] Just as a piece of wood submerged in a swimming pool is the sort of thing that could be set on fire, although the circumstances it is in preclude it from being so, so likewise Christ's human nature is the sort of thing with which a person could sin, although the circumstances it is in preclude this. On Aquinas's theology, Christ's will – or perhaps better to say Christ according to his human nature (specifically, his will) – was free, tempted, yet unable to sin.[49]

CHRIST'S HUMAN PASSIONS

Aquinas believed that Christ had the appetites common to humanity, but he did not have them in a disordered manner. Again emphasizing the reality of Christ's humanity, Aquinas argues that Christ felt sorrow, fear, wonder, and anger.[50] He wrote:

> [B]y a certain dispensation the Son of God before His Passion *allowed His flesh to do and suffer what belonged to it.* And in like manner He allowed all the powers of His soul to do what belonged to them.[51]

Christ's passions, then, are genuine. He was not play acting in the garden. Rather, he felt real fear, fear of the same sort you or I would feel at foreseen crucifixion.

Christ had all the appetites that a normal human has. This includes not only a will – a rational appetite – as mentioned earlier. He also had both an irascible and a concupiscible appetite – although, as mentioned above in the discussion of temptation, the concupiscible appetite is importantly not the same thing as the tradition means by 'concupiscence.' Christ had a concupiscible appetite, but no inordinate dispositions with respect to it, and so no concupiscence. Moreover, he had the emotions and passions that humans have; yet, again, due to his divinity, not in a sinful manner.[52]

THE FUNDAMENTAL PHILOSOPHICAL PROBLEM OF THE INCARNATION

The Incarnation doctrine seems flatly contradictory, for, as we have seen, it requires that one and the same person, the Word, the Son of God, be predicated by predicates drawn from his human nature – 'suffered,' 'died' – and predicates drawn from his divine nature – 'immutable,' 'eternal.' There are some attributes that seemingly must be had by anything divine, namely the attributes of classical theism, which, again, seemingly no human could have. For instance, God must be omnipotent, but any human is limited in power in at least some ways; God must be impassible, and yet any human is able to be causally affected in at least some ways. If God must be *this way*, and no human can be *this way*, it follows that nothing can be both God and human. But, then, since the traditional Christianity that Aquinas inherited explicitly requires that something, namely Jesus, be both God and man, it follows that the Incarnation doctrine is false.[53]

Aquinas saw the force of this variety of objection, which he discussed in multiple texts. For instance, he has an objector argue:

> Further, Christ is something passible and something impassible. But the passible is not impassible. Therefore Christ is something and something else. Therefore, Christ is not one.[54]

And again, in the *Summa theologiae*, he has an objector argue:

> It would seem that what belongs to the human nature cannot be said of God. For contrary things cannot be said of the same. Now, what belongs to human nature is contrary to what is proper to God, since God is uncreated, immutable, and eternal, and it belongs to the human nature to be created temporal and mutable. Therefore what belongs to the human nature cannot be said of God.[55]

One can get clearer on Aquinas's approach to this problem by seeing the methods of response that he explicitly rejects.

One option which some have taken is to deny that a divine thing must be *this way* or that a human thing must not be *this way*. For instance, one might deny that a divine person must be impassible. In such a case, the responder says that while it is true that nothing can be impassible and passible, and it is true that Christ is passible, it is false that he is impassible, and so the contradiction does not follow. Aquinas does not accept this maneuver as a general response to this problem. He writes:

> All the properties of the human, just as of the Divine Nature, may be predicated equally of Christ. Hence Damascene says (*De Fide Orth*. iii, 4) that "Christ Who [is] God and Man, is called created and uncreated, passible and impassible."[56]

The strategy of denying one of the potentially contradictory predicates of Christ is one that Aquinas is unwilling to employ universally. This makes sense, given Aquinas's desire to remain within the bounds of orthodoxy and the examples where the early ecumenical councils employed apparently contradictory predicates of Christ.[57]

Aquinas's method of response begins by reminding the reader that, for predicates to be contradictory, they must be said at the same time, in the same way. Since Christ is both God and human at the same time, Aquinas is willing to assert the predicates of Christ at the same time. But that still leaves the final clause, "in the same way." It is that clause which Aquinas emphasizes in his response to the fundamental problem. He writes:

> [O]pposites cannot be said truly of the same thing in the same way: the divine and human things said of Christ are, of course, in opposition, suffering and incapable of suffering, for example, or dead and immortal, and the remainder of this kind; therefore, it is necessarily in different ways that the divine and the human are predicated of Christ.[58]

And again, in his response to the fundamental problem as he raises it in the *Summa*, he writes:

> It is impossible for contraries to be predicated of the same in the same respects, but nothing prevents their being predicated of the same in different aspects. And thus contraries are predicated of Christ, not in the same, but in different natures.[59]

The first quotation notes that different respects for predication are required; the second notes the source of the difference – they are said *in different natures*. How exactly these different respects are meant to insulate Christ from contradiction is contested. Aquinas provides examples in which the *according to this or that* modifiers are used when one needs to disambiguate that in virtue of which a person is a certain way. We need such modifiers for 'white,' he says, since a person's skin or teeth could be white, but not 'curly,' as only hair can be curly. Such an example makes it seem as if it is the natures of Christ that are certain ways, and these ways are derivatively said of the whole person – they are *borrowed*, as some Thomistic exegetes put it.[60] Hauser argues that such borrowing is not the whole Thomistic story, and that one needs a non-uniform account of how to deal with the allegedly problematic pairs of predicates attributable to Christ in virtue of his two natures.[61]

CONCLUSION

This chapter has examined Aquinas's view of personhood – that a person is a *suppositum* with a rational nature. It has presented his view of the assumed nature of Christ – that it is a concrete composite of substantial form and matter. It presented Aquinas's understanding of the hypostatic union – it is that by which the divine and human natures are united in the person of the Word, and that which ontologically undergirds the communication of idioms. It presented Aquinas's view of who became incarnate and why – while all three divine persons could become incarnate, it was most fitting that the Son do so. Finally, it showcased Aquinas's emphasis on the integrity of Christ's humanity along with the prerogatives Christ had in virtue of his divinity in three ways: by means of his assumed human intellect, through which he genuinely learned, and in which he had impressive, infused knowledge; by means of his will, which was free and able to be tempted, yet impeccable; and by means of his passions, which were of the same sort and variety as a mere human, though without the inordinate dispositions common to humanity post-fall. Finally, it presented the fundamental philosophical problem of the Incarnation and an outline of Aquinas's response to it.[62]

NOTES

1 See also N. Breiner, "Punishment and Satisfaction in Aquinas's Account of the Atonement," *Faith and Philosophy* 35 (2018): 237–56; P. L. Quinn, "Aquinas on Atonement" in R. J. Feenstra (ed.), *Trinity, Incarnation, and Atonement* (South Bend, IN: University of Notre Dame Press, 1989),

pp. 153–77; E. Stump, "Atonement according to Aquinas" in T. Morris (ed.), *Philosophy and the Christian Faith* (South Bend, IN: University of Notre Dame Press, 1988), pp. 61–91; E. Stump, "Justifying Faith, Free Will, and the Atonement" in R. Velkley (ed.), *Freedom and the Human Person* (Washington, DC: The Catholic University of America Press, 2007), pp. 90–105; E. Stump, *Atonement* (Oxford: Oxford University Press, 2018).

2 See, for instance, the following *Quodlibetal Questions*: I, q.2; II q.1; III, q.2; IV, q.5; V, q.3; VII, q.2; IX q.1 and q.2. For more on the historical context of Aquinas's Christology, see J. Wawrykow, "The Christology of Thomas Aquinas in Its Scholastic Context" in F. Murphy and T. Stefano (eds.), *The Oxford Handbook of Christology* (Oxford: Oxford University Press, 2015), pp. 233–49. For Aquinas's own emphasis on the Council of Chalcedon and Leo's Tome, see C. L. Barnes, "Thomas Aquinas's Chalcedonian Christology and Its Influence on Later Scholastics," *The Thomist* 78 (2014): 189–217; P. Gondreau, *The Passions of Christ's Soul in the Theology of St. Thomas Aquinas* (Providence, RI: Cluny Media, 2018), p. 141, 150.

3 I discuss Aquinas's view of personhood more fully in T. Pawl, *In Defense of Conciliar Christology: A Philosophical Essay* (Oxford: Oxford University Press, 2016), pp. 30–4. For other helpful discussions of Aquinas's view of personhood, see R. Cross, "Nature and Personality in the Incarnation," *The Downside Review* 107 (1989): 237–54; R. Cross, "Aquinas on Nature, Hypostasis, and the Metaphysics of the Incarnation," *The Thomist* 60 (1996): 171–202; A. Freddoso, "Human Nature, Potency and the Incarnation," *Faith and Philosophy* 3 (1986): 27–53; M. Gorman, "Uses of the Person–Nature Distinction in Thomas's Christology," *Recherches de Théologie et Philosophie médiévales* 67 (2000): 58–79; E. Stump, "Aquinas's Metaphysics of the Incarnation" in S. T. Davis, D. Kendall, and G. O'Collins (eds.), *The Incarnation* (Oxford: Oxford University Press, 2004), pp. 197–218; E. Stump, *Aquinas* (New York and London: Routledge, 2003), pp. 415–22.

4 *In Rom* cap. 1, lect. 2, n.36. All quotations from *In Rom* are from Aquinas, *Commentary on the Letter of Saint Paul to the Romans*, translated by F. R. Larcher, J. Mortensen, and E. Alarcón (Lander, WY: Aquinas Institute for the Study of Sacred Doctrine, 2012). See also *CT* I.212.

5 *ST* III q.16 a.12 ad 2. See also *CT* I.210–11; *ST* I q.29 a.2. All quotations from *ST* are taken from Aquinas, *The* Summa theologica *of St. Thomas*

Aquinas, translated by the Fathers of the English Dominican Province (South Bend, IN: Christian Classics, 1981).

6 *CT* I.211.

7 See, for instance, J. W. Carlson, *Words of Wisdom: A Philosophical Dictionary for the Perennial Tradition* (South Bend, IN: University of Notre Dame Press, 2012), p. 204; Pawl, *In Defense of Conciliar Christology*, pp. 33–4; T. Pawl, *The Incarnation* (Cambridge: Cambridge University Press, 2020), p. 7; J. Pohle, *The Divine Trinity: A Dogmatic Treatise* (St. Louis, MO: B. Herder Book Co., 1911), pp. 226–7; A. Stevenson, "The Unity of Christ and the Historical Jesus: Aquinas and Locke on Personal Identity," *Modern Theology* 37 (2021): 851–64.

8 I discuss Aquinas's view of natures more fully in Pawl, *In Defense of Conciliar Christology*, pp. 34–9; T. Pawl, "The Metaphysics of the Incarnation: Christ's Human Nature" in T. Marschler and T. Schärtl (eds.), *Herausforderungen und Modifikationen des klassischen Theismus. Volume 1: Die Trinität* (Münster: Aschendorff, 2020), pp. 131–48, here pp. 139–47. For other treatments of Aquinas's view of natures, see M. M. Adams, *What Sort of Human Nature? Medieval Philosophy and the Systematics of Christology* (Milwaukee: Marquette University Press, 1999); Cross, "Aquinas on Nature, Hypostasis, and the Metaphysics of the Incarnation"; Freddoso, "Human Nature, Potency and the Incarnation"; Stump, *Aquinas*, ch. 14; T. J. White, *The Incarnate Lord: A Thomistic Study in Christology* (Washington, DC: The Catholic University of America Press, 2016), chs. 2–3.

9 Aquinas discusses and denies that the assumption was of something universal in *ST* III q.4 aa.4–5.

10 See, for instance, *ST* III. q.2 a.5; *CT* I.209.

11 For the relevant texts from Aquinas, see: visible (*ST* III q.8 a.1 ad 3), passable (*ST* III q.14 a.1 ad 2), and corporeal defects (*ST* III q.14 a.3 ad 2). I discuss such robust predications of the human nature in T. Pawl, *In Defense of Extended Conciliar Christology: A Philosophical Essay* (Oxford: Oxford University Press, 2019), pp. 28–31; Pawl, "The Metaphysics of the Incarnation"; Pawl, *The Incarnation*, pp. 13–23.

12 See *CT* I.212.

13 *ST* III q.19 a.1.

14 *CT* I.212. All quotations from *CT* are taken from Aquinas, *Compendium of Theology*, translated by C. Vollert (St. Louis: B. Herder Book Co., 1948).

15 See *ST* III q.19 a.1.

16   *QDUVI* a.2 ad 10. This translation is from Jason L. A. West, available at
     https://isidore.co/aquinas/QDdeUnione.htm.

17   *ST* III q.2 a.8.

18   See *ST* III q.2 a.7. I discuss the hypostatic union in more detail at Pawl, *In
     Defense of Conciliar Christology*, pp. 20–3; Pawl, *The Incarnation*,
     pp. 23–8. For other useful resources on the union, see M. Gorman,
     Aquinas on the Metaphysics of the Hypostatic Union (Cambridge:
     Cambridge University Press, 2017); White, *The Incarnate Lord*, ch. 1.

19   See *ST* III q.2 a.7 ad 1.

20   *In Rom* cap. 1, lect. 2, n.37.

21   *ST* III q.33 a.3.

22   I discuss the communication of idioms more deeply in Pawl, *In Defense of
     Conciliar Christology*, pp. 23–7, 54–5, 62–5; Pawl, *In Defense of Extended
     Conciliar Christology*, pp. 17–19; Pawl, *The Incarnation*, pp. 24–8. For
     other discussions of the communication of idioms, see R. Cross,
     Communicatio Idiomatum: *Reformation Christological Debates* (Oxford:
     Oxford University Press, 2019); J. Aldama and I. Solano, *Sacrae Theologiae
     Summa IIIA: On the Incarnate Word, On the Blessed Virgin Mary*,
     translated by K. Baker (Saddle River, NJ: Keep The Faith, 2014), pp. 170–1;
     J. Pohle, *Christology: A Dogmatic Treatise on the Incarnation* (St. Louis,
     MO: B. Herder Book Co., 2013), p. 186.

23   *ST* III q.16, especially a.4.

24   *SCG* IV.38; see also *CT* I.211. All quotations from *SCG* are from Aquinas,
     Summa Contra Gentiles. Book Four: Salvation (South Bend, IN:
     University of Notre Dame Press, 1989).

25   *CT* I.211.

26   *ST* I q.3 a.6.

27   See *ST* III q.50 a.2 for the continuation of the union; *ST* III q.50 a.4 for
     Christ's not being a man during that time. I discuss the death of Christ
     and the hypostatic union more deeply in Pawl, *In Defense of Extended
     Conciliar Christology*, ch. 4. For more on the death of Christ, see T. C.
     Nevitt, "Aquinas on the Death of Christ," *American Catholic
     Philosophical Quarterly* 90 (2016): 77–99.

28   I discuss the possibility of multiple incarnations in T. Pawl, "Thomistic
     Multiple Incarnations," *The Heythrop Journal* 57 (2016): 359–70; Pawl, *In
     Defense of Extended Conciliar Christology*, chs. 2–3. There I formalize
     Aquinas's arguments that I discuss here. In those works I claim that

Aquinas was committed to a thesis that I call *Thomistic Multiple Incarnations*: There could be three simultaneously existing concrete rational natures, each of which is assumed by all three of the divine persons, at the same time.

29 *ST* III q.3 a.5 s.c.

30 *ST* III q.3 a.8.

31 *ST* III q.12 a.2.

32 *ST* III q.11 a.3.

33 I discuss Christ's human knowledge more deeply in Pawl, *In Defense of Extended Conciliar Christology*, chs. 7–8. For other discussions of Christ's human knowledge, see S. F. Gaine, "Christ's Acquired Knowledge according to Thomas Aquinas: How Aquinas's Philosophy Helped and Hindered His Account," *New Blackfriars* 96 (2015): 255–68; S. F. Gaine, *Did the Saviour See the Father?* (London: T&T Clark, 2015); S. F. Gaine, "The Veracity of Prophecy and Christ's Knowledge," *New Blackfriars* 98 (2017): 44–62; R. Moloney, "Approaches to Christ's Knowledge in the Patristic Era" in T. Finan and V. Twomey (eds.), *Studies in Patristic Christology* (Portland, OR: Four Courts Press, 1998), pp. 37–66; R. Moloney, *Knowledge of Christ* (New York: Bloomsbury Academic, 2000); J. C. Murray, *The Infused Knowledge of Christ in the Theology of the 12th and 13th Centuries* (Windsor, Ontario: Privately printed PhD thesis, 1963).

34 *ST* III q.11 a.1 ad 3; see also *QDV* q.8 a.4; *QDV* q.20 aa.2–3.

35 See *ST* III q.11 a.5, especially ad 1.

36 For evidence of this claim, see Aldama and Solano, *Sacrae Theologiae Summa IIIA*, p. 142; T. W. Bartel, "Like Us in All Things, Apart From Sin?," *Journal of Philosophical Research* 16 (1991): 19–52, here p. 35; Murray, *The Infused Knowledge of Christ*; W. Pannenberg, *Jesus, God and Man* (Philadelphia: Westminster Press, 1968), p. 333; Pawl, *In Defense of Extended Conciliar Christology*, pp. 176–9; Pohle, *Christology*, pp. 266–70. Aquinas was not unaware of the scriptural passages that seem in tension with this infused knowledge. For instance, "But of that day or that hour no one knows, not even the angels in heaven, nor the Son, but only the Father" (Mark 13:32, Revised Standard Version) and "Jesus increased in wisdom and in stature, and in favor with God and man" (Luke 2:52 RSV). Aquinas discusses these passages in *QDV* q.20 a.1 s.c.; *CT* I.216, 242; *ST* III q.7 a.12 obj.3 and ad 3; *ST* III q.10 a.2 obj.1 and ad 1; *ST* III

q.12 a.2 s.c. and ad 3; *In John* I 1.14, para. 264. He follows the lead of Augustine in *De Trinitate* I.12.23.

37 *ST* III q.10 a.4. For more discussion of Christ's possession of the beatific vision, see T. Weinandy, "Jesus' Filial Vision of the Father," *Pro Ecclesia* 13 (2004): 189–201; T. Weinandy, *Jesus: Essays in Christology* (Ave Maria, FL: Sapientia Press, 2014); T. J. White, "The Voluntary Action of the Earthly Christ and the Necessity of the Beatific Vision," *The Thomist* 69 (2005): 497–534; White, *The Incarnate Lord*, ch. 5.

38 *CT* I.216; cf. *ST* III q.9 a.2.

39 I discuss these three points more deeply in Pawl, *In Defense of Extended Conciliar Christology*, chs. 5–6.

40 *ST* III q.41. For the scriptural passages, see Matthew 4:1–11; Mark 1:13; Luke 4:1–13.

41 See *ST* III q.41 a.1 ad 3; *In Matt* IV.1.

42 For more on Aquinas's view of temptation, see Gondreau, *The Passions of Christ's Soul*, p. 326; P. Hoffman, "Aquinas on Threats and Temptations," *Pacific Philosophical Quarterly* 86 (2005): 225–42; Pawl, *In Defense of Extended Conciliar Christology*, ch. 6. For broader recent work on the topic of Christ's temptation, see J. E. McKinley, *Tempted for Us: Theological Models and the Practical Relevance of Christ's Impeccability and Temptation* (Eugene, OR: Paternoster, 2009); J. E. McKinley, "Four Patristic Models of Jesus Christ's Impeccability and Temptation," *Perichoresis* 9 (2011): 29–66; A. Pelser, "Temptation, Virtue, and the Character of Christ," *Faith and Philosophy* 36 (2019): 81–101; D. Werther, "Freedom, Temptation, and Incarnation" in D. Werther and M. Linville (eds.), *Philosophy and the Christian Worldview: Analysis, Assessment and Development* (New York: Continuum, 2012), pp. 252–65.

43 This teaching, called dyothelitism, is defined at the Third Council of Constantinople in 681 and quoted by Aquinas in *ST* III q.18 a.6 s.c.

44 See *ST* III q.18 a.6. For more on Aquinas's view of Christ's freedom, see C. L. Barnes, *Christ's Two Wills in Scholastic Thought: The Christology of Aquinas and Its Historical Contexts* (Toronto: Pontifical Institute of Mediaeval Studies, 2012); White, *The Incarnate Lord*, p. 253.

45 *SCG* IV.36.

46 *ST* III q.15 a.1. For more on Aquinas's view of impeccability, see A. Echavarría, "Aquinas on Divine Impeccability, Omnipotence, and Free Will," *Religious Studies* 56 (2020): 256–73; Stump, *Aquinas*, pp. 102–7.

47 *ST* III q.50 a.2.

48 O. D. Crisp, "Was Christ Sinless or Impeccable?," *Irish Theological Quarterly* 72 (2007): 168–86, here p. 175.

49 For discussions of how these three attributes are not inconsistent, see T. Pawl, "The Freedom of Christ and Explanatory Priority," *Religious Studies* 50 (2014): 157–73; T. Pawl, "The Freedom of Christ and the Problem of Deliberation," *International Journal for Philosophy of Religion* 75 (2014): 233–47; Pawl, *In Defense of Extended Conciliar Christology*, chs. 5, 6, and 8.

50 *ST* III q.15.

51 *ST* III q.18 a.5; emphasis in the original.

52 I discuss this more deeply in Pawl, *In Defense of Extended Conciliar Christology*, pp. 148–51; Pawl, *The Incarnation*, p. 31. For more on Aquinas's views of Christ's passions, see P. Gondreau, "St. Thomas Aquinas, the Communication of Idioms, and the Suffering of Christ in the Garden of Gethsemane" in J. F. Keating and T. J. White O. P. (eds.), *Divine Impassibility and the Mystery of Human Suffering* (Grand Rapids, MI: William B. Eerdmans, 2009), pp. 214–45; Gondreau, *The Passions of Christ's Soul*; D. Schrader, "Christ's Fear of the Lord According to Thomas Aquinas," *Heythrop Journal* 62 (2021): 1052–64. For more on Aquinas's view of passions more generally, see R. Miner, *Thomas Aquinas on the Passions: A Study of* Summa Theologiae, *Ia2ae 22–48* (Cambridge: Cambridge University Press, 2011).

53 I have discussed this problem more deeply in T. Pawl, "A Solution to the Fundamental Philosophical Problem of Christology," *Journal of Analytic Theology* 2 (2014): 61–85; T. Pawl, "Conciliar Christology and the Problem of Incompatible Predications," *Scientia et Fides* 3 (2015): 85–106; T. Pawl, "Temporary Intrinsics and Christological Predication" in J. Kvanvig (ed.), *Oxford Studies in Philosophy of Religion: Volume 7* (Oxford: Oxford University Press, 2016), pp. 157–89; Pawl, *In Defense of Conciliar Christology*; T. Pawl, "Conciliar Christology and the Consistency of Divine Immutability with a Mutable, Incarnate God," *Nova et Vetera* 16 (2018): 913–37; Pawl, *In Defense of Extended Conciliar Christology*; Pawl, *The Incarnation*. For other discussions of Aquinas's response to this problem, see A. T. Bäck, "Scotus on the Consistency of the Incarnation and the Trinity," *Vivarium* 36 (1998): 83–107; A. T. Bäck, "Aquinas on the Incarnation," *The New Scholasticism* 56 (2008): 127–45;

R. Cross, *The Metaphysics of the Incarnation: Thomas Aquinas to Duns Scotus* (Oxford: Oxford University Press, 2005), pp. 195–8; M. Gorman, "Christological Consistency and the Reduplicative Qua," *Journal of Analytic Theology* 2 (2014): 86–100; M. Gorman, "Classical Theism, Classical Anthropology, and the Christological Coherence Problem," *Faith and Philosophy* 33 (2016): 278–92; Gorman, *Aquinas on the Metaphysics of the Hypostatic Union*; C. Hauser, "On Being Human and Divine: The Coherence of the Incarnation," *Faith and Philosophy* 37 (2020): 3–31; G. Klima, "Libellus Pro Sapiente," *New Scholasticism* 58 (1984): 207–19; Stump, "Aquinas's Metaphysics of the Incarnation"; Stump, *Aquinas*, ch. 14.

54 *In III Sent.*, d.6, q.2, a.1 obj.5.

55 *ST* III q.16 a.4 obj.1.

56 *ST* III q.16 a.8 ad 2.

57 For discussion of the councils, see Pawl, *In Defense of Conciliar Christology*, chs. 1 and 4.

58 *SCG* IV.39.

59 *ST* III q.16 a.4 ad 1.

60 See Stump, *Aquinas*, pp. 412–15, for instance.

61 See C. Hauser, "Aquinas on Persons, Psychological Subjects, and the Coherence of the Incarnation" [manuscript] (n.d.). For other discussions of the property borrowing strategy, see Cross, *The Metaphysics of the Incarnation*, pp. 196–203; W. Hasker, "A Compositional Incarnation," *Religious Studies* 53 (2017): 433–47, here pp. 436–7; M. A. Hight, "The Son More Visible: Immaterialism and the Incarnation," *Modern Theology* 26 (2010): 120–48; J. Hill, "Aquinas and the Unity of Christ: A Defence of Compositionalism," *International Journal for Philosophy of Religion* 71 (2012): 117–35; B. Leftow, "Composition and Christology," *Faith and Philosophy* 28 (2011): 310–22; T. D. Senor, "The Compositional Account of the Incarnation," *Faith and Philosophy* 24 (2007): 52–71; Stump, "Aquinas's Metaphysics of the Incarnation," pp. 205–6, 212–17.

62 I thank Eleonore Stump and Fr. Thomas Joseph White for helpful comments on this chapter.

15 Evil, Sin, and Redemption

Thomas Williams

THE PROBLEM OF EVIL, COSMIC AND ANGELIC

We recognize one of a pair of opposites by means of the other, Aquinas says. Just as we understand what darkness is only by reference to the notion of light, we must understand what evil is by reference to the notion of good. What is good is what is desirable. Every nature desires its own being and perfection, so we can conclude that "the being and perfection of every nature has the character of goodness."[1] Evil, then, cannot be a being or nature; it must be an absence of good. Not every absence of good counts as evil, however. A stone lacks the power to see, but its "blindness" is not evil: The nature of a stone has no aptitude for sight, and so it is no part of the perfection of a stone that it should see. Thus, evil is not a simple *negation* of good, but a *privation* of good; and we recognize a privation by comparing it with the fullness of being that is characteristic of a thing's nature.[2] Evil is a *defectus*: a falling short of, or falling away from, what is good.

The fact that evil is not a positive reality but instead a *defectus* does not mean that evil requires no explanation. On the contrary, evil is in a sense *unnatural*, and "the fact that something falls short of its natural and appropriate condition"[3] calls out for explanation. A part of the explanation is that, in order to be perfect, the whole of creation must contain creatures of every possible level of being, including creatures that can fall away from good; and from the fact that they *can* fall away from good, it follows that they sometimes *do* fall away from good.[4] The work of divine providence is not to override nature, but to preserve it, and many goods would be lost if God did not allow creatures to fall away from being as their natures allow them to do: "Fire would not be generated if air were not destroyed, and the lion's life would not be preserved if the ass were not killed."[5] In this way, the *defectus* that is unnatural for a *given* thing has its appropriate place in the good of the whole, and God is the *per accidens* agent cause of evil: agent cause in that he gives things their corruptible natures, *per accidens* because he does so with a view to the good of the universe and not for the sake of the *defectus* itself. In fact, no evil of any kind has a per se agent cause; no agent acts for the sake of evil, but only for the sake of a good thing that brings some evil with it.

Some evil, then, is simply built into the system of the universe. Such evil – the evil that is found among what Aquinas calls "natural things" – in no way calls into question the goodness or justice of God. But there is also evil found in what Aquinas calls "voluntary things" – that is, "rational creatures that have a will" – and this evil is theoretically and practically much more troublesome.[6] Creatures endowed with will can, and sometimes do, fall short of the good that they are apt to have and should have, not merely in the way natural things fall short, but by acts of their own wills. Such voluntary defections from the good have an explanation as well: Creatures with wills are themselves the *per accidens* causes of their own wrongdoing by the exercise of their free choice. (For more on the nature of the will's freedom, see Chapters 9 and 10.) But voluntary defection demands more than an explanation; it calls out for a remedy. For voluntary defection is doubly unnatural: Not only is it contrary to the nature of the individual, just as natural defections are, but it is also not necessary for the order of the universe. Nothing about the good of the whole creation requires that any individual creature have a disordered will.

Both angels and human beings have disordered wills, but there is no remedy for the disordered angelic will, which is fixed in evil (*obstinata in malo*). Aquinas explains:

> To investigate the cause of this fixity in evil, we must observe that the appetitive power in all things is proportioned to the

apprehensive power by which it is moved ... Now an angel's apprehension differs from a human being's apprehension in that an angel through his intellect apprehends immovably – just as we too immovably apprehend first principles, of which there is intellectual understanding – whereas human beings through reason apprehend in a movable way, reasoning discursively from one thing to another, which leaves open a path to either of two opposites. Hence, the human will also cleaves to something in a movable way, as having the power to withdraw from it and cleave to its contrary, whereas an angel's will cleaves to something fixedly and immovably. Accordingly, if the angelic will is considered before it cleaves to something, it can freely adhere to that thing and to its opposite (as regards objects that it does not will naturally); but once it has cleaved to something, it cleaves immovably. For this reason it has customarily been said that human free choice is capable of turning to the opposite both before choice and after it, whereas an angel's free choice is capable of turning to the opposite before choice, but not after it. And thus the good angels, always cleaving to justice, are confirmed in justice, whereas the evil angels, once they sin, are fixed in sin.[7]

There can be, therefore, no remedy for the disorder of (some) angelic wills, short of the annihilation of the evil angels, a prospect Aquinas does not contemplate.

Some Christian writers, taking their cue from a passage in Paul's Letter to the Romans, have held that the fall of rational creatures caused disorder in the rest of creation as well. Paul wrote:

> The expectation of creation awaits the revelation of the sons and daughters of God. For the creation was subjected to futility, not willingly, but on account of the one who subjected it in hope, because creation itself will also be set free from enslavement to corruption, into the freedom of the glory of the sons and daughters of God. For we know that all creation groans and is in labor even until now.[8]

Irenaeus of Lyons interpreted this passage to mean that the fall rup-
tured the Edenic perfection of the material creation, which will be
restored when humanity too is fully restored. For Ambrosiaster, the
fallen material creation suffers both because of humanity and in
solidarity with humanity, and it cries out for redemption alongside
us. By contrast, Augustine read "all creation" as referring only to
humanity: Human beings, who as spiritual, animal, and material
contain within themselves every level of creation, await redemption,
but the wider material universe does not share in the fall. Aquinas's
reading of the passage is broadly Augustinian, though he does allow
that one possible meaning of "creation" includes the sensible creation. If we take the expression in that way, the "futility" (*vanitas*)
to which creation is subjected is simply the *defectus* that comes along
with mutability, which (as we have seen) is contrary to the natural
appetite of each particular thing but in accordance with the general
nature of things as created and ordained by God. Paul speaks of the
sensible creation as "groaning," Aquinas says, because such fallings
away are contrary to the natural appetite of individual creatures; he
speaks of it as "awaiting" and "in labor" because the sensible creation
is destined to be made new – not restored to a pristine natural perfection injured by the fall, as Irenaeus and Ambrosiaster would have it,
but brought to a state of fulfillment that exceeds their natural capacity, just as the glory of redeemed humanity will exceed the capacity
of human nature ("They will be like the angels of heaven," as Aquinas
likes to quote from Matthew 22:30).[9]

THE PROBLEM OF EVIL: HUMAN SINFULNESS

With the angelic creation either excluded from the possibility of
redemption or beyond the need for it, and the non-rational creation
"groaning" only under the mutability and corruptibility that is its
natural condition, only humanity's disorder has both the need and
the possibility of correction. Although this disorder entered the
human race by a sin – that is, by "a thought, deed, or desire, contrary
to the eternal law"[10] – on the part of our first parents, the disorder
itself goes beyond individual sinful acts; it ramifies into a complex

system that we could call "sinfulness." Our sinful condition includes original sin, the *fomes* of sin, and actual sinful acts, as well as ignorance, along with our liability to judgment and eternal condemnation. Some explanation of each of these aspects of our sinful condition will be necessary in order to understand God's plan of repair as Aquinas expounds it.

Original sin is transmitted to all who derive their human nature by generation from Adam, which is to say, to every human being other than Jesus.[11] All human beings descended from Adam are like members of a single body; we can even be "considered as a single human being insofar as we agree in the nature that we receive from our first parent."[12] Accordingly, the vitiation of our nature that Adam's fall produced is found in all of Adam's natural descendants, and along with it the guilt or blameworthiness (*culpa*) that attaches to it. To have original sin is therefore to be guilty and worthy of punishment.[13]

Original sin is in part a privation – a *defectus* of the righteousness with which our first parents were originally created – but it has also a positive aspect: It is a disordered disposition of the parts of the soul. Aquinas compares it to bodily sickness, which likewise is both privative, in that it is a *defectus* of health, and positive, in that it is a disordered disposition of the body, an imbalance of the humors.[14] From this spiritual sickness follow disordered desires and disordered acts: They follow from it indirectly, insofar as the righteousness of which original sin is a privation would prevent such disordered desires and acts[15] and ensure that the human mind is subject to God.[16] Original sin vitiates every power of the soul that can possess virtue – it produces ignorance in reason, wickedness in the will, weakness in the irascible appetite, and immoderate desire in the concupiscible appetite[17] – and even affects the body, making it subject to various deficiencies and ultimately to death. All of these deficiencies of both body and soul are punishments for original sin, imposed by God according to his justice.[18] If borne voluntarily, however, for the sake of the salvation of the soul and for God's glory, they are no longer penal, strictly speaking, but medicinal.[19]

Not only are both soul and body wounded by sin, but the relationship between soul and body is disrupted. Commenting on Paul's lament, "I am carnal, sold as a slave under sin" (Rom. 7:14), Aquinas says that there are two senses in which human beings are carnal. The first is that the body is in rebellion against the spirit; this carnality is part of the propensity to sin – called the *fomes* – that derives from Adam's sin. (*Fomes* means "kindling" or "tinder." The idea is that in our damaged state only a small spark of temptation is needed to kindle the fire of rebellion against God.) The second sense in which human beings are carnal is that we sometimes consent to the wayward desires that arise from the body; this carnality derives not solely from original sin but also from actual sin. The first kind of carnality is present even in those who have been restored by grace, although the second is not. Paul says that we have been "sold as slaves under sin" because "sinners sell themselves into slavery to sin as the price of fulfilling their own wills."[20]

ATONEMENT: THE REMEDY FOR HUMAN SINFULNESS

The sinful condition of human beings is therefore very dire indeed, and Paul cries out to be set free from the enslavement into which Adam's sin and our own sins have thrust us. "Wretched human being that I am, who will deliver me from the body of this death?" he asks; and the answer comes immediately, "The grace of God through Jesus Christ our Lord" (Rom. 7:24–5). But how does this grace work, and in what sense does it come through Jesus Christ?

In order to appreciate Aquinas's answer to these questions, it is useful to contrast his views with those of Anselm of Canterbury, whose speculations in *Cur Deus Homo* (1094–8) informed much of the later medieval discussion of the Atonement. Anselm had argued that the breach between God and humanity introduced by Adam's sin could be repaired only if humanity offered adequate satisfaction to God. Only a God-man, by the voluntary self-offering of his own infinitely precious life, could make adequate satisfaction for human sin, which is of infinite disvalue because it is an offense against the infinite majesty of God. Therefore, God had to become incarnate and offer his life for the sins of humankind in order to reconcile us to God and restore us to that fellowship with God which was God's intention for us in creation. Only by means of this satisfaction can God's justice be served and his loving purposes for humanity be realized.[21]

In certain contexts Aquinas can sound very much like Anselm. In his commentary on Romans 3, Aquinas argues that, because of the sin of our first father, the whole human race has become enslaved to sin and is liable to punishment. By making satisfaction for sin, someone can redeem us – buy us out of our slavery and wipe out our liability to punishment – in the way that someone who paid another person's fine would be said to redeem him from his debt. Only Christ can offer satisfaction for the whole human race and thereby redeem it, because only Christ is free from all sin. The satisfaction Christ offers

> has efficacy both for justifying and for redeeming because God had ordained him for this purpose according to his own plan ... God put him forward for the sake of all people, because the human race did not have the wherewithal to make satisfaction unless God himself gave them a redeemer and satisfier.[22]

Yet although Aquinas affirms that only Christ can offer adequate satisfaction for the sin of the human race, he (along with almost all other medieval writers on the Atonement) denies that any such satisfaction was necessary: "[I]f God had willed to liberate human beings from sin without any satisfaction, he would not have acted contrary to justice."[23] Even so, Aquinas argues, it was more fitting for humanity to be set free by Christ's passion and death than by God's will alone:

> A way of attaining a given end is more fitting to the extent that that way incorporates more things that are serviceable for that end. And the liberation of humanity through Christ's passion incorporates several things that pertain to human salvation, in addition to liberation from sin. First, through Christ's passion human beings recognize how much God loves them and are thereby stirred to love God, which is what constitutes the completion of human salvation ... Second, by his passion he gave us an example of obedience, humility,

constancy, justice, and other virtues ... Third, through his passion Christ not only freed human beings from sin but also merited for them justifying grace and the glory of happiness ... Fourth, his passion declares to human beings a greater urgency in keeping themselves unstained by sin ... Fifth, his passion brought greater dignity to humanity: just as human beings had been overcome and deceived by the devil, it would also be a human being who overcame the devil; and just as human beings had deserved death, so too a human being, by dying, would overcome death.[24]

Since the superiority of Christ's death as a means of reconciliation is at least in part a matter of the abundance of ways in which it effects human salvation and brings us to our ultimate end, there is no single controlling concept that does the systematic work for Aquinas that satisfaction had done for Anselm.

Note that Aquinas identifies both objective and subjective dimensions of Christ's saving work.[25] The objective aspects are realized independently of any human response: Christ makes satisfaction, merits grace and glory, and brings greater dignity to humanity simply by suffering and dying in the way that he did. The subjective aspects encompass the ways in which Christ's passion effects changes in human beings: It shows the love of God and stirs us to love God in return, it gives us an example of outstanding virtue, and it impresses upon us the serious cost of sin and thereby the urgency of avoiding it. The systematic character of Aquinas's account of Atonement is found, not in its use of a single controlling concept, but rather in the fusing together of multiple aspects of Atonement, both objective and subjective aspects, into a coherent whole. As I shall now show in detail, the objective aspects of Atonement are, for Aquinas, inextricably linked both with each other and with the subjective aspects.

MERIT, SATISFACTION, SACRIFICE, AND REDEMPTION

In the *Summa theologiae*, Aquinas asks two central questions about Christ's atoning work. First, how does his passion accomplish its effects? Second, what are those effects? Aquinas's answer to the first question is that Christ's passion accomplishes its effects in four different ways: by way of merit, by way of satisfaction, by way of sacrifice, and by way of redemption. Consider first the notion of merit. To merit is to earn a reward. Charity is the root of merit, and Christ's human soul was graced with meritorious charity from the very moment of his conception.[26] That merit was by itself sufficient to earn eternal salvation for us, because "Christ was given grace, not merely as an individual person, but as Head of the Church, so that grace would overflow from him into the members" of the Church.[27] Why, then, did Christ need to suffer? Not because his charity would otherwise be too small or his merit insufficient, but because "there were obstacles on our part that were preventing us from attaining the effect of those previous merits; hence, it was fitting for Christ to suffer in order to remove those obstacles."[28] Sinful human beings need a vivid demonstration of God's love that awakens an answering love in them; they need a pre-eminent example of "humility, obedience, constancy, justice, and other virtues";[29] they need to be shaken out of their complacency by being confronted with the horror of sin and its cost. All these needs are met, as we have seen, by the passion of Christ, which thus allows the objective merit of Christ to have its subjective effect.

Whereas to merit is to earn a reward, to make satisfaction for an offense is to offer to the offended party something that he loves as much as or more than he hates the offense. "By suffering out of charity and obedience," Aquinas explains, "Christ offered God something greater than was required as a recompense for the whole offense of the human race."[30] It is "not merely a sufficient but indeed a super-abundant satisfaction for the sins of the human race" because of the greatness of the charity with which he bore his suffering, the worth of the divine-human life that he laid down as a satisfaction, and the scope of his suffering and the greatness of his pain.[31] And because head and members are one mystical person, the satisfaction that Christ makes belongs to all the baptized as members of Christ.[32]

Thus, note that the mystical union between Christ and his Church, into which human beings are incorporated by baptism, is a key part of the mechanism (so to speak) by which both merit and satisfaction effect human salvation. In this way, Aquinas develops the Pauline theme of Christ as a second Adam. Sin is transmitted to us because we are members of one body with Adam, salvation because we are members of one body with Christ; and the dignity of human nature is restored, and more than restored, because a human being recapitulates perfectly the obedience that the first human being refused to offer.[33]

The fact that the Incarnation was intended as a means of satisfaction helps explain why Christ, though not himself subject to original sin, was subject to the bodily failings that are the penal consequences (*poenalitates*) of original sin. Someone makes satisfaction on another's behalf, Aquinas says, by taking upon himself the requisite punishment for the other's sin. Bodily failings such as death, hunger, and thirst are "punishments for the sin that was introduced into the world by Adam."[34] It was therefore fitting that in taking on human flesh for the sake of making satisfaction, Christ should also take upon himself our liability to pain and death. But failings in the powers of the soul would have impeded his work of satisfaction, so Christ did not take on the *fomes* of sin or any of our inherited defects in the sensory appetite, will, or intellect.[35]

Christ's death also effects human salvation as a sacrifice:

Something done for the honor that is properly owed to God, in order to conciliate him, is properly called a sacrifice ... "Now Christ offered himself for us in his passion," and this very deed – Christ's voluntarily undergoing suffering – was in the highest degree acceptable to God, because it proceeded from charity. Thus it is clear that Christ's passion was a true sacrifice.[36]

It might seem that sacrifice, so understood, is difficult to distinguish from satisfaction; and, indeed, in the next question the notion of

sacrifice is discussed in the same language, and with the same definition, that Aquinas uses to explain satisfaction.[37] Rather than indicat-
ing conceptual fuzziness in Aquinas's account of Atonement,
however, this connection between the notions of satisfaction and
sacrifice effects an integration of the Anselmian language of satisfaction with the more scriptural language of sacrifice.

Aquinas accomplishes a still larger synthesis with the theories
of his predecessors by the way he talks about redemption, the final
way in which Christ's passion effects human salvation. Redemption,
like sacrifice, is a scriptural image: To redeem is to buy back (redi-
mere), to pay a price to free captives. "You were bought with a great
price," Paul says; Aquinas comments, "[A]nd therefore you are ser-
vants of the one who redeemed you from enslavement to sin."[38] In
some places Aquinas understands redemption as Anselm did, in terms
of satisfaction: "Because Christ's passion was a sufficient and super-
abundant satisfaction for the sin and guilt of the human race, his
passion was a sort of price by which we were set free" both from
enslavement to sin and from our liability to punishment in accordance with God's justice.[39] Elsewhere he explains redemption in terms
of merit, invoking again the mystical union between Christ and the
Church.[40]

One way of understanding human enslavement to sin is as
enslavement to the devil, and Aquinas engages in a most subtle way
with the venerable understanding of Christ's passion as a payment to
buy us back from the devil's control.[41] Some authorities held that the
devil, by successfully tempting our first parents, had acquired rights
over humanity. It was either necessary or at least fitting – accounts
differed – for God to redeem us from Satan's power in a way that
respected Satan's rightful claim on us. Anselm had expressed nothing
but scorn for the idea that the devil had any such claim on us:
Although God justly handed us over to Satan's dominion to punish
us, and it was just that we be punished, Satan himself was always
acting unjustly, and we remained under God's dominion, not the
devil's.[42]

Aquinas is enough of an Anselmian on this point that he does not even entertain the idea that the devil had *rights* over humanity. He speaks instead of the devil's *power* over humanity, and here he shows a defter hand than Anselm's in preserving what he can of the patristic theory. The devil's power over humanity had three aspects: on humanity's part, on God's part, and on the devil's part. Humanity deserved to be handed over to the devil, who had overcome us by tempting us; God in his justice left us in the power of the devil because we had offended against God by sinning; and the devil "by his utterly wicked will thwarted human beings from attaining salvation."[43] The passion of Christ frees us from the power of the devil in its first aspect by bringing about the forgiveness of sins,[44] and in its second aspect by reconciling us with God. As for its third aspect,

> Christ's passion freed us from the devil because in Christ's passion the devil overstepped the boundaries of the power that God had handed over to him, by conniving at the death of Christ who, being sinless, did not deserve death. This is why Augustine says in *De Trinitate* XIII that "the devil was overcome by the justice of Christ, because he found nothing worthy of death in Christ, yet he killed him. And indeed it is just that the debtors whom he had in his control should be set free by believing in the one whom he killed even though no debt was owed."[45]

Note that the justice at issue here is not the rights of the devil, but the righteousness of Christ, along with the poetic justice that those in Satan's power would be set free by believing in the righteous one whom Satan unrighteously killed.

FAITH, CHARITY, AND THE SACRAMENTAL LIFE

Believing in Christ, then, is a crucial notion in Aquinas's account of the economy of redemption. It is precisely "through faith in his blood" (Rom. 3:25) that the redemptive effect of Christ's death reaches us. And it was only through the blood of Christ that both present and past sins could be forgiven (*remitti*), "because the power of the blood of Christ works through human faith, a faith that those who lived before the passion of Christ had, just as we too have it."[46]

Faith in Christ is not the only means by which the benefits of Christ's merit, satisfaction, sacrifice, and redemption are made available to human beings. Aquinas also lays great stress on participation in the sacramental life of the Church as mediating both the objective transaction and the subjective transformation that represent the completeness of Christ's atoning work. As we have already seen, the sacrament by which we are joined to Christ and become members of his mystical body, and thereby first receive the fruits of his redeeming work, is baptism. Aquinas speaks of our being shaped or fashioned after Christ in baptism (*conformari, configurari*). We are fashioned after his death in that we die to sin. What Paul calls "the old human being" – that is, the decrepitude introduced by sin, by which our nature is corrupted – is crucified with Christ, "put to death by the cross of Christ."[47] The guilt and stain of original sin are completely removed, and the power of the *fomes* (and even of the habit of sinning, in the case of those baptized late enough in life to have committed actual sins) is diminished.[48] In this way we are also fashioned after the resurrection of Christ, raised to a new life of wholeness.[49] The baptized person is liberated from enslavement to sin and has the power never to surrender to it again.[50] Thus, the grace of baptism does not merely free human beings from past sin, both Adam's sin and our own sins; it also gives us strength to resist future sins.[51]

The newness of life into which the faithful are baptized is not, however, a complete restoration to Edenic perfection. The desires of the flesh remain, and although reason can resist them sometimes, it cannot resist them always; venial sin, at least, is therefore inevitable. And because of those desires, "many objects strike us in such a way that we draw back from God in order to attain or to avoid them, in contempt of his commandment, and thus we sin mortally."[52] No one, Aquinas says, has made such spiritual progress as to be beyond the need for constant vigilance in guarding against sin.[53]

The new life that is inaugurated in baptism is strengthened, renewed, and replenished in the Eucharist: "In this sacrament the whole mystery of our salvation is contained."[54] It is therefore the central sacrament of the Christian life and the means by which Christ's redeeming work is made present and effective in us again and again.[55] Spiritual life requires spiritual food, for the fervor of charity in us is depleted daily by the fire of concupiscence in much the same way that our body is depleted by its natural fire.[56] The eucharistic food, which is Christ himself, becomes one with us, just as physical food becomes one with those who are nourished by it.[57] Through our union with Christ in the Eucharist we receive forgiveness of past sins, and our charity is increased so that we are better able to avoid future sins.

Yet we receive the effects of the Eucharist in a way commensurate with our human condition: Unlike the angels, we have free choice that can be turned to either good or evil.[58] When we freely choose evil, "the abundance of divine mercy and the efficacy of Christ's grace do not allow the sinner to be left without recourse." We have a remedy in the sacrament of penance. As baptism imparts spiritual life and the Eucharist spiritual nourishment, penance effects spiritual healing through Christ, "the physician of our souls." Christ's merit is sufficient to take away all sins, but not all who approach the sacrament of penance receive the full effect of his merit; each penitent receives forgiveness and healing to the extent that he or she is joined with Christ as suffering for our sins.[59]

It is initially surprising to see Aquinas speaking of penitents as making satisfaction for their sins by carrying out the punishment imposed on them by the judgment of the confessor, who acts with judicial power as Christ's representative. If Christ's suffering really was "not merely a sufficient but indeed a superabundant satisfaction for the sins of the human race,"[60] how can there be a place for works of satisfaction on our part? The answer to this question highlights a thread that runs throughout Aquinas's account of Christ's atoning work and its sacramental appropriation. What Christ does is done *for* us, but not *to* us, except insofar as we freely cooperate with divine grace in appropriating the benefits of Christ's passion. And that appropriation is a matter of becoming more Christlike: like Christ in his death, like Christ in his resurrection, like Christ in his perfect charity (by which alone any offering is acceptable to God), like Christ in his unstinting conformity with the divine will. When we freely submit to divine judgment and carry out a work of satisfaction, we become more like Christ in his suffering, in that we suffer something for his sake as he suffered for ours: "[Y]et a much lesser suffering than is commensurate with the sin is sufficient, because the satisfaction made by Christ works together with our own satisfaction."[61]

NOTES

1 *ST* I q.48 a.1; see also *ST* I q.5 a.1. All translations are my own.

2 *ST* I q.48 a.5 ad 1.

3 *ST* I q.49 a.1.

4 For the conception of possibility at work here, see S. Knuuttilla, *Modalities in Medieval Philosophy* (New York: Routledge, 2019), pp. 99–137.

5 *ST* I q.48 a.2 ad 3.

6 *ST* I q.48 a.5.

7 *ST* I q.65 a.2.

8 Romans 8:19–22 (translated from the Vulgate). Tyra provides a helpful overview of patristic exegesis of this passage. S. W. Tyra, "When Considering Creation, Simply Follow the Rule (of Faith): Patristic Exegesis of Romans 8:9–12 and the Theological Interpretation of Scripture," *Journal of Theological Interpretation* 8 (2014): 251–73.

9 *In Rom* cap. VIII, lect. 4, n.665, 668, 671. For a discussion of the issues raised by Aquinas's account of perfect happiness and our likeness to angels, see C. Van Dyke, "Aquinas's Shiny Happy People: Perfect Happiness and the Limits of Human Nature," *Oxford Studies in the Philosophy of Religion* 6 (2014): 269–91.

10 *ST* I-II q.71 a.6.

11 *ST* I-II q.81 a.3. Aquinas denies that the mother of Jesus was conceived without original sin: *ST* III q.27 a.2. Theologians who affirm that doctrine

are nonetheless in agreement with Aquinas that, but for a miraculous intervention on God's part, original sin would have been transmitted to Mary in the usual way, and that the virginal conception of her Son meant that he was free from original sin.

12 *ST* I-II q.81 a.1.

13 *ST* I-II q.81 a.1 and ad 1, 2, 3.

14 *ST* I-II q.82 a.1 and ad 1, 2; *In Rom* cap. V, lect. 2, n.395.

15 *ST* I-II q.82 a.1.

16 *ST* I-II q.82 a.2, 3.

17 *ST* I-II q.85 a.3.

18 *ST* I-II q.85 a.5; *ST* I-II q.87 a.2.

19 *ST* I-II q.87 a.7.

20 *In Rom* cap. VIII, lect. 3, nn.560–1.

21 See S. Visser and T. Williams, *Anselm. Great Medieval Thinkers* (Oxford: Oxford University Press, 2009), pp. 213–32, for an exposition of Anselm's argument in *Cur Deus Homo*.

22 *In Rom* cap. III, lect. 3, nn.307–8.

23 *ST* III q.46 a.2 ad 3. Likewise, at *ST* III q.1 a.2 Aquinas denies the Anselmian claim that the Incarnation was necessary for humanity to be reconciled with God: "God, in virtue of his almighty power, could have restored human nature in many other ways." Oddly, Aquinas says at *CT* l.1 c.200 that "if God had restored human beings by his own will and power, the order of divine justice, according to which satisfaction is required for sin, would have been preserved"; whatever might account for the appearance of this claim in *CT*, it is clearly not Aquinas's considered view. For a survey of medieval accounts of the Atonement, including a number of authors who deny the necessity of any satisfaction, see T. Williams, "Atonement" in R. Cross and J. T. Paasch (eds.), *The Routledge Companion to Medieval Philosophy* (New York: Routledge, 2021).

24 *ST* III q.46 a.3.

25 See O. D. Crisp, *Approaching the Atonement: The Reconciling Work of Christ* (Downers Grove, IL: IVP Academic, 2020), pp. 22–3, for a brief explanation of the use of "objective" and "subjective" in contemporary discussions of accounts of the Atonement.

26 *ST* III q.34 a.3.

27 *ST* III q.48 a.1.

28 *ST* III q.48 a.1 ad 2.

29 *ST* III q.46 a.3.

30 *ST* III q.48 a.2.

31 *ST* III q.48 a.2.

32 *ST* III q.48 a.2 ad 1. See also *ST* III q.49 a.3.

33 Aquinas explores the theme of Christ as second Adam most fully in his commentaries on Paul. See especially *In Rom* cap. V, lect. 3–5; *In I Cor* cap. XV, lect. 3.

34 *ST* III q.14 a.1.

35 *ST* III q.15, a.2. See also *CT* l.1 c.226.

36 *ST* III q.48 a.3, quoting Augustine, *City of God* X.6.

37 *ST* III q.49 a.4.

38 *In I Cor* cap. VI, lect. 3, 310. "Great" appears in the Vulgate but not in the Greek text or in most English translations. Aquinas explains, "The price of redemption is said to be great because it is not corruptible: no, it has eternal power, because it is the blood of the eternal God himself."

39 *ST* III q.48 a.4.

40 *ST* III q.49 a.1.

41 So subtle, indeed, that my own account of it in Williams, "Atonement," is mistaken; the remainder of this section clears up my confusion.

42 *Cur Deus Homo* I.7.

43 *ST* III q.49 a.2.

44 The passion of Christ brings about forgiveness of sins in three ways: by enkindling charity; by redeeming us as members of his mystical body; and insofar as his flesh is an instrument of Godhead and therefore its passions and actions are effective by divine power in driving out sin. *ST* III q.49 a.1.

45 *ST* III q.49 a.2. See also *ST* III q.46 a.3 ad 3.

46 *In Rom* cap. III, lect. 3, n.310.

47 *In Rom* cap. VI, lect. 2, n.479.

48 *In Rom* cap. VI, lect. 2, n.480.

49 *In Rom* cap. VI, lect. 1, n.476.

50 *In Rom* cap. VI, lect. 2, nn.484–91.

51 *In Rom* cap. VI, lect. 1, n.468.

52 *ST* I-II q.109 a.8.

53 *In I Cor* cap. XV, lect. 4, n.963.

54 *ST* III q.103 a.4.

55 I do not have space to do justice to Aquinas's account of the Eucharist as the ordinary vehicle by which the benefits of Christ's passion are made available to us. For fuller accounts, see R. Van Nieuwenhove, "The Saving Work of Christ" in B. Davies and E. Stump (eds.), *The Oxford Handbook of Aquinas* (Oxford: Oxford University Press, 2012), pp. 436–47, here pp. 442–4; E. Stump, *Aquinas* (New York and London: Routledge, 2003), pp. 445–52.

56 *ST* III q.79 a.3.

57 *ST* III q.79 a.5.

58 *ST* III q.79 a.6 ad 1.

59 *SCG* IV.72.

60 *ST* III q.48 a.2.

61 *ST* III q.49 a.4 ad 2.

16 **Resurrection and Eschatology**

Simon Francis Gaine, OP

INTRODUCTION

Toward the end of his life, Aquinas delivered a series of catechetical talks in the vernacular on the Apostles' Creed to an Italian audience, which were preserved in Latin by his secretary, Reginald of Piperno. Its eschatological themes, including the resurrection, would have been of huge importance to Aquinas's audience.[1] His exposition shows his commitment in faith to the future resurrection of all the dead for judgment, and to an eternal reward bestowed on those who die in a state of grace and an eternal punishment for those who die in sin. In our own times there has been widespread theological debate over whether an eternal hell will ever be populated, especially in view of those passages in Scripture that suggest a renewal of creation. In Aquinas's time and place there was no such controversy about hell. But while the beatitude of heaven enjoyed priority over hell in his theological thinking, with infernal punishment understood to consist primarily in the eternal loss of the beatific vision, fundamental to each was the bodily resurrection common to both the blessed and the wretched.

At the same time Aquinas was committed in faith to the teaching that souls, separated from their bodies at death, when their wills were fixed, would not have to wait for reunion with their bodies to enter eternal beatitude or punishment. Prior to the general judgment, there was a particular judgment for each soul at death, with that soul forever either consigned to hell or admitted to the vision of God following whatever purification might be needed.[2] While Aquinas's treatments of eschatology accorded systematic priority to bodily resurrection over the state of the separated soul, the chronological priority of particular judgment and recompense clearly urged the question of what more is added by the resurrection, when separated souls already experience everlasting misery or felicity. It was thus a challenge for theologians to articulate the resurrection's specific contribution to judgment, reward, and retribution.[3] This Aquinas did by drawing not only on the teaching of Scripture as interpreted by the Fathers of the Church, but also on his philosophical anthropology and cosmology, which were much indebted to Aristotle.

Aquinas never completed his systematic masterpiece, the *Summa theologiae* (*ST*), with its concluding treatise on eschatology. He confided to Reginald that he could write no more, having experienced a vision after which his writing seemed to him as though straw. Reginald attempted to make up for this lacuna with the addition of a supplement, lifting material from Aquinas's early *Commentary on the Sentences*, and rearranging it, so that treatment of the separated soul now preceded that of resurrection.[4] The present chapter addresses the contribution of resurrection to Aquinas's eschatology by drawing not simply on the unfinished *Summa* and his early commentary, but also on other works, especially the mature systematic treatments in the *Summa contra Gentiles* and *Compendium theologiae* (*CT*). While each takes the material in its own order, this chapter follows none of them exclusively, but examines first how resurrection contributes to judgment, then how the resurrection body is both continuous and discontinuous with the body of this life, and finally what it contributes to the twin recompense of heaven and hell.

JUDGMENT AND THE RESURRECTION

For Aquinas, no recompense can properly take place without a judgment being made, and everlasting recompense cannot be made without a final judgment.[5] While he holds that the last judgment and the eternal recompense consequent on it will take place simultaneously,[6] the final judgment has a natural priority over reward and punishment.

Aquinas clarifies why it is to Christ that God has committed this judgment, and how, already risen from the dead, he returns to earth to execute it.[7] This section concentrates, however, on Aquinas's account of the need for a final judgment that involves the bodily resurrection of those to be judged.

Although Aquinas did not investigate the last judgment as such in the *ST*, he did treat Christ's power to judge. One might suppose that a general judgment of souls alone would be sufficient to render judgment final and perfect, and yet what Aquinas envisages is, in accordance with Christian belief, a judgment of bodies as well as souls. When treating of this judiciary power, he asked why the general judgment was required.[8] After all, Christ was already exercising his judiciary power in the here and now. Souls judged at death are judged definitively, since there is no longer any possibility for them in their fixed state of will of performing acts that either merit or demerit such that they require further judgment.

However, while all such acts have been completed, Aquinas notes that at the point of the individual's death full account is not taken of their acts' effects that still lie in the future. And so, while the individual's life has been ended per se, in a certain way it is still bound up with what is yet to come. One example is that the memory of someone lives on in the world, and yet their reputation may not accord with the truth. Then there is the question of effects that live on in one's children, when good people have bad children and vice versa. A third point is that effects of one's actions can also live on for good or ill in the lives of others. Aquinas gives the example of the wicked teaching of heresiarchs and the preaching of the apostles. His fourth point relates to treatment of the corpse, which may or may not be honorable. And, finally, there are temporal matters on which one's heart was set, and which may or may not endure. All this leaves a great deal of unfinished business for divine judgment, which was not dealt with at the particular judgment. Aquinas concludes that a perfect and public judgment of all these things is only possible at the last day, when everything that concerns everyone will be perfectly and publicly judged by Christ. In this way his is a perspective that is not individualistic but one that is appreciative of the social and interdependent character of our humanity. Whereas the particular judgment gives each one certainty regarding personal reward or punishment, the general judgment will make known to each the recompense of all.[9]

Why, though, should the bodies of those judged be required for this final judgment? One might suppose that a general judgment of souls on the last day could be enough to satisfy the foregoing considerations, and yet what Aquinas envisages is a judgment of bodies as well as souls. Doubtless Aquinas would have scrutinized this in the *ST*'s section on eschatology, but his approach can be found elsewhere in his writings. He states in the *CT* that the recompense of any human being must require recompense in both body and soul, and since all recompense requires judgment, judgment must extend to the body as well as to the soul.[10] In other words, for one to be recompensed in the body, one must be judged in the body. But why is it that recompense should extend to the body as well as the soul?

For Aquinas, human beings are recompensed on the last day for what they have done in this life. Those who act well or wrongly are composed of soul and body, and acted as they did in body as well as in soul, and hence deserve recompense in both.[11] With such a recompense to be delivered, the presupposed judgment must extend to body and as well as to soul. This furnished Aquinas with a supporting argument for the reality of the resurrection from reason. Given that reason can establish that, by divine providence, sinners deserve punishment and those who do good a reward, and that both have acted in body as well as in soul, the fact that such recompense does not always take place in this life, as is evident, points to resurrection taking place in the next.[12]

In making his argument, Aquinas invoked his conviction that a human being is a composite of soul and body. This he consistently articulated in Aristotelian terms such that the soul is the single substantial form of the body.[13] Aquinas does not treat the body as something extraneous to a human being. The soul is not a complete substance in its own right, but part of one, and the soul is not identical to a complete human being. The upshot is that, were the soul alone ultimately recompensed, then the complete human being, body and soul, would be neither recompensed nor judged.[14] Hence, if the judgment of human beings on the last day is not to be deficient, a bodily resurrection is required.

However, one might suppose that resurrection will provide for the final recompense of complete human beings, while asserting that a further judgment at the moment of resurrection is superfluous. This appears to be the position of an objection Aquinas put in the *ST* to Christ's judicial power being exercised in a judgment beyond the particular judgment. The objection argues that no further judgment is required for the sake of the body, because the body is open to recompense only insofar as it is the instrument of the soul. In other words, the body never performs an act that may be judged for its morality, except insofar as the body has acted under the influence of the soul. The soul, however, has already been sufficiently judged at death, such that no further judgment is required for a human being in the body. What would take place at the resurrection, on this view, is not any fresh judgment of human beings in their risen bodies, but each risen body simply shares in the recompense already assigned its soul at the particular judgment. In contrast to a general judgment of souls without a resurrection, the objection appears to be rooting for a resurrection without any new judgment.

Against the objection, however, Aquinas reasons that, while the recompense of the body is linked to that of the soul, it is only because of union with the body that the soul is changeable. Such mutability does not belong to the immaterial soul as such, but only insofar as it is united to the material body. Once the soul is separated from the body in death, it leaves this changeability behind. Aquinas's point is that there cannot be a definitive judgment on something so long as its relevant mutability persists, but such judgment takes place once a fixed state arrives. Hence, on entering its immutable state after separation from the body, the soul receives its particular judgment. The same principle Aquinas applies to the body, which, he says, remains subject to change until the end of time, and then is recompensed at the general judgment.[15] In taking this view, Aquinas argues against not only a general judgment of souls without a resurrection, but also a resurrection of the dead without an accompanying judgment. When the bodies of all are raised from the dead, they are raised together in such a way that a judgment can take place that is perfect and public, where complete human beings are judged both in body and in soul, and the recompense of all is known to each.

JUDGMENT REQUIRES THE SAME BODY ...

In the section after this, we shall see that Aquinas follows Scripture in distinguishing the resurrection body from the earthly body: They are not the same in every way. However, this does not mean he thinks that the body assumed by the soul at the resurrection is a different body from the one to which the soul was united prior to death. For Aquinas, not only must those judged on the last day be bodily, but their bodies must be the same bodies as their bodies during their earthly lifetimes. It is evident that, if a soul resumes a different body from the one it had in this life, then a different body will be recompensed at the resurrection from the body in which the acts deserving of recompense were performed. Were that to be the case, the justice of the final judgment would be compromised, at least as regards the body. While the body deserving of recompense will have gone unjudged, a body in which the relevant acts had not been performed would have been judged.

Aquinas explores various ways in which one might think that the soul could take up a different kind of body from the one it had before.[16] Resurrection bodies of a different kind cannot, however, meet the criteria exhibited by the risen Christ, who had flesh and bones configured in a human way, able to be touched by his disciples. An aerial body is not possible, on Aquinas's analysis, because air cannot provide the determination of shape, as a whole and in its parts, that is required by a human body. Moreover, air cannot provide any animal body, including the human body, with its characteristic sense of touch. A heavenly body – such as Aquinas supposed to exist in the sun, moon, and stars – fared no better on this Aristotelian analysis.

Moreover, Aristotle had demonstrated, he says, that the shape due to such bodies by nature is spherical, such that they cannot receive the figure due by nature to a human body. In that case, it would be impossible that the bodies of the risen be the same in nature as the bodies of the stars. Aquinas also ruled out a purely spiritual body – that is, one that is totally immaterial, as the soul is. He does not think it possible for anything bodily to be transformed into something purely spiritual: To think otherwise is to misconstrue the difference between the material and the immaterial. Likewise, it is impossible for one individual to be composed of two spiritual substances; and if one of these were absorbed into the other, the resurrection would end up making no significant difference to the soul. Finally, a purely spiritual body could not be physically touched, as Christ's was.

What we will see in our resurrection, then, is the same as is found in Christ's: a human body of flesh and bones, one of human shape that can be touched by others. This is precisely what is provided by the union of the resurrection body with the soul. The definition of a human being, as with any natural material being, includes its matter, and were human beings to rise not with human flesh and bones but with some other matter, they would be of a different species. On Aquinas's anthropology, the soul is united to body as form to matter, and since there must be a proportion between act and potency, every form must have its determinate matter. The soul, then, which is human in species, must have matter which is of the same species. Hence, the resurrection body will be human in species, just as the pre-mortem body was.

The restoration of human nature in the resurrection body means that it will be made up of flesh and bone, and of all the same organs possessed by the body in this life. Without such a complete restoration of parts, Aquinas holds, the resurrection body would not have its proper integrity and be defective.[17] As we shall see in the next section, Aquinas does not hold that all these organs will retain their former functions at the resurrection. Nevertheless, they have a crucial contribution to make. Without their presence, a large portion of bodily members would be wanting, and the integrity of the natural human body compromised. Aquinas makes a point of emphasizing that this will include sexual organs, whether male or female. He explicitly rejects the view that no resurrection body will be female, linking this to his conviction that the distinction of the sexes, according to divine wisdom, is part of the intention of nature rather than a defect in it. Should all risen bodies be male, the resurrection itself would be deficient.[18]

It is not enough, however, for Aquinas to be assured that the bodies taken up at the resurrection will be genuinely human in species. For Aquinas, each body that is judged and recompensed must be precisely the same body in which the acts under judgment were performed. The soul of one cannot resume the body of another. Rather, each resurrection body must be, according to Aristotle's terminology, numerically identical with that soul's pre-mortem body. It must be the same one.[19]

How, though, is such identity to be guaranteed? Aquinas acknowledges that there are many points of continuity between the body of this life and the next which are not the guarantee of such identity. One example he gives is the proper accident of the ability to laugh, which will exist in the next life, he says, as well as in this. Other examples are accidents such as individual hair color, which continue the natural variation of this world. However, it is not such characteristics that guarantee numerical identity, but rather these characteristics are possessed by the same subject and presuppose that subject's numerical identity, which is in fact explained by its essential principles. Aquinas holds that, for a material thing to be numerically identical, its formal and material principles must be numerically identical. In the case of a human being, whose essential principles are body and soul, numerical identity is guaranteed at the resurrection by the uniting of numerically the same soul with numerically the same matter.[20]

Aquinas rejects the suggestion that restoration of numerical identity is impossible because some of its essential principles are reduced at death to nothing. Instead, he holds that none of a human being's essential principles entirely yields to nothing. The substantial form is the subsistent immaterial soul which continues to exist, separated from the body. While the corpse is not a body, strictly speaking, according to Aquinas's hylomorphism, in terms of their dimensions these remains nevertheless exhibit a certain continuity with the pre-mortem body.[21] Their subsequent history up to and through the conflagration Aquinas holds will engulf all things at the judgment,[22] and of any matter that had previously been present in that individual during his or her earthly lifetime, is known to the omniscient God. Hence, the resurrection body of each can be drawn by divine power from what had been present in that individual during this life. Aquinas's adoption of an Aristotelian account of a body's numerical identity over its lifetime, where its matter was gradually replaced, liberated him from older theological accounts that had supposed that bodily identity must involve the continual presence of some special portion of matter.[23] Moreover, not all the matter that had been present in any one body during its entire lifetime, he supposed, would be resumed at the resurrection, but only as much as would result in the correct quantity due to it. Where the same matter had been present in more than one body, he concluded that it would be resumed by the one to whom it had belonged most intimately, and he presents criteria for assessing this. Should someone be left without a full complement of matter from their earthly lifetime, Aquinas surmised that it would be supplied by divine power.[24]

The appeal to divine power is crucial for Aquinas's account of the resurrection. The power of nature is insufficient to bring about a resurrection with numerical identity, but rather continues a species by bringing into existence new members as others die.[25] Not that he sees the resurrection as motivated simply for the sake of a display of divine power. The resurrection will in fact take place for the purpose of judgment and recompense, and so Aquinas identifies divine justice as the principal efficient cause of our resurrection. Moreover, given God's choice to save us through the Incarnation of the Word, Christ's own rising in his humanity is identified as the secondary and instrumental efficient cause of the general resurrection. Thus, while Christ's rising acts here under the impetus of divine power, it is applied as an instrument suited precisely to achieve the resurrection of others. Moreover, since the principal cause is divine justice, from which Christ according to his humanity derives his judicial power, he thus causes the resurrection of all who are subject to his judgment, whatever their moral status.[26] Finally, identification of Christ's own rising as the cause of ours helps Aquinas to explain the difference between the body in this life and the body in the next.

... AND DIFFERENT

Despite his emphasis on the continuity of nature and the individual in the resurrection, Aquinas hardly supposes that the resurrection body will not differ from the pre-mortem body at all. For example, risen bodies are free of the natural defects encountered in this life. This is because divine power accomplishes a natural perfection of each body that the power of nature itself is unable to achieve. Bodily defects have their source in deficiencies found in the natural power of human generation. Moreover, as the products of material generation, human beings are also vulnerable to the loss of bodily parts, senses, and so on. According to Aquinas, the complete restoration of human nature involves the removal of all such things. Should any remain, he thinks, they would harm the human integrity of those who rise.[27]

Unlike the human power of generation, divine power is altogether perfect and cannot admit of any deficiency. One is reminded of how Aquinas argues that Christ's body was perfectly formed at his Incarnation, since it was formed not by human fatherhood but by the power of the Holy Spirit.[28] Since it is divine power that is responsible for resurrection, it causes human beings to rise with a perfect integrity that surpasses any defects of their pre-mortem state. Although Christ's body still bore the scars of his passion, Aquinas refuses to treat these as defects but rather as beautiful enhancements of Christ's glorified body, with the possibility that the glorified bodies of the martyrs may be similarly enhanced.[29] While one might have thought that natural defect would have suited the bodies of those punished in hell, Aquinas refuses that option:

Although their wills had turned to evil, the soul in itself, to which the resurrection body is united, is created good, and to that extent the bodies even of those in hell have their natural integrity without defect.[30] Hence, Christ's rising with a body in its natural integral perfection is the cause of the future rising of all bodies to such perfection. The resurrection body will differ from this life, then, in terms of its perfection of nature, with former defects removed.

Connected to the natural perfection of these bodies is a further way that they will differ from bodies in the pre-mortem state. Through divine power, once again, all will have a common age. While as products of natural generation, human beings grow toward perfection in childhood and then withdraw from it in old age, at the resurrection they benefit from divine power, which causes them all to have bodies in the age of youth.[31] It is in this age, Aquinas says, that the perfection of nature is found, consequent on childhood growth to perfection and prior to its decline. According to Aquinas, this begins around the age of thirty, and it is because of this perfection both that Christ began his earthly ministry at this age,[32] and that all are caused by him to rise with the perfect age. This is the case for all, whether their recompense is to be reward or retribution.

The most important way in which risen bodies will differ from those of this life is in their immortality and incorruptibility. Aquinas acknowledges that those who had thought of the risen body as aerial, spiritual, or heavenly were trying to come to terms with the fact that the resurrection body will not be subject to corruption and death.[33] While he disagrees with their conclusions, Aquinas is adamant that the resurrection body will never die again. God's plan is not for human beings to rise only to die again, perhaps subject to something like a cyclical infinitude of dying and rising, with no determinate end. Rather, God has determined an everlasting recompense for human beings, body and soul, which requires that they be immortal.[34] Were their bodies subject to mortality, they would be unable to be judged for reward or punishment without end. Hence Christ, in rising from the dead never to die again (Rom. 6:4), causes the risen to be likewise immortal, the effect being likened to its cause. Were it otherwise, Aquinas thinks, death would not be entirely conquered by Christ. Hence, everyone shares in the immortality Christ merited by his passion, whether they are admitted to heaven or not. Nevertheless, he insists that this does not mean that human nature has been changed or numerical identity undermined. For Aquinas, mortality is not, strictly speaking, part of the definition of a human being. While we sometimes speak as though it were, Aquinas says that is because mortality is being used to indicate matter.[35] Moreover, the body, in and of itself, remains mortal as far as its nature is concerned.[36]

The reason, therefore, why human beings will rise immortal is not because they have assumed a body which is different in nature from their earthly bodies. It is because the formerly corruptible body has itself been made incorruptible through Christ's own rising to an incorruptible life. This explains why Aquinas says that the body is the same in nature but has a different disposition, and he holds that this counts for both the good and the wicked: All are incorruptible and so immortal. Incorruptibility is required so that, in each case, they can receive everlasting recompense in the body for deeds done in the body. Aquinas takes the view that the natural corruptibility of the material human body is derived from the fact that it is composed of contrary elements. However, this corruptibility is not overcome in the resurrection by any change to the natural composition of the human body. Rather, this is achieved by divine power, from which it follows that the soul will have a perfect dominion over the body in terms of giving it life.[37] This natural life, lived in a body of perfect age without danger of decline or loss of integrity, is thus indestructible and without end. Disposed as each soul requires, such a body persists forever according to the soul's fixity of will, and thus the body is fit to be judged for an everlasting recompense.

The question of how life in the resurrection body will differ more broadly from life in the body in the present can be more fully answered only in the light of a consideration of eternal reward and punishment, to which we shall turn in the next section. However,

Aquinas argues for certain future differences shared by all the risen on account of their common incorruptibility. There are some activities, he says, that will not play a part in an incorruptible human life, such as the consumption of food and sexual intercourse, which both serve our present corruptible life. We saw in the previous section that the organs relevant to these are present in the resurrection body in order to contribute to its integrity. They will not, however, perform their former functions, since their proper purposes play no part in incorruptible life. Aquinas appeals to the principle that it is fitting that the means to an end be removed when the end itself is removed. There will be no need to maintain an incorruptible body through the consumption of food, and no need for a body already in possession of its due quantity to consume food to grow. Aquinas is aware that the risen Christ ate and drank in the presence of his disciples, but the purpose of that eating and drinking was not to support the body but to demonstrate its reality. Likewise, scriptural references to feasting in the kingdom of heaven and the like are to be interpreted figuratively.[38]

Aquinas adds that, since sperm is produced from food, the fact that food is no longer consumed implies the cessation of sexual reproduction.[39] The purpose of sexual intercourse, he says, is the generation of new members of a species to preserve in the species what cannot be preserved in the individual. Nature cannot cause the eternal preservation of individuals intact, but is limited to generating new members of a species as others die. With the resurrection of incorruptible and immortal bodies, however, the reproduction of the species is no longer required.[40] Aquinas rejects the suggestion that intercourse, as well as eating and drinking, might be pursued for pleasure alone, which he regards as immoral.[41] Those in heaven could not so wish to act, and those in hell are unable to act on their sinful desires. Finally, were new human beings to be produced after the last judgment, there would be the troubling question of their status now that the divine plan of redemption from original sin had been fulfilled, where all rise together for an eternal recompense before the judgment seat of Christ.[42] What befits final judgment is a resurrection to incorruptible life without further reproduction.

Before moving on to the differences between the resurrection bodies of those in heaven and hell, it should be noted that, for Aquinas, just as there are consequences for future human life based on the common future state of incorruptibility, so there are fitting consequences for the material world in which human beings have lived. As he concluded to the future absence of various aspects of human life necessary in the present, so he concludes to the future absence of current features of the earth and the heavens above the earth, where the sun, moon, and stars are found.[43] On Aquinas's theological principles, everything in the world is ordered to the service of humankind. On his cosmology, the heavens are turned around the earth in order to exercise a principal causal role in human corruption and reproduction, thus similarly causing corruption and reproduction in the other animal and plant species needed by human beings for food. However, given that human beings will be incorruptible, and that neither human reproduction nor the reproduction of any other species will any longer be required, God sees to it that the heavens will no longer turn. Aquinas concludes that, apart from humanity, the species of living things, together with minerals, will cease to be, although the different elements from which they were composed will persist. Although the sun, moon, and stars no longer revolve, they, too, continue in existence, since they are not naturally composed in such a way as to corrupt. Thus, Aquinas attempted to depict a renewed heaven and earth that were a fit with a resurrection of human beings to an incorruptible life. This renewal is not so much an exclusively heavenly renewal, but one that undergirds the twofold recompense of heaven and hell.

THE BODY'S CONTRIBUTION TO REWARD AND RETRIBUTION

Not only are there differences between the body of this life and the next, but Aquinas also distinguished between glorified bodies in heaven and non-glorified bodies in hell. At the moment of resurrection and judgment, Christ will separate those bound for heaven and those who are not. The latter are left behind on earth, while the former are taken up.[44] Those rewarded with eternal life are given a place proportionate to them with Christ in the empyrean heaven above the heavens that formerly turned. Those not in heaven are correspondingly located very low, although Aquinas does note that those who died in original sin only are placed together above the wicked who had turned inordinately from God to creatures through sins of their own.[45]

With resurrection taking place, recompense can be made in bodies as well as in souls, and so resurrection adds something to Aquinas's account of ultimate beatitude and misery. Prior to the resurrection, a soul already enjoyed its essential beatitude by contemplating God's essence, together with further non-essential rewards, or suffered the penalty of loss of this vision, together with further punishments of sense insofar as souls had turned inordinately to creatures. While it was agreed that beatitude increased at the resurrection by its being somehow extended from soul to body, an intensive increase in the soul's beatitude was debated. Since the body did not contribute to the intellect's act of beatific vision, Aquinas changed his mind and concluded that the resumption of the body did not increase the soul's essential beatitude. While reunion with the body completes the subject that enjoys beatitude, it does not complete the soul's essential happiness. Likewise, it could make no sense to Aquinas to attribute an increase in a non-glorified soul's loss of the beatific vision to the resurrection. In both cases, the presence of the body adds to recompense by way of extension.[46]

Aquinas's hylomorphic understanding of the close union between soul and body underlines their mutual impact, such that an intellectual discovery can cause a good feeling in us or physical pain can affect us mentally. In the case of the beatified soul, Aquinas says that its glory redounds or overflows onto the body. In the case of Christ, whose intellect was blessed with glory throughout his earthly life, its overflow was prevented from taking place until he rose from the dead.[47] While his rising was the instrumental efficient cause of the resurrection of all others, Aquinas says that he was properly the exemplary cause only of those resurrected to heaven.[48] Their resurrection, as well as their state of soul, was thus more completely modeled on his. Aquinas lists four gifts thereby bestowed on the body: subtlety, agility, impassibility, and clarity.[49] Souls which are not glorified receive none of these gifts. Given that a soul is wracked and frustrated in its natural desire for happiness through its own actions, a corresponding negative impact on the body will follow.[50]

While the soul of every resurrection body has dominion over it by divine power in terms of its being, by divine power the glory of the blessed soul gives it a more extended dominion, where the body is subject to the soul in every way and nothing bodily interferes with the life of eternal contemplation. For Aquinas, the more the form of anything successfully rules its matter, the more perfect it is. This is how he interprets the spiritual body of 1 Corinthians 15:44: one entirely subject to the spirit. Aquinas also speaks of this body as subtle. He distances himself from the opinion that such subtlety is what allowed Christ's risen body to enter a room when the doors were shut: The presence of two bodies in one place is always a miracle wrought by divine power. A better example of subtlety would be Christ's ability to make himself appear and disappear from his disciples' sight. However, where a body is not glorified, it is not made subtle according to Christ's exemplary causality, and so it can continue to dominate the soul in many ways. Where one is turned inordinately to creatures, it is not so much that the body is made spiritual as that the soul is made carnal.

When Christ disappeared from his disciples' sight, that could be attributed not only to his body's subtlety but also to its agility. Aquinas interprets the body's power referred to in 1 Corinthians 15:43 as this ability for rapid movement. Since power overflows from any glorified soul to its risen body, whenever the glorified soul wills its body to move, that body will be utterly obedient to this wish. While bodily movement had previously served the active life, in heaven it will serve the contemplative life. A saint can thus move rapidly for a better view of, say, a star or the body of another saint, and perceive God's presence and power within it. Those who are not glorified, however, will be unable to move about with such ease: Rather, they will experience difficulty in movement, finding their bodies heavy by comparison.

A glorified body is furthermore clothed by a kind of beautifying clarity, as glory redounds to it from a soul adorned with spiritual light. This is how Aquinas interprets 1 Corinthians 15:43's rising in glory and Christ's saying that the just will shine like the sun in the Father's kingdom (Matt. 13:43). His own transfiguration is understood as a transient appearance of this clarity.[51] The risen Christ appeared to his disciples without such clarity, and Aquinas takes the saints also to be able to appear with or without such clarity, as they wish. Different degrees of clarity are proportioned to the different levels of intensity in the beatific vision enjoyed by them (somewhat as some people can see the same physical object better than others because of sharper eyesight), which is itself proportioned to the different degrees of charity in which they died.[52] In this way, "star differs from star in glory" (1 Cor. 15:41). And just as non-glorified souls do not have the light of divine knowledge, so non-glorified bodies are not gifted with clarity. In comparison with glorified bodies, they are clothed in darkness.

Although all risen bodies are incorruptible, Aquinas refers 1 Corinthian 15:42's incorruptibility to the further gift of impassibility. Overflowing from the glory of the soul, it guarantees that glorified bodies are free from suffering. Aquinas is careful to distinguish such suffering from the passivity required for the body's enhanced senses to operate. He reasons that, just as the glorified soul's desires are fulfilled in the achievement of every good, so its desires are fulfilled in the removal of every evil, whether actual or potential. Hence, over and above its actual integrity, its body will be incapable of suffering potential harm. Without this gift, the body retains its passibility. In the case of those who died in original sin only, Aquinas thinks that as a matter of fact they will not experience anything harmful to their bodies, even though they do not have the gift of impassibility. In the case of those who deserve retribution for the sins they themselves committed, the possibility of the body lays them open to appropriate suffering. We are not to suppose that Aquinas held that it is the resumption of the body itself that in the first place enabled punishment by material fire, which is how Scripture was normally interpreted. Since God can unite a material body to an immaterial soul, Aquinas has no trouble in supposing that an immaterial soul can be punished materially in some way.[53] What Aquinas takes trouble to explain is that the eternally punished body cannot corrupt. While fire destroys a corruptible body, and intense sorrow can separate the soul from the body, the incorruptibility of the body means that there can be no removal of its substantial form, such that the body's potential to be changed into something else is restricted. Thus, the body's incorruptibility and its lack of impassibility combine to make sense of the eternity of its punishment.

CONCLUSION

For Aquinas, since human beings acted well or badly in the body, they are to be recompensed in the body. Through the general resurrection they are judged in the very same body in which they had formerly so acted. Resurrection thus contributes something across the subject matter of eschatology, to judgment, final reward, and retribution. While glorified and non-glorified bodies differ, they share at the judgment an immortality and incorruptibility that mark off the risen from the pre-mortem body. Aquinas does not associate the renewal of the world only with heaven; instead it befits an incorruptible life of everlasting just punishment as well as perfect eternal beatitude.

NOTES

1 *Expositio in Symbolum Apostolorum* 7, 11–12. On the broad significance of resurrection belief for medieval Western Christians, see C. W. Bynum, *The Resurrection of the Body in Western Christianity, 200–1336* (New York: Columbia University Press, 1995).

2 *SCG* IV.91.

3 For comparison with Bonaventure and Ockham, see M. M. Adams, "Why Bodies as Well as Souls?" in G. T. Doolan (ed.), *The Science of Being as Being: Metaphysical Investigations* (Washington, DC: The Catholic University of America Press, 2012), pp. 264–98.

4 C. Leget, "Eschatology" in R. van Nieuwenhove and J. Wawrykow (eds.), *The Theology of Thomas Aquinas* (South Bend, IN: University of Notre Dame Press, 2005), pp. 386–406, here p. 365.

5 *SCG* IV.96.1.

6 *CT* I.244.

7 *CT* I.241–2.

8 *ST* III q.59 a.5.

9 Cf. *In IV Sent.*, d.47, q.1, a.1. On Aquinas's development here, see B. Kromholtz, *On the Last Day: The Time of the Resurrection of the Dead according to Thomas Aquinas* (Fribourg: Academic Press Fribourg, 2010), pp. 393–6.

10 *CT* I.242.

11 *SCG* IV.79.12.

12 B. Davies, *Thomas Aquinas's* Summa Contra Gentiles*: A Guide and Commentary* (Oxford: Oxford University Press, 2016), p. 384, notes that Aquinas does not claim in his arguments from reason to have demonstrated philosophically that resurrection will occur.

13 For example, *SCG* II.68.

14 *Quodl* VII q.5 a.1 ad 3.

15 *ST* III q.59 a.5 ad 3.

16 *SCG* IV.84.

17 *CT* I.157.

18 *SCG* IV.88.

19 *CT* I.153.

20 *Quodl* XI q.6 a.1.

21 *SCG* IV.80–1; *CT* I.153; *Quodl* XI q.6 a.1 ad 2.

22 *SCG* IV.97.6; *In IV Sent.*, d.47, q.2.

23 *CT* I.159.

24 *SCG* IV.81; *CT* I.160–1. How Aquinas secured bodily numerical identity in philosophical terms is debated (see S. Langley, "Aquinas, Resurrection, and Material Continuity," *Proceedings of the American Catholic Philosophical Association* 75 (2001): 135–47). Aquinas never had the opportunity to address this in the uncompleted *ST*. Fitzpatrick contends that Aquinas's appeal to dimensions was based on Averroes's theory of matter and is in tension with

his Aristotelian principles. See A. Fitzpatrick, *Thomas Aquinas on Bodily Identity* (Oxford: Oxford University Press, 2017). Others hold that Aquinas's hylomorphism commits him to bodily identity at the resurrection being secured by identity of substantial form. See Chapter 6 in this volume.

25 *CT* I.154.

26 *ST* III q.56 a.1. Aquinas's application of instrumental causality to Christ's sufferings and human activity distinguishes him from his contemporaries.

27 *CT* I.158.

28 *ST* III q.33 a.1.

29 *ST* III q.54 a.4.

30 *SCG* IV.89.2.

31 *SCG* IV.88.5.

32 *ST* III q.39 a.3.

33 *SCG* IV.84.1.

34 *SCG* IV.82.

35 *CT* I.155.

36 *Quodl* XI q.6 a.1.

37 *SCG* IV.85.

38 *SCG* IV.83; *CT* I.156. On the role of food, see P. L. Reynolds, *Food and the Body: Some Peculiar Questions in High Medieval Theology* (Boston, MA: Brill, 1999), pp. 391–5.

39 *SCG* IV.83.5.

40 *CT* I.156.

41 *SCG* IV.83.9–14.

42 *SCG* IV.82.6–8.

43 *SCG* IV.97; *CT* I.170–1. On the compatibility of his writings on the world's renewal, see Kromholtz, *On the Last Day*, pp. 165–237.

44 *CT* I.244.

45 *SCG* IV.87, 89.8. On the limbo of infants, see *In II Sent.*, d.33, q.2; C. Beiting, "The Idea of Limbo in Thomas Aquinas," *The Thomist* 62 (1998): 217–44.

46 *ST* I-II q.4 a.5. For his former view, see *In IV Sent.*, d.49, q.1, a.4.

47 *ST* III q.14 a.1 ad 2.

48 *ST* III q.56 a.1 ad 3.

49 *SCG* IV.86; *CT* I.168; *In I Cor* 15.

50 *SCG* IV.89; *CT* I.176.

51 *ST* III q.45 a.2.

52 *ST* I-II q.5.

53 *SCG* IV.90.

Bibliography

Acar, R. 2005. *Talking about God and Talking about Creation: Avicenna's and Thomas Aquinas' Positions.* Islamic Philosophy, Theology and Science. Texts and Studies 58 (Leiden and Boston: Brill).

Adams, M. M. 1999. *What Sort of Human Nature? Medieval Philosophy and the Systematics of Christology* (Milwaukee: Marquette University Press).

    2012. "Why Bodies as Well as Souls?" in G. T. Doolan (ed.), *The Science of Being as Being: Metaphysical Investigations* (Washington, DC: The Catholic University of America Press), pp. 264–98.

Aertsen, J. 1996. *Medieval Philosophy and the Transcendentals: The Case of Thomas Aquinas* (Leiden, New York, and Cologne: Brill).

Aldama, J. and I. Solano. 2014. *Sacrae Theologiae Summa IIIA: On the Incarnate Word, On the Blessed Virgin Mary,* K. Baker (trans.) (Saddle River, NJ: Keep The Faith).

Anderson, J. M. 2020. *Virtue and Grace in the Theology of Thomas Aquinas* (Cambridge: Cambridge University Press).

Aristotle. 1984. *The Complete Works of Aristotle,* J. Barnes (ed.) (Princeton: Princeton University Press).

Augustine. 1950. *The City of God,* M. Dods (trans.) (New York: Random House).

    1982. *The Literal Meaning of Genesis,* 2 vols., J. H. Taylor (trans. and annotation) (New York: Newman Press).

    1992. *Sermons,* vol. 4, E. Hill (trans.) (Brooklyn: New City Press).

    1994. "The Spirit and the Letter," P. Holmes and R. Wallis (trans.), in P. Schaff (ed.), *The Nicene and Post-Nicene Fathers,* vol. 5 (Peabody, MA: Hendrickson Publishers).

Avicenna. 1977. *Liber de Philosophia Prima sive Scientia Divina, I–IV,* S. Van Riet ed. (Leuven and Leiden: Peeters and Brill).

    2003. *The Metaphysics of the Healing,* M. Marmura (trans.) (Provo, UT: Brigham Young University Press).

Ayala, F. J. 2007. *Darwin's Gift to Science and Religion* (Washington, DC: Joseph Henry Press).

Bäck, A. T. 1998. "Scotus on the Consistency of the Incarnation and the Trinity," *Vivarium* **36**: 83–107.

2008. "Aquinas on the Incarnation," *The New Scholasticism* **56**: 127–45.

Barker, M. 2012. "Experience and Experimentation: The Meaning of *Experimentum* in Aquinas," *The Thomist* **76**: 37–71.

Barnes, C. L. 2012. *Christ's Two Wills in Scholastic Thought: The Christology of Aquinas and Its Historical Contexts* (Toronto: Pontifical Institute of Mediaeval Studies).

2014. "Thomas Aquinas's Chalcedonian Christology and Its Influence on Later Scholastics," *The Thomist* **78**: 189–217.

Bartel, T. W. 1991. "Like Us in All Things, Apart From Sin?," *Journal of Philosophical Research* **16**: 19–52.

Bataillon, L. J. 2014. "Introduction" in *Sancti Thomae de Aquino Opera omnia: iussu Leonis XIII P.M. edita* ("Leonine edition"), vol. 44/1 (Rome: Commissio Leonina).

Bateson, M., D. Nettle, and G. Roberts. 2006. "Cues of Being Watched Enhance Cooperation in a Real-World Setting," *Biology Letters* **2**: 412–14, https://doi.org/10.1098/rsbl.2006.0509.

Beiting, C. 1998. "The Idea of Limbo in Thomas Aquinas," *The Thomist* **62**: 217–44.

Belo, C. 2016. "Freedom and Determinism" in R. Taylor and L. X. López-Farjeat (eds.), *Routledge Companion to Islamic Philosophy* (New York: Routledge), pp. 325–36.

Bliss, R. and K. Trogdon. 2016. "Metaphysical Grounding" in E. N. Zalta (ed.), *The Stanford Encyclopedia of Philosophy* [online], https://plato.stanford.edu/archives/win2016/entries/grounding/.

Block, B. 2019. "Thomas Aquinas on How We Know Essences: The Formation and Perfection of Concepts in the Human Intellect." Dissertation, The Catholic University of America.

Boland, V. 1996. *Ideas in God according to Saint Thomas Aquinas: Sources and Synthesis* (New York: Brill).

Bouillard, H. 1944. *Conversion et grâce chez S. Thomas d'Aquin* (Paris: Éditions Aubier-Montaigne).

Boyle, L. 2002. "The Setting of the *Summa Theologiae* of St. Thomas – Revisited" in S. J. Pope (ed.), *The Ethics of Aquinas* (Washington, DC: Georgetown University Press), pp. 1–17.

Bradley, D. 1997. *Aquinas on the Twofold Human Good: Reason and Human Happiness in Aquinas's Moral Science* (Washington, DC: The Catholic University of America Press).

Breiner, N. 2018. "Punishment and Satisfaction in Aquinas's Account of the Atonement," *Faith and Philosophy* **35**: 237–56.

Brower, J. 2005. "Aquinas's Metaphysics of Modality: Reply to Leftow," *Modern Schoolman* **83**: 201–12.

2014. *Aquinas's Ontology of the Material World: Change, Hylomorphism, and Material Objects* (Oxford: Oxford University Press).

Brown, C. 2005. *Aquinas and the Ship of Theseus: Solving Puzzles about Material Objects* (London: Continuum).

Buber, M. 1923. *Ich und Du*, 1st edn. (Leipzig: Insel-Verlag).

Burnyeat, M. 2001. "Aquinas on Spiritual Change" in D. Perler (ed.), *Ancient and Medieval Theories of Intentionality* (Leiden: Brill), pp. 129–53.

Burrell, D. B. 1993. *Freedom and Creation in Three Traditions* (South Bend, IN: University of Notre Dame Press).

(ed.). 2010. *Creation and the God of Abraham* (New York: Cambridge University Press).

Bynum, C. W. 1995. *The Resurrection of the Body in Western Christianity, 200–1336* (New York: Columbia University Press).

Calo, P. 1917. "Vita S. Thomae Aquinatis, c. 7" in D. Prümmer (ed.), *Fontes Vitae S. Thomae Aquinatis* (Toulouse: Privat).

Calvin, J. 1989. *Institutes of the Christian Religion*, H. Beveridge (trans.) (Grand Rapids, MI: William B. Eerdmans).

Carl, M. 1997. "Law, Virtue, and Happiness in Aquinas's Moral Theory," *The Thomist* **61**: 425–47.

Carlson, J. W. 2012. *Words of Wisdom: A Philosophical Dictionary for the Perennial Tradition* (South Bend, IN: University of Notre Dame Press).

Chenu, M.-D. 2002. *Aquinas and His Role in Theology*, P. Philibert (trans.), (Collegeville: Liturgical Press).

Christianson, J. 1988. "Aquinas: The Necessity and Some Characteristics of the Habit of First Indemonstrable (Speculative) Principles," *New Scholasticism* **62**: 249–96.

Clayton, P. 2004. "Natural Law and Divine Action: The Search for an Expanded Theory of Causation," *Zygon* **39**: 615–36.

Cohoe, C. 2013. "There Must Be a First: Why Thomas Aquinas Rejects Infinite, Essentially Ordered, Causal Series," *British Journal for the History of Philosophy* **21**: 838–56.

Colton, R. 2006. "Two Rival Versions of Sexual Virtue: Simon Blackburn and John Paul II on Lust and Chastity," *The Thomist* **70**: 71–101.

Cory, D. 2018. "Agency and Materiality in Aquinas's Soul Theory." PhD thesis, The Catholic University of America.

Cory, T. S. 2013. "What Is an Intellectual Turn? The *Liber de Causis*, Avicenna, and Aquinas's Turn to Phantasms," *Tópicos* **45**: 129–62.

2015. "Rethinking Abstractionism: Aquinas's Intellectual Light and Some Arabic Sources," *Journal of the History of Philosophy* **53**: 607–46.

2014. *Aquinas on Human Self-Knowledge* (Cambridge: Cambridge University Press).

2016. "Attention, Intentionality, and Mind-Reading in Aquinas's *De malo* 16.8" in M. V. Dougherty (ed.), *Aquinas's Disputed Questions on Evil: A Critical Guide* (Cambridge: Cambridge University Press), pp. 164–91.

2020. "Aquinas's Intelligible Species as Formal Constituents," *Documenti e studi sulla tradizione filosofica medievale* **31**: 261–309.

Crisp, O. D. 2007. "Was Christ Sinless or Impeccable?," *Irish Theological Quarterly* **72**: 168–86.

2020. *Approaching the Atonement: The Reconciling Work of Christ* (Downers Grove, IL: IVP Academic).

Cross, R. 1989. "Nature and Personality in the Incarnation," *The Downside Review* **107**: 237–54.

1996. "Aquinas on Nature, Hypostasis, and the Metaphysics of the Incarnation," *The Thomist* **60**: 171–202.

2005. *The Metaphysics of the Incarnation: Thomas Aquinas to Duns Scotus* (Oxford: Oxford University Press).

2019. *Communicatio Idiomatum*: Reformation Christological Debates (Oxford: Oxford University Press).

Dahm, B. 2015. "The Acquired Virtues Are Real Virtues: A Response to Stump," *Faith and Philosophy* **32**: 453–70.

Davies, B. 2016. Thomas Aquinas's *Summa contra Gentiles*: A Guide and Commentary (Oxford: Oxford University Press).

De Haan, D. 2014. "Perception and the *Vis Cogitativa*: A Thomistic Analysis of Aspectual, Actional, and Affectional Percepts," *American Catholic Philosophical Quarterly* **88**: 397–437.

2019. "Approaching Other Animals with Caution: Exploring Insights from Aquinas's Psychology," *New Blackfriars* **100**: 715–37.

2019. "Aquinas on Sensing, Perceiving, Thinking, Understanding, and Cognizing Individuals" in E. Băltuţă (ed.), *Medieval Perceptual Puzzles: Theories of Sense-Perception in the 13th and 14th Centuries* (Leiden: Brill), pp. 238–68.

Descartes. 1984. *The Philosophical Writings of Descartes*, J. Cottingham, R. Stoothoff, and D. Murdoch (trans.) (Cambridge: Cambridge University Press).

Dewan, L. 1999. "St. Thomas and the Causes of Free Choice," *Acta Philosophica* **8**: 87–96.

DeYoung, R., C. McCluskey, and C. Van Dyke. 2009. *Aquinas's Ethics: Metaphysical Foundations, Moral Theory, and Theological Context* (South Bend, IN: University of Notre Dame Press).

Dodds, M. J. 2012. *Unlocking Divine Action: Contemporary Science and Thomas Aquinas* (Washington, DC: The Catholic University of America Press).

Echavarría, A. 2020. "Aquinas on Divine Impeccability, Omnipotence, and Free Will," *Religious Studies* **56**: 256–73.

Emery, G. 2007. *The Trinitarian Theology of St. Thomas Aquinas* (Oxford: Oxford University Press).

Fabro, C. 1950. *La nozione metafisica di partecipazione secondo s. Tommaso d'Aquino* (Turin: Società Editrice Internazionale).

　1961. *Participation et causalité selon s. Thomas d'Aquin* (Leuven and Paris: Publications Universitaires de Louvain and Béatrice-Nauwelaerts).

Fakhry, M. 2008 [1958]. *Islamic Occasionalism and Its Critique by Averroes and Aquinas* (Abingdon and New York: Routledge).

Farrer, A. 1967. *Faith and Speculation: An Essay in Philosophical Theology* (London: Adam and Charles Black).

Feingold, L. 2016. "God's Movement of the Soul Through Operative and Cooperative Grace" in S. A. Long, R. W. Nutt, and T. J. White (eds.), *Thomism and Predestination: Principles and Disputations* (Ave Maria, FL: Sapientia Press), pp. 166–91.

Feser, E. 2019. *Aristotle's Revenge: The Metaphysical Foundations of Physical and Biological Science* (Haverton, PA: Editiones Scholasticae).

Fisher, K. 2017. "Thomas Aquinas on Hylomorphism and the In-Act Principle," *British Journal for the History of Philosophy* **25**: 1053–72.

Fitzpatrick, A. 2017. *Thomas Aquinas on Bodily Identity* (Oxford: Oxford University Press).

Freddoso, A. 1986. "Human Nature, Potency and the Incarnation," *Faith and Philosophy* **3**: 27–53.

Frost, G. 2021. "Aquinas on Passive Powers," *Vivarium* **59**: 33–51.

　2022. *Aquinas on Efficient Causation and Causal Powers* (Cambridge: Cambridge University Press).

Furlong, P. 2015. "Aquinas, the Principle of Alternative Possibilities, and Augustine's Axiom," *International Philosophical Quarterly* **55**: 179–96.

Gaine, S. F. 2003. *Will There Be Free Will in Heaven? Freedom, Impeccability, and Beatitude* (London: T&T Clark).

2015. "Christ's Acquired Knowledge according to Thomas Aquinas: How Aquinas's Philosophy Helped and Hindered His Account," *New Blackfriars* **96**: 255–68.

2015. *Did the Saviour See the Father?* (London: T&T Clark).

2017. "The Veracity of Prophecy and Christ's Knowledge," *New Blackfriars* **98**: 44–62.

Gallagher, D. 1994. "Free Choice and Free Judgment in Thomas Aquinas," *Archiv für Geschichte der Philosophie* **76**: 247–77.

Garfinkel, A. 1993. "Reductionism" in R. Boyd, P. Gasper, and J. D. Trout (eds.), *The Philosophy of Science* (Cambridge, MA: MIT Press), pp. 443–59.

Garrigou-Lagrange, R. 1946. *La synthèse thomiste.* Bibliothèque Française de Philosophie (Paris: Desclée de Brouwer).

Geiger, L.-B. 1942. *La participation dans la philosophie de S. Thomas d'Aquin* (Paris: Librairie Philosophique J. Vrin).

Gilson, É. 1952. *Being and Some Philosophers* (Toronto: Pontifical Institute of Mediaeval Studies).

1994. *L'être et l'essence* (Paris: Librairie Philosophique J. Vrin).

Gondreau, P. 2009. "St. Thomas Aquinas, the Communication of Idioms, and the Suffering of Christ in the Garden of Gethsemane" in J. F. Keating and T. J. White O. P. (eds.), *Divine Impassibility and the Mystery of Human Suffering* (Grand Rapids, MI: William B. Eerdmans), pp. 214–45.

2018. *The Passions of Christ's Soul in the Theology of St. Thomas Aquinas* (Providence, RI: Cluny Media).

Gorman, M. 2000. "Uses of the Person–Nature Distinction in Thomas's Christology," *Recherches de Théologie et Philosophie médiévales* **67**: 58–79.

2014. "Christological Consistency and the Reduplicative Qua," *Journal of Analytic Theology* **2**: 86–100.

2016. "Classical Theism, Classical Anthropology, and the Christological Coherence Problem," *Faith and Philosophy* **33**: 278–92.

2017. *Aquinas on the Metaphysics of the Hypostatic Union* (Cambridge: Cambridge University Press).

Gould, S. J. 1997. "Nonoverlapping Magisteria," *Natural History* **106**: 16–22.

Grant, W. M. 2001. "Aquinas among Libertarians and Compatibilists: Breaking the Logic of Theological Determinism," *Proceedings of the American Catholic Philosophical Association* **75**: 221–35.

Grimm, S. 2021. "Understanding" in E. N. Zalta (ed.), *The Stanford Encyclopedia of Philosophy* [online], https://plato.stanford.edu/archives/sum2021/entries/understanding/.

Gui, B. 1959. "Vita S. Thomae Aquinatis, c. 6" in K. Foster (ed.), *The Life of St. Thomas Aquinas: Biographical Documents* (Baltimore, MD: Helicon Press).

Hasker, W. 2017. "A Compositional Incarnation," *Religious Studies* **53**: 433–47.

Hause, J. 1997. "Thomas Aquinas and the Voluntarists," *Medieval Philosophy and Theology* **6**: 167–82.

Hause, J. 2007. "Aquinas on the Function of Moral Virtue," *American Catholic Philosophical Quarterly* **81**: 1–20.

Hauser, C. n.d. "Aquinas on Persons, Psychological Subjects, and the Coherence of the Incarnation" [manuscript].

Hauser, C. 2020. "On Being Human and Divine: The Coherence of the Incarnation," *Faith and Philosophy* **37**: 3–31.

Hibbs, T. 1988. "Against a Cartesian Reading of Intellectus in Aquinas," *The Modern Schoolman* **66**: 55–69.

Hight, M. A. 2010. "The Son More Visible: Immaterialism and the Incarnation," *Modern Theology* **26**: 120–48.

Hill, J. 2012. "Aquinas and the Unity of Christ: A Defence of Compositionalism," *International Journal for Philosophy of Religion* **71**: 117–35.

Hobson, P. 2005. "What Puts Jointness into Joint Attention?" in N. Eilan, C. Hoerl, T. McCormack, and J. Roessler (eds.), *Joint Attention: Communication and Other Minds: Issues in Philosophy and Psychology* (Oxford: Oxford University Press), pp. 185–204.

Hofer, A. 2009. "Balthasar's Eschatology on the Intermediate State: The Question of Knowability," *Logos: A Journal of Catholic Thought and Culture* **12**: 148–72.

Hoffman, P. 1990. "St. Thomas Aquinas on the Halfway State of Sensible Being," *Philosophical Review* **99**: 73–92.

Hoffman, P. 2005. "Aquinas on Threats and Temptations," *Pacific Philosophical Quarterly* **86**: 225–42.

Hoffmann, T. 2021. *Free Will and the Rebel Angels in Medieval Philosophy* (Cambridge: Cambridge University Press).

Hoffmann, T. and P. Furlong. 2016. "Free Choice" in M. V. Dougherty (ed.), *Aquinas's Disputed Questions on Evil: A Critical Guide* (Cambridge: Cambridge University Press), pp. 56–74.

Hoffmann, T. and C. Michon. 2017. "Aquinas on Free Will and Intellectual Determinism," *Philosophers' Imprint* **17**: 1–36.

International Theological Commission. 2004. *Communion and Stewardship*, https://www.vatican.va/roman_curia/congregations/cfaith/cti_documents/rc_con_cfaith_doc_20040723_communion-stewardship_en.html.

Jenkins, J. 1997. *Knowledge and Faith in Thomas Aquinas* (Cambridge: Cambridge University Press).

Jensen, S. 2017. "Libertarian Free Choice: A Thomistic Account," *The Thomist* **81**: 315–43.

Johnson, J. 2021. "Final Causality, Cognition, and Self-Motion in Aquinas's Natural Philosophy" [manuscript].

Johnson, J. 2021. "Nature Does Nothing in Vain: Reexamining Aquinas's Fifth Way" [manuscript].

Kerr, G. 2012. "Ontological Commitment and Thomistic Realism" in J. McEvoy, M. Dunne, and J. Hynes (eds.), *Thomas Aquinas: Teaching and Scholar* (Dublin: Four Courts Press), pp. 211–29.

Kerr, G. 2012. "A Thomistic Metaphysics of Creation," *Religious Studies* **48**: 337–56.

Kerr, G. 2015. Aquinas's Way to God: The Proof in *De Ente et Essentia* (New York: Oxford University Press).

Kerr, G. 2019. *Aquinas and the Metaphysics of Creation* (New York: Oxford University Press).

Kitcher, P. 1984. "1953 and All That: A Tale of Two Sciences," *The Philosophical Review* **93**: 335–73.

Klima, G. 1984. "Libellus Pro Sapiente," *New Scholasticism* **58**: 207–19.

Klubertanz, G. 1952. The Discursive Power: Sources and Doctrine of the *Vis Cogitativa* according to St. Thomas Aquinas (Saint Louis: The Modern Schoolman).

Klubertanz, G. P. 1952. "St. Thomas and the Knowledge of the Singular," *New Scholasticism* **26**: 135–66.

Knobel, A. M. 2021. *Aquinas and the Infused Moral Virtues* (South Bend, IN: University of Notre Dame Press).

Knuuttila, S. 2019. *Modalities in Medieval Philosophy* (New York: Routledge).

Krause, K. 2020. *Thomas Aquinas on Seeing God: The Beatific Vision in His Commentary on Peter Lombard's Sentences IV.49.2* (Milwaukee: Marquette University Press).

Kretzmann, N. 1993. "Philosophy of Mind" in N. Kretzmann and E. Stump (eds.), *The Cambridge Companion to Aquinas* (Cambridge and New York: Cambridge University Press), pp. 128–59.

Kretzmann, N. 1997. The Metaphysics of Theism: Aquinas's Natural Theology in *Summa Contra Gentiles I* (Oxford: Clarendon Press).

Kretzmann, N. 1998. The Metaphysics of Creation: Aquinas's Natural Theology in *Summa Contra Gentiles II* (Oxford: Clarendon Press).

Kroll, N. 2017. "Teleological Dispositions," *Oxford Studies in Metaphysics* **10**: 3–37.

Kromholtz, B. 2010. *On the Last Day: The Time of the Resurrection of the Dead according to Thomas Aquinas* (Fribourg: Academic Press Fribourg).

Kvanvig, J. L. and H. J. McCann. 1988. "Divine Conservation and the Persistence of the World" in T. V. Morris (ed.), *Divine and Human Action* (Ithaca, NY: Cornell University Press), pp. 13–49.

Lamb, M. L. 2004. "The Eschatology of St. Thomas Aquinas" in T. G. Weinandy, D. A. Keating, and J. P. Yocum (eds.), *Aquinas on Doctrine: A Critical Introduction* (New York: T&T Clark), pp. 225–40.

Langley, S. 2001. "Aquinas, Resurrection, and Material Continuity," *Proceedings of the American Catholic Philosophical Association* **75**: 135–47.

Leftow, B. 2011. "Composition and Christology," *Faith and Philosophy* **28**: 310–22.

Leget, C. 2005. "Eschatology" in R. van Nieuwenhove and J. Wawrykow (eds.), *The Theology of Thomas Aquinas* (South Bend, IN: University of Notre Dame Press), pp. 386–406.

Levering, M. W. 2017. *Engaging the Doctrine of Creation: Cosmos, Creatures, and the Wise and Good Creator* (Grand Rapids, MI: Baker Academic).

Lisska, A. 2016. *Aquinas's Theory of Perception: An Analytic Reconstruction* (Oxford: Oxford University Press).

Lonergan, B. J. F. 2000. *Grace and Freedom: Operative Grace in the Thought of St. Thomas Aquinas. Collected Works of Bernard Lonergan*, vol. 1 (Toronto: University of Toronto Press).

Long, S. A., R. W. Nutt, and T. J. White (eds.). 2016. *Thomism and Predestination: Principles and Disputations* (Ave Maria, FL: Sapientia Press).

López-Farjeat, L. X. 2012. "Avicenna's Influence on Aquinas' Early Doctrine of Creation in 'In Sent.', D. 1, Q. 1, A. 2," *Recherches de Théologie et Philosophie médiévales* **79**: 307–37.

Loughran, S. 1999. "Aquinas, Compatibilist" in F. W. McLain and W. M. Richardson (eds.), *Human and Divine Agency: Anglican, Catholic, and Lutheran Perspectives* (Lanham, MD: University Press of America), pp. 1–39.

Löwe, C. L. 2021. *Thomas Aquinas on the Metaphysics of the Human Act* (Cambridge: Cambridge University Press).

MacDonald, S. 1991. "Ultimate Ends in Practical Reasoning: Aquinas's Aristotelian Moral Psychology and Anscombe's Fallacy," *Philosophical Review* **100**: 31–66.

1993. "Theory of Knowledge" in N. Kretzmann and E. Stump (eds.), *The Cambridge Companion to Aquinas* (Cambridge and New York: Cambridge University Press), pp. 160–95.

1998. "Aquinas's Libertarian Account of Free Choice," *Revue Internationale de Philosophie* **52**: 309–28.

MacIntyre, A. 2007. *After Virtue: A Study in Moral Theory*, 3rd edn. (South Bend, IN: University of Notre Dame Press).

Matava, F. J. 2016. *Divine Causality and Human Free Choice: Domingo Báñez, Physical Premotion and the Controversy de Auxiliis Revisited* (Leiden: Brill).

McCluskey, C. 2002. "Intellective Appetite and the Freedom of Human Action," *The Thomist* **66**: 421–56.

2013. "Thomism" in R. Crisp (ed.), *Oxford Handbook of the History of Ethics* (Oxford: Oxford University Press), pp. 147–66.

2017. *Thomas Aquinas on Moral Wrongdoing* (Cambridge: Cambridge University Press).

McFadden, R. D. and A. Macropoulos. 2008. "Wal-Mart Employee Trampled to Death," *New York Times*, November 28, 2008, http://www.nytimes.com/2008/11/29/business/29walmart.html [accessed February 9, 2012].

McGilchrist, I. 2009. *The Master and His Emissary: The Divided Brain and the Making of the Western World* (New Haven, CT and London: Yale University Press).

McKinley, J. E. 2009. *Tempted for Us: Theological Models and the Practical Relevance of Christ's Impeccability and Temptation* (Eugene, OR: Paternoster).

2011. "Four Patristic Models of Jesus Christ's Impeccability and Temptation," *Perichoresis* **9**: 29–66.

Miner, R. 2009. *Thomas Aquinas on the Passions* (Cambridge: Cambridge University Press).

2011. Thomas Aquinas on the Passions: A Study of *Summa Theologiae*, Ia2ae 22–48 (Cambridge: Cambridge University Press).

Moloney, R. 1998. "Approaches to Christ's Knowledge in the Patristic Era" in T. Finan and V. Twomey (eds.), *Studies in Patristic Christology* (Portland, OR: Four Courts Press), pp. 37–66.

2000. *Knowledge of Christ* (New York: Bloomsbury Academic).

Morard, M. 2005. "Thomas d'Aquin lecteur des Conciles," *Archivum Franciscanum Historicum* **98**: 211–365.

Murray, J. C. 1963. *The Infused Knowledge of Christ in the Theology of the 12th and 13th Centuries* (Windsor, ON: Privately printed PhD thesis).

Nevitt, T. C. 2016. "Aquinas on the Death of Christ," *American Catholic Philosophical Quarterly* **90**: 77–99.

Noone, T. and R. E. Hauser. 2020. "Saint Bonaventure" in E. N. Zalta (ed.), *The Stanford Encyclopedia of Philosophy* [online], https://plato.stanford.edu/archives/win2020/entries/bonaventure/.

Norris Clarke, W. 1994. "Action as the Self-Revelation of Being: A Central Theme in the Thought of St. Thomas" in *Explorations in Metaphysics: Being – God – Person* (South Bend, IN: University of Notre Dame Press), pp. 45–65.

1994. "The Limitation of Act by Potency in St. Thomas: Aristotelianism or Neoplatonism?" in *Explorations in Metaphysics: Being – God – Person* (South Bend, IN: University of Notre Dame Press), pp. 89–101.

2001. *The One and the Many: A Contemporary Metaphysics* (South Bend, IN: University of Notre Dame Press).

O'Callaghan, J. 2003. *Thomist Realism and the Linguistic Turn* (South Bend, IN: University of Notre Dame Press).

Oelze, A. 2018. *Animal Rationality: Later Medieval Theories 1250–1350* (Leiden: Brill).

Oliva, A. 2006. *Les débuts de l'enseignement de Thomas d'Aquin et sa conception de la* Sacra Doctrina *avec l'édition du prologue de son Commentaire des Sentences* (Paris: Librairie Philosophique J. Vrin).

Olson, C. E. and D. Meconi. 2016. *Called To Be the Children of God: The Catholic Theology of Human Deification*, annotated edn. (San Francisco: Ignatius Press).

O'Neill, T. P. 2019. *Grace, Predestination, and the Permission of Sin: A Thomistic Analysis* (Washington, DC: The Catholic University of America Press).

O'Rourke, F. 2019. *Ciphers of Transcendence: Essays in Philosophy of Religion in Honour of Patrick Masterson* (Newbridge: Irish Academic Press).

Ortiz, J. 2019. *Deification in the Latin Patristic Tradition* (Washington, DC: The Catholic University of America Press).

Owens, J. 1970. "Judgment and Truth in Aquinas," *Mediaeval Studies* **32**: 138–58.

1985. *An Interpretation of Existence* (Houston, TX: Center for Thomistic Studies, University of St. Thomas).

Paluch, M. 2004. *La profondeur de l'amour divin: La prédestination dans l'œuvre de saint Thomas d'Aquin* (Paris: Librairie Philosophique J. Vrin).

Pannenberg, W. 1968. *Jesus, God and Man* (Philadelphia: Westminster Press).

Pasnau, R. 2002. *Thomas Aquinas on Human Nature* (Cambridge: Cambridge University Press).

Pasnau, R. and C. Shields. 2004. *The Philosophy of Aquinas* (Boulder, CO: Westview Press).

Pawl, T. 2014. "A Solution to the Fundamental Philosophical Problem of Christology," *Journal of Analytic Theology* **2**: 61–85.

2014. "The Freedom of Christ and Explanatory Priority," *Religious Studies* **50**: 157–73.

2014. "The Freedom of Christ and the Problem of Deliberation," *International Journal for Philosophy of Religion* **75**: 233–47.

2015. "Conciliar Christology and the Problem of Incompatible Predications," *Scientia et Fides* **3**: 85–106.

2016. "Temporary Intrinsics and Christological Predication" in J. Kvanvig (ed.), *Oxford Studies in Philosophy of Religion: Volume 7* (Oxford: Oxford University Press), pp. 157–89.

2016. *In Defense of Conciliar Christology: A Philosophical Essay* (Oxford: Oxford University Press).

2016. "Thomistic Multiple Incarnations," *Heythrop Journal* **57**: 359–70.

2018. "Conciliar Christology and the Consistency of Divine Immutability with a Mutable, Incarnate God," *Nova et Vetera* **16**: 913–37.

2019. *In Defense of Extended Conciliar Christology: A Philosophical Essay* (Oxford: Oxford University Press).

2019. "The Metaphysics of the Incarnation: Christ's Human Nature" in T. Marschler and T. Schärtl (eds.), *Herausforderungen und Modifikationen des klassischen Theismus. Volume 1: Die Trinität* (Münster: Aschendorff), pp. 131–48.

2020. *The Incarnation* (Cambridge: Cambridge University Press).

Peifer, J. F. 1952. *The Concept in Thomism* (New York: Bookman Associates).

Pelser, A. 2019. "Temptation, Virtue, and the Character of Christ," *Faith and Philosophy* **36**: 81–101.

Pinckaers, S. 2001. *Morality: The Catholic View*, M. Sherwin (trans.) (South Bend, IN: St. Augustine's Press).

Pinsent, A. 2012. *The Second-Person Perspective in Aquinas's Ethics: Virtues and Gifts* (New York and Abingdon: Routledge).

2014. "Avarice and Liberality" in K. Timpe and C. A. Boyd (eds.), *Virtues and Their Vices* (Oxford and New York: Oxford University Press), pp. 157–76.

2014. "Neurotheological Eudaimonia" in N. Levy and J. Clausen (eds.), *Handbook of Neuroethics* (Dordrecht: Springer).

2017. "Who's Afraid of the Infused Virtues? Dispositional Infusion, Human and Divine" in H. Goris and H. Schoot (eds.), *The Virtuous Life: Thomas Aquinas on the Theological Nature of Moral Virtues* (Leuven, Paris, and Bristol, CT: Peeters), pp. 73–96.

2020. "Temperance and the Second-Person Perspective," *European Journal for Philosophy of Religion* **12**: 101–15.

Plotinus. 1991. *The Enneads*, S. McKenna (trans.) (London: Penguin).

Pohle, J. 1911. *The Divine Trinity: A Dogmatic Treatise* (St. Louis, MO: B. Herder Book Co.).

1913. *Christology: A Dogmatic Treatise on the Incarnation* (St. Louis, MO: B. Herder Book Co.).

Polkinghorne, J. 1989. *Science and Providence: God's Interaction with the World* (Boston, MA: New Science Library).

1996. "Chaos Theory and Divine Action" in W. M. Richardson and W. J. Wildman (eds.), *Religion and Science: History, Method and Dialogue* (New York: Routledge), pp. 243–52.

Porro, P. 2016. *Thomas Aquinas: A Historical and Philosophical Profile*, J. G. Trabbic and R. W. Nutt (trans.) (Washington, DC: The Catholic University of America Press).

Porter, J. 1992. "The Subversion of Virtue: Acquired and Infused Virtues in the 'Summa Theologiae,'" *Annual of the Society of Christian Ethics* **12**: 19–41.

2019. "Moral Virtues, Charity, and Grace: Why the Infused and Acquired Virtues Cannot Co-Exist," *Journal of Moral Theology* **8**: 40–66.

Prudlo, D. S. 2020. *Thomas Aquinas: A Historical, Theological, and Environmental Portrait* (Mahway, NJ: Paulist Press).

Pseudo-Dionysius. 1987. *The Complete Works*, K. Froehlich (trans.) (Mahway, NJ: Paulist Press).

1987. "The Divine Names," C. Luibheid (trans.), in *The Complete Works*, K. Froehlich (trans.) (Mahway, NJ: Paulist Press).

Quinn, P. L. 1989. "Aquinas on Atonement" in R. J. Feenstra (ed.), *Trinity, Incarnation, and Atonement* (South Bend, IN: University of Notre Dame Press), pp. 153–77.

Reichberg, G. 2002. "The Intellectual Virtues" in S. Pope (ed.), *The Ethics of Aquinas* (Washington, DC: Georgetown University Press).

Reynolds, P. L. 1999. *Food and the Body: Some Peculiar Questions in High Medieval Theology* (Boston, MA: Brill).

Richardson, K. 2020. "Causation in Arabic and Islamic Thought" in E. N. Zalta (ed.), *The Stanford Encyclopedia of Philosophy* [online] https://plato.stanford.edu/archives/win2020/entries/arabic-islamic-causation/.

Rigby, P. 2015. *The Theology of Augustine's Confessions* (Cambridge: Cambridge University Press).

Rota, M. 2004. "Substance and Artifact in Thomas Aquinas," *History of Philosophy Quarterly* **21**: 241–59.

2012. "Causation" in B. Davies and E. Stump (eds.), *The Oxford Handbook to Aquinas* (Oxford: Oxford University Press), pp. 104–14.

Sammon, B. T. 2014. *The God Who Is Beauty: Beauty as a Divine Name in Thomas Aquinas and Dionysius the Areopagite* (Cambridge: James Clarke & Co.).

Schmidt, R. W. 1966. *The Domain of Logic according to St. Thomas Aquinas* (The Hague: Martinus Nijhoff).

Schrader, D. 2021. "Christ's Fear of the Lord according to Thomas Aquinas," *Heythrop Journal* **62**: 1052–64.

Senor, T. D. 2007. "The Compositional Account of the Incarnation," *Faith and Philosophy* **24**: 52–71.

Shanley, B. J. 1998. "Divine Causation and Human Freedom in Aquinas," *American Catholic Philosophical Quarterly* **72**: 99–122.

1998. "Aquinas on God's Causal Knowledge: A Reply to Stump and Kretzmann," *American Catholic Philosophical Quarterly* **72**: 447–57.

2008. "Beyond Libertarianism and Compatibilism: Thomas Aquinas on Created Freedom" in R. Velkley (ed.), *Freedom and the Human Person* (Washington, DC: The Catholic University of America Press), pp. 70–89.

Sherwin, M. S. 2005. *By Knowledge and by Love: Charity and Knowledge in the Moral Theology of St. Thomas Aquinas* (Washington, DC: The Catholic University of America Press).

Silva, I. 2013. "Thomas Aquinas Holds Fast: Objections to Aquinas within Today's Debate on Divine Action," *Heythrop Journal* **48**: 658–67.

Silva, J. F. 2014. "Medieval Theories of Active Perception: An Overview" in J. F. Silva and M. Yrjönsuuri (eds.), *Active Perception in the History of Philosophy* (Cham: Springer), pp. 117–46.

Smiley, M. 2020. "Collective Responsibility" in E. N. Zalta (ed.), *The Stanford Encyclopedia of Philosophy* [online], https://plato.stanford.edu/entries/collective-responsibility/.

Spiering, J. A. 2015. "'What Is Freedom?': An Instance of the Silence of St. Thomas," *American Catholic Philosophical Quarterly* **89**: 27–46.

Stenberg, J. 2016. "'*Considerandum est quid sit beatitudo*': Aquinas on What Happiness Really is," *Res Philosophica* **93**: 161–84.

Stevenson, A. 2021. "The Unity of Christ and the Historical Jesus: Aquinas and Locke on Personal Identity," *Modern Theology* **37**: 851–64.

Stump, E. 1988. "Atonement according to Aquinas" in T. Morris (ed.), *Philosophy and the Christian Faith* (South Bend, IN: University of Notre Dame Press), pp. 61–91.

1993. "Biblical Commentary and Philosophy" in N. Kretzmann and E. Stump (eds.), *The Cambridge Companion to Aquinas* (Cambridge: Cambridge University Press), pp. 252–68.

1995. "Non-Cartesian Substance Dualism and Materialism without Reductionism," *Faith and Philosophy* **12**: 505–31.

2003. *Aquinas* (New York and London: Routledge).

2004. "Aquinas's Metaphysics of the Incarnation" in S. T. Davis, D. Kendall, and G. O'Collins (eds.), *The Incarnation* (Oxford: Oxford University Press), pp. 197–218.

2006. "Resurrection, Reassembly, and Reconstitution: Aquinas on the Soul" in B. Niederbacher and E. Runggaldier (eds.), *Die menschliche Seele: Brauchen wir den Dualismus?* (Frankfurt: Ontos Verlag), pp. 151–71.

2007. "Justifying Faith, Free Will, and the Atonement" in R. Velkley (ed.), *Freedom and the Human Person* (Washington, DC: The Catholic University of America Press), pp. 90–105.

2011. "The Non-Aristotelian Character of Aquinas's Ethics: Aquinas on the Passions," *Faith and Philosophy* **28**: 29–43.

2013. "Emergence, Causal Powers, and Aristotelianism in Metaphysics" in R. Groff and J. Greco (eds.), *Powers and Capacities in Philosophy: The New Aristotelianism* (New York and Oxford: Routledge), pp. 48–68.

2016. *The God of the Bible and the God of the Philosophers: Aquinas Lecture* (Milwaukee: Marquette University Press).

2018. *Atonement* (Oxford: Oxford University Press).

2019. "Aquinas's Ethics: The Infused Virtues and the Indwelling of the Holy Spirit," *Ephemerides Theologicae Lovanienses* **95**: 269–81.

Stump, E. and N. Kretzmann. 1998. "Eternity and God's Knowledge: A Reply to Shanley," *American Catholic Philosophical Quarterly* **72**: 439–45.

ten Klooster, A. 2018. *Thomas Aquinas on the Beatitudes: Reading Matthew, Disputing Grace and Virtue, Preaching Happiness* (Leuven, Paris, and Bristol, CT: Peeters).

2019. "Aquinas on the Fruits of the Holy Spirit as the Delight of the Christian Life," *Journal of Moral Theology* **8**: 80–94.

Thomas Aquinas. 1911. The *"Summa Theologica"* of St. Thomas Aquinas, Literally Translated by the Fathers of the English Dominican Province (London: Burns, Oates and Washbourne).

1982. *Quaestiones disputatae De malo* (Rome: Commissio Leonina; Paris: Librairie Philosophique J. Vrin).

1965. *Quaestiones disputatae. Volume 2: Quaestiones disputatae de potentia.* P. M. Pession (ed.), 10th edn. (Turin and Rome: Marietti), pp. 1–276.

1970–76. *Quaestiones disputatae De veritate* (Rome: Editori di san Tommaso).

1929–47. *Scriptum super libros Sententiarum* (Paris: Lethielleux).

1971. *In duodecim libros Metaphysicorum Aristotelis expositio.* M. R. Cathala and R. M. Spiazzi (eds.), 2nd edn. (Turin and Rome: Marietti).

1979. *Opera omnia iussu Leonis XIII P. M. edita. Volume 42: Compendium theologiae seu Brevis compilatio theologiae ad fratrem Raynaldum* (Roma: Editori di San Tommaso), pp. 5–205.

1889–1906. *Opera omnia iussu impensaque Leonis XIII P. M. edita. Summae theologiae. Volumes 4–5: Pars prima; volume 6–7: Prima secundae; volumes 8–10: Secunda secundae; volumes 11–12: Tertia pars* (Rome: Ex Typographia Polyglotta S. C. de Propaganda Fide).

1953. *Super Epistolas S. Pauli lectura. Volume 1: Super Epistolam ad Romanos lectura.* R. Cai (ed.), 8th edn. (Turin and Rome: Marietti), pp. 1–230.

1953. *Super Epistolas S. Pauli lectura. Volume 1: Super secundam Epistolam ad Corinthios lectura.* R. Cai (ed.), 8th edn. (Turin and Rome: Marietti), pp. 437–561.

1953. *Super Epistolas S. Pauli lectura. Volume 2: Super Epistolam ad Ephesios lectura.* R. Cai (ed.), 8th edn. (Turin and Rome: Marietti), pp. 1–87.

1953. *Super Epistolas S. Pauli lectura. Volume 2: Super primam Epistolam ad Timotheum lectura.* R. Cai (ed.), 8th edn. (Turin and Rome: Marietti), pp. 211–264.

1965. *Quaestiones disputatae. Volume 2: Quaestio disputata de caritate.* E. Odetto (ed.), 10th edn. (Turin and Rome: Marietti, 1965), pp. 753–790.

1972. *Super Evangelium S. Ioannis lectura.* R. Cai (ed.), 6th edn. (Turin and Rome: Marietti).

1996. *Opera omnia iussu Leonis XIII P. M. edita. Volume 25/1: Quaestiones de quolibet.Préface. Quodlibet VII, VIII, IX, X, XI; volume 25/2: Quaestiones de quolibet. Quodlibet I, II, III, VI, IV, V, XII.* (Rome: Commissio Leonina; Paris: Les Éditions du Cerf).

1947. *Summa theologica,* Fathers of the English Dominican Province (trans.) (New York: Benzinger Brothers).

1948. *Compendium of Theology*, C. Vollert (trans.) (St. Louis: B. Herder Book Co.).

1950. *In librum Beati Dionysii De divinis nominibus Expositio* (Turin: Marietti).

1954. *The Disputed Questions on Truth (in Three Volumes)*, R. Schmidt (trans.) (Chicago: Henry Regnery Co.).

1956. *Summa contra Gentiles*, vol. II, J. Anderson (trans.) (Garden City, NJ: Doubleday).

1961. *Summa contra Gentiles* (Turin: Marietti).

1962. *Tractatus de substantis separatis* (West Hartford, CT: St. Joseph College).

1976. *De ente et essentia* (Rome: Editori di San Tommaso).

1981. *The* Summa theologica *of St. Thomas Aquinas*, Fathers of the English Dominican Province (trans.) (South Bend, IN: Christian Classics).

1989. *Summa contra Gentiles. Book Four: Salvation* (South Bend, IN: University of Notre Dame Press).

1992. *Super Boethium De trinitate et expositio libri Boethii De ebdomadibus* (Rome: Commissio Leonina).

1998. "On Being and Essence" in R. McInerny (trans.), *Thomas Aquinas Selected Writings* (London and New York: Penguin).

2005. *Disputed Questions on the Virtues*, E. M. Atkins and T. Williams (eds. and trans.) (Cambridge: Cambridge University Press).

2011. "On Creation: *Quaestiones disputatae De potentia Dei*, Q.3" in S. Selner-Wright (trans.), *Thomas Aquinas in Translation* (Washington, DC: The Catholic University of America Press).

2012. *Commentary on the Letter of Saint Paul to the Romans*, F. R. Larcher, J. Mortensen, and E. Alarcón (trans.) (Lander, WY: Aquinas Institute for the Study of Sacred Doctrine).

2012. *The Power of God*, R. J. Regan (trans.) (Oxford: Oxford University Press).

Tocco, W. 1996. *Ystoria Sancti Thome de Aquino* (critical edition prepared by C. le Brun-Gouanvic, *Ystoria Sancti Thome de Aquino de Guillaume de Tocco (1323)*) (Toronto: Pontifical Institute of Mediaeval Studies).

Tolomeo of Lucca. 1968. "*Historia Ecclesiastica Nova* 22.24," in A. Ferrua (ed.), *S. Thomae Aquinatis Vitae Fontes Precipuae* (Alba: Edizioni Domenicanae).

Toner, P. 2009. "Personhood and Death in St. Thomas Aquinas," *History of Philosophy Quarterly* **26**: 121–38.

Torrell, J.-P. 2003. *Saint Thomas Aquinas. Volume 1: The Person and His Work*, R. Royal (trans.) (Washington, DC: The Catholic University of America Press).

2003. *Saint Thomas Aquinas. Volume 2: Spiritual Master*, R. Royal (trans.) (Washington, DC: The Catholic University of America Press).

2015. *Initiation à saint Thomas d'Aquin: Sa personne et son œuvre*, new edn. (Paris: Les Éditions du Cerf).

2017. *Saint Thomas d'Aquin, maître spirituel*, 3rd edn. (Paris: Les Éditions du Cerf).

Tugwell, S. 1988. *Albert and Thomas: Selected Writings* (New York: Paulist Press).

Tuttle, J. 2016. "Suárez's Non-Reductive Theory of Efficient Causation," *Oxford Studies in Medieval Philosophy* **4**: 125–58.

Tyra, S. W. 2014. "When Considering Creation, Simply Follow the Rule (of Faith): Patristic Exegesis of Romans 8:9–12 and the Theological Interpretation of Scripture," *Journal of Theological Interpretation* **8**: 251–73.

Ugobi-Onyemere, M. 2015. *Knowledge of the First Principles in Saint Thomas Aquinas* (Oxford: Peter Lang).

Valuet, B. 2018. *Dieu joueur d'échecs? Prédestination, grâce et libre arbitre. Volume 2: Relecture de saint Thomas d'Aquin* (Le Barroux: Éditions Sainte-Madeleine).

2019. "Prédestination, grâce et libre arbitre, tentative de synthèse personnelle," *Revue thomiste* **119**: 67–90.

Van Dyke, C. 2014. "Aquinas's Shiny Happy People: Perfect Happiness and the Limits of Human Nature," *Oxford Studies in the Philosophy of Religion* **6**: 269–91.

Van Inwagen, P. 1994. "Composition as Identity" in J. Tomberlin (ed.), *Philosophical Perspectives 8* (Altascadero, CA: Ridgeview Publishing Co.), pp. 207–19.

1998. "Resurrection" in E. Craig (ed.), *Routledge Encyclopedia of Philosophy 8* (London: Routledge).

Van Nieuwenhove, R. 2012. "The Saving Work of Christ" in B. Davies and E. Stump (eds.), *The Oxford Handbook of Aquinas* (Oxford: Oxford University Press), pp. 436–47.

Visser, S. and T. Williams. 2009. *Anselm. Great Medieval Thinkers* (Oxford: Oxford University Press).

Wallace, W. A. 1974. "Aquinas on Creation: Science, Theology, and Matters of Fact," *The Thomist* **38**: 485–523.

Wawrykow, J. P. 1995. *God's Grace and Human Action: "Merit" in the Theology of Thomas Aquinas* (South Bend, IN: University of Notre Dame Press).

Wawrykow, J. 2015. "The Christology of Thomas Aquinas in Its Scholastic Context" in F. Murphy and T. Stefano (eds.), *The Oxford Handbook of Christology* (Oxford: Oxford University Press), pp. 233–49.

2018. "Aquinas and Bonaventure on Creation" in G. Anderson and M. Bockmuehl (eds.), *Creation ex nihilo: Origins, Development, Contemporary Challenges* (South Bend, IN: University of Notre Dame Press), pp. 173–94.

Weinandy, T. 2004. "Jesus' Filial Vision of the Father," *Pro Ecclesia* **13**: 189–201.

2014. *Jesus: Essays in Christology* (Ave Maria, FL: Sapientia Press).

Weisheipl, J. A. 1974. *Friar Thomas d'Aquino: His Life, Thought, and Work* (New York: Doubleday).

Werther, D. 1993. "The Temptation of God Incarnate," *Religious Studies* **29**: 47–50.

2012. "Freedom, Temptation, and Incarnation" in D. Werther and M. Linville (eds.), *Philosophy and the Christian Worldview: Analysis, Assessment and Development* (New York: Continuum), pp. 252–65.

Westberg, D. 1994. *Right Practical Reason: Aristotle, Action, and Prudence in Aquinas* (New York: Oxford University Press).

1994. "Did Aquinas Change His Mind about the Will?," *The Thomist* **58**: 41–60.

White, T. J. 2005. "The Voluntary Action of the Earthly Christ and the Necessity of the Beatific Vision," *The Thomist* **69**: 497–534.

2009. *Wisdom in the Face of Modernity* (Washington, DC: The Catholic University of America Press).

2016. "Divine Simplicity and the Holy Trinity," *International Journal of Systematic Theology* **18**: 66–93.

2016. "Nicene Orthodoxy and Trinitarian Simplicity," *American Catholic Philosophical Quarterly* **90**: 727–50.

2016. *The Incarnate Lord: A Thomistic Study in Christology* (Washington, DC: The Catholic University of America Press).

Williams, T. 2012. "Human Freedom and Agency" in B. Davies and E. Stump (eds.), *The Oxford Handbook of Aquinas* (Oxford: Oxford University Press), pp. 199–208.

2021. "Atonement" in R. Cross and J. T. Paasch (eds.), *The Routledge Companion to Medieval Philosophy* (New York: Routledge).

Wippel, J. F. 1977. "The Condemnations of 1270 and 1277 at Paris," *Journal of Medieval and Renaissance Studies* **7**: 169–201.

1989. "Truth in Thomas Aquinas: Part 1," *Review of Metaphysics* **43**: 295–326.

1990. "Truth in Thomas Aquinas: Part 2," *Review of Metaphysics* **43**: 543–67.

1995. "Thomas Aquinas and the Condemnation of 1277," *The Modern Schoolman* **72**: 233–72.

1995. "Divine Knowledge, Divine Power, and Human Freedom in Thomas Aquinas and Henry of Ghent" in *Metaphysical Themes in Thomas Aquinas* (Washington, DC: The Catholic University of America Press), pp. 213–41.

2000. *The Metaphysical Thought of Thomas Aquinas: From Finite Being to Uncreated Being* (Washington, DC: The Catholic University of America Press).

2003. "Norman Kretzmann on Aquinas's Attribution of Will and Freedom to Create to God," *Religious Studies* **39**: 287–98.

2007. "Truth in Thomas Aquinas" in *Metaphysical Themes in Thomas Aquinas II* (Washington, DC: The Catholic University of America Press), pp. 65–113.

2007. "Thomas Aquinas and the Axiom 'What Is Received Is Received according to the Mode of the Receiver'" in *Metaphysical Themes in Thomas Aquinas II* (Washington, DC: The Catholic University of America Press), pp. 113–23.

2007. "Thomas Aquinas and the Axiom that Unreceived Act Is Unlimited" in *Metaphysical Themes in Thomas Aquinas II* (Washington, DC: The Catholic University of America Press), pp. 123–52.

2007. "Thomas Aquinas on Our Knowledge of God and the Axiom that Every Agent Produces Something Like Itself" in *Metaphysical Themes in Thomas Aquinas II* (Washington, DC: The Catholic University of America Press), pp. 152–71.

2011. "Thomas Aquinas on the Ultimate Why Question: Why Is There Anything At All Rather Than Nothing Whatsoever" in J. Wippel (ed.), *The Ultimate Why Question: Why Is There Anything At All Rather Than Nothing Whatsoever?* (Washington, DC: The Catholic University of America Press), pp. 84–109.

Wittman, T. R. 2019. *God and Creation in the Theology of Thomas Aquinas and Karl Barth* (Cambridge: Cambridge University Press).

Wood, A. 2020. *Thomas Aquinas on the Immateriality of the Human Intellect* (Washington, DC: The Catholic University of America Press).

Index

accidental change, 32; substances and accidents in, 33
acquired virtues, 287
actionable appearance, 162
acts of cognition, 166
Adam, 235, 309–11, 313–14, 316–17, 347–8, 352, 355
al-Ash'arī, 113
Albert the Great, 9, 14, 25, 85
Alexander of Hales, 85, 109
Ambrosiaster, 346
angel, 128
Anselm of Canterbury, 240, 348; *Cur Deus Homo*, 348
apophaticism, 66
Apostles' Creed, 361
appetite(s), 154, 261; estimative sense and, 161; natural, 346; original sin and, 347; rational, 258, 261; sensory, 236, 261, 352; sensory appetite, 242, 259; will as a rational appetite, 258
appetitive powers, 268
apprehension, 197–8; simple, 197
Aristotle, xv, 7, 9, 14, 18, 20–1, 24, 31, 33, 60, 62, 67, 85–7, 96–7, 99, 103, 105, 108, 127–8, 133, 140, 145, 184, 243, 246–8, 258, 260–1, 280, 285–8, 290, 310, 362, 367–8; *Nicomachean Ethics*, 9, 286
Atonement, 348
Augustine, 66, 109
autonomy, 21
Averroes (Ibn Rushd), 108
Avicenna, 7, 11, 59, 86–7, 111, 114

baptism, 247, 289, 313, 352, 355–6
beatitudes, 267, 269, 271, 285, 288, *see also* VGBF (virtues, gifts, beatitudes, and fruits); and resurrection, 375; describing actions or activities, 269; happiness, *see* happiness; second-person relatedness and, 296

being: account of, 85; different grades of, 88; general mode of, 88; goodness, 94, 99; participation in, 95; substance and accident, 88; transcendentals, *see* transcendentals; truth, 93; unity, 91
Benedict, St., 7
Benedictine monks, 7
benignity, 298
Block, Benjamin, 197
bodily forms, 39
bodily intellectual being, 156; sensory experience, 157
Boethius, 96, 99
Bonaventure (Giovanni di Fidanza), 109
Buber, Martin, 294

Cartesian dualism, 131, 133, 135
Catholic faith, 13, 15, 24–5
causal powers, 39
causes: efficient, 47; final, 49; formal, 43; fourfold division of, 31, 43; material, 43
celestial bodies, 214
Celestial Hierarchy (Pseudo-Dionysius), 9
change, 32; accidental, 32; fundamental principles of, 32; in general, 33; sameness and difference, 33
charity, 236, 244–6; acts of, 247; as root of merit, 351; infusion of, 247; mortal sin, 246; mortal sins, 236; spiritual life and, 356
choice: free, 211
Christ, 363; as subject to the bodily failings, 352; communication of idioms, 326–7; divinity of, 22, 329, 332, 335; faith in, 355, *see also* faith; free will of, 243; freedom of, 331; human intellect of, 329; human nature of, 243, 323–4; human will of, 243, 330; hypostatic union, 77, 326; impeccability of, 331; judiciary power, 363; passions of, 332; temptation of, 330; union of natures in, 11

Lightning Source UK Ltd.
Milton Keynes UK
UKHW020633110822
407169UK00010B/932